A Practical Guide
to Infant and Preschool
Assessment in Special
Education

The Psychoeducational Assessment of Preschool Children, Second Edition
Bruce A. Bracken (Editor)
ISBN: 0-205-12520-4

Clinical Assessment of Children's Intelligence
Randy W. Kamphaus
ISBN: 0-205-13934-5

Clinical Evaluation of Young Children with the McCarthy Scales
Alan S. Kaufman and Nadeen L. Kaufman
ISBN: 0-205-10122-4

Clinical Interpretation of the Woodcock-Johnson Tests of Cognitive Ability—Revised
Kevin S. McGrew
ISBN: 0-205-14801-8

Assessing and Screening Preschoolers: Psychological and Educational Dimensions
Ena Vazquez Nuttall, Ivonne Romero, and Joanne Kalesnik
ISBN: 0-205-13280-4

Assessment of Cognitive Processes: The PASS Theory of Intelligence
J. P. Das, Jack A. Naglieri, and John J. Kirby
ISBN: 0-205-14164-1

A Practical Guide to Infant and Preschool Assessment in Special Education

Judith A. Bondurant-Utz
State University College at Buffalo

Lenore B. Luciano
School Psychologist, Buffalo, New York

Allyn and Bacon
Boston • London • Toronto • Sydney • Tokyo • Singapore

Copyright © 1994 by Allyn and Bacon
A Division of Paramount Publishing
160 Gould Street
Needham Heights, Massachusetts 02194

Library of Congress Cataloging-in-Publication Data

Bondurant-Utz, Judith A.
   A practical guide to infant and preschool assessment in special
education / Judith A. Bondurant-Utz and Lenore B. Luciano.
       p.   cm.
   Includes bibliographical references and index.
   ISBN 0-205-15205-8
   1. Handicapped children–Education (Preschool)–United States.
   2. Handicapped children–Services for–United States.
   3. Handicapped–United States–Functional assessment. I. Luciano,
   Lenore B.
LC4019.2.B66   1994
371.9'0472'0973--dc20   93-28916
                                                              CIP

Printed in the United States of America

10 9 8 7 6 5 4 3 2 1   97 96 95 94 93

About the Authors

JUDITH A. BONDURANT-UTZ, Ed.D., is an associate professor in the Department of Exceptional Education at the State University College at Buffalo. Her primary teaching responsibilities are in infant/preschool special education, which involves teaching graduate courses in early intervention and assessment as well as in the areas of learning disabilities and behavior disorders. She is currently project director for federal and state funded personnel preparation grants in early childhood special education and severe emotional disabilities. Dr. Bondurant-Utz is involved in research in personnel preparation for early interventionists, whole language learning, and social skills. She directs student research in a variety of areas of early childhood special education.

LENORE B. LUCIANO, M.S., N.C.S.P., is a school psychologist specializing in early childhood education. She currently resides in western New York state where she has worked with a number of early intervention programs. Her primary roles include assessment; program development and implementation; teacher/team consultation; and family counseling with respect to infants, toddlers, and pre-schoolers presenting with a variety of developmental disabilities. Ms. Luciano also has served as psychologist at the Center for Neuromuscular and Developmental Disorders Hospital for Joint Diseases/Orthopedic Institute in New York City and as coordinator of the Infant/Toddler Personnel Preparation Program at East Tennessee State University.

Contributors

BARBARA WEITZNER-LIN, Ph.D., is a tenured assistant professor in the Department of Speech Language Pathology at the State University College at Buffalo with expertise in the areas of personnel preparation and program development for infants, toddlers, and young children with communicative disabilities. Dr. Weitzner-Lin currently teaches courses in language development, facilitating infant communication, and the assessment/management of augmentative or alternative communication systems for individuals who are physically, cognitively, and/or linguistically disabled. Dr. Weitzner-Lin is involved in clinical research as well as directing students' research in areas such as routines in intervention, involving families in the intervention process, and the development of intentionality in children at-risk for communication delay.

SHELLY J. LANE, Ph.D., is an assistant professor at the State University of New York at Buffalo, Department of Occupational Therapy. In this capacity, she is responsible for developing and teaching the pediatric graduate curriculum and covering assessment and intervention with children ages birth to 21 years. She has practiced occupational therapy for over 15 years and has focused her clinical skills on infants and children at-risk for developmental delay and learning disabilities. Dr. Lane is a frequent national and international guest speaker on issues pertinent to both pediatric occupational therapy and the neurosciences as applied to this discipline. Recently, she completed research on sensory and motor development in four-year-old children who were born prematurely. Her current research and clinical efforts focus on sensory and motor development, caregiver/infant interaction, and behavior in infants and toddlers exposed to cocaine prenatally.

EMILY MARGULIS-EISENBAUM, M.S. Ed., has been involved in the field of special education for 14 years, both teaching at an early childhood center and conducting educational seminars for professionals. She is currently a college practicum supervisor for a federally funded master's program in early childhood special education at the State University College at Buffalo, which involves both lecturing and supervision on many practicum educational sites. Ms. Margulis-Eisenbaum has written articles for educational publications and been responsible for the organization and development of the Very Special Arts Festival for children with disabilities in western New York state and also coordinates several parent/child playgroup programs.

Contents

Preface

The passage of P.L. 99-457 in 1986 has brought the education of infants and preschoolers with special needs to the forefront. Implementation of this law now requires early childhood educators, special educators, and other professionals working with infants and preschoolers to constantly make decisions about the nature and amount of services to provide to those children who need some form of special help.

This resource book is intended for early intervention teachers, evaluators, related service staff, supervisors, and professionals involved in training personnel who make these service delivery decisions. The purpose of *A Practical Guide to Infant and Preschool Assessment in Special Education* is to provide basic guidelines for early childhood assessment, an overview of the variety of assessment instruments available, and a rationale for decision making when choosing an instrument to use. The development of this book was stimulated by the recognition that assessing very young children is a process that requires different skills and knowledge than does the process of assessing school-aged children. The focus here is on assessment for the practical purpose of intervention or instructional programming.

Over the years, the authors have been confronted with a large amount of important information that needs to be presented in a usable format. There is a deluge of assessment instruments available to early childhood special education professionals, and new tests are being published constantly. In addition, many professionals are not familiar with the skills and abilities of infants and preschoolers, having had minimal training and experience with any young children. To gain the most from the information presented in this book, the following four premises should be kept in mind.

First, the book is meant to be a practical resource guide for professionals who are responsible for designing and implementing individualized early intervention programs for infants, toddlers, and preschoolers as well as individuals responsible for training early intervention personnel. It is our hope that it will be especially useful for teachers, evaluators, and supervisors in early childhood settings serving both normal preschoolers and those with special needs.

Second, *A Practical Guide to Infant and Preschool Assessment in Special Education* is designed to be a condensation of an information-gathering process that should take place when planning intervention. Although various tests are presented, this manual is intended only as a beginning. Every child is different and programs have different philosophies; therefore, each professional must choose what is needed for each *individual* child. Assessing infants and preschoolers always involves multiple disciplines. The format here is designed to encourage the individual user to add sections as needed.

Third, competence in the evaluation process comes with experience and supervised practice. This book is intended to be a good beginning in this difficult task but is not meant as a substitute for comprehensive training.

Last, a comprehensive, multidisciplinary introduction to assessment in early childhood from a variety of respected authorities is presented. The material provides basic guidelines and also is designed to be functional, providing an overview of important points to consider, a compilation of resources, examples, and practical suggestions for individuals, families, and training personnel.

Part I provides an introduction to the purpose and characteristics of a comprehensive, multidisciplinary assessment. Part II discusses basic considerations that should be given to: the examining situation, making qualitative observations of behavior, cultural diversity, the assessment of infants and young children— those with sensory or physical impairments—who require adaptation of materials or instruments, and family involvement in the assessment process.

The stages in the assessment process from the very beginning to end— screening to program evaluation—are addressed in Part III. Norm- and curriculum-based assessment are discussed with examples of each type of assessment and recommendations for their use. Ecological and environmental assessments that may be done at various stages in the process are included in this part. Assessing environments and seeing the child from multiple perspectives enables the examiner to better understand her or his behavior. Direct observation and informal assessment procedures are described along with a variety of examples for use by parents and professionals. Finally, the last chapter in this part discusses program evaluation, especially as it relates to curriculum.

Part IV presents assessment within specific areas that are key developmental domains. The domains presented are cognition, language, social-emotional, gross- and fine-motor skills, and self-help capabilities. The communication and language chapter is written by a speech/language pathologist; and the gross- and fine-motor skills chapter is written by an occupational therapist. These viewpoints provide a more comprehensive understanding of the domains and further emphasize the need for an interdisciplinary approach to assessment of infants and preschoolers with special needs.

For those readers who have experiences with very young children with disabilities and their families, we hope this will be a useful resource book. For those who are new to the field of early childhood special education, we hope that *A Practical Guide to Infant and Preschool Assessment in Special Education* will be an excellent beginning point.

Acknowledgments

Special words of appreciation go to Lenore B. Luciano who not only contributed to the writing of the manuscript but also provided many hours of reading, editing, and professional expertise for most of the chapters. Special thanks for reviewing the information on cultural diversity is given to Dr. Isaura Barrera at the University of New Mexico, Albuquerque, New Mexico, and for adding her expertise in the area of infants and preschoolers who are culturally and/or linguistically diverse. My gratitude also to Barbara Weitzner-Lin and Shelly J. Lane for contributing the chapters on Communication and Language and Sensorimotor Development. I am grateful to Emily Margulis-Eisenbaum for the development of activities that may be used in personnel development. Her creativity and fresh approach provide an excellent addition to this book.

Thanks to Carol Julian for the many hours of typing, writing for permissions, and all the other secretarial assistance needed in the development of a manuscript; to Debbie Zellinger, Bette Anne Domilici, and Joan Tedesco-Blair, who helped in the location of resources, typing, proofreading, and citing of references; and to Rebecca Smith for layout, design, and typing many of the charts.

My appreciation also goes to the following professionals who reviewed the manuscript: Susan R. Sandall, University of Delaware, Newark, Delaware; Janet S. Chamberlain, Family, Infant and Preschool Program, Western Carolina Center, Morganton, North Carolina; and Linda L. Gil, Northwest Child Development Center, Seattle, Washington. The author would like to acknowledge the individuals at Allyn and Bacon who believed in this project, Laurie Lombard and Mylan Jaixen, and Susan Hutchinson who assisted in the development of this manuscript.

Finally, I would like to express my appreciation to my husband, Russell, who constantly supported and encouraged me in this long and time-consuming endeavor.

*To Russ who reminded me that
winners take chances;
they don't give up;
they make the most of their strengths;
and they keep on climbing.*

JBU

*To Madeline, Fred, and Charlie whose
love and wisdom have brought
much to this work.*

LBL

An Overview of the Assessment Process

This resource guide or manual is intended for early intervention teachers, evaluators, related service staff, supervisors, and professionals involved in the training of these personnel. Special education professionals working in early childhood settings are swamped with new tests and information being published, and many are not familiar with infants and preschoolers, having had minimal training and experience with young children.

The purpose of this manual is to provide basic guidelines for early childhood assessment, an overview of the variety of assessment instruments available, and a rationale for decision making when choosing an instrument. Its development was stimulated by the recognition that assessing very young children is a process that requires different skills and knowledge than does the process of assessing school-age children. The focus here is on assessment for the practical purpose of intervention or instructional programming. Faced with the large amount of important information that needs to be presented in a usable format, this book is not intended to be a comprehensive text, but rather a basic informational guide that can refer an individual to more comprehensive sources. Certain *warnings* and *limitations* need to be stated at the outset.

First, this guide is designed to be a practical resource for professionals who are responsible for designing and implementing individualized early intervention programs for infants, toddlers, and preschoolers as well as the individuals responsible for training early intervention personnel. The hope is that it will be especially useful for teachers, evaluators, and supervisors in early childhood settings serving both normal preschoolers and those with special needs.

Second, this guide is designed to be a condensation of the overall information-gathering process that needs to take place when planning intervention. Although references are made to various tests, the information here is intended to be only a beginning. As every child presents with a unique set of characteristics and needs, and as programs espouse different philosophies, each professional must be selective in choosing what is needed for each individual child and program. Multiple disciplines are involved in assessing infants and preschoolers. Each professional may amass a wealth of information and materials that are relevant to early childhood assessment and intervention. The individual reader may wish to add to the parts as needed.

Third, competence in the evaluation process comes with experience and supervised practice. This guide is intended to be used as a good beginning in this difficult task; it is not meant to be a substitute for comprehensive training.

This manual presents a comprehensive multidisciplinary overview of assessment in early childhood from a variety of respected authorities. The material here is a compilation of resources, examples, and practical suggestions and group activities for use by early childhood professionals and training personnel and is meant to provide basic guidelines as well as a functional overview of important points to consider.

C h a p t e r 1

Introduction

Purpose of Assessment

The purpose of assessment in early childhood is the same as it is for an individual of any age, i.e., to derive information to facilitate decision making with respect to that individual. Such decisions revolve around the potential existence, implications, and treatment needs of a problem(s) for the child and the family. Direct or indirect assessment procedures may be used. The target may be a single child, a group of children, the family members, or an inanimate entity such as the physical setting (Bailey & Simeonsson, 1988).

In 1990, P.L. 99-457 (the 1986 amendments to the Education for All Handicapped Children Act) was retitled the Individuals with Disabilities Education Act (IDEA) P.L. 101-476. The IDEA amendment to P.L. 99-457 requires a timely, comprehensive, multidisciplinary evaluation, including assessment activities related to the child and the child's family.

The components of evaluation and assessment are defined as follows:

Evaluation refers to the procedures used by appropriate qualified personnel to determine a child's initial and continuing eligibility for services as a child with a developmental delay. The criteria and procedures for defining the term *developmental delay* must be determined by each individual state. The delay may occur in one or a combination of these areas: cognitive development, physical and sensory development, language and speech development, psychosocial development, development of self-help skills.

The term *assessment* refers to the ongoing procedures used throughout the period of a child's eligibility to identify: (a) the child's unique needs; (b) the family's strengths and needs related to development of the child; and (c) the nature and extent of early intervention services that are needed by the child and the family to meet the needs determined in the evaluation process (Fewell, 1991).

Assessment assists with decisions regarding:

Screening: Accessing the population of families with children from birth to five years of age who may be in need of early intervention services.

3

Diagnosis: Confirmation or disconfirmation of a diagnostic entity, e.g., autism, mental retardation, and so on. The purpose is to verify a particular problem.

Prognosis: Implications and predictions regarding future development based on documentation of current capabilities and deficits.

Placement or Prescription: A prescription for appropriate intervention matched to assessed needs of the child based on the educational assessment.

Program Evaluation: Monitoring of the intervention program for the child and family in order to track ongoing progress, determine program effectiveness, and make modifications as needed.

The Stages in Assessment Process

Bagnato, Neisworth, and Munson (1989) offer a model that provides a process for making these decisions and more clearly linking evaluation and assessment to intervention. The steps or stages in this model are (1) screen/identify, (2) assess/link, (3) program/intervene, and (4) monitor/evaluate. Appropriate assessment measures must be used to accomplish each function, but the steps are interrelated. Bagnato and Neisworth (1989) have published *LINK: A Developmental Assessment/Curriculum Linkage System for Special Needs Preschoolers*, which is available from Developmental Innovations in Julian, Pennsylvania. As shown in Figure 1–1, this model is similar to a magnifying lens.

The stages in this process, adapted from Bagnato, Neisworth, and Munson (1989), are as follows:

Screening

- Examines a child's skills for a broad look at overall functioning.
- Looks for signs of developmental concern in patterns of peaks and lows.
- Identifies areas of development that are in need of closer examination.

Assessment and linkage

- Increases the magnification and provides more attention to detail.
- Provides a comprehensive and detailed analysis of child-developmental capabilities that establish the goals for intervention.
- Yields a score or product, but more important it gathers qualitative information about how the child earned that score.
- Produces a profile of strengths and limitations with suggestions about the best way in which the child learns.
- More precisely analyzes development by focusing on the problem areas identified during the screening and then profiles the specific factors that impact on the developmental areas requiring intervention (e.g., visual-perceptual deficits that hinder a child's ability to imitate and copy drawn forms).

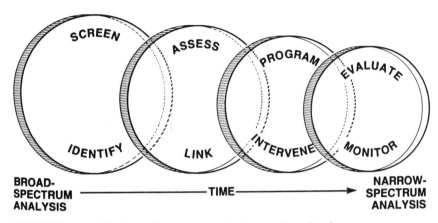

FIGURE 1-1 **Linking Assessment-Intervention Goals**

Source: From *Linking Developmental Assessment and Early Intervention: Curriculum-Based Prescriptions*, 2e, by S. J. Bagnato, J. T. Neisworth, and S. M. Monson. New York: Plenum Publishing Corporation. Copyright ©⅔ 1987 by Plenum Publishing Corporation. Reprinted by permission.

Programming and intervention

- Is the planning of individualized curricular activities and adaptive strategies for teaching.
- Analyzes the child's skills into subskills that can be taught more easily
- Establishes the objectives as well as the particular instructional strategies for intervention.

Evaluation of progress

- Must take a wide view as well as pay attention to detail.
- Uses repeated assessment to provide information on developmental gains across time.
- Examines the child's progress in specific curricular areas in order to determine program effectiveness and to allow for subsequent modifications as indicated.
- Determines program effectiveness from the perspective of family needs and expectations.

Methods for Obtaining Information

Assessment information may be gathered by formal and informal observation of the child. The information needs to be obtained from the family members and teachers as well as any other professionals who are involved with the child. Bailey and Wolery (1984) identify three broad methods to obtain information about children: (1) direct testing, (2) naturalistic observation, and (3) interviews.

Direct Testing

In direct testing a set of standard tasks is presented using predetermined administration procedures and then interpreted in a prescribed or standard manner. Direct testing may employ norm-referenced and/or curriculum-referenced tools. The consistency in administering and scoring allows for communication and meaningful interpretation of test results. A variety of standardized tests have been developed for different purposes. The decision to use a certain test should be consistent with the original purpose of the instrument. Various tests may be used for screening, diagnosis, educational assessment, and program evaluation.

Naturalistic Observation

Naturalistic or direct observation is the recording of behavior as it occurs in a variety of settings, either natural or contrived. Bailey and Wolery (1984) define observation as ". . . a means of discerning what behaviors are performed by children, under what conditions those behaviors appear, and which stimuli are related to those behaviors" (p. 65). Various methods of observational recording are available, including commercially published checklists, informal anecdotal notes, and so on.

Direct observation complements direct testing throughout the assessment process from initial screening to placement and programming decisions. Bailey and Wolery (1989, p. 67) summarize the rationale for direct observation in assessment. Direct observation can:

1. Assess difficult-to-test skills
2. Validate information collected from other measurement strategies
3. Extend assessment activities to other settings and routines
4. Identify functional relationships between the child's behavior and environmental stimuli
5. Provide ongoing assessment of program effectiveness.

Family Interview

Active family participation is an essential component in early childhood assessment. The child's caregivers are the most expert informants about his or her behavior. The role of the family in the assessment process is a central feature of P.L. 99-457—family members are an integral part of the assessment team and have a voice in all decision making. The family interview sets the tone of the working relationship for all future interactions and should be conducted by a skilled professional.

An interview may be structured and formal or unstructured and informal.

A number of procedures have been developed for the assessment of young children with special needs; they will be discussed in Chapter 4 in a section on family involvement in the assessment process.

Bailey and Wolery (1984) summarize the advantages and disadvantages of direct testing, naturalistic observation, and parent interviewing as shown in Table 1–1. They emphasize that a comprehensive assessment should combine all of these procedures, which would capitalize on the unique strengths of each.

Characteristics and Qualities of Multidimensional Assessment

Assessment, programming, and evaluation information needs to be based on different types of data obtained from multiple sources (McCune, Fleck, Kalmanson, Glazewski, & Sillari, 1990). Neisworth and Bagnato (1988) define multidimensional assessment as "a comprehensive and integrated approach that employs multiple measures, derives data from multiple sources, surveys multiple domains, and fulfills multiple purposes" (p. 24).

Multiple Assessment Measures

A variety of assessment measures should be used by early interventionists. Using multiple measures provides more information and, therefore, a more comprehensive assessment of the child. Preschool teachers most commonly use curriculum-based assessments. School psychologists and related service professionals (i.e., speech and language pathologists, occupational therapists, physical therapists, often employ norm-referenced scales.

Many early interventionists may not be aware of the number of assessment instruments currently available in early childhood special education. When faced with so many assessment instruments, the decision becomes very difficult, and a wrong choice may yield misleading information or be inadequate in detecting important variations in behavior. A thorough diagnostic battery of tests for a child might include norm-based, curriculum-based, and clinical judgment scales that require impressions of developmental or behavioral traits (Neisworth & Bagnato, 1988). Researchers have attempted to categorize these diverse instruments to help the practitioner make appropriate selections. The multidimensional model presented by Neisworth and Bagnato (1988) provides a practical guide of these categories by matching assessment measures to the needs of the early interventionist (see Table 1–2).

Curriculum-based

Curriculum-based assessment allows the early interventionist to track a child's performance on specific program objectives and compare current performance to past performance, thus monitoring the child's progress. The curriculum-based

TABLE 1-1   Advantages and Disadvantages of Testing, Naturalistic Observation, and Interviews

Procedure	Advantages	Disadvantages
Testing	Standard procedures allow meaningful comparisons of children. Necessary for diagnostic needs Facilitates transfer of information	Alternate procedures for children with sensory or motor impairments are not generally allowed. Some tests require considerable training. Lack of validated measures for educational planning Skills sampled are limited to those included as the test.
Observation	Measures what children do in real world settings Sensitive to changes over time Can be done during regular classroom activities	Time-consuming Requires a certain amount of skill to design a good observation system Lack of guidelines to interpret data gathered
Interview	Information comes from another's perspective Efficient use of time	Not a direct measure of child behavior The interviewee may not accurately report skills.

Source: Reprinted with the permission of Merrill Publishing Company an imprint of Macmillan Publishing Company, Inc. from *Teaching Infants and Preschoolers with Handicaps* by Donald B. Bailey, Jr. and Mark Wolery. Copyright © 1984 by Merrill Publishing Company.

assessment provides specific developmental objectives that make up the instructional curriculum for the child. The teacher determines if the child has acquired the skills addressed in the curriculum.

Adaptive-to-handicap
Assessments that are designed to be adapted to a disability are used to obtain a more valid or fair estimate of the capability of the child who has a sensorimotor impairment. Procedures are provided for excluding biased items, rescoring performance, or using new technologies such as computers, assistive devices, and interactive laser discs. These modifications are necessary to avoid penalizing a child who cannot see, hear, or make voluntary movements. Assessments that provide adaptions for disabilities give a more representative assessment of the child's functioning and true capabilities than do those that rely solely on comparisons to the norm.

TABLE 1-2   Dependent variables in early intervention assessment

Type of Dependent Variable	Definition	Illustrative Dependent Measures	Appropriate Purpose Research/Practice	Illustrative Studies
Curriculum-based (CBA)	. . . child mastery of objectives within a continuum of objectives	Learning Accomplishment Profile (Sanford & Zelman, 1981) HICOMP Preschool Curriculum Willoughby-Herb & Neisworth, 1983)	Identify individual treatment objectives. Track child progress/provide feedback for instructional changes. Offer common base to interdisciplinary diagnosis and treatment.	MacTurk & Neisworth, 1978 Bagnato, 1984
Adaptive-to-handicap (AH)	. . . modification of assessment content to include or permit alternative sensory or response modes	Oregon Project Curriculum (Brown, Simmons, & Methvin, 1979) Uniform Performance Assessment System (White, Edgar, Haring, Affleck, Hayden, & Bendersky, 1981) Early Intervention Developmental Profile (Rogers, D'Eugenio, Brown, Donovan, & Lynch, 1981) Carolina Curriculum (Johnson-Martin, Jens, & Attermeier, 1986)	Obtain valid assessment by circumventing handicap. Identify goals for instruction. Specific strategies for learning.	Kiernan & Dubose, 1974

(Continued)

TABLE 1-2   *(Continued)*

Type of Dependent Variable	Definition	Illustrative Dependent Measures	Appropriate Purpose Research/Practice	Illustrative Studies
Process (PA)	. . . detection of changes in child related to changes in stimulus events; qualitative changes in cognitive status	Information-Processing Approach (Zelazo, 1982) Infant Learning (Dunst, 1981)	Probe possible capabilities when more direct, conventional assessment is not feasible.	Kearsley, 1981 Dunst, 1983
Norm-based (NBA)	. . . comparison of a child's skills and characteristics relative to an appropriate referent group	Battelle Developmental Inventory (Newborg, Stock, Wnek, Guidubaldi, & Svinicki, 1984) McCarthy Scales of Children's Abilities (McCarthy, 1972)	Diagnostic screening and description of child characteristics relative to peers.	Sciarillo, Brown, Robinson, Bennett, & Sells, 1986 Dubose, 1976
Judgment-based (JBA)	. . . impressions of developmental/behavioral traits (e.g., reactivity, motivation, normalcy)	Carolina Record of Individual Behavior (Simeonsson et al., 1982) Perceptions of Developmental Status (Bagnato & Neisworth, 1987	Detect perceptions and bias. Estimate nebulous/difficult to observe processes. Enhance scope of assessment battery.	Blacher-Dixon & Simeonsson, 1981 Bagnato, 1984
Ecological (EA)	. . . evaluation of the physical, social, and psychological features of a child's developmental context	Early Childhood Environment Rating Scale (Harms & Clifford, 1980) Home Observation for Measurement of the Environment (Caldwell & Bradley, 1978)	Describe nature of reciprocal interactives. Identify environmental variables that suggest needed changes in interactions.	Bailey, Clifford, & Harms, 1982 Dunst, Trivette, & Cross, 1986

TABLE 1–2   *(Continued)*

Type of Dependent Variable	Definition	Illustrative Dependent Measures	Appropriate Purpose Research/Practice	Illustrative Studies
Interactive (IA)	. . . examination of social capabilities of the infant and caregiver and the content and extent of synchrony between them	Brazelton Neonatal Behavioral Assessment Scale (Brazelton, 1984) Parent Behavior Progression (Bromwich, 1978)	Appraise parent-child reciprocity; discover match between child competencies and tasks presented.	Crockenberg & Acredolo, 1983 Mahoney, Finger, & Powell, 1985
Systematic observation (SO)	. . . structured procedures for collecting objective and quantifiable data on ongoing behavior	Pla-Check (Doke & Risley, 1972) Mapping (Ruggles, 1982)	Analyze functional relations among antecedents, child behavior, and consequences; provide close-ups of strengths and weaknesses, and detect small changes.	Madle, Neisworth, & Kurtz, 1980

Source: Neisworth, J. T., & Bagnato, S. J. (1988). Assessment in early childhood special education. In S. L. Odom and M. B. Karnes (Eds.), *Early Intervention for Infants and Children with Handicaps: An Empirical Base* (pp. 26–27). Baltimore, MD: Paul H. Brookes Publishing Co. Reprinted with permission.

Process

Process assessment provides a means to estimate the capabilities of children with severe impairments who seem to be untestable. It looks at the changes in a child's reactions, such as smiling or vocalizing, as a result of changes in stimulus events. These responses are used to infer the child's capacity to understand concepts or events. Process assessment allows the examiner to estimate the status of children who have absent or impaired response modalities.

Norm-based

Norm-based assessment compares a child's developmental skills to those of a referent or normative group that is similar to the child and the child's demographic dimensions (Neisworth & Bagnato, 1988). Norm-based assessment will be discussed further in Chapter 9.

Judgment-based

Judgment-based assessment quantifies the perceptions and clinical judgments of professionals and caregivers about a child's environmental characteristics. These assessment measures may require actual observation of a child and immediate judgment, or they may be the result of accumulated impressions across time, people, and situations. Although these measures are retrospective and highly subjective, judgment-based assessments may provide social validity if a variety of people in different settings have similar judgments (Neisworth & Bagnato, 1988).

Ecological
Ecological assessment looks at a child's development on the basis of the physical, social, and psychological features, including preschool and home environments, peer interactions, caregiver responsiveness, family program participation, and so on. Ecological assessment is based on an interactive model that stresses behavior as a function of personal variables (Neisworth & Bagnato, 1988). (See also Chapter 11.)

Interactive
The interactive assessment method is a result of the discovery that caregiver-child interactions are reciprocal. There are instruments to assess the content and effect of interactions and the capabilities of both partners in this process. Interactive assessment provides information regarding the content and quality of these interactions (Neisworth & Bagnato, 1988).

Systematic Observation
Systematic observation is the direct observation and recording of behavior. It is a structured way to collect data on observable, measurable behaviors. The child may be observed in his or her natural setting, a situation that has been staged or in a role-play or setting that has been prompted.

Multiple Source

The assessment of an infant or preschooler needs to include information and findings from several professionals and caregivers. Young children tend to be person- and situation-specific. Information from the family and a variety of professionals allows the early interventionist to evaluate the child's behavior in a variety of situations. This input should validate findings from norm-referenced and curriculum-based assessments and thus provide a more accurate appraisal of the child's skills. Team members who can provide relevant information from a variety of settings include caregivers, psychologist, teacher, speech/language pathologist, occupational and/or physical therapist, nurse, pediatrician, social worker, and any paraprofessionals who are familiar with the child.

Multiple Domain

Assessment of multiple domains refers to examining the child's strengths and weaknesses in several developmental and behavioral areas. Curriculum-based assessments usually examine such areas as cognitive, language, socioemotional, gross- and fine-motor skills, and self-care domains. Behavioral processes to assess include mastery motivation, social competence, play, temperament, attention, emotional expression, and early coping behavior. Information on the processes the child is employing in his learning or how the child learns as well as the product of his learning (the demonstration of a skill) should be included the assessment. These domains and behavioral processes are discussed in later chapters.

Multiple Purpose

Multiple-purpose measurement allows the early interventionist to screen, diagnose, place, prescribe, predict, or evaluate. *LINK: A Developmental Assessment/Curriculum Linkage System for Special Needs Preschoolers* (Bagnato, 1981, 1984; Bagnato & Neisworth, 1981, 1989) coordinates the instruments used from screening through to program evaluation. The measurement instrument chosen must be consistent with the purpose of the assessment. For example, a screening instrument is not appropriate when diagnosing, placing, or prescribing for a preschooler. All assessment measures also need to be compatible with the goals and content of the curriculum. If increasing the quality of parent-child interaction is a goal of the curriculum, then choose an assessment that measures this interaction. The framework or typology shown in Table 1–2 should assist in the choice of an appropriate assessment instrument.

Summary

Assessment is a process that needs to be family driven. The overall purpose of this process is to facilitate decision making with respect to the child and family. These decisions focus on determining the provision of any special services that might be necessary to help the child develop to his or her full potential. Assessment must be a continuous process, with each stage in the process linked to the next stage. It is important to use an interdisciplinary or transdisciplinary approach involving the family and professionals from across several disciplines based on the individual needs of the child and the family. The assessment process should be multidimensional—employing multiple measures from multiple sources, fulfilling multiple purposes, and allowing for the diversity of cultures in our society.

Suggested Group Activities

1. Find a partner and write down two observations about him or her. Draw some conclusions from these observations. What follow-up assessment could be conducted to verify or disprove these conclusions? While dyads are giving feedback, the instructor should note on the board the different types of observations, e.g., physical, affective, and so on, and the different ways of validating the conclusions they drew.

2. Define screening, diagnosis, prognosis, placement/prescription, and program evaluation. Give the purpose of each process.

3. Differentiate between direct testing, naturalistic observation, and family interview. Describe situations that would warrant each procedure.

4. Discuss the implications for a multidimensional approach to testing. Review what kinds of measures should be included and why.

References

Bagnato, S. J. (1981). Developmental scales and developmental curricula: Forging a linkage for early intervention. *Topics in Early Childhood Education, 1*(2), 1–8.

Bagnato, S. J. (1984). Team congruence in developmental diagnosis and intervention: Comparing clinical judgment and child performance measures. *School Psychology Review, 13*, 7–16.

Bagnato, S. J., & Neisworth, J. T. (1981). *Linking developmental assessment and curricula: Prescriptions for early intervention*. Rockville, MD: Aspen.

Bagnato, S. J. & Neisworth, J. T. (1989). *LINK: A developmental assessment/curriculum linkage system for special needs preschoolers*. Julian, PA: Developmental Innovations.

Bagnato, S. J., Neisworth, J. T., & Munson, S. M. (1989). *Linking developmental assessment and early intervention: Curriculum-based prescriptions*. Rockville, MD: Aspen.

Bailey, D. B., & Simeonsson, R. J. (1988). *Family assessment in early intervention*. Columbus, OH: Merrill.

Bailey, D. B., & Wolery, M. (1984). *Teaching infants and preschoolers with handicaps*. Columbus, OH: Merrill.

Bailey, D. B., & Wolery, M. (1989). *Assessing infants and preschoolers with handicaps*. Columbus, OH: Merrill.

Fewell, R. R. (1991). Trends in the assessment of infants and toddlers with disabilities. *Exceptional Children, 58*(2), 166–173.

McCune, L., Fleck, M., Kalmanson, B., Glazewski, B., & Sillari, J. (1990). An interdisciplinary model of infant assessment. In S. J. Meisels & J. P. Shonkoff (Eds.), *Handbook of early childhood intervention* (pp. 221–245). New York: Cambridge University Press.

Neisworth, J. T., & Bagnato, S. J. (1988). Assessment in early childhood special education: A typology of dependent measures. In S. L. Odom & M. B. Karnes (Eds.), *Early intervention for infants and children with handicaps: An empirical base* (pp. 23–51). Baltimore: Paul H. Brookes.

$$P \; a \; r \; t \quad II$$

Basic Considerations for Assessment

To measure the skills and behaviors of a child, the examiner should demonstrate basic competencies in assessment techniques as well as have a thorough knowledge of early childhood development. Knowing the salient features of a given population can help to better prepare the examiner for an optimally successful assessment experience.

The examiner needs to remember that the purpose of assessment is to derive information to facilitate appropriate decision making for the individual child. The task is to gather data that are representative of the child's typical functioning.

This part is designed to prepare the examiner for the challenges posed in the assessment of the very young child. The basic considerations raised here are relevant to early childhood assessment regardless of the particular tests and measures selected to gather the information needed. These considerations are also applicable to the various stages in the assessment process (i.e., initial identification, reevaluation, monitoring of a child's progress, and so on).

Chapter *2*

The Assessment Experience

LENORE B. LUCIANO

Assessing the skills and behaviors of a very young child offers a special challenge to the teacher/practitioner. The child should be observed under a variety of conditions (i.e., home, day care, nursery/preschool, play group) in order to ensure a representative sampling of abilities and behaviors. The more naturalistic the setting, the more likely typical functioning will be observed.

Components of the Evaluation

Steps in the evaluation process should include: (1) passive observation of the child or infant in a familiar setting (i.e., home, play group, preschool), (2) unstructured play with the child, (3) gathering information regarding the child's typical functioning through interviews with family members, and (4) individual assessment of the child's skills.

Observation

Observation of the child's natural responses to situations and persons will provide valuable information about his or her developmental skills as well as shed light on the temperament and interactive style of the child or infant. A child with specific disabilities prompts additional considerations and modifications that will be addressed later (see chapter 7, Children with Severe Disabilities). Paget (1991) reminds us that each child presents with unique needs that require an examiner to adapt the evaluation situation. She notes that every attempt should be made to adjust and optimize the assessment experience for each child.

Play

Through observation and play, the examiner can note under what conditions the child appears most responsive: Does he or she initiate interaction with others or wait for them to approach? Are there apparent disabilities that are likely to impact upon the child's functioning as well as raise special considerations for assessment? Is the child active and inquisitive in exploring the environment and engaging with objects and toys? Does the child seem to sit passively on the sidelines until drawn into activity by an adult or peer? Is the child's tendency to remain engaged in one activity or task for minutes at a time or does he or she rapidly flit from one item to the next? In the case of an infant: Is he or she alert and responsive to smiles and playfulness, or more passive and seemingly inattentive to social approach? Is the infant's demeanor different with familiar family members than with unfamiliar practitioners (as one might expect)?

Family Interview

The descriptions and suggestions of the family members also offer much information about the child's preferences and style. The examiner may wish to use structured checklists and developmental inventories as well as an open-ended interview to gather relevant information (see also chapter 4, Family Involvement). The family's perceptions of the child's development and behavior, compared with other children in the family, are crucial to an understanding of the expectations of the assessment and intervention as well as the overall impact of the child's potential disabilities on the family.

Individual Assessment

The individual assessment session allows the examiner to gather valuable information about a child's functioning within a relatively confined space and time. Whether in a classroom, the child's home, or another designated area, individualized assessment provides an opportunity to observe and interact closely with the child or infant as well as stimulate the performance of specific tasks or skill-behaviors by structuring or directing the activity.

Assessment of Young Children

It is important to remember that infants and preschoolers typically have had little experience with a testing situation. They cannot conceptualize the purposes and expectations of such an event. The preschool child is less familiar with the social and performance demands and expectations of assessment than the child already enrolled in a school program. The infant has even less understanding of our expectations or of performance on demand. How well the child adapts to the testing situation will depend on: (1) the child's own resources, (2) the skill and demeanor of the examiner, (3) the appropriateness and conduciveness of the setting, and (4) the support of the caregiver.

The Child

Each child is certainly an individual with specific behaviors, preferences, and temperamental style. Nonetheless, general characteristics and developmental features that impact on the nature and tendencies of the very young child must be taken into account when staging the evaluation. (The special considerations that specific disabilities bring to the assessment process will be discussed in chapter 7.)

Variability

The most important characteristic to keep in mind with respect to the young child is variability. Infants, toddlers, and preschoolers develop at varying rates across a number of domains. Motor, language, cognitive, and social skills develop rapidly in the early years. The norms and expectations for attaining milestones in each of these areas are quite broad. It is recognized that children come to an evaluation with varying degrees of exposure to developmentally stimulating materials and experiences outside the home environment (Romero, 1992). Infants and young children are also more likely to show unevenness in levels of endurance/fatigue, attentiveness/distractibility, and separation tolerance/anxiety than are their school-age counterparts.

Verbal Limitations

Language development is limited as well as variable for young children. Most preschoolers are in the process of struggling with verbal effectiveness in communicating their wants, needs, and thoughts. For the preverbal infant, the challenge of communicating preferences, needs, and recognition is even greater, and the burden of understanding or interpreting these communications is all the more difficult for the practitioner.

Self-direction

The very young child often is inquisitive and self-directed by nature. This is an age of exploration and discovery. While some structured, directed activity is helpful in gathering specific data about a child's abilities, opportunities for the child to freely explore and manipulate the environment and its contents should be offered or built into the assessment sessions. The infant may not yet be mobile enough to physically explore the surroundings. It is critical, however, to note the infant's responsiveness to visual stimuli, sounds, and events. Inquisitiveness or "exploration" need not be demonstrated through mobility alone. Observation of the child at such times will reveal much valuable information about her skills and interests as well as behavioral and learning styles. (See also chapter 3, Qualitative Observations of Assessment Behavior.)

Stranger Anxiety

It is important to remain aware of the stages of normal development when testing young children. For example, an infant of approximately 7 to 10 months typically is becoming more alert to and anxious about strangers. A period of gradual warm-up and acceptance of the practitioner as "safe" will be crucial to meaningful data collection. Observing the infant in nonthreatening, naturalistic settings as well as working in a cooperative effort with caregivers in order to elicit the child's responses to assessment situations may be the most effective ways to sample his typical skills. Nonrecognition of this normal phase of "stranger anxiety" could lead a practitioner to conclude that a child is unduly withdrawn or irritable or even incapable of many tasks well within his repertoire if sensitively elicited.

Autonomy

Similarly, it is important to recognize that assertion of autonomy is typical of the toddler attempting to increase her independence and separation tolerance. Being unaware of this normal behavior could lead to inaccurate conclusions about a child's refusal to perform on demand. Testing limits is an important part of this stage of development and should not be dismissed as defiance. A young child often will reveal many more skills when examined using structured choices instead of rigid directions and demands. (See also chapter 3 on qualitative observation.)

Mobility

Young children typically need and enjoy mobility. Sitting at a table for more than about 15 minutes at a time usually fatigues or bores a child (including the infant in a high chair or on a caregiver's lap). Attention span is fairly short, particularly for activities not selected by the child. Varying the activities such that seated tasks are alternated with motor tasks (and, of course, free exploration described earlier) often serves to increase the young child's willingness to participate. Even the nonambulatory infant needs a change of position periodically or an opportunity to lie on or crawl on the carpet whenever fidgetiness or boredom are noted.

The Examiner

The teacher/practitioner/examiner is one of the most important tools in the assessment of the young child. The materials selected become unimportant if the examiner cannot relate to and elicit responsiveness from the child.

Professional Competence

The examiner's familiarity with the materials to be employed is essential to effective assessment and data gathering. Having an organized plan or sequence of activities to use makes for smoother interaction between practitioner and child. Flexibility to change the order of tasks as necessary is encouraged but not at the expense of well-prepared and organized goals of assessment.

The examiner must possess a good working knowledge of normal child development as well as a respect for the diverse variations among children (see the previous section). "Reading" the child's responses and reactions will guide the examiner in "fine-tuning" when to begin an activity, when to end a task, when to support and encourage, and when to leave the child alone.

Rapport

Remembering that the young child has little experience with assessment and limited motivation to perform on demand, it is essential that the examiner stimulate and engage the child as well as establish a trusting rapport. In the case of infants, keep in mind that it is quite typical for the child to be hesitant to engage in any activity with an unfamiliar adult. A patient, kind, and friendly demeanor is as much an asset to the examiner as is competent handling of the test materials. Making the caregiver a partner in the assessment process, such that the infant or toddler can maintain needed security, is also a useful and recommended technique.

Rapport-building is a skill that is more readily developed intrinsically than taught to the examiner. It is a skill vital to effective interaction with the family as well as with the child. Allotting enough time for play and diversions will make for a less pressured assessment, enhance rapport, and allow for a better look at the child's potential. It is during these less structured times that the examiner may make many qualitative observations that are important to an understanding of the child as well as gain greater insight into the family perspective (see chapter 3 on qualitative observation).

Style and Demeanor

While each examiner/practitioner's personal style should be respected, several suggestions may prove helpful with regard to assessment of very young children. Comfortable, less formal clothes communicate greater ease and are more practical when working with this age group; be prepared to be on the floor, to hold the child, and to frolic occasionally. Although some children respond well to enthusiasm and animation, most young children confronted with their first assessment situation seem to prefer a calm, quiet demeanor and voice. One is less likely to alarm or overstimulate a young child this way, and one can always "pump up" the enthusiasm and volume to meet the needs or style of a particularly perky child.

Young children seem to prefer higher-pitched voices, but avoid squealing and shrillness. A friendly, warm banter, which includes facial expression and humor, proves quite successful most of the time. Keep language appropriate to the developmental level of the child, avoiding baby talk and euphemistic terms. Frequent eye contact is crucial as are smiles. Following a warm-up period, touch may be used judiciously to increase rapport, offer encouragement, or help bring a child back to task. The gentle touch of a hand or shoulder can be an effective prompt for some children.

Sensitivity to Family

Of particular importance is the practitioner's sensitive inclusion of and responsiveness to family/caregivers as members of the team evaluating the child's functioning. Recognition of and respect for the expertise of the family/caregivers as participants in the assessment process facilitates effective and productive program decisions as well as ensures greater investment of the family in the programming and follow-through of goals. Further, not only is such a practice productive and ethical, it is mandated in P.L. 94-142 and 99-457 (Bagnato & Neisworth, 1991).

The Setting

Another important "tool" in evaluating young children is the room or area in which one performs an assessment. Portions of the assessment may be done in a separate room, in the child's classroom, or in the child's home. Certain general guidelines apply to the assessment settings regardless of the specific location.

Comfort and Quiet

The setting needs to be comfortable but functional. It should accommodate infants and small children as well as their caregivers and be cheerful and warm but not too distracting. An excessive number of toys and wall hangings are discouraged because they will draw the child's attention away from the desired activities. The noise level should not be distracting either. Avoid settings that are subject to variations in sound level (i.e., unusual outbursts, loud machinery, noisy plumbing).

Furniture

Use furniture appropriate to the size of the child during the assessment activities. Chairs should allow the child's feet to rest on the floor with her back resting against the back of the chair. The height of the testing table should allow for comfortable manipulation of materials, block building, and drawing. A suggested height is waist-level to the child (Bagnato & Neisworth, 1991). If adaptive positioning equipment or modified materials are needed to meet the special needs of an infant or child with a specific disability, this needs to be ascertained prior to beginning the assessment and appropriate devices should be available during all evaluation sessions (see chapter 7).

An adult-size table and comfortable chairs should be available for meeting with caregivers and sharing assessment data. Such a table also might be used to accommodate an infant supported on a parent/caregiver's lap to allow participation in tabletop activities.

A carpeted area is recommended as it is natural for infants and young children to play on the floor. An examiner often can learn a great deal about a child's skills, as well as increase rapport, from this vantage point.

Lighting

Lighting should be bright enough for picture activities but not too harsh. Flickering lights, such as the fluorescent types so often found in schools and clinics, may be distracting to both the examiner and the child. These lights often have a tendency to "hum." They may induce self-stimulatory behaviors in children who are so predisposed.

Homelike Setting

When testing very young children, a rule of thumb is to keep the setting as "homelike" as possible (Bagnato & Neisworth, 1991). This is the most natural environment for the child and the one most conducive for her to readily display skills. It is also a more comfortable and sensitive setting for the caregivers, who are such a vital part of the assessment process.

Caveat

Keep in mind that the only comparable experiences many young children may have had are visits to a physician's office, and these may have involved uncomfortable, invasive, or painful procedures. As a result, a child may be fearful. Certain assessment settings, such as a separate testing room, may be reminiscent of those experiences. Home or classroom settings are more natural and less threatening to the young child. Patience and sensitivity are useful tools in creating an effective assessment setting for each child.

Parent/Caregiver Support

In addition to the valuable information gathered through the input of the caregivers as members of the evaluation team, the presence of these members is of great importance to the well-being of the child.

Adaptability

Caregiver support and encouragement play a large part in a young child's ability to adapt to the assessment experience. This support may take the form of the presence or proximity of the caregiver during the assessment activities. For an infant, being held in the caregiver's lap may be preferred for much of the assessment. The caregiver's reassurance communicates that engaging with the practitioner/examiner and participating in the assessment activities is important. A caregiver who has been fully and sensitively informed about the goals and procedures of the assessment is likely to be more at ease and will communicate that ease to the child, both verbally and nonverbally.

Separation and Security

At no time should the child's separation from the caregiver be a source of confrontation. It is important to remember that the infant or young child is still working through issues of stranger anxiety, separation tolerance, and independence. Children will vary in their level of mastery of such issues. They will exhibit different degrees of security and comfort in novel situations both with and without the immediate presence of their caregivers. It is important to "read" the child and the caregiver and to establish assessment procedures that are responsive to their needs and comfort. Caregiver and child should be respected and accepted in their choices during the assessment. The rapport established with each is essential to the assessment process (see also chapter 4 on family involvement).

Summary

Effective assessment of infants and young children necessitates paying attention to the special conditions and considerations that such a task entails. The various components of assessment—observation, play, family interview, and individual testing—must be addressed in order to learn about the child's skills and needs. It is important to know and recognize the developmental characteristics and behaviors specific to infants and young children. It also is essential that the examiners/practitioners attend to their own skills, the settings in which they assess children, and the relationships they develop with the families and caregivers they serve. In an effort to understand and meet the needs of young children, the challenge of the task itself must be appreciated.

Suggested Group Activities

1. Divide into groups and assign an age to each group (e.g., 0 to 6 months, 6 to 12 months, 12 to 24 months, and so on). Each group should compile a list of appropriate motivating toys that would hold the interest of a child in that age range. Share the lists with the class. The lists can be copied and distributed later to help students start an activity file.

2. Have each participant select a partner and take turns role-playing the part of an examiner and a cooperative, reluctant, shy, or overly active child. The examiner must adjust his or her interactional skills to address each personality. Use an appropriate assessment instrument to test the "child."

3. Think of ways to involve and encourage the caregiver's support during the assessment activities. Include suggestions on how to explain the assessment results.

4. Discuss reasons why caregivers may have preconceived and/or negative attitudes toward professionals. Generate a list to dispel these ideas (e.g., develop a newsletter; avoid technical jargon; write a questionnaire to help determine caregiver's interest, concerns, and suggestions).

References

Bagnato, S., & Neisworth, J. T. (1991). *Assessment for early intervention: Best practices for professionals.* New York: Guilford Press.

Paget, K. (1991). The individual assessment situation: Basic considerations for preschool-aged children. In B. A. Bracken (Ed.), *The psychoeducational assessment of preschool children* (pp. 32–39). Boston: Allyn and Bacon.

Romero, I. (1992). Individual assessment procedures with preschool children. In E. V. Nuttall, I. Romero, & J. Kalesnick (Eds.), *Assessing and screening preschoolers: Psychological and educational dimensions* (pp. 55–66). Boston: Allyn and Bacon.

Chapter 3

Qualitative Observations of Assessment Behavior

LENORE B. LUCIANO

A great deal of meaningful information can be gathered during the assessment. Qualitative observations of the child's physical, behavioral, and developmental characteristics are as important as the scores, percentiles, and age levels derived from the scales utilized.

Features and Caveats

Bracken (1991) describes several important features of behavioral observations and shares some caveats as well. His major points may be summarized in four considerations. First, observations and clinical judgments are subjective and tend to be more fragile than standard test scores. Second, *normalcy* is difficult to define with respect to young children, given their rapid rate of growth and the broad range of ages at which many skills typically emerge. Third, it is more useful and valid to make descriptive statements about what a child does and what behaviors seem to enhance or impede test performance than to make interpretations or broad generalizations about the implications of those behaviors. Finally, one's observations and descriptions of the child can do a great deal to enhance, round out, fill in, and generally enrich the assessment information if they are sensitively and appropriately viewed in light of the aforementioned features.

Importance of Observation

Observation is an important part of assessment across all settings in which the child is evaluated. Viewing the child in his or her home, preschool, day care center, or play group is likely to yield more typical behavior and functioning than might be displayed in an unfamiliar setting such as a local evaluation site or a practitioner/examiner's testing room. Note, however, that the mere presence of an observer or examiner may alter the child's behavior somewhat. Certainly in the case of individual assessment in a testing area, a child's behavior should not be assumed to be generalizable to other settings. The influence of surroundings (persons, places, and things) on behavior always should be taken into account.

Recording

Given the general considerations regarding behavioral observations, suggestions for increasing the effectiveness of the essential recording component of assessment need to be mentioned.

The individual practitioner/examiner may find a style of recording valuable observations that suits her or him best. One might make notations in margins of developmental inventories or test forms, write anecdotal statements on an accompanying sheet of paper, or even devise a useful checklist to allow quick identification and notations on a broad variety of observations. Romero (1992) offers one such format that is shown in Table 3–1.

Regardless of the system chosen, it is helpful to consider that observations fall in major categories, including physical characteristics, temperament and behavioral style, interactive and communicative style, problem-solving and learning style, and adaptive behavior. It also is essential to remain mindful of developmental issues typical to the age of the child being assessed. The following points are to be considered during observation.

Physical Characteristics

The examiner needs to take note of what immediately meets the eye when observing the child. The child's size or stature for her age may have an impact on how she interacts with peers. Relative size and weight also can be helpful clues to a child's rate of development and health, particularly when compared to familial traits of size and stature. Excesses in one direction or another also can have an impact on a child's strength, endurance, coordination, and so on. Bracken (1991) points out that a meaningful observation would include how excessive weight, for example, appeared to interfere with the way a child performed certain fine and gross-motor tasks, rather than merely mention that the child is overweight.

Other aspects of the child's general appearance also need to be noted: Does the child appear well or ill? Does he or she seem unusually pale or tired? Are there notable dark circles under the child's eyes or a marked redness of the nose or ears (possibly suggesting sleeplessness, a cold, or allergies)? While such obser-

TABLE 3–1   Behavioral Observation Checklist for Different Domains: Language, Motor, Task Approach, Social/Emotional, General*

Name _____ DOB _____ Age _____ Gender _____

Primary Language _____ Ethnicity _____ Hand preference _____

Examiner _____ Date(s) of Evaluation _____

Referral Reason _____

Place an X under the appropriate number for each behavior. Omit items for behaviors not observed or not applicable.

Descriptions of Child's Test Behavior

Test Behavior	Adequate (Not Problematic) 1	2	Occasionally Problematic 3	4	Problematic 5
Language: Expressive					
Syntax	_____	_____	_____	_____	_____
Grammar	_____	_____	_____	_____	_____
Voice quality (volume, pitch)	_____	_____	_____	_____	_____
Speech intelligibility	_____	_____	_____	_____	_____
Articulation	_____	_____	_____	_____	_____
Vocabulary (extent, word choice)	_____	_____	_____	_____	_____
Spontaneous communication (vs. limited to answering)	_____	_____	_____	_____	_____
Ability to express ideas (fluency)	_____	_____	_____	_____	_____
Latency of response	_____	_____	_____	_____	_____
Elaboration of response	_____	_____	_____	_____	_____
Use of unusual language (echolalia, bizarre, ritualistic, obscene)	_____	_____	_____	_____	_____

*Designed by Ivonne Romero. May be reproduced without permission.

(Continued)

TABLE 3-1 *(Continued)*

	Descriptions of Child's Test Behavior				
	Adequate (Not Problematic)		Occasionally Problematic		Problematic
Test Behavior	1	2	3	4	5
Language: Receptive					
Understanding of spoken information	———	———	———	———	———
Need for modified language (repetitions, clarifications)	———	———	———	———	———
Motor: Fine Motor					
Fluidity of movement (fumbling, tremor)	———	———	———	———	———
Bilateral hand coordination (dexterity and speed)	———	———	———	———	———
Hand grasp	———	———	———	———	———
Motor: Gross Control					
Gait	———	———	———	———	———
Posture	———	———	———	———	———
Movement in space (precise vs. knocks objects, awkward)	———	———	———	———	———
Motor: Graphomotor					
Pencil grip (tripod vs. fisted, pencil held loosely or too tight)	———	———	———	———	———
Handwriting/drawing (fluid vs. labored)	———	———	———	———	———
Line quality (trembly, overshoots)	———	———	———	———	———

TABLE 3-1 *(Continued)*

Test Behavior	Descriptions of Child's Test Behavior				
	Adequate (Not Problematic)		Occasionally Problematic		Problematic
	1	2	3	4	5
Task Approach					
Initiation (deliberate vs. impulsive)	——	——	——	——	——
Style (organized vs. disorganized)	——	——	——	——	——
Problem solving (efficient vs. inefficient)	——	——	——	——	——
Ability to benefit from feedback	——	——	——	——	——
Attention	——	——	——	——	——
Persistence	——	——	——	——	——
Flexibility	——	——	——	——	——
Ability to shift	——	——	——	——	——
Interest	——	——	——	——	——
Effort	——	——	——	——	——
Social-Emotional					
Affect	——	——	——	——	——
Mood	——	——	——	——	——
Ability to separate from parents	——	——	——	——	——
Relationship with parents (warm vs. detached)	——	——	——	——	——
Expression of feelings	——	——	——	——	——
Sociability (confident vs. insecure)	——	——	——	——	——
Ability to regulate and modulate behaviors	——	——	——	——	——
Bizarre or unusual behaviors	——	——	——	——	——

(Continued)

TABLE 3-1 *(Continued)*

| | Descriptions of Child's Test Behavior | | | | |
| | Adequate (Not Problematic) | | Occasionally Problematic | | Problematic |
Test Behavior	1	2	3	4	5
General					
Appearance:	—	—	—	—	—
Grooming	—	—	—	—	—
Height	—	—	—	—	—
Weight	—	—	—	—	—
Facies	—	—	—	—	—
Visual acuity	—	—	—	—	—
Hearing acuity	—	—	—	—	—
Eye contact	—	—	—	—	—
Activity level	—	—	—	—	—
Compliance	—	—	—	—	—
Need for limit setting	—	—	—	—	—
Need for reassurance	—	—	—	—	—
Need for structure	—	—	—	—	—
Response to praise	—	—	—	—	—
Reaction to examiner	—	—	—	—	—
Reaction to test materials	—	—	—	—	—
Approach to a new situation (relaxed vs. tense)	—	—	—	—	—
Curiosity	—	—	—	—	—
Degree of cooperation	—	—	—	—	—

Other observed test behaviors not mentioned above (please describe):

_____

_____

Source: From Romero, I. (1992). Individual assessment procedures with preschool children. In E.V. Nuttall, I. Romero, & J. Kalesnik (Eds.). *Assessing and Screening Preschoolers: Psychological and Educational Dimensions* (pp. 55–66). Boston: Allyn and Bacon. Reprinted with permission.

vations cannot lead to diagnostic conclusions, they may prompt the examiner to more fully discuss the child's sleep and feeding habits as well as general medical history with the family or caregivers. Knowing whether the child is currently medicated for an ailment or allergy is helpful information. The child's level of energy, activity, or attention to task may be directly affected by some medications, and this impact must be considered when conducting the assessment as well as when drawing any conclusions from its results.

Other appearance characteristics might include a child's overall grooming. This is particularly useful when assessing a child with emerging self-help skills: Is the child asserting more autonomy in his or her bathing, dressing, and feeding activities? Is the parent encouraging the child to be more independent and tolerating the temporary imperfections in the end result? Again, while the first glance may not provide conclusive information, it may prompt appropriate developmental inquiry.

Observations of the child's apparent sensorimotor skill, coordination and balance for age, gait, and seating posture are important as well: Does the child appear secure and confident when walking and sitting? Do you note frequent falling or bumping into barriers? Is the child's fine-motor dexterity impacted by shakiness or apparent tremors? Does the child's exploration of the environment or assessment materials seem impeded by motor awkwardness or sensory limitation? Does the child move closer to materials to see them better or turn his or her head in a consistent way when looking or listening? Does the child seem to rely on visual cues or on verbal repetitions? Is squinting observed? Observations of such physical characteristics may provide helpful clues to the child's overall functioning and preferred learning styles, as well as to cue the examiner to make appropriate assessment modifications.

It is important to keep in mind that the child may not have had prior experience with or exposure to activities and materials such as those typically used in developmental assessment (i.e., crayons, pencils, scissors, paper folding). In some cases, observing the child perform more familiar tasks, such as putting on shoes, buttoning a coat, or eating with a utensil, may be a helpful way to examine a child's motor dexterity. Again, even if not always conclusive, observations can prompt further investigation of suspected areas of difficulty as they arise (see chapter 7, Children with Severe Disabilities).

Temperament and Behavioral Style

Observations of the child's personal style and characteristics are vital to an understanding of that child's experience in educational situations. The child's responsiveness to others and to events may reveal much about his or her preferences, strengths and weaknesses, self-confidence, self-esteem, and coping strategies. Noting how the child reacts to new persons, places, and materials can suggest how a child may respond to learning new tasks. Once again, describing rather than interpreting the child's behaviors is valid and useful.

The child's apparent interest in the environment and his or her motivation to explore it may be an indication of levels of trust, curiosity, and even intelligence.

Of course, the extent to which the child may act on those inclinations also may be a function of sensorimotor ability, family style and practices, and previous experiences outside the home: Does the child seem at ease in new or challenging settings? Does he or she respond with apparent fear, hesitance, caution, or eagerness? How is separation from the family/caregivers tolerated? During the assessment activities, does the child greet new tasks head-on or hang back, observing for a while? Do you detect much frustration as the child attempts difficult tasks, or even in response to less obvious obstacles? How does the child seem to comfort or relieve perceived pressure (i.e., ask for help, retreat, distract, cry, strike out at someone or something)? How does the child respond to limit-setting by the practitioner/examiner or by family members? How does he or she respond to praise and/or encouragement from others? How the child initiates, responds, and reacts may provide clues about the educational effectiveness of different programming plans.

It is helpful to note the child's behavioral state, preferably observed on different occasions and under different circumstances: Does the child present as energetic, overly active, or lethargic for his or her age? Is the child alert or are there signs of sleepiness? If sleepiness is noted, might it correlate with the child's typical nap time or has he or she endured a long assessment session? Is the child seeming more irritable or anxious than most same age peers? Is he or she more active or distractible than expected for the age? Observations made with respect to these tendencies are critical components of the assessment process; they shed light on assessment behavior and performance as well as on the child's effectiveness in dealing with others.

Communication and Interaction

The child's verbal and nonverbal communications during interpersonal contacts provide some of the most important information about him or her. Observations such as how approachable the child is, how readily rapport is established, and how the child reacts to unfamiliar people and settings are important keys to the child's personal-social development and coping skills: Does the child initiate contact or wait for another's lead? Does the child present as independent for his or her age or more reliant on the attention of adults? These observations may aid in understanding the child's self-confidence or self-esteem: Is eye contact frequent? Is it steady or fleeting? Such behaviors may reflect self-esteem, trust, or attention span.

The child's communication effectiveness is important to note. How the child makes his or her wants and needs known will have a great impact on getting them met: If communicating verbally, is the child easily understood? Do articulation errors and poor grammar impede intelligibility? Is speech fluent or does it contain stuttering or stammering? These observations may help determine the need for an in-depth speech/language evaluation if one has not already been planned. Noting whether the child tries alternate means of expressing a particular thought or response also is important. This behavior may indicate flexibile thinking as well as responsiveness to the social cues of others (i.e., an indication that the other does not understand the communication): Does the child seem aware of and/or frustrated by the expressive limitations? If nonverbal, does the child gesture and point to communicate? How effective does this seem to be in getting his or her needs met? What is the family's perspective on the effectiveness of the child's communication efforts?

His or her temperamental style impacts on the child's interactional style. The verbal child who converses openly and at length may be revealing his or her comfort and ease in the assessment situation. The child with known verbal ability who remains reticent throughout the sessions may be revealing notable anxiety or discomfort (Bracken, 1991). Whether a child is outgoing or cautious, confident or hesitant, active or lethargic, his or her personal characteristics will influence and guide interactions. Remember that it is important to note and describe the child's tendencies rather than evaluate or judge them.

Problem-solving and Learning Style

During the assessment activities, the practitioner/examiner needs to note how the child approaches and completes tasks as well as whether or not he or she succeeds. Some children use a trial-and-error approach to new activities. Some examine the materials and plan a strategy. Some avoid or hesitate to perform unfamiliar tasks. The examiner should observe the patterns of the child's performance. It is important to try to distinguish between an inability to perform a task and a lack of understanding of the directions and demands of the task.

While observing the patterns of performance, the examiner gains insight into the child's preferred or most efficient means of learning: Does the child do better with visual cues? Are verbal directions followed? Is an actual demonstration needed and is it helpful? Is a specific handicapping condition interfering with performance of some or all tasks and might modifications be made to optimize success? Does the child talk herself through a task, possibly compensating for a perceptual limitation with language strengths? The examiner will obtain much helpful information about the child's receptiveness to various methods of learning. The child may demonstrate consistent preference for the visual modality, or perhaps a tactile or hands-on approach to tasks. Again, it is critical to observe how the child performs in addition to what he or she performs.

Another observation made in this realm is that of persistence and perseverance: Does the child stay with a task for a while or give up easily? Does he or she jump rapidly from task to task? Does the child demonstrate a preference for one type of activity (i.e., blocks) and a willingness to engage in that activity for a longer period of time than noted during other activities? Might avoidance of a particular type of activity (i.e., crayons) be due to relative deficit in a skill needed to perform that task (in this case, fine motor, visual, visual-motor)? Such observations may prompt further inquiry into the specifics of the child's developmental strengths and weaknesses.

The child's style of problem solving also will be revealed through careful observation: Does the child try different and creative angles in approaching a challenging task? Does the child seem to do the same thing with most materials offered (i.e., bang the objects together, or stack them) and perseverate on that action? Bagnato and Neisworth (1991) note that such behavior may be present when a child has learned only one way to play with toys or objects. They suggest that demonstrating or teaching a new response to materials, i.e., cause-effect actions, may be helpful in reducing perseveration while also providing an indication of the child's short-term learning abilities. The child's cognitive ability and flexibility often is reflected in his or her manipulation of the materials in the environment and responsiveness to the challenge of the unfamiliar. By noting these observations, further investigation into the child's overall functioning may be explored as needed.

Adaptive Behavior

Observing how the child adapts to new settings and circumstances will shed light on the child's flexibility as well as on his or her tendency to compensate for weaknesses with strengths. This is particularly true in young children with specific disabilities who are adopting alternative means of exploring and interacting with the environment. For example, a child with a visual impairment relies more heavily on tactile and auditory cues in his or her contact with objects and people in the environment. If hearing impaired, a child relies on visual cues and physical prompts in order to perform. Movement disabilities, gross or fine in nature, greatly impede a child's free exploration of the surroundings and manipulation of objects.

Noting how the child deals with each situation is important: Does the child ask for assistance? Does the child request that an object be brought to him or her? Does he or she seem to give up trying to obtain it? The child may have established adaptive ways of moving, grasping, and problem-solving. It is essential to provide ample time and opportunity for the child to achieve his or her goal.

A great variety of compensatory tendencies may be noted. As each child's needs, resources, and style will vary, it is important not to stereotype one's expectations of what a child with a given disability will do to adapt to challenges. Again, the family/caregiver perspective of the child's independence, adaptive behavior, and problem-solving techniques, as well as the family's own part in the dependence/independence issue, will offer critical information.

Developmental Issues for Young Children

When observing and recording behavior, it is important to know those behaviors that are within typical expectations for the young child. In many cases, it is the extent to which a behavior is demonstrated that may be considered remarkable. For example, a behavior that is somewhat typical for a young child (i.e., short attention span) but so excessive that it interferes with the establishment of rapport or the performance of expected skills is notable. One might suggest that the child's attention span was particularly short for age and that this seemed to interfere with his or her participation in the assessment activities. Three major developmental issues that affect young children and their potential to engage in assessment activities are: (1) separation, (2) autonomy, and (3) activity level/ attention span.

Separation Issues

It is typical for young children to be hesitant and apprehensive with strangers and in unfamiliar settings. For those portions of the assessment that may entail testing in a separate room, care should be taken to reduce or avoid the stresses of separation for a child uncomfortable with this arrangement. By about age 3 to 3½, however, many children can be expected to separate from a family member for a brief period of time.

In most cases, giving the child some time (i.e., 10 to 15 minutes) to become familiar with the surroundings and the expectations of the assessment situation will yield greater comfort. Giving the child and family a period of adjustment time in a waiting area often can suffice in helping the child make the transition to a testing area. Telling a child about the "games" and activities to be shared while family members wait with a magazine may ease a child's concern. This transitional conversation with the child also allows for initial rapport-building between practitioner/examiner and child.

For a particularly shy or hesitant child, the family member's presence may be invited. For a very young child, i.e., under three years of age, this is preferred. If the child cannot establish rapport with the examiner or accommodate to any of the activities in his or her expected level of functioning despite caregiver support and encouragement, then the separation issues may be notable. Certainly, one should attempt several assessment sessions to determine whether the child might eventually adapt to the situation.

Autonomy Issues

Young children are normally testing out their growing independence. As they become increasingly competent (or so perceive themselves), they assert the "I do" or "my way" principle. They are naturally inquisitive and enjoy self-directed exploration of a new environment. A short amount of time (i.e., 5 to 10 minutes) to freely explore the assessment area helps the child adjust and feel secure as well as offers an opportunity for the practitioner/examiner to make some meaningful observations about the child's style and preferences. However, the child who cannot be directed in structured activity even for brief moments by a creative and skilled examiner may be experiencing a greater-than-usual struggle with autonomy issues. It is this child who may refuse tasks, or seem noncompliant in general, even when offered a variety of tasks otherwise performed independently.

Bagnato and Neisworth (1991) point out that this apparent negativism and opposition is understandable given the young child's natural drive toward autonomy and independence coupled with his or her lack of experience with the demands of assessment. In cases such as this, the examiner should record as many of the skills the child spontaneously demonstrates during self-directed activity and arrange multiple assessment sessions in order to observe for eventual adaptation to evaluation efforts.

Bracken (1991) reminds us that unwillingness is not to be confused with inability. Careful observation of the child's behavior patterns, particularly with facile versus difficult tasks, helps distinguish between the two. Also, consider the possible influence of the child's activity level and attention span on his or her difficulty with being directed in structured tasks.

Activity Level and Attention Span

It is developmentally appropriate for young children to be highly active as they are learning and performing more and more skills every day. They also may seem to attend only briefly to some tasks, moving instead from one activity to another quite rapidly. It is important to distinguish between a naturally high activity level, which may not interfere with learning and task performance, and excessively high activity or impulsivity, which may suggest a limited ability to inhibit a response that does interfere with task performance.

In the latter case, a child's haste may be such that he or she knocks down his or her own block tower during an attempt to make it taller; or a child may quickly blurt out a response before hearing the entire direction or question. The result may be poor test performance despite potentially adequate abilities. Similarly, while a young child's attention span is normally short (i.e., usually less than 15 minutes), this should be distinguished from distractibility. A child may be able to attend to an activity or a short story for 10 minutes if nothing occurs in the environment to distract him, but may go off task within seconds at the slightest sound down the hall or a fly buzzing by. Another child may be able to attend to an activity for only seconds at a time despite the absence of environmental distractions. Again, note the nature and extent of the behavior that is being observed and describe how it impacts on typical performance.

Summary

Qualitative observation of a young child's behavior during any assessment attempt enriches and rounds out the data obtained. As the examiner/practitioner acquires increased experience and skill in the assessment of infants and preschoolers, he or she will find that observations are made spontaneously—they become a natural and integral part of the assessment process. Initially, however, the use of a structured observation system can assist the examiner/practitioner in gathering information for appropriate interventions.

Suggested Group Activities

1. *Normalcy* is an important issue when discussing evaluative observations. How can educators keep subjectivity to a minimum and make their judgments as useful as possible? Design a brief list of guidelines to keep the assessment results objective.

2. Assign a task to a fellow classmate and carefully observe all   behaviors (i.e., physical characteristics, interactions, and overt attitudes). Write the observations in a report-style description. Be as objective as possible.

3. Make a list of techniques that can help children make the transition from the caregiver to the examiner. Role-play several ideas and write down helpful phrases and activities.

4. Why is it essential for children to develop problem-solving strategies? This is an important developmental skill and should be addressed in the assessment process. Think of various situations that could be presented to different ages to help elicit this skill.

5. Design a behavioral checklist that includes as many nonverbal areas as possible. Share the checklist with classmates and improve the original list with additional suggestions.

References

Bagnato, S. J., & Neisworth, J. T. (1991). *Assessment for early intervention: Best practices for professionals.* New York: Guilford Press.

Bracken, B. A. (1991). The clinical observation of preschool assessment behavior. In B. A. Bracken (Ed.), *The psychoeducational assessment of preschool children* (pp. 40–52). Boston: Allyn and Bacon.

Romero, I. (1992). Individual assessment procedures with preschool children. In E. V. Nuttall, I. Romero, & J. Kalesnik (Eds.), *Assessing and screening preschoolers: Psychological and educational dimensions* (pp. 55–66). Boston: Allyn and Bacon.

Chapter *4*

Family Involvement

JUDITH A. BONDURANT-UTZ
LENORE B. LUCIANO

The family unit is important to the assessment, program planning, and intervention processes for any child. This is particularly true with respect to the infant and young child whose life experiences are largely family-directed. In recent years, the field of early childhood education and intervention has come to recognize the child as a member of a family unit that is best regarded in its entirety.

The federal government has furthered the practice of family involvement in early childhood special education by mandating the inclusion of families in the assessment of and program development for infants and toddlers with disabilities (P.L. 99-457, The Education of the Handicapped Act Amendments, and P.L. 102-119, Individuals with Disabilities Education Act Amendments of 1991). As a result of this legislation, families are an integral part of the process of evaluating a young child's potential needs through their participation in assessment activities relating to the child's development and family functioning as well as in the planning of any intervention program. The family assessment, which strives to identify family strengths and needs, is one component of the early intervention process. Caregivers then work with professionals in the development of an Individualized Family Service Plan (IFSP) that defines the treatment program for the child and family (Fewell, 1991). (See, Developing an Individualized Family Service Plan, later in this chapter.)

Dunst, Johanson, Trivette, and Hamby (1991) encourage us to become increasingly *family-centered* in the policies and practices of our early intervention programs. Orienting assessment, planning, and treatment toward families as units is recommended for intervention with all young children and is mandated for those from birth to two years of age.

Dunst, Trivette, and Deal (1988) point out that the family—not the individual child—must be the focus of any plan and system of intervention in order to maximize its effectiveness. This recognition stems, in part, from an awareness that the success of any early intervention program is dependent on the efforts coming from within as well as from outside the family unit.

Dunst, Trivette, and Deal (1988) also champion respect for families and meaningfulness of intervention in their commitment to enabling and empowering families. *Enabling* is defined as creating opportunities for all families to display and acquire competencies that strengthen family functioning; and *empowerment* is the family's ability to meet needs and aspirations in a way that promotes a clear sense of intrafamily mastery and control over important aspects of family functioning. The key point is that family members must maintain ownership of their powerful, positive impact on one another, including the child with disabilities. The efficacy of early intervention programs will be enhanced to the extent that professionals can assist in meeting the needs and reaching the special goals of the family.

Domains of Family Assessment

Bailey and Simeonsson (1988) present and describe a number of specific tools that may be useful in conducting a family assessment. They point out that selecting an assessment tool for families should be based on individual program philosophies as well as individual family needs. They outline the levels of child and family assessment that may be conducted (see Table 4–1). These range, in focus, from the individual level, which addresses personal characteristics, to the community level, which considers supportive resources and legislation. They also suggest five domains that are potentially the most important areas to consider in family assessment. These are:

1. Child characteristics and needs likely to affect family functioning
2. Parent-child interactions
3. Family needs
4. Critical events
5. Family strengths

All the domains are not examined during each family assessment. The particular areas of focus should be determined on an individual family basis, depending on the presenting concerns and identified potential needs.

Child Characteristics and Needs

Children differ in behavioral and personality characteristics. Consequently, caregivers react and cope differently. Bailey and Simeonsson (1988) suggest

TABLE 4–1 Levels of Child and Family Assessment

Level	Description	Focus of Assessment
1	Individual clients: handicapped or at-risk infants and preschoolers, and individual members of their families	Children's skills in socialization, communication, thought, self-help, play, and motor ability. Children's behavioral characteristics (e.g., endurance, consolability, ability to deal with frustration, reactivity) Characteristics of individual family members
2	Demographic and environmental characteristics of families	Family size and membership Home environment
3	Interactions that occur within families	Parent-child interactions Relations between spouses Family roles and functions Family cohesion and decision-making strategies
4	External forces that directly create stress *or* provide support for families	Family needs Family resources Critical events Professional services
5	External factors that indirectly affect families or have the potential for providing support	Legislation Untapped state and community resources Agency policies

Source: From Simeonsson, R. J., *Psychological and Developmental Assessment of Special Children*, p. 11. Copyright © 1986. Boston: Allyn and Bacon. Reprinted with permission of Allyn and Bacon.

documentation of the child's behavior and temperament characteristics in order to gain a better understanding of family dynamics. Child variables that may affect family relationships include: child responsiveness, temperament, repetitive behavior patterns, the presence of unusual caregiving demands, consolability, regularity, responsiveness to others, endurance, and motivation (Bailey & Simeonsson, 1988).

Parent-Child Interactions

The emotional bonds that are established between caregivers and children during the preschool years can last a lifetime. Although many caregivers are able to develop and use appropriate interactional styles with their special needs children, potential problems may occur. Bailey and Simeonsson (1988) summarize the research in areas in which caregivers often need assistance. These areas include how to teach the child specific skills, how to respond appropriately to the child, and how to develop and maintain strong emotional bonds.

Family Needs

An important dimension to family assessment is the identification and documentation of specific needs with which each family would like assistance. These needs range from wanting information about their child's disability, including current and future services available, to developing strategies for teaching their child, obtaining babysitting services, and accessing specialized adaptive equipment, to finding and accessing financial assistance owing to medical complications. The early interventionist should be able to help families meet certain needs; refer them to other professionals, agencies, or resources; and help family members build and reinforce their own resources for meeting needs (Bailey & Simeonsson, 1988).

Critical Events

The purpose of this area of family assessment is to help professionals anticipate events that are likely to cause stress or problems. Examples of these events include the initial diagnosis or realization of a disability, stages of parental reactions and adjustment to the diagnosis, medical crises, transitions from one program to another, and a child's failure to achieve obvious developmental milestones (e.g., talking and walking). Awareness of these events in relation to the family will help the interventionist better understand the family and help them to plan coping strategies (Bailey & Simeonsson, 1988).

Family Strengths

Bailey and Simeonsson (1988) suggest three categories of family strengths and resources:

Personal resources: These are the personal characteristics that give meaning to life and allow individuals to address problems constructively. Examples of these resources might include an outgoing and assertive personality, a strong sense of competence and control over life, and religious or philosophical beliefs.

Within-family resources: These resources are obtained within the nuclear or extended family, e.g., from a spouse, sibling, parents, or in-laws. Within-family resources include help with specific tasks, such as child care or housekeeping, and socioemotional support, such as listening and responding empathically.

Extra-family resources: This type of resource comes from outside the family. Individuals or groups who might be a resource include neighbors, friends, professionals, social agencies, churches, and so on.

Benefits of Family Involvement

The importance of family involvement in the young child's assessment far exceeds compliance with federal mandates. The family's input and participation are highly valued for many reasons. The family constitutes the young child's predominant environment. Even those children who attend nursery and preschool programs do so for only small portions of the day or week. Also, few preschool-age children are either offered or ready for the social independence needed to establish a community of peers/friends outside the family circle. Most of the young child's functioning occurs within, or closely related to, family life. Therefore, it is difficult to meaningfully assess a child's functioning without considering him or her in the context of that primary environment. An excellent model for including the family in the assessment process is presented in *Transdisciplinary Play-based Assessment* (Linder, 1990).

Source of Information

The family's input also is highly valued because of the wealth of information it offers—families, parents, and caregivers, in particular, are the greatest source of information about the child. They are the experts with respect to this individual; birth, medical, and early developmental histories are vital to an understanding of the young child and his or her needs. Parent/caregiver responses to checklists, questionnaires, and inventories provide a host of information regarding the child's overall development, skills, and behaviors. Adaptive and daily functioning measures are an important part of the child's developmental assessment and are best provided by those with whom the child lives.

Most Naturalistic Setting

Our assessment of the child becomes fuller and richer when we examine the way the child functions within that most important and natural setting. Direct observation of the child-caregiver-family interactions leads to a better understanding of the child's interpersonal relating skills, personality, temperament, and communication effectiveness. Developmental, behavioral, and social skills assessments are served well by family participation and report.

Family Investment in Program

The parents, caregivers, and family also benefit from their involvement in the assessment process. By becoming active members of the assessment and intervention team, the parents/caregivers learn more about the child's functioning, strengths, and needs. The perspectives of the professional members of the multidisciplinary team add to the family's knowledge base by confirming what they observed, ruling out suspected concerns, and/or offering new observations and impressions. Furthermore, by participating in the development of the intervention plan (IFSP), the family's personal investment in the plan is increased. Through increased understanding of and agreement with the assessed needs and how to address them, family members become increasingly committed to the plan they help devise. Their competencies are enhanced in the process, enabling them to effectively meet the needs of their own child and family system.

Child Comfort and Security

Among the greatest benefits of family involvement in the assessment process is what it affords the child. The young child's feelings of comfort, safety, and security are important if an adequate sample of the child's capabilities is to be assumed. The young child's perceptions of safety and security often depend on parent feedback and support and, in the case of infants, on the parent's own demeanor and feelings of comfort in the unfamiliar setting. The parent/caregiver's presence and participation in the assessment process can hasten the child's establishment of trust and rapport with the other members of the team.

Respect for the Family

Recognition of the importance and value of the family's involvement in the assessment process must be matched by a respect for the family system and its unique set of circumstances. It is recommended that the examiners/practitioners strive for the following when assessing an infant or young child:

- Recognize and be sensitive to the family's values, attitudes, and feelings, especially as they relate to the child.
- Respect and communicate awareness of the family's *expertness* with respect to the child.
- Come to understand the family's expectations, wishes, and goals regarding the child.
- Respect the culture of the family, including its beliefs, customs, and parenting styles.
- Note how the family's style and expectations impact on the child and how adaptive the child is in the context of the family and its routine practices.
- Assist and empower the family while not diminishing or disregarding its responsibility for the child.
- Recognize the particular stresses the assessment must present to the parents/caregivers. The assessment may confirm or refute some concerns raised about the child. Sensitivity and respect for the family's tension at this time is crucial to accurate data collection as well as to effective decision making regarding the child's potential programming.

Developing an Individualized Family Service Plan

The requirement mandated by P.L. 99-457 for the development of an Individualized Family Service Plan (IFSP) emphasizes the view of the child in the context of the family. Children from birth to two years of age who receive services through Part H must have an IFSP.

The law provides some guidance with respect to the development and completion of the IFSP process. Information is included about the content, participants, meetings, and timelines of the process. The IFSP must include these seven elements:

1. Statement of the child's functioning
2. Statement of family strengths and needs
3. Statement of outcomes
4. Early intervention plans
5. Dates for services
6. Designated case managers
7. A transition plan

No specific format is required for the IFSP except that it must be a written plan. The emphasis is on the process rather than the completion of a standardized form.

Slentz and Bricker (1992) advocate a family-guided rather than a family-focused approach to family assessment and early intervention. With a family-guided approach, the child remains the primary focus of intervention and assessment. Resolution of family issues is facilitated by the interventionist as concerns or priorities related to the child's development are raised. Family outcomes are included in the IFSP as they arise rather than being identified at the time of entry into the program. The family guides the content of assessment and intervention so that services are individualized according to family members' priorities, values, culture, and activities.

Slentz and Bricker (1992) recommend an initial interview and a brief needs assessment. Discussing family strengths sets a positive tone and allows the family the opportunity to participate in the intervention planning. A series of topics or questions such as those posed by Kaiser and Hemmeter (1989) are recommended (see Table 4–2). The questions should be discussed with the family in the context of assessing their needs and planning to meet those needs (Kaiser & Hemmeter, 1989). The family also could be given the opportunity to complete a formal or informal needs assessment at this time or at a later meeting.

In essence, families are responsible for their children. Needs and concerns, as identified by the family, determine the professional's role. Families do not have to participate in the family assessment in order for their children to receive services. However, the most effective method of obtaining useful information for early intervention depends on collaboration between caregivers and professionals (Benner, 1992).

TABLE 4-2 Checklist for Intervenors

Part I: Questions about the Intervention

1. Does the intervention enhance family participation in the community?
2. Does the intervention improve the family's ability to meet its developmental tasks?
3. Does the intervention enhance the family's social support?
4. Does the intervention provide essential minimum resources?
5. Does the intervention promote shared responsibility between parents and service provider?
6. Will the intervention provide opportunities for family members to enhance their skills and competence?
7. Will the intervention deprive any family member of care or support?
8. Does the intervention include only procedures that are nonaversive, safe, and development-promoting?

Part II: Questions about the appropriateness of a particular intervention for a family

1. Is the intervention based on a valid needs assessment?
2. Did the family indicate this as a priority need?
3. Is the intervention likely to be sufficient to meet the priority need?
4. Is the level of intervention appropriate for the problem?
5. Does the intervention plan include a comprehensive evaluation of its effects?
6. Is the ratio of benefits to costs (resources, time, intrusion) acceptable to the family?
7. Are the family members willing and able to meet the costs?
8. Is the intervention consistent with the family's values?
9. Does the intervention fit with the family's context in the community and the prevailing social norms?
10. Is the amount of change, relative to the status quo, required of the family acceptable to them?

Source: From Kaiser, A., & Hemmeter, M. (1989). Value-based approaches to family intervention. *Topics in Early Childhood Special Education, 8*(4):72–86. Copyright © 1992 by PRO-ED, Inc. Reprinted by permission.

Assessing Family Strengths and Needs

Families report that one of the most threatening and uncomfortable aspects of early intervention services is the process of family assessment (Slentz, Walker, & Bricker, 1989). The process of identifying family strengths and needs must be done on an individual basis. The purpose is to identify strengths, resources, needs, and concerns relevant to an individual family's ability to enhance the development of the child (Johnson, McGonigel, & Kaufmann, 1989).

Professionals seeking information should always explain why the information is needed and how it will be used. Professionals must always assure caregivers of their right not to provide information they consider irrelevant or to answer questions they consider intrusive.

Methods and Techniques for Gathering Information

The early interventionist must view the family as a system and assess the different factors influencing it (Ostfeld & Gibbs, 1990). A variety of methods may be used to assess the family. These methods include interviews, observations, and self-report questionnaires and test instruments. The law does not mandate that formal surveys, indices, scales, and questionnaires be used (Slentz & Bricker, 1992). The method and the content area of the assessment should be chosen to fulfill the program's goals.

Interviews
Parent/caregiver interviews may be used either to gather or clarify information from other sources, such as caregiver's perceptions about specific events and identification of priorities for services. The interview may be either nondirected or structured/focused. Nondirected interviews provide the opportunity to build rapport but make data gathering and goal setting difficult. Inexperienced staff may have difficulty interpreting data from unstructured interviews. A structured or focused interview has specific questions or goals. The questions may have forced-choice responses or be open-ended. This type of interview may be helpful for families who are uncomfortable with a questionnaire (Ostfeld & Gibbs, 1990).

Observations
Observations also may be structured or unstructured. Observations may be used to determine the rate, quality, or pattern of behavior (e.g., caregiver–child interactions) in natural and/or clinical settings. Structured observations are helpful when specific information is needed. For example, a coding system may be used to measure a predetermined behavior or category of behaviors—e.g., displays of affection, initiation of interactions by caregiver (Benner, 1992). A running record of observations is another technique that may be useful. (Running records are discussed further in chapter 11, Ecological and Behavior Assessment.) The professional should always remember that it is difficult to be natural when one is being observed. These techniques should be compatible with family functioning style and the types of information needed.

Questionnaires and Test Instruments
Standardized instruments as well as less formal self-report checklists and scales provide an efficient, uniform way of gathering information (Ostfeld & Gibbs, 1990). Some instruments are designed to identify family strengths, needs, resources, and sources of support. Other instruments are designed to determine family functioning in specific areas such as stress, knowledge of infant development, or depression. Assessment of family functioning should be used only if specific areas of concern arise during the process of identifying strengths and needs.

Professionals should remember that self-report questionnaires may have items that parents see as being intrusive, and they have the right to choose not to respond. When administering a questionnaire, the professional needs to provide a general statement of purpose and allow parents/caregivers not to answer. Staff members should be available to clarify questions that are unclear or not understood.

Many types of assessments are available that may or may not be appropriate for use in some early intervention programs with particular families. Some of the various instruments and strategies that can be used to assess families are listed in Table 4–3. Ostfeld and Gibbs (1990) recommend that professionals: (1) know what a test purports to measure, (2) avoid interpretations that go beyond the data, and (3) recognize and respect individual differences. These authors further recommend, when selecting and evaluating an assessment method, that a review of the literature on the selected instrument or method be conducted to ascertain the reliability and validity for the particular families with which it will be used. They also suggest that interpretation of findings and making appropriate recommendations based on these instruments should be directed to a mental health practitioner who has the clinical experience in counseling families with special needs children.

Simeonsson (1986) cautions professionals to be aware of the subjectivity of their philosophies and value systems in order to avoid imposing them on family demands that are incompatible with the family's lifestyle and belief system. For example, instruments developed by and for the Western Caucasian population reflect a set of cultural norms and beliefs about children, parenting, and the role of families. The cultural values of families from diverse backgrounds may differ from Western, Caucasian middle-class standards (Hanson, Lynch, & Wayman, 1990).

Models of Family-oriented Strengths and Needs Assessment

Two comprehensive, family-focused models have been developed for assessment and intervention. These models may be used to assist in the data-gathering process for IFSP development. The models are similar and use the interview process to obtain information (Benner, 1992).

The first model is the Family-Focused Intervention Model, which is presented in depth in *Family Assessment in Early Intervention* (Bailey & Simeonsson, 1988). These steps are delineated in the model: (1) initial family assessment, (2) focused interview, (3) follow-up assessments, (4) IFSP meeting, (5) implementation of needed services, and (6) evaluation.

The second model is the Family Systems Assessment and Intervention Model. This model is explained in *Enabling and Empowering Families: Principles and Guidelines for Practice* (Dunst, Trivette, & Deal, 1988). The four steps outlined in this model are: (1) identification of family needs, (2) identification of family functioning styles and strengths, (3) identification of sources of support and resources, and (4) professional's role as help-giver. A number of assessment scales used in this model (listed on page 55) are included in this text.

TABLE 4-3   Assessment of Family Context

Title/Author	Source
Parent/Caregiver–Child Interactions	
Dyadic Parent-Child Interaction Coding System (Robinson & Eyberg, 1981	*Journal of Consulting and Clinical Psychology, 49,* 245–250
Social Interaction Assessment/Intervention (McCollum & Stayton, 1985)	*Journal of the Division for Early Childhood, 9*(2), 125–135
Parent Behavior Progression (Bromwich, 1981)	*Working with parents and infants: An interactional approach.* Baltimore: University Park Press
Nursing Child Assessment Teaching and Feeding Scales (Bee, Barnard, Eyres, Gray, Hammond, Spietz, Snyder, & Clark, 1982)	*Child Development, 53,* 1134–1156
The Assessment of Parent-Infant Interaction by Observation of Feeding and Teaching (Barnard & Bee, 1984)	In T. B. Brazelton and B. Lester (Eds.), *New approaches to developmental screening in infants.* New York: Elsevier, North Holland
Interaction Rating Scales (Clark & Siefer, 1985)	*Infant Mental Health Journal, 6,* 214–225
Social Interaction Assessment/Intervention (McCollum, 1984; McCollum, & Stayton, 1985)	Infant/Parent Interaction: Studies and Intervention Guidelines Based on the SIAI Model. *Journal of the Division for Early Childhood, 9*(2), 125–135
Teaching Skills Inventory (Rosenberg, Robinson & Beckman, 1984)	*Journal of the Division for Early Childhood, 8,* 107–113
Material Behavior Rating Scale (Mahoney, Finger, & Powell, 1985)	*American Journal of Mental Deficiency, 90,* 296–302
Parent/Caregiver Involvement Scale (Farran, Kasari, Yoder, Harber, Huntington, & Comfort-Smith, 1987)	In T. Tamir (Ed.), *Stimulation and intervention in infant development.* London: Freund.
Family Strengths and Needs	
Family Needs Survey (Bailey & Simeonsson, 1986)	*Family assessment in early intervention.* Columbus, OH: Merrill.

(Continued)

TABLE 4–3 *(Continued)*

Title/Author	Source
Parent Needs Survey (Seligman & Darling, 1989)	*Ordinary families, special children: A systems approach to childhood disability.* New York: Guilford
How Can We Help? (1988)	Child Development Resources, P.O. Box 299, Lightfoot, VA 23090-0299
Family Information Preference Inventory (Turnbull & Turnbull, 1986)	*Families, professionals, and exceptionality: A special partnership.* Columbus, OH: Merrill
Family Strengths Scale (Olson, Portner, & Bell, 1982)	Family Adaptation and Cohesion Evaluation Scales. Unpublished rating scales, School of Family and Social Sciences, University of Minnesota, St. Paul, MN
Family Adjustment Survey (Abbott & Meredith, 1986)	*Family Relations, 35,* 371–375
Family Functioning	
Family-Systems-Test (Gehring & Wyler, 1986)	*Child Psychiatry and Human Development, 16,* 235–248
Beavers-Timberlawn Family Evaluation Scale (Lewis, Beavers, Gossett, & Austin-Phillips, 1976)	In J. Lewis, et al., *No single thread: Psychological health in family systems.* New York: Bruner/Mazel
Family Assessment Device (Epstein, Baldwin, & Bishop, 1983)	*Journal of Marital and Family Therapy, 9,* 171–180
Family Assessment Measure (Skinner, Steinhauser, & Santa-Barbara, 1983)	*Canadian Journal of Community Mental Health, 2,* 91–105
Family APGAR (Smilkstein, 1978)	*Journal of Family Practice, 6,* 1231–1239
Family Adaptability and Cohesion Evaluation Scales (FACES, I, II, and III) (Olson, Portner, & Lavee, 1985)	In P. H. Olson, H. I. McCubbin, H. Barnes, A. Larsen, M. Muxen, and M. Wilson (Eds.), *Family inventories in a national survey of families across the family life cycle.* St. Paul, MN: University of Minnesota, Family Social Sciences

TABLE 4-3   *(Continued)*

Title/Author	Source
Family Environment Scale (Moos & Moos, 1981)	Palo Alto, CA: Consulting Psychologists Press
Social Support and Resource Scales	
Psychosocial Kinship Inventory (Pattison, DeFrancisco, Wood, Frazier, & Crowder, 1975)	*American Journal of Psychiatry, 132,* 1246–1251
Perceived Support Network Inventory (Oritt, Paul, & Behrman, 1985)	*American Journal of Community Psychology, 13,* 565–582
Exercise: Social Support (Summers, Turnbull, & Brotherson, 1989)	In B. H. Johnson, M. J. McGonigel, and R. K. Kaufman (Eds.), *Guidelines and recommended practices for the individualized family service plan.* National Early Childhood Technical Assistance System and Association for the Care of Children's Health, Bethesda, MD
Social Network Questionnaire (Levitt, Weber & Clark, 1986)	*Developmental Psychology, 22,* 310–316
Stress	
Questionnaire on Resources and Stress (Holroyd, 1974)	*Journal of Community Psychology, 2,* 92–94
Questionnaire on Resources and Stress for Families with a Chronically Ill or Handicapped Member: Manual (short form) (Holroyd, 1986)	Brandon, VT: Clinical Psychology Publishing
Parenting Stress Index (2d ed.) (Abidin, 1986)	Charlottesville, VA: Pediatric Psychology Press
Impact-on-Family Scale (Stein & Reissman, 1980)	*Medical Care, 18,* 465–472
Impact-on-Family Scale Adapted for Families of Children with Handicaps (McLinden-Mott & Braeger, 1988)	*Journal of the Division for Early Childhood, 12*(3), 217–223
Functional Status Measure (Stein & Jessop, 1982)	*Public Health Report, 97,* 354–362

(Continued)

TABLE 4-3   *(Continued)*

Title/Author	Source
Life Events	
Recent Life Changes Questionnaire (Rahe, 1978)	*Psychosomatic Medicine, 40,* 95–98
Life Experiences Survey (Sarason, Johnson, & Siegel, 1978)	*Journal of Consulting and Clinical Psychology, 46,* 932–946
Family Inventory of Life Events and Changes (McCubbin & Patterson, 1987)	In H. M. McCubbin and A. I. Thompson (Eds.), *Family assessment inventories for research and practice,* 79–98. Madison, WI: University of Wisconsin–Madison
Spouse Relations	
Measuring Dydadic Adjustment: New Scales for Assessing the Quality of Marriage and Similar Dyads (Spanier, 1976)	*Journal of Marriage and the Family, 38,* 15–28
Perceptions of Support from Spouse	
The Division of Responsibilities in Families with Preschool Handicapped Children (Gallagher, Scharfman, & Bristol, 1984)	*Journal of the Division for Early Childhood, 8,* 3–12
Parental Perceptions of Children's Characteristics	
Revision of the Infant Temperament Questionnaire (Carey & McDevitt, 1978)	*Pediatrics, 61,* 735–738
Locus of Control	
Development and Validation of the Child Improvement Locus of Control Scales (DeVillis, DeVillis, Revicki, Lurie, Runyan & Bristol, 1985)	*Journal of Social and Clinical Psychology, 3,* 308–325
Parental Satisfaction with Services	
Assessment of Client Parent Satisfaction: Development of a General Scale (Larsen, Attkinsson, Hargreaves & Nguyen, 1979)	*Evaluation and Program Planning, 2,* 197–207
Family Coping	
Parent Perception Inventory (Hymovich, 1988)	King of Prussia, PA: D. Hymovich

- Needs-based Assessment Scales

    Family Resource Scale (Dunst & Leet)
    Support Functions Scale (Dunst & Trivette)
    Resource Scale for Teenage Mothers (Dunst, Leet, Vance, & Cooper)
    Family Needs Scale (Dunst, Cooper, Weeldreyer, Snyder, & Chase)

- Social Support Scales

    Family Support Scales (Dunst, Trivette, & Jenkins)
    Inventory of Social Support (Trivette & Dunst)
    Personal Network Matrix (Trivette & Dunst)

- Family Functioning Style Scale (Deal, Trivette, & Dunst)
- Profile of Family Needs and Social Support (Trivette, Dunst, & Deal)
- Family Strengths Profile (Trivette, Dunst, & Deal)

Summary

Best practice, as well as federal mandates, encourages focusing on the family unit when evaluating the developmental functioning of infants and young children. An assessment of family strengths, needs, cultural values, and preferences plays a significant role in the development and delivery of early childhood special education services. Collaboration between caregivers and professionals is essential to meaningful program planning and intervention.

A variety of levels and domains of family assessment are germane to the field of early intervention. The benefits of family involvement in the assessment of and programming for young children are many. A critical aspect of effective family–practitioner relationships is respect for family values, practices, and decisions, especially as they relate to the child.

Ten guiding principles underlying the IFSP process have been developed by the National Early Childhood Technical Assistance System (Johnson, McGonigel, & Kaufman, 1989). These guiding principles are:

1. *Infants and toddlers are uniquely dependent on their families for their survival and nurturance. This dependence necessitates a family-centered approach to early intervention.*
2. *States and programs should define* family *in a way that reflects the diversity of family patterns and structures.*
3. *Each family has its own structure, roles, values, beliefs, and coping styles. Respect for and acceptance of this diversity is a cornerstone of family-centered early intervention.*
4. *Early intervention systems and strategies must reflect a respect for the racial, ethnic, and cultural diversity of families.*

5. *Respect for family autonomy, independence, and decision making means that families must be able to choose the level and nature of early intervention's involvement in their life.*
6. *Family/professional collaboration and partnerships are the keys to family-centered early intervention and to successful implementation of the IFSP process.*
7. *An enabling approach to working with families requires that professionals reexamine their traditional roles and practices and develop new practices when necessary—practices that promote mutual respect and partnerships.*
8. *Early intervention services should be flexible, accessible, and responsive to family needs.*
9. *Early intervention services should be provided according to the normalization principle—that is, families should have access to services provided in as normal a fashion and environment as is possible and that promote the integration of the child and family within the community.*
10. *No one agency or discipline can meet the diverse and complex needs of infants and toddlers with special needs and their families. Therefore, a team approach to planning and implementing the IFSP is necessary. (p. 6)*

Considering these underlying principles, early intervention should be based on a family-guided, family-centered, or family-focused philosophy. There needs to be a direct link between assessment and intervention strategies. The information collected through child and family assessments should assist in developing IFSP objectives and enhance the effectiveness of intervention strategies for the child and the family (Slentz & Bricker, 1992).

Suggested Group Activities

1. Interview some parents/caregivers of children with developmental disabilities. Try to determine if each family feels included in the child's assessment and educational process. Compare notes with other classmates about the results of these discussions and devise a list of suggestions to help caregivers feel they are a part of this process. An informal needs assessment could be used here.

2. Role-play the position of an interventionist explaining to a caregiver some of the following:

- How to teach his or her child a particular skill
- Response options to the child's behavior
- How to encourage emotional support
- Describing the child's strengths and weaknesses

3. Using a real or imagined case study of an infant or young child, develop an Individualized Family Service Plan (IFSP). Address each of the seven elements mentioned in this chapter. Share these with other groups and be prepared to explain or defend the goals.

4. Compile a directory of local support services that could be useful to parents/caregivers of children with special needs. Try to include agencies and organizations that would address a variety of IFSP goals. Provide the names of contact people, locations, telephone numbers, criteria for acceptance, any fees, and the type(s) of services provided.

5. Distribute some sample Individual Education Plans of students and discuss where the goals could have been rewritten to include family involvement and participation.

6. Ten principles that support the IFSP process were outlined in this chapter. After dividing into small groups, generate statements, examples, or ideas to support each of these important principles.

References

Bailey, D. B., & Simeonsson, R. J. (1988). *Family assessment in early intervention*. Columbus, OH: Merrill.

Benner, S. (1992). *Assessing young children with special needs: An ecological perspective*. New York: Longman.

Dunst, C. J., Johanson, C., Trivette, C. M., & Hamby, D. (1991). Family-oriented early intervention policies and practices: Family-centered or not? *Exceptional Children, 58*(2), 115–126.

Dunst, C., Trivette, C., & Deal, A. (1988). *Enabling and empowering families: Principles and guidelines for practice*. Cambridge, MA: Brookline.

Fewell, R. R. (1991). Trends in the assessment of infants and toddlers with disabilities. *Exceptional Children, 58*(2), 166–173.

Hanson, M. J., Lynch, E. W., & Wayman, K. I. (1990). Honoring the cultural diversity of families when gathering data. *Topics in Early Childhood Special Education, 10*(1), 112–131.

Johnson, B. H., McGonigel, M. J., & Kaufmann, R. K. (Eds.). (1989). *Guidelines and recommended practices for the individualized family service plan*. Chapel Hill, NC: National Early Childhood Technical Assistance System and the Association for the Care of Children's Health.

Kaiser, A., & Hemmeter, M. (1989). Value-based approaches to family intervention. *Topics in Early Childhood Special Education, 8*(4), 72–86.

Linder, T. W. (1990). *Transdisciplinary play-based assessment: A functional approach to working with young children*, Baltimore: Paul H. Brookes.

Ostfeld, B. M., & Gibbs, E. D. (1990). Use of family assessment in early intervention. In E. D. Gibbs & D. M. Teti (Eds.), *Interdisciplinary assessment of infants: A guide for early intervention professionals* (pp. 249–271). Baltimore: Paul Brookes.

Simeonsson, R. J. (1986). *Psychological and developmental assessment of special children*. Boston: Allyn and Bacon.

Slentz, K., & Bricker, D. (1992). Family-guided assessment for IFSP development: Jumping off the family-assessment bandwagon. *Journal of Early Intervention, 16*(1), 11–19.

Slentz, K., Walker, B., & Bricker, D. (1989). Supporting involvement in early intervention: A role-taking model. In G. Singer & L. Irvin (Eds.), *Support for caregiving families: Enabling positive adaptations to disability* (pp. 221–238). Baltimore: Paul H. Brookes.

Chapter 5

The Team Process

The Team Approach

The provisions of P.L. 99-457 require that services for a child with a disability include a multidisciplinary assessment and a written Individualized Family Service Plan (IFSP) that is developed by a multidisciplinary team that includes the family. The team approach reflects the early interventionists' view of human development as an integrated and interactive whole and not simply a collection of separate parts (Golin & Duncanis, 1981). This interrelated nature of developmental domains is prompting early interventionists to recognize the need for professionals to work together as a team (Woodruff & McGonigel, 1988).

Early intervention teams use a variety of disciplines. The roles and functions of the disciplines outlined in P.L. 99-457 are summarized in Table 5-1. All of these disciplines have several common tasks or services, including assessment of the child's developmental status and the development and implementation of a program to meet identified needs. The way these services are incorporated into a plan by a multidisciplinary team differs

There are three team structures for providing services to children who are at risk or have a disability—multidisciplinary, interdisciplinary, and transdisciplinary models. These team approaches differ in philosophy and in the way they function. Table 5–2 outlines the differences between these team approaches to intervention.

Multidisciplinary

The multidisciplinary approach to providing services frequently is used to describe an evaluation and management process in which many individual evaluations from different disciplines are obtained, but they are done independent of each other with little opportunity for the various professionals to interact. Each

TABLE 5-1   Roles and Functions of Service Providers under P.L. 99-457

Role	Functions
Infant special educator	Generally takes responsibility for the child's overall educational growth and development. Planning and educational programming, monitoring infant development, educational assessment, child and family advocacy, and referral to ancillary services (Ensher & Clark, 1986).
Speech/language pathologist and audiologist	Has primary responsibility for the child's development of communicative abilities. In working with infants, this specialist is concerned with oral-motor facilitation, feeding therapy, and development of preverbal communication (Hanson & Harris, 1986; Mueller, 1972)
Occupational therapist	Takes primary responsibility for the child's sensory development and integration. The motor focus overlaps with communicative development, thus necessitating the close working relationship with the speech/language pathologist and audiologist (Mather & Weinstein, 1988), yet the emphasis on sensory information processing distinguishes the functions of this professional (Jenkins, Fewell, & Harris, 1983).
Physical therapist	Focuses on the neurologic functioning underlying gross motor development (Harris, 1982). With the occupational therapist, the physical therapist takes primary responsibility for the child's positioning, handling, and movement; the emphasis is on the facilitation of normal movement and the suppression of abnormal movement (Bobath & Bobath, 1972).
Psychologist	Responsible for the child's behavior, cognitive, and social-emotional development. As such, the psychologist has a strong interest in the family's psychological climate. Primary responsibilities include psychological assessment, child and family counseling, and consultation with other team members concerning the child's behavior and development.
Social worker	Provides a close link between home and program, which is critical to successful intervention. Knowledge of the family's dynamics, information about siblings and grandparents of the handicapped young child, and an understanding of family stresses.
Nurse	Takes responsibility for the medical well-being of the child and family. This may involve both general preventive measures, such as regular physical examinations and routine innoculations, as well as more specific treatment of medical disorders, such as supervising prescriptive medication for a seizure disorder (Peterson, 1987).
Nutritionist	Works with the parents or other caregivers to ensure optimal nutrition for the handicapped infant or toddler. Provides guidance in food purchase, preservation, and preparation to help ensure proper diet and treat dietary problems (Thurman & Widerstrom, 1990).

Source: From B. A. Mowder, A. H. Widerstrom, & S. R. Sandall, 1989. School psychologists serving at-risk and handicapped infants, toddlers and their families. *Professional School Psychology* 4(3), p. 161. Reprinted with permission of Guilford Publications, Inc.

TABLE 5–2 Three Models for Early Intervention

	Multidisciplinary	Interdisciplinary	Transdisciplinary
Assessment	Separate assessments by team members	Separate assessments by team members	Team members and family conduct a comprehensive developmental assessment together
Parent participation	Parents meet with individual team members	Parents meet with team or team representative	Parents are full, active, and participating members of the team
Service plan development	Team members develop separate plans for their discipline	Team members share their separate plans with one another	Team members and the parents develop a service plan based on family priorities, needs, and resources
Service plan responsibility	Team members are responsible for implementing their section of the plan.	Team members are responsible for sharing information with one another as well as for implementing their section of the plan	Team members are responsible and accountable for how the primary service provider implements the plan
Service plan implementation	Team members implement the part of the service plan related to their discipline	Team members implement their section of the plan and incorporate other sections where possible	A primary service provider is assigned to implement the plan with the family
Lines of communication	Informal lines	Periodic case-specific team meetings	Regular team meeting where continuous transfer of information, knowledge, and skills are shared among team members
Guiding philosophy	Team members recognize the importance of contributions from other disciplines	Team members are willing and able to develop, share, and be responsible for providing services that are a part of the total service plan	Team members make a commitment to teach, learn, and work together across discipline boundaries to implement unified service plan
Staff development	Independent and within their discipline	Independent within as well as outside of their discipline	An integral component of team meetings for learning across disciplines and team building

Source: From Woodruff, G. A., & Hanson, C. (1987). Project KAI, 77B Warren Street, Brighton, MA 02135. Funded by U.S. Department of Education, Special Education Programs, Handicapped Children's Early Education Program. Reprinted with permission of the Council for Exceptional Children.

discipline uses an instrument(s) specifically designed to measure development in that discipline. Team members develop the part of the service plan that is related to their own discipline. Peterson (1987) compares the way multidisciplinary team members interact to parallel play; they work side by side but separately. This approach omits the possibility of group synthesis and can result in duplicate services for families.

Interdisciplinary

An interdisciplinary team is composed of both parents/caregivers and professionals representing several disciplines. Professionals and caregivers/parents work together cooperatively to plan and deliver services to the child or caregiver/parent. Interdisciplinary teams have formal channels of communication that encourage team members to share their information and discuss individual results (Fewell, 1983; Peterson, 1987). Separate assessments are conducted by each discipline's specialist, who is basically responsible for the part of the service plan in his or her area at scheduled therapy or consultation times. Regular meetings are held to discuss the results of individual assessments and to develop plans for intervention. This approach outlines a process in which professionals from different but related disciplines work together to assess and manage problems by actively participating in mutual decision making. The team members share information with one another but independently implement their section of a plan. The emphasis is on teamwork and interaction among the team members to provide well-coordinated, integrated services for the child and family.

Transdisciplinary

The transdisciplinary approach describes what many professionals believe to be the ideal type of interdisciplinary team functioning. Woodruff and McGonigel (1988) recommend the transdisciplinary approach as a sound, logical, and valid system for offering coordination and comprehensive services to young children and their families. The transdisciplinary approach involves the mutual sharing of assessment results and dictates professional involvement and participation that crosses traditional discipline boundaries. Professionals from any of the disciplines involved in early intervention—nursing, nutrition, psychology, social work, special education, occupational and physical therapy, and speech/language and hearing—may be included in a transdisciplinary team approach.

Two basic beliefs are integral to this approach. First, the child's development must be seen as integrated and interactive. Second, a child needs to be served within the context of the family (Woodruff & McGonigel, 1988). Families are seen as part of the transdisciplinary team and participate in goal-setting and program decisions because they have the greatest influence on the child's development. With this approach, professionals work together with the direct guidance of the family to develop a unified and integrated plan for the child and the family. The service plan is carried out by the family and one other team member who is designated as the primary service provider.

Description of the Transdisciplinary Approach

Rationale

The basic rationale for the transdisciplinary approach to serving children and families with disabilities is the desire to have fewer people work directly with the family and child, to improve continuity in programming, to attain maximum consistency of services in the home and center, and to improve integration of parent participation (Raver, 1991).

The transdisciplinary approach attempts to meet the needs of the child and family without compartmentalization and fragmentation of planning and services. The interaction that takes place between team members allows professionals to get a more balanced and integrated picture of the whole child. Each discipline cannot be concerned only with the needs that a particular professional sees. For example, the physical therapist cannot look just at the motor needs of the child; how motor status impacts on the child's functioning in other areas (i.e., educational performance, personal-social interactions, play skills) need to be considered as well.

Role of Transdisciplinary Team Members

The team members systematically cross traditional discipline boundaries to better understand other disciplines and provide services to families who require skills outside their own discipline when appropriate and necessary. The shared responsibilities of transdisciplinary teamwork is not easily achieved. The approach demands flexibility, tolerance, and understanding among and between those involved (Garland, Woodruff, & Buck, 1988).

Transdisciplinary team members have many responsibilities. They conduct assessments and develop service plans as a team with the direct collaboration of families, focusing on the families' priorities. A primary service provider is authorized by the team to work directly with the family and implement the plan. Each team member is accountable for how the primary service provider implements the plan. Many meetings are needed to discuss assessment, diagnosis and goal setting, planning and program implementation, and evaluation of the program and the child.

Team members are responsible for organizing regular staff development meetings to teach their discipline's skills to other members and to share discipline-specific information. An integral part of the transdisciplinary approach is learning across discipline lines. The program is developed by the whole team and implemented by each member not just the primary service provider.

Role Release

Role release is the sharing of responsibilities and roles across disciplines by more than one team member. This process is what distinguishes transdisciplinary teaming from interdisciplinary teaming. The transdisciplinary model requires administrators and other professionals to commit themselves to teaching, learning, and working across discipline boundaries. Role release allows professionals to teach discipline-specific skills to other team professionals from different discipline backgrounds. The process of role release demands professional and personal change and a continuous dialogue between team members.

Program Components

Transdisciplinary procedures need to be utilized throughout each phase of service delivery from intake to reassessment. Administrators and team members must be aware of how the model affects program operation in each phase. The components of the transdisciplinary approach, outlined by Woodruff and Hanson (1987), are shown in Table 5–3.

Arena Assessment

Transdisciplinary teams often use an assessment process known as arena assessment. In an arena assessment, one professional (the facilitator) does the testing while the other team members sit on the floor around the child and caregiver(s), and observe. The role of the facilitator is to engage the child in activities that demonstrate the child's developmental strengths and weaknesses.

Team members meet before an arena assessment and identify behaviors for the facilitator that they would like to see for their individual evaluations. After the assessment, if the professionals in the arena did not observe all they needed, parent report items are used or a time for another assessment is arranged. Following the arena assessment, the team meets to discuss the results and plan an intervention; this sharing becomes natural and continuous. Professionals who use arena assessment report that it saves time and with training they can see what they need for their discipline-specific evaluations while also observing the child's overall functioning.

The arena assessment is a major component of the transdisciplinary model but occasionally this format may not be the best for an individual child or family. For example, a sensitive or distractible child may not be able to perform well in an arena. Some families may be very uneasy in the presence of more than one person at a time, and, therefore, they may not be willing to participate. Programs should be sensitive to this possibility and alter assessments as needed (Woodruff & McGonigel, 1988). The use of one-way mirrors, with caregiver knowledge and permission, can get around this problem.

Advantages

An arena assessment offers advantages for the child, the family and the whole team (Woodruff, 1980). Advantages for the family include: (1) communication to caregivers that they are fully functioning members of the team, (2) decreasing

TABLE 5-3 Components of the Transdisciplinary Model

Intake
Responsibility rotated among team members.
Rapport established with family.
Family information and child data gathered.
Transdisciplinary model explained.

Pre-arena preparation
Facilitator and coach chosen for assessment.
Case presentation provided.
Team members coach facilitator.
Team members share information across disciplines.
Staff members chosen to lead post-arena feedback to parent.

Arena assessment
Arena facilitator works with child and parents.
Team members observe all aspects of child's behavior and parent. child interaction.
Team members observe and record across all developmental areas.
Arena facilitator works to reassure parent and gain involvement.

Post-arena feedback to family
Child's strengths and needs are established.
Family's goals and priorities are discussed.
Activities are recommended for home implementation.

Post-arena discussion of team process
Primary service provider (PSP) assignment is made.
Team evaluates assessment process and provides feedback to one another.

IFSP development
Team develops goals, objectives, and activities.
Parents and PSP reach consensus on which IFSP goals, objectives, and activities will be initiated first.

Activity planning
Team establishes regular meetings to monitor the implementation of the IFSP, to assign daily or weekly activities, and to make revisions in the plan.

Program implementation
PSP implements the plan.
Team members monitor the implementation, maintain accountability for their discipline, provide role support, and when needed, supervision.

Reassessment
Team follows pre-arena, arena, and post-arena procedures.

Program continues to repeat cycle

Source: From Woodruff, G. A., & Hanson, C. (1987). Project KAI, 77B Warren Street, Brighton, MA 02135. Funded by the U.S. Department of Education, Special Education Programs, Handicapped Children's Early Education Program. Reprinted with permission of the Council for Exceptional Children.

the possibility of service providers asking the same questions, and (3) communication that efforts to assist the child are a series of problem-solving experiences. Advantages for the child are that only one assessment time is needed instead of separate domain-specific assessments; and the child is able to demonstrate strengths under a natural, more global set of circumstances.

Advantages for the team include: (1) provision of a comprehensive, integrated assessment of the child; (2) team sharing of knowledge about the child's development based on the same observation of the child, leading to easier consensus; and (3) expansion of the knowledge of all team members because they all are able to see the child from their discipline's perspective and simultaneously receive a perception of the child from another discipline.

Selection of Assessment Instruments
The team needs to choose the appropriate assessment instrument. Each professional should identify the essential information he or she wishes to learn from the evaluation and specify the sample of behavior that will allow him or her to draw the required inferences. The team then constructs a general outline of the assessment categories (Foley, 1990). Foley provides an example of such an outline for an arena assessment of an infant (see Table 5–4), he cautions that this list is not exhaustive.

Foley (1990) encourages the team to strive to identify a single arena instrument. This instrument should contain the broadest item pool, sample the most representative range of behaviors, and cover the most categories in the general outline. This is just one part of the multidimensional, multisource assessment process. This single instrument is then supplemented with more in-depth assessments in particular areas that require additional information.

Conducting an Arena Assessment
There is no definite script for an arena assessment. Exactly how the assessment is carried out varies according to the needs of child and family. This process develops for each team after members work together for a time. Foley (1990) suggests a more structured sequence that can be followed with older toddlers (see Table 5–5).

Linder's (1990) transdisciplinary, play-based assessment (TPBA) model is designed to provide an arena assessment. Observation guidelines for cognitive, social-emotional, communication and language, and sensorimotor development are outlined in her book. Linder also outlines a flexible six-phase process. Table 5–6 gives an overview of the format used in the TPBA model.

Criteria for Effective Transdisciplinary Teams

Hutchinson (1974), a primary advocate of this approach, stressed several criteria for working effectively in a transdisciplinary team. Peterson (1987, p. 487) summarizes these criteria as follows (see bottom of page 69):

TABLE 5-4 Outline of Assessment (observations to be made in arena evaluation)

Behavior and style	Communication	Sensorimotor
Appearance	Mode of communication	Sensory
Temperament	Frequency/duration	Tactile responsivity/
State regulation	Echolalia	sensitivity
Rhythmicity	Speech	Auditory/visual
Reactivity	Respiration	perception
Attention	Voice	Vestibular/propriocep-
Frustration tolerance	Vocalization	tive responsivity
Level of organization	Intonation	Body image
Kinetics	Word approximation	Gross motor
Object interaction/Cognition	Intelligibility	Primitive reflexes
Schema use	Articulation	Postural tone
Symbolic object use	Rate	Symmetry
Discrimination	Fluency	Components of
Object classification	Receptive language	movement
Reality testing	Receptive vocabulary	Head control
Learning style	Comprehension—direc-	Trunk control
Sensory assimilation	tion/questions	Proximal joint control
Imitation	Comprehension—con-	Weight shifting
Trial and error	nected discourse	Dynamic equilibrium
Planned problem solving	Expressive language	Rotation
Learning modalities	Spontaneity	Antigravitional control
Social/Emotional	Vocabulary/retrieval	Transitional postures
Contact/cueing style	Knowledge level	Bilateral integration
Reaction to strangers	Length and quality of	Locomotion
Predominant affect/mood	connected discourse	Motor planning
Affective range	Pragmatics	Fine motor
Attachment/separation	Communicative intent	Prehension
behavior	Turn taking	Tool use
Individual/autonomy	Topic maintenance/	Visual-motor accuracy
Coping strategies	expansion	Oral motor
Defensive strategies	Felicity	Infantile reflexes
Play style	Syntax	Sucking/drinking/
Solitary	Grammatical form	chewing
Observer	Overgeneralization	Tongue/jaw control
Parallel		Oral motor planning
Associative		**Self-help**
Adaptability		Feeding
Social appropriateness		Dressing
		Toileting
		Activities of daily living

Source: From Foley, Gilbert M., Portrait of the arena evaluation: Assessment in the transdisciplinary approach. In E. D. Gibbs and D. M. Teti (Eds.), *Interdisciplinary Assessment of Infants: A Guide for Early Intervention Professionals*, p. 281. Copyright © 1990. Baltimore, MD: Paul H. Brookes Publishing. Reprinted with permission.

TABLE 5-5 Sequence for Arena Assessment

Greeting and warm up
Family and team get acquainted time. Child may explore area with guidance and interact with various team members. Team may observe child's coping strategies, style, and mood and may decide on preliminary strategies about space, sequence, style of interaction, instrumentation, and location of the team.

Formal task-centered segment
Chosen instrument is administered by the chosen facilitator and scored by a colleague. Other professionals may be scoring discipline-specific instruments and making clinical notes and comments.

Snack breaks and refueling
Child has snacks with his or her caregivers. This is a good chance to observe self-help skills, oral motor functioning, spontaneous language, and social interaction.

Separation and reunion
After the snack break, the facilitator takes the child for a bathroom break which provides the team the opportunity to observe separation behavior and spontaneous movement.

Story time or teaching samples
This time is used to collect additional samples of behavior as needed. Key assessment items that may have failed earlier may be reintroduced. The length and content of this segment depends on the age and functional level of the child.

Free play
During this segment, the team observes spontaneous movement and interaction with toys. The physical and occupational therapists may enter the assessment at this time to assess the child.

Closing and physical exam
The facilitator and parents help the child unwind. If a physical exam is to be given, it may be completed at this time.

Brief staffing and feedback
Team meets to form impressions while the family worker collects the parents comments about the encounter. This allows the parents to have some closure and feedback so they do not leave with unnecessary anxiety and ambiguity.

Formal staffing and interpretation
This segment occurs after the team has had time to analyze and reflect on the data collected. The results are reviewed at this time and a composite report and preliminary intervention plan are organized. If the caregivers are not present at this session, a formal feedback session must be held with them later.

Source: Adapted from Foley, Gilbert M. (1990). Portrait of the arena evaluation: Assessment in the transdisciplinary approach. In Elizabeth D. Gibbs and Douglas M. Teti (Eds.), *Interdisciplinary Assessment of Infants: A Guide for Early Intervention Professionals* (pp. 171–186). Baltimore, MD: Paul H. Brookes Publishing Co. Used with permission.

TABLE 5-6   TPBA Play Session

	Time Allotted
Phase I—Unstructured facilitation Child takes lead. Facilitator interacts in response to the child. Attempts to move child to higher skill levels through modeling.	20.25 minutes
Phase II—Structured facilitation Involves the cognitive and language activities that did not occur in the first phase. Facilitator takes direct approach, making specific requests to the child with play continuing to be the mode for assessment.	14.15 minutes
Phase III—Child . child interaction Child-to-child interactions are observed in an unstructured situation. A slightly older child without disabilities, familiar to the child being assessed and of the same sex, should be chosen.	5.10 minutes
Phase IV—Parent. child interaction Parent has opportunity to play with child as is routinely done at home. After this unstructured play, the caregiver leaves the room for a few minutes and then returns. Team members note separation and greeting behaviors. When caregivers return, they are asked to teach child an unfamiliar task.	10 minutes
Phase V—Motor play Includes both structured and unstructured motor play.	10.20 minutes
Phase VI—Snack Facilitator may allow the other child used in the assessment to join in with the snack. This provides the opportunity to observe social interactions.	5.10 minutes

Source: Adapted from Linder, Toni W. (1990). *Transdisciplinary Play-Based Assessment: A Functional Approach to Working with Young Children* (p. 43). Baltimore, MD: Paul H. Brookes Publishing Co. Used with permission.

1. *A team member must have depth and be particularly strong in his or her own discipline. Without this knowledge the member is in no position to make decisions or to pass on information in a form that another professional can implement.*
2. *Each team member's role must be continuously enriched by expanding his or her knowledge through training and supervision provided by other team members. For this to occur, the appropriate disciplinary representative must give "role release" and authorization of the designated team member to act as the direct service agent with a particular child in behalf of each discipline.*
3. *Team members must provide continuous consultative back-up to one another. Ongoing problem solving, information exchange, and feedback between the*

consulting discipline and the primary service agent of the team for a given child are critical. Procedures or new information may have to be tested by a disciplinary representative before being passed on to the overall team and prescribed as the treatment strategy for the primary service agent to use.

4. *Throughout the transdisciplinary process each team member must remain accountable for the information and directives delivered to others. Each disciplinary representative also must remain accountable for how well the primary service agent learns the service delivery strategy for that discipline and carries it out with the child. Finally, every discipline involved must remain accountable for the child's progress under their own prescription.*

Summary

The transdisciplinary approach is recommended as a reasonable, practical, and efficient method for providing services to young children with special needs and their families (Woodruff & McGonigel, 1988). However, Woodruff and McGonigel caution early interventionists that the transdisciplinary approach is not an easy process and may not be useable for every program. This process requires tremendous planning, effort, time, and expense at the outset. The arena assessment model is presented to demonstrate how the transdisciplinary approach may be incorporated into the assessment process.

More research needs to be conducted around this approach. As this model of service delivery is expanded, refined, and applied by more early intervention programs, it is hoped that teams will become better equipped to provide the integrated, family-driven services needed by infants, toddlers, and preschoolers with special needs and their families.

Suggested Group Activities

1. Divide into groups and have each individual assume the identity of a service provider (refer to Table 5-1). Select or create a case study of an infant or child and conduct a team meeting to discuss the child's assessment results and instructional goals. Be sure to include a member of the family in the team. Compare how the process changes for multidisciplinary, interdisciplinary, and transdisciplinary approaches.

2. Discuss and compile a list of advantages and disadvantages for the multidisciplinary, interdisciplinary, and transdisciplinary team approaches. Then discuss the list considering a hypothetical early intervention setting.

3. Compile a list of difficulties that may arise in the process of role release. Discuss several options for overcoming the obstacles (e.g., inservicing teachers on various occupational/physical therapist terms and procedures).

4. Generate a list of activities and situations that could be used with an infant, toddler, or preschooler to allow for an arena assessment observation; include a wide variety of toys that address competencies in each domain.

References

Fewell, R. R. (1983). The team approach to infant education. In S. G. Garwood & R. R. Fewell (Eds.), *Educating handicapped infants: Issues in development and intervention* (pp. 299–322). Rockville, MD: Aspen.

Foley, G. M. (1990). Portrait of the arena evaluation: Assessment in the transdisciplinary approach. In E. D. Gibbs & D. M. Teti (Eds.), *Interdisciplinary assessment of infants: A guide for early intervention professionals* (pp. 271–286). Baltimore: Paul H. Brookes.

Garland, C. W., Woodruff, G., & Buck, D. (1988). *Case management* (Division for Early Childhood White Paper). Reston, VA: The Council for Exceptional Children.

Golin, A. K., & Duncanis, A. J. (1981). *The interdisciplinary team*. Rockville, MD: Aspen.

Hutchinson, D. A. (1974). *A model for transdisciplinary staff development. A nationally organized collaborative project to provide comprehensive services to atypical infants and their families* (Technical Report #8). New York: United Cerebral Palsy Association.

Linder, T. W. (1990). *Transdisciplinary play-based assessment: A functional approach to working with young children*. Baltimore: Paul H. Brookes.

Peterson, N. (1987). *Early intervention for handicapped and at-risk children: An introduction to early childhood special education*. Denver: Love.

Raver, S. A. (1991). *Strategies for teaching at-risk and handicapped infants and toddlers: A transdisciplinary approach*. New York: Merrill, Macmillan.

Woodruff, G. (1980). Transdisciplinary approach for preschool children and parents. *The Exceptional Parent, 10*(1), 13–16.

Woodruff, G., & Hanson, C. (1987). *Project KAI training packet*. Unpublished manuscript.

Woodruff, G., & McGonigel, M. J. (1988). Early intervention team approaches: The transdisciplinary model. In J. B. Jordan, J. J. Gallagher, P. L. Hutinger, & M. B. Karnes (Eds.), *Early childhood special education: Birth to three* (pp. 164–181). Reston, VA: The Council for Exceptional Children.

Chapter 6

Cultural Diversity

JUDITH A. BONDURANT-UTZ

In the next decade early intervention services and programs will be called on to meet the needs of many children with special needs and families from a variety of cultures and languages. These children and families will require services that are comprehensive, flexible, and family-focused. Service providers will need to see children in the context of their families and the families in the context of their communities.

The process of assessment should be individualized for each child and family in order to maintain relevance and minimize bias. Even within cultures it may not be possible to develop a truly nonbiased instrument sensitive enough to be used effectively with all individuals (Anderson & Goldberg, 1991). Individualized assessment and intervention is required for each child and family unit within a given cultural context. In order to meet the needs of children and families from diverse backgrounds, professionals need to familiarize themselves with the guidelines and questions that encourage an individualized, nonbiased perspective.

Legislative Mandates

P.L. 99-457 outlines the nondiscriminatory assessment procedures that must be followed:

- All tests and other procedures must be administered in the child's or the parent's home language or their preferred mode of communication.
- Test procedures and materials must not be culturally or racially discriminatory.

- More than one procedure must be used for determining a child's eligibility for special services.
- Assessments must be completed by qualified personnel.

Early childhood special education professionals should be extremely careful when assessing children who are culturally diverse, especially when identifying the need for special services. A biased assessment could result in the classification of a child as disabled when in fact the insensitivity of the test itself contributed to the low score attained by the child. Screening and assessment need to be sensitive to the cultural biases that could lead to over- or under-identification of perceived deficits in children from various cultural and linguistic groups.

Family Perspective

Part H and Part B, Section 619, of IDEA (retitled P.L. 99-457) are family-focused. Children must be viewed as having strengths, weaknesses, needs, and resources that are part of a larger family and social context. Assessment procedures should recognize the critical role of the family as well as its cultural and linguistic background. Caregivers are the constants in children's lives and the chief decision makers. All relevant family members, as defined by the culture, need to be considered and encouraged to be full partners in the intervention process.

Not all families are prepared for or feel comfortable with the degree of family participation expected in early intervention programs. However, one must not assume that they do not wish to be involved or that they are not involved from their perspective.

Several culturally influenced variables are language and communication, childrearing practices, definition of family, and beliefs about wellness and disability. Other conditions, such as socioeconomic and educational status, are not characteristics of specific cultures but rather are cross-cultural. A combination of these factors may impact on children and families and influence the assessment process (Anderson & Goldberg, 1991).

Language and Communication

Effective communication is essential to the family-professional relationship. Members of some cultures may be reticent to go to a facility unless someone who speaks the language that they are most comfortable with will be there. Communication can be verbal and nonverbal. Nonverbal communication has important and varied cultural meanings. Cultures rely on situational cues, established hierarchies, and nonconfrontational responses differentially. Thus, important information may not be adequately communicated when translated.

Body language and other forms of communication are important considerations in the assessment process. Professionals need to have an understanding of the different meanings attached to the body language they may use. For example, eye contact, personal space, and touching are forms of body language that have different meanings in different cultures. Effective assessment relies on sharing information through observation and written and spoken language. When language differences occur, the real meanings may not be understood even with translation.

Childrearing

Cultures have varying ideas about the family member who cares for and educates children of various ages and sexes. Expectations of children may vary with respect to the types of competence and behaviors regarded as normal or ideal for a particular age or sex group. These expectations may require children to become competent in areas other than those needed in the social mainstream (Anderson & Fenichel, 1989).

Family Membership

The view of what constitutes a family, including its structures and relationships, differs from culture to culture. In many cultures, the family is extended in different ways; various relatives, and frequently non-relatives or temporary relatives, may make up the primary closely knit group. The family membership may be constant, with changes occurring only as a result of birth or death, or it may be somewhat fluid. Situations and relationships may vary among distant relatives or non-relatives who are considered family members. Family roles and relationships vary from culture to culture and may change over time. Family members may or may not constitute an important support network for one another. There may be a strict hierarchy among family members and/or rigidly defined gender roles (Anderson & Fenichel, 1989).

Wellness/Disability

Cultural groups differ greatly in their views of health, prevention of illness or disability, medicine, and health care. The occurrence of a disability is given different meaning by different cultures. Some cultures emphasize the role of fate; others may place responsibility on the person with the disability or his or her family. There may be guilt or shame or a feeling that the disability is a punishment for sins or results from some action by the mother or father during pregnancy or by a remote ancestor. Other cultures attribute the disability to a person's bad luck or misfortune. Disabilities may cause different levels of concern in different cultures. A disability that is common to a particular cultural group may be seen as little cause for concern. Such perceptions will influence the family's willingness to seek help or participate in any intervention program (Hanson, Lynch & Wayman, 1990).

The Child's Language Competence

Sufficient information about the cultural and language patterns in the home must be obtained prior to screening or assessment. It is important to know not only what language is spoken in the home, but the degree of bilingualism, and the nature and patterns of language practices. For example, a bilingual child may have been bilingual only a year or two; the family may speak one language at home, but the child is with a sitter all day who speaks another language. The degree of proficiency in one or more languages must be assessed (Barrera Metz, 1991).

The child must be evaluated in the area of language prior to any other testing; it should include an assessment of competence not only in English but also in the child's home language. This also is true for children who are nonverbal or severely disabled. Differences in affect and muscle tone have been noted in children who are nonverbal and severely disabled when using the child's home language (Barrera Metz, 1991). Scores obtained for minority children on assessment instruments for language are most often minimal indications of abilities.

Looking at language proficiency alone is too simplistic when assessing a child's ability to use language in interactions. Language competence is connected to the issue of cultural knowledge of the child and family and how people interpret situations and guide their communicative behavior as a result.

Research has suggested that the successful functioning of Hispanic and other ethnic-minority students can be affected dramatically by the interactional competencies that extend beyond the knowledge of the structural features of the language (Goldman & Trueba, 1987). These interactional competencies involve such skills as knowing when and how to respond to a teacher's questions, how to ask for clarifications of information, and the appropriate demeanor for using language in the activities of the classroom. The communicative competence of a child also is affected by the communicative strategies used by other students, the teacher, and the differences in social relations among the speakers (Duran, 1989). Garcia and Ortiz (1988) compiled a number of variables that need to be considered. These variables are shown in Table 6–1, which has been adapted for use with young children.

Problems with Test Translations and Using Interpreters

Translating Assessment Instruments

Examiners often evaluate the child with the help of an interpreter who should have experience in administering tests. If using a standardized instrument, the examiner must remember that normed samples may not have included individuals from this child's home population. In order to assess a culturally diverse child, the examiner needs to do more than simply translate the test into the child's dominant language. A summary of the problems inherent in test translations and in using an interpreter follows on page 79 (Sattler, 1988):

TABLE 6-1   Child Variables

Experiential background

Are there any factors in the child's school history that may be related to the current difficulty?
- Attendance/mobility
- Opportunities to learn
- Program placement(s)
- Quality of prior instruction

Are there any variables related to family history that may be affecting the child's performance?
- Lifestyle
- Length of residence in the United States
- Stress (e.g., poverty, lack of emotional support)

Are there any variables related to the child's medical history that may have affected performance?
- Vision
- Nutrition
- Illness
- Hearing
- Trauma or injury

Culture

How is the child's cultural background different from the culture of the school and larger society? (Mattes & Omark, 1984; Saville-Troike, 1978)
- Family (family size and structure, roles, responsibilities, expectations)
- Aspirations (success, goals)
- Language and communication (rules for adult, adult. child, child. child communication, language use at home, nonverbal communication)
- Religion (dietary restriction, roles expectation)
- Traditions and history (contact with homeland, reason for immigration)
- Decorum and discipline (standards for acceptable behavior)

To what extent are the child's characteristics representative of the larger group?
- Continuum of culture (traditional, dualistic atraditional [Ramirez & Castaneda, 1974])
- Degree of acculturation or assimilation

Is the child able to function successfully in more than one cultural setting?

Is the child's behavior culturally appropriate?

Language proficiency

What is the child's dominant language? Which is the preferred?
- Settings (school, playground, home, church)
- Topics (at school, day-to-day interactions)
- Speakers (parents, teachers, siblings, peers)
- Aspects of each language (syntax, vocabulary, phonology, use)
- Expressive versus receptive

What is the child's level of proficiency in the primary language and in English? (Cummins, 1984)
- Interpersonal communication skills
- Cognitive/preacademic-related skills

(Continued)

TABLE 6-1 *(Continued)*

Language proficiency *(Continued)*

Are the styles of verbal interaction used in the primary language different from those most valued in English? (Heath, 1986)
- Label quests (e.g., what's this? who?)
- Meaning quests (adult infers for child, interprets or asks for explanation)
- Accounts (generated by teller, information new to listener—e.g., show and tell, creative writing)
- Eventcasts (running narrative on events as they unfold, or forecast of events in preparation)
- Stories

If so, has the child been exposed to those that are unfamiliar to him or her?

What is the extent and nature of exposure to each language?

What language(s) do the parents speak to each other?

What language(s) do the children use with each other?

What television programs are seen in each language?

Are stories read to the child? In what language(s)?

Are student behaviors characteristic of second-language acquisition?

What types of language intervention has the student received?
- Bilingual versus monolingual instruction
- Language development, enrichment, remediation
- Additive versus subtractive bilingualism (transition versus maintenance)

Learning style

Does the child's learning style require curricular/instructional accommodation?
- Perceptual style differences (e.g., visual versus auditory learner)
- Cognitive style differences (e.g., inductive versus deductive thinking)
- Preferred style of participation (e.g., teacher versus child-directed, small versus large group)

If so, were these characteristics accommodated, or were alternative styles taught?

Motivational influences

Is the child's self-concept enhanced by school experiences?
- School environment communicates respect for culture and language
- Child experiences preacademic and social success

Is schooling perceived as relevant and necessary for success in the child's family and community?
- Aspirations
- Realistic expectations based on community experience
- Culturally different criteria for success
- Education perceived by the community as a tool for assimilation

Source: Adapted from Student variables in Garcia, S., & Ortiz, A. (1988). *Preventing inappropriate referrals of language minority students to special education. New Focus* 5:7. The National Clearinghouse for Bilingual Education Occasional Papers in Bilingual Education. Used with permission.

- The interpreter may not be equally fluent in both languages, resulting in incorrect translations
- Many concepts have either no equivalent in another language or are difficult to translate without causing ambiguity; thus, the meaning of important phrases may be lost in translation
- The interpreter may not use the particular dialectical or regional variation with which the child is familiar. Some words may have different meanings for Chinese-Americans who originate from the People's Republic of China, Hong Kong, or Taiwan.
- The language familiar to the child may be a combination of two languages, so a monolingual translation may be inappropriate.
- The level of difficulty of words may change as a result of translation. For example, the Spanish equivalent of the common English word *pet* is *animal doméstico*, not commonly used in conversational Spanish.
- Translation can alter the meaning of words. For example, seemingly harmless English words may translate into Spanish profanity. *Huevo* is the literal translation of the word *egg*, but the Spanish term has more earthy connotations.
- The interpreter may inadvertently prompt the child through translation attempts, gestures, and/or intonations common to the language in question.
- Interpreters usually are not trained in or familiar with administering tests.

The major concern with translations is to ensure that each translated phrase is equivalent to the phrase in the original language. An important rule in translating is that the translator must be familiar with the language as it is used by the prospective examinee.

Conducting an Interview

Lynch (1992, pp. 55–56) summarizes the guidelines for conducting an assessment or interview with the help of interpreters suggested by previous researchers. (See also: Hagen, 1989; Randall-David, 1989; Schilling & Brannon, 1986.) These guidelines are:

- Learn proper protocols and forms of address (including a few greetings and social phrases) in the family's primary language, the names they wish to be called, and the correct pronunciation.
- Introduce yourself and the interpreter, describe your respective roles, and clarify mutual expectations and the purpose of the encounter.
- Learn basic words and sentences in the family's language and become familiar with special terminology they may use so you can selectively attend to them during interpreter-family exchanges.
- During the interaction, address your remarks and questions directly to the family (not the interpreter); look at and listen to family members as they speak and observe their nonverbal communication.
- Avoid body language or gestures that may be offensive or misunderstood.

- Use a positive tone of voice and facial expressions that sincerely convey respect and your interest in the family; and address them in a calm, unhurried manner.
- Speak clearly and somewhat more slowly, but not louder.
- Limit your remarks and questions to a few sentences between translations and avoid giving too much information or long complex discussions of several topics in a single session.
- Avoid technical jargon, colloquialisms, idioms, slang, and abstractions.
- Avoid oversimplification and condensing important explanations.
- Give instructions in a clear, logical sequence; emphasize key words or points; and offer reasons for specific recommendations.
- Periodically check on the family's understanding and the accuracy of the translation by asking a family member to repeat instructions or whatever has been communicated in her or his own words, with the interpreter facilitating, but avoid asking, "Do you understand?"
- When possible, reinforce verbal information with materials written in the family's language and use visual aids or behavioral modeling if appropriate. Before introducing written materials, tactfully determine the client's literacy level through the interpreter.
- Be patient and prepared for the additional time that inevitably will be required for careful interpretation.

An interpreter or mediator may be hired by an intervention program to assist in the screening or assessment. A mediator is a person who helps to buffer or connect across cultures (Barrera, 1992). The mediator or interpreter should meet with the assessor prior to the assessment to be shown the test to be used and trained in giving it; the mediator needs to be familiar with the purpose of the test items. Mediators may present the test items or simply watch. The mediator explains what is happening to the family. After the assessment, the mediator may add what the family has offered about their language or culture. The mediator participates for the benefit of both the family and the intervention program.

The Cultural Competence of the Examiner

Roberts (1990) defines cultural competence as the ability to honor and respect the beliefs, interpersonal styles, attitudes, and behaviors of families. When addressing the issue of cultural diversity, caution must be exercised in trying to describe any group in a generalized sense. There often are as many and as wide a variation within a group as there are between groups. In an attempt to better understand cultural difference and variability, always be careful not to perpetuate stereotypes (McAdoo, 1978).

Anderson and Fenichel (1989) describe culture as the specific framework of meanings in which a population, individually and as a group, shapes its life. A cultural framework is not absolute; it is an ongoing process. The cultural framework must be seen as a set of possible tendencies from which to choose. As Ortiz (1987) indicated, culture exists on a continuum. Early intervention must discern where on the continuum of assimilation into the majority culture a family functions and recognize that this may change. Individual families may accept, deny, modify, or situationally exhibit various cultural tendencies.

The culturally competent individual values diversity, is able to self-assess, is conscious of the dynamics involved when cultures interact, has acquired cultural knowledge, and has developed adaptations to diversity (Bazron, Dennis & Isaacs, 1989). Anderson and Fenichel (1989) state that cultural sensitivity cannot mean knowing everything about a culture. Cultural sensitivity is being aware that cultural differences and similarities exist, learning about the cultures in a region, and realizing that cultural differences affect every family's participation in an intervention program because all of us are influenced by the culture of our ancestors.

To become culturally competent early interventionists need to: (a) clarify their values and assumptions, (b) gather and analyze ethnographic information about the cultural community of the family, (c) determine the degree of assimilation of the family into the majority culture, and (d) examine the family's orientation to specific childrearing issues (Hanson, Lynch & Wayman, 1990). In this chapter, no attempt is made to describe individual cultural groups. The content applies to everyone regardless of the particular culture from which he or she originates, i.e., Hispanic, Anglo-Saxon, Asian, Native American, and so on. References to additional informative resource materials are provided for the reader to begin to understand cultural differences that occur between individuals and groups. Here, emphasis is placed on general considerations for assessing individuals from culturally diverse backgrounds.

General Recommendations for Providing a Multicultural Assessment

It is unlikely that a truly unbiased test will ever be developed. Bailey (1989) and Lynch and Hanson (1992) recommend the following strategies to ensure that assessments are as fair as possible. The recommendations apply to the assessment of any child and family, but are emphasized here because they are even more crucial when assessing a child and family who are culturally and/or linguistically diverse. These recommendations include:

- Use multiple measures and gather data in naturalistic contexts to ensure that the best representation of the child and his or her abilities is obtained.
- Use a multidisciplinary team approach to evaluation so that one area of development is not the sole focus.
- Involve parents as significant partners in the assessment process and focus intervention goals and objectives on those areas viewed as particularly important to parents. Gather information in the areas in which the family has expressed concern. This shows respect for all families.

- Focus on skills rather than on a label when describing a child's functioning.
- Examine test items or questions to ensure that they are not biased against children of a certain sex or cultural background.
- Use commercial assessment instruments when available. Examine test manuals to determine if evidence is presented supporting the fair use of the test with minority children and both boys and girls. Choose only those that are appropriate for the language and culture of the child and family.
- Have knowledge of cultural factors, and be aware of one's own strengths and limitations.
- Use the skills of interpreters or mediators effectively. The interpreter should be able to interpret both language and cultural cues.
- Limit the number of forms, questionnaires, and other paperwork. Gather only the data necessary to begin working with the child and family. Families who have minimal competence in English may be overwhelmed by forms, questionnaires, tests, and so on.

Anderson and Goldberg (1991) compiled a set of strategies for professionals working with families from culturally or linguistically diverse backgrounds (see Table 6–2). These strategies are a result of interviews, a review of the literature, and the experiences of individuals from diverse backgrounds. These suggestions will help the professional to be more culturally competent in assessing the child and the family.

Assessment Methods and Instruments

It is not possible to select or develop a test that is perfect for every cultural or linguistic group. However, the use of standardized psychometric tests cannot be totally eliminated from the assessment process. Leung (1986) suggests that the examiner needs to: (a) understand the limitations of tests in general, (b) know the technical limitations of commonly used tests and weigh the results accordingly, (c) choose test measures based on the kinds of information needed, and (d) administer the test in a nonstandardized manner (e.g., use the test-teach-test technique and avoid applying inappropriate norms).

Walton and Nuttall (1991) provide an extensive review of specific instruments used for assessing preschoolers. In their chapter "Preschool Evaluation of Culturally Different Children," they summarize the research on instruments used for screening, cognition, language, perceptual performance, social-emotional-adaptive skills, and curriculum-based assessment. Table 6–3 is an example of the type of information contained in their chapter. The authors also discuss the research findings in regard to various culturally different populations.

Culturally Fair Assessment

Various alternatives have been sought to create culturally fair tests (Duran, 1989; Laosa, 1977; Nuttall, Landurand & Goldman, 1984). These assessment alternatives

TABLE 6-2   Strategies for Professionals Working with Families from Various
Cultural and/or Linguistic Groups

1. Individualize the screening and assessment process for parents as well as for children. Children and other family members may be at various levels of acculturation and may require similar or varying degrees of modifications, adaptations, or support such as language interpretation.
2. Do a self-assessment of your own cultural background, experiences, values, and biases. Examine how they may impact your interactions with people from other cultural groups.
3. Begin the screening and assessment process at the point where the parents are. Find out their concerns, why they are coming to you, and what they hope you can provide.
4. Take time to establish the trust needed to fully involve the family in the screening and assessment process.
5. Use bilingual and bicultural staff, or mediators and translators, whenever needed. Try to maintain a consistency of providers to allow the family to establish ongoing communication.
6. Allow for flexibility of the process and procedures. You may need to meet with parents at their job site, or call them when they return home from their job. You may need to modify test items to ensure cultural competency.
7. Conduct observations and other procedures in environments familiar to the child. These may be at the home of their grandmother, outdoors, or at their parents' work site.
8. Provide assistance and be flexible in establishing meetings with parents. This might include providing for child care of siblings, transportation to a meeting site, or meeting the family in their home.
9. Participate in staff training on cultural competence skills in screening and assessment. Strive to achieve standards for professional cultural competence.
10. Conduct ongoing discussions with practitioners, parents, policymakers, and members of the cultural communities you serve.

Source: From *Cultural Competence in Screening and Assessment: Implications for Services to Young Children with Special Needs Ages Birth Through Five,* pp. 22, 23. Copyright © 1991 by NECTAS and PACER Center, 4826 Chicago Ave., S., Minneapolis, MN 55417; (612) 827-2966. Used with permission.

are presented here to provide a direct connection between assessment and instruction.

Criterion-referenced or Curriculum-based Tests

Criterion-referenced or curriculum-based tests that measure the child against her or his previous performance rather than against the majority may be less biased. However, a criterion-referenced test needs to be evaluated as to who determines what the objective will be and who establishes the criterion. This type of test may also may be culturally biased if the objectives and criteria reflect majority standards and values. The developmental sequences in these tests have not been researched for cultural differences with the exception of the Portage Classroom Curriculum Checklist (Brinkerhoff, 1976; Walton & Nuttall, 1991). One advantage of the criterion-referenced test is that it yields specific information regarding

TABLE 6-3 General Cognitive Ability Tests

> **Key**
> A. Name of instrument
> B. Age range
> C. Psychometric data
> D. Description
> E. Administration time
> F. Year, author, publisher

A. *Kaufman Assessment Battery for Children*
B. 2-6 to 12-5.
C. Standard scores. Reliability and validity data presented. National norming group included proportional representation of minority children. Norms for two levels of parent education, and for black and white samples. Nonverbal norms well standardized.
D. Measures two styles of thinking, simultaneous and sequential, and some academic readiness at the early level. Directions in Spanish are given in the manual. Teaching the tasks is encouraged and standardized.
E. 45 minutes.
F. 1983a and 1983b, Kaufman and Kaufman, American Guidance Service.

A. *McCarthy Scales of Children's Abilities*
B. 2-5 to 8-7.
C. Standard scores. National norming group with proportional minority children (based on ''color''). Reliability and validity data.
D. Measures general cognitive ability. Separate measures of verbal, perceptual, quantitative, memory, and motor skills
E. One hour.
F. 1972, McCarthy, Psychological Corporation.

A. *Stanford-Binet Intelligence Scale—LM*
B. 2–6 to adult
C. Standard scores (deviation IQ scores). Minority children included in the 1972 national norming group. Reliability and validity data presented.
D. Measures general cognitive ability with various tasks arranged by half-year age levels at the preschool level.
E. 45 minutes.
F. 1973, Terman and Merrill, Riveside Publishing Company.

A. *Wechsler Preschool and Primary Scale of Intelligence—Revised*
B. 3-0 to 7-0.
C. Standard scores. National norming group included minority children proportionally. Items biased against blacks or Hispanics were eliminated.
D. Measures general cognitive ability with verbal and nonverbal problems.
E. 45 minutes.
F. 1989, Wechsler, Psychological Corporation.

Source: From Walton, J. R., & Nuttall, E. V., Preschool evaluation of culturally different children. In E. V. Nuttall, I. Romero, and J. Kalesnik (Eds.), *Assessing and Screening Preschoolers: Psychological and Educational Dimensions* (p. 288). Copyright © 1991. Boston: Allyn and Bacon. Reprinted with permission of Allyn and Bacon.

skills the child can and cannot perform. This information is more useful for educational programming than is the numerical score that the standardized test yields.

Neo-Piagetian Task Performance
The child may be tested on his or her ability to perform Piagetian tasks. Stages associated with these tasks occur across cultures and, therefore, tests associated with them are less likely to contain bias. The Ordinal Scales of Psychological Development developed by Uzgiris and Hunt (1975) is an appropriate example of such a test for young children.

Another assessment of Piagetian task performance is the Concept Assessment Kit—Conservation (Goldschmid & Beatler, 1968). The Concept Assessment Kit is intended for four- to seven-year-olds. It tests their ability to conserve. This test is individually administered. Using Piaget's research technique, the examiner demonstrates a phenomenon that the child is then asked to explain. The test is normed and provides validity and reliability data. Several studies reveal some positive correlations between performance on these Piagetian-based scales and more traditional tests of intelligence (Goodwin & Driscoll, 1980).

Other tests of specific cognitive skills suggested by Walton and Nuttall (1991) include the *Columbia Mental Maturity Scale* (CMMS) (Burgemeister, Blum & Lorge, 1972), the *Bracken Basic Concepts Scale* (BBCS) (Bracken, 1984), the *Boehm Test of Basic Concepts—Preschool Version* (BTBC—P) (Boehm, 1986), and the *Arthur Adaptation of the Leiter International Performance Scale* (Leiter, 1966).

Diagnostic Tests
Diagnostic tests, which assess specific areas such as fine-motor and visual-motor coordination, perception, and so on rather than general ability, also may be used. These tests tend to be nonverbal, performance-oriented, symbolic responses to relationships among figures or designs. The information they yield is, therefore, less likely to be culturally biased and less likely to be used to label children. The *Bender Gestalt Visual Motor Test* (Bender, 1946) and the *Developmental Test of Visual Motor Integration* (Beery, 1982) can be used with minority children. These tests do not depend on language skills and thus make them more appropriate for testing linguistically different children.

This approach has been criticized because of its lack of predictability for academic performance (Mercer, 1979) and its lack of assessment of psychological characteristics (Oakland & Matuszek, 1977).

Observational Techniques
Informal observational techniques are recommended to assess the child's behavior. This approach is very appropriate for preschool children, because they are less inhibited by adult observers than older children and, thus, can provide much valuable information to the trained observer. Of course, the information from informal observation is only as biased as the observer who records it. The child's entire learning environment should be taken into account.

Observational techniques are discussed in chapter 11. To provide a better understanding of the child, the examiner should make qualitative observations as noted in chapter 3. However, the examiner should be cautioned not to make value judgments about the behavior, but simply to observe to learn more about the child and his interactions with others around him.

Assisted Performance

Tharp and Gallimore (1988) suggest a very different idea of assessment as part of effective instruction. Teaching happens only when a student is assisted in accomplishing previously unattained elements of a learning task. This teaching requires the teacher to carefully assess the learning performance of a child and then offer assistance to the learner. The learner then attains skills that would otherwise not have been possible.

Tharp and Gallimore's approach is based on Vygotsky (1978). In the beginning the learner is capable of learning only when a teacher or more capable other actively supports the learning performance by providing useful hints. Gradually, the child internalizes these cues and then becomes able to provide them on her own. The child then becomes capable of performing the task automatically. This type of assessment would be very useful for teachers and parents in early childhood settings.

Dynamic Assessment

Figueroa (1989) proposes a model based on the information-processing research of Campione, Brown, and Ferrara (1982). These researchers believe that the building blocks of intelligence are speed of processing, knowledge base, strategies, metacognition, and executive control. Using these constructs, the focus changes from standardized assessment instruments to modifications of the learning environment. Prominent researchers in this field include Embretson, Feuerstein, Bransford, Budoff, Campione, and Brown.

Dynamic assessment approaches employ a fundamental test-train-test cycle; there is a strong link between testing and teaching. The teacher is encouraged to use clinical judgment in the evaluation of the child's performance. The teacher observes the child's growth from assisted performance to unassisted performance. There can be great variation in the target skills and content areas for learning and in the testing and training procedures.

Two general approaches to conducting of dynamic assessment can be seen. One of these emphasizes clinical probing of a student's readiness to master new skills. The teacher relies on clinical judgment in diagnosing the readiness of a student to learn and determines which hints and cues can promote new learning. A second approach relies on a pre-established set of hints and cues that represent skill levels in a problem-solving task. Each response of the child is matched against the learning hierarchy, and the child is given an appropriate set cue or hint.

These approaches can easily be used in the classroom every day. If a pre-ordered set of cues that go from general to specific is used, the lower the number of hints and cues the student needs, the greater their potential for learning.

Children can be compared on their readiness to learn on the same problem-solving tasks. Dynamic assessment can be used to teach general cognitive or thinking skills and specific content skills.

Task Analysis Approach

When using the task analysis approach, the teacher analyzes the skills and behaviors the child needs to accomplish the task and then determines why he or she is not able to do the task. The child is then trained in the areas of weakness and retested (Kaufman, 1977). Children are treated as individuals and not compared to others. The method is a test-teach-test approach (Mercer & Ysseldyke, 1977). This approach becomes difficult when tasks are complex.

Considerations for More Effective Assessment

The Examiner

The individual conducting the assessment is the most important variable in the process and needs to possess not only the necessary skills, knowledge, and experience but be sensitive and open to working with families from another culture. This openness includes the willingness to acknowledge one's limitations. Recognize any stereotypes you may have about the child's ethnic group. Be sure your preconceived images or notions do not interfere with your work.

Questions an assessor might ask include: How do I feel about this (Asian, Hispanic) child? Will my attitude unfairly affect this child's performance? Can I evaluate this child fairly without positive or negative prejudice or preconceived notions? If I can't, should I refer the child to someone else? (Leung, 1986). Anderson and Goldberg (1991) compiled a list of questions for professionals to ask themselves in order to ensure cultural competence (see Table 6–4).

Learn as much as possible about the child's ethnic group and culture. Try to understand the ethnic group's viewpoint and accept the premise that each child must be given an equal opportunity to achieve to the limits of his or her capacity.

It is important to establish contact with diverse cultural groups before working with children and families. A network needs to be established and programs need to get to know the cultural community and establish credibility before screening and assessment begins.

A multidisciplinary or transdisciplinary team approach to assessment can provide much needed assistance in order to conduct a nonbiased assessment, especially between bilingual and early childhood special educators. The evaluator should rely on a multidisciplinary approach to assessment and gather relevant information about the child from a variety of sources. This will result in a more accurate assessment of the child's strengths and weaknesses. Using an ongoing assessment of the child within the classroom, using a method such as the TPBA, provides a more accurate picture of the child's strengths and needs.

TABLE 6–4 Questions for Professionals to Ask When Conducting a Culturally Sensitive Screening and Assessment

1. With what cultural group was this screening or assessment tool normed? Is it the same culture as that of the child I am serving?
2. Have I examined this screening and assessment tool for cultural biases? Has it been reviewed by members of the cultural group being served?
3. If I have modified or adapted a standardized screening or assessment tool, have I received input on the changes to be certain it is culturally appropriate? If using a standardized tool, or one to which I have made changes, have I carefully scored and interpreted the results in consideration of cultural or linguistic variation? When interpreting and reporting screening and assessment results, have I made clear reference that the instrument was modified and how?
4. Have representatives from the cultural community meet to create guidelines for culturally competent screening and assessment for children from that group? Has information about childrearing practices and typical child development for children from that community been gathered and recorded for use by those serving the families?
5. What do I know about the childrearing practices of this cultural group? How do these practices impact child development?
6. Am I aware of my own values and biases regarding childrearing practices and the kind of information gathered in the screening and assessment process? Can I utilize nondiscriminatory and culturally competent skills and practices in my work with children and families?
7. Do I utilize parents and other family members in gathering information for the screening and assessment? Am I aware of the people with whom the child spends time, and the level of acculturation of these individuals?
8. Do I know where or how to find out about specific cultural or linguistic information that may be needed in order for me to be culturally competent in the screening and assessment process?
9. Do I have bilingual or bicultural skills, or do I have access to another person who can provide direct service or consultation? Do I know what skills are required of a quality interpreter or mediator?
10. Have I participated in training sessions on cultural competence in screening and assessment? Am I continuing to develop my knowledge base through additional formal training and by spending time with community members to learn the cultural attributes specific to the community and families I serve? Is there a network of peer and supervisory practitioners who are addressing these issues, and can I become a participating member?

Source: Reprinted from *Cultural Competence in Screening and Assessment: Implications for Services to Young Children with Special Needs Ages Birth Through Five.* Copyright © 1991, by NECTAS and PACER Center, 4826 Chicago Ave., S. Minneapolis, MN 55417; (612) 827-2966. Used with permission.

Establishing Rapport and Getting to Know the Family

When developing the IFSP, a thorough assessment of the family's present needs and resources is essential. It is important to gather information on family resources (information on family members, cultural values, beliefs about school), family interactions (reactions to the child with a disability, family activities, family interests and hobbies, family routines), family functions (division of family chores, home-intervention activities, community activities), and family life cycle (information on past life events and future goals). For the professional working with culturally diverse families, it also is beneficial to expand the family assessment into the following areas (Fradd & Weismantel, 1989):

- Family experiences in the native country, where applicable.
- The role of extended family members and siblings.
- The amount of community support available.
- Religious, spiritual, and/or cultural beliefs.
- Parenting practices (discipline versus independence).

Chan (1983) suggests that the types of Asian cultural information useful to an assessor might include the following: (1) perception of the child, (2) childrearing practices, (3) behavior management, (4) communication styles, (5) views of handicapping conditions, (6) coping strategies, and (7) expectations. Such variables should be considered as part of any effective family assessment.

Wayman, Lynch, and Hanson (1990) designed a set of "Guidelines for the Home Visitor" that can be used to learn more about the family's cultural values and preferences (see Table 6–5). Lynch (1992) points out that these guidelines were not designed to use as a checklist or interview protocol. These guidelines may help interventionists determine the kinds of questions and issues that are often mediated by culture. Knowing more about the family's attitudes, beliefs, and practices will assist the interventionist in matching the program's services to the family's way of life.

Optimizing the Testing Situation

The assessment always should be arranged at a time that allows the individuals who are important to the family to be present. This may include not only the direct caregivers, but also any other individual who has responsibility for decision making in the family, e.g., a grandmother.

The assessment should occur in a setting where the family feels most comfortable. This might be in the home, at the early intervention program site, or a neutral location.

Be sure to explain every part of the assessment and its purpose to the family. These explanations need to be made frequently and in a variety of ways.

Remember the child's behavior during a testing situation may be influenced by the way his or her culture defines learning, by past experiences with taking tests, whether she or he is being raised in a cooperative or competitive environment, his or her cognitive style, and the cultural values of the family.

Take care to determine whether the child understands the verbal test instructions and questions; repeat the instructions and questions where permitted by the test manual. Ask the child to repeat the instructions or questions to be sure that he or she understands them. On nonstandardized tests, also give the

TABLE 6–5   Guidelines for the Home Visitor

Part I—Family structure and childrearing practices

Family structure

- Family composition
  - Who are the members of the family system?
  - Who are the key decision makers?
  - Is decision making related to specific situations?
  - Is decision making individual or group oriented?
  - Do family members all live in the same household?
  - What is the relationship of friends to the family system?
  - What is the hierarchy within the family? Is status related to gender or age?

- Primary caregiver(s)
  - Who is the primary caregiver?
  - Who else participates in the caregiving?
  - What is the amount of care given by mother versus others?
  - How much time does the infant spend away from the primary caregiver?
  - Is there conflict between caregivers regarding appropriate practices?
  - What ecological/environmental issues impinge on general caregiving (i.e., housing, jobs, etc.)?

Childrearing practices

- Family feeding practices?
  - What are the family feeding practices?
  - What are the mealtime rules?
  - What types of foods are eaten?
  - What are the beliefs regarding breastfeeding and weaning?
  - What are the beliefs regarding bottle feeding?
  - What are the family practices regarding transitioning to solid food?
  - Which family members prepare food?
  - Is food purchased or homemade?
  - Are there any taboos related to food preparation or handling?
  - Which family members feed the child?
  - What is the configuration of the family mealtime?
  - What are the family's views on independent feeding?
  - Is there a discrepancy among family members regarding the beliefs and practices related to feeding an infant/toddler?

- Family sleeping patterns
  - Does the infant sleep in the same room/bed as the parents?
  - At what age is the infant moved away from close proximity to the mother?
  - Is there an established bedtime?
  - What is the family response to an infant when he or she awakes at night?
  - What practices surround daytime napping?

- Family's response to disobedience and aggression
  - What are the parameters of acceptable child behavior?
  - What form does the discipline take?
  - Who metes out the disciplinary action?

- Family's response to a crying infant
  - Temporal qualities—How long before the caregiver picks up a crying infant?
  - How does the caregiver calm an upset infant?

TABLE 6–5   *(Continued)*

Part II—Family perceptions and attitudes

Family perception of child's disability

- Are there cultural or religious factors that would shape family perceptions?
- To what/where/whom does the family assign responsibility for their child's disability?
- How does the family view the role of fate in their lives?
- How does the family view their role in intervening with their child? Do they feel they can make a difference or do they consider it hopeless?

Family's perception of health and healing

- What is the family's approach to medical needs?
  - Do they rely solely on Western medical services?
  - Do they rely solely on holistic approaches?
  - Do they utilize a combination of these approaches?
- Who is the primary medical provider or conveyer of medical information?
  - Family members? Elders? Friends? Folk healers? Family doctor? Medical specialists?
- Do all members of the family agree on approaches to medical needs?

Family's perception of help-seeking and intervention

- From whom does the family seek help—family members or outside agencies/individuals?
- Does the family seek help directly or indirectly?
- What are the general feelings of the family when seeking assistance—ashamed, angry, demand as a right, view as unnecessary?
- With which community systems does the family interact (educational/medical/social)?
- How are these interactions completed (face-to-face, telephone, letter)?
- Which family member interacts with other systems?
- Does that family member feel comfortable when interacting with other systems?

Part III—Language and communication styles

Language

- To what degree:
  - Is the home visitor proficient in the family's native language?
  - Is the family proficient in English?
- If an interpreter is used:
  - With which culture is the interpreter primarily affiliated?
  - Is the interpreter familiar with the colloquialisms of the family members' country or region of origin?
  - Is the family member comfortable with the interpreter? Would the family member feel more comfortable with an interpreter of the same sex?
- If written materials are used, are they in the family's native language?

Interaction styles

- Does the family communicate with each other in a direct or indirect style?
- Does the family tend to interact in a quiet manner or a loud manner?
- Do family members share feelings when discussing emotional issues?
- Does the family ask you direct questions?
- Does the family value a lengthy social time at each home visit unrelated to the early childhood services program goals?
- Is it important for the family to know about the home visitor's extended family? Is the home visitor comfortable sharing that information?

Source: From Home-based early childhood services: Cultural sensitivity in a family systems approach by K. Wayman, E. Lynch, & M. Hanson, 1990, *Topics in Early Childhood Special Education,* 10(4): 56–75. Copyright © 1992 by PRO-ED, Inc. Reprinted by permission.

instructions in a different way to see if this enhances the child's responsiveness. If it seems that language variations are interfering with a child's ability to repeat accurately, ask the child to repeat or elaborate on his or her response.

Try to enhance the child's motivation and interest by helping him or her feel as comfortable as possible in the assessment situation. Take as much time as necessary to enlist the child's cooperation. If at all possible, the examiner should be someone who is familiar to the child.

Curriculum-based assessment and ongoing data collection within the classroom will provide a better picture of a child's abilities. Standardized tests should be supplemented with information obtained from observations, interviews, and anecdotal information from a variety of sources and contexts.

Using Tests Appropriately

In testing children who have learned a language other than English in the home, administer a language test in the primary language of the child and use a nonlanguage performance scale. Never use a nonlanguage scale or a language test exclusively. In testing a bilingual child, administer intelligence tests in both languages on the assumption that the ability repertoires in the separate languages will rarely overlap completely.

After giving a test item according to the standardized procedures, try teaching a missed test item to see how quickly the child can learn and what kind of teaching is effective.

Interpreting Data Appropriately

Know when to include the child's extended family in the interviews, in the gathering of assessment data, and in the interpreting of test information. Assessment needs to go beyond the test itself; it should take into account the child's entire learning environment.

The validity and reliability of tests may be reduced because of factors such as the child's limited language proficiency in the language of the test, lack of familiarity with the content of the test items, lack of social and cultural sensitivity on the part of the test administrator, and the child's lack of familiarity with test-taking strategies.

Be flexible when making interpretations. Know the research findings about how children from specific ethnic groups perform on the tests that have been selected. Recognize that principles of test interpretation that apply to the nonminority group may not be applicable to all ethnic minority groups.

Take into account the degree of acculturation in the child and the child's family. Recognize that acculturation will take various forms among different individuals, ethnic groups, and subgroups.

A Global Approach

Nuttall, Landurand, and Goldman (1984) advocate the global approach to decrease test bias. Nonbiased assessment is viewed as a process rather than a set of instruments. This approach values language dominance, adaptive behavior, and sociocultural background. The assessment process is evaluated at each stage for possible sources of bias.

A global approach involves a multidisciplinary team assessment that includes at least one person who speaks the child's language and is familiar with the child's culture and one person experienced in bilingual education, preferably in the child's language.

Before any assessment begins, the child's level of proficiency in both the home language and in English must be determined. Assessment of proficiency should include both receptive and expressive language. Assessment instruments need to be chosen carefully. If no instruments exist to test proficiency in the child's home language, an informal assessment should be made.

Observe the child in a variety of settings, and describe the child's behavior or functioning in each. Behavior-rating scales may give a measure of a child's adaptation to his or her own environment. (See chapter 11, Ecological and Direct Observation.)

The team member who is knowledgeable about the child's culture and language should visit the child in his or her home to determine the language the family normally speaks, what language(s) is spoken in the neighborhood, and what exposure the child has had to English, and then prepare a home survey summary. This information about the child's history and experience is important to cross-cultural assessment.

When conducting an interview, the team members need to work and talk with specific personnel who have had contact with the child and family. Leung (1986) suggests some general guidelines for use with Asian families that could apply to all interviews regardless of cultural background:

- Give the family the option of where the interview is to take place.
- Offer to bring an interpreter if unsure about the primary language.
- Accept hospitality; this conveys acceptance of the family.
- Spend time building rapport.
- State the purpose clearly and often, so there are no misunderstandings about the visit.
- Be aware that nonverbal cues may be more important than verbal cues, especially if the parents are unfamiliar with English.
- When in doubt, adjust communication style and body language to that of the family.
- Be sure to follow up on the visit with updates of information and decisions.
- Most important, be patient. There are many potential barriers to cross-cultural communication; the examiner can be an important link.

A medical exam should be part of the assessment process. Physical problems that may be undetected and could be easily corrected need to be ruled out.

Nuttall and Landurand (1984) also recommend that an educational assessment be done. For infants, toddlers, and preschoolers use a criterion- or curriculum-based assessment to determine what skills the child performs in the native or second language.

All assessments need to focus on determining how the child functions both socially and cognitively in both English and the home language. An integral part of this is the inclusion of a team member who is familiar with the child's culture and speaks the child's language. If no appropriately qualified professional is familiar with the child's home language, an interpreter needs to be found and trained to work with the monolingual assessor (Nuttall & Landurand, 1984).

The Behavioral-Ecological Perspective

Vincent and colleagues (1990) present a behavioral-ecological approach. This approach would use naturalistic observation in the full range of environments with the full range of people with whom the child usually interacts. This would, of course, necessitate the inclusion of parents as equal members of the assessment team.

The behavioral-ecological approach requires the early childhood interventionist to evaluate the environments where the child functions daily to determine what skills she or he needs now and in the future in order to be successful. The direct observation of the environments in which the young child functions would be conducted based on an analysis with the family of what settings are most important to them (Vincent et al., 1990). This analysis is based on the behavioral approach discussed in chapter 11.

The ecological focus of this approach requires that assessment also include a look at family needs. A combination of methods is necessary to gather this information, including family self-report, structured interviews, and direct observation (Vincent et al., 1990). Chapters 4 and 11 provide information on assessing family needs and resources and ecological assessment. The fundamental basis of the assessment is the concept that all families have needs and resources.

Summary

The role of direct testing, naturalistic observation, and parent interviewing are advocated as appropriate methods of assessment for children who are culturally diverse. Observation and interview are the foundation of assessment. The emphasis needs to be on the interaction between the child and his or her world rather than simply the interaction between the child and the test items. A genuine sensitivity to and appreciation for the uniqueness of each child, the child's family and their needs should be established as an integral part of screening and assessment.

An important fact for the examiner to keep in mind is that the purpose of the assessment is to learn more about the child and family to determine if special assistance is needed in order for the child to develop to his or her full potential. Professionals in assessment need to be advocates for children and families as opposed to agents who legitimize the location of the problem within the child. As an advocate, the early interventionist examines the societal and educational contexts in which the child has developed.

Cultural diversity should be viewed as a strength not as a deficit. Stressing the use and importance of family interviews and observation procedures as sources of information for planning is important. If children who are culturally/linguistically different from the norm are to receive appropriate assessments, placements, and programs, emphasis needs to be placed on administrative coordination, finding trained personnel who speak minority languages, providing descriptive data, and clearly articulating guidelines and procedures.

Suggested Group Activities

1. Generate a "Do/Don't's list" for the evaluator, early interventionist, or classroom teacher to help facilitate cultural sensitivity and support.

2. Devise a survey that could be used to elicit necessary information from the family regarding their child and cultural environment. Include open-ended questions inviting the opportunity for additional knowledge.

3. Examine commercial assessment instruments for items with cultural bias. Rewrite the items to make them more culturally fair.

4. How could the culture of poverty affect the test performance of children who are culturally and/or linguistically different? What could be done to counteract this disparity?

5. Discuss the various characteristics of a culturally competent individual. Provide specific examples that indicate an awareness of cultural sensitivity.

6. Describe an example of the use of assisted performance in an assessment situation. If possible, role-play the activity with a peer.

7. Discuss the advantages and disadvantages of utilizing a dynamic assessment. When would this technique be appropriate? Does it lend itself to various settings and situations?

8. Imagine needing to explain the behavioral-ecological perspective to a reluctant evaluator. What arguments can be presented to describe this approach?

References

Anderson, P. P., & Fenichel, E. S. (1989). *Serving culturally diverse families of infants and toddlers with disabilities.* Arlington, VA: The National Center for Clinical Infant Programs.

Anderson, M., & Goldberg, P. F. (1991). *Cultural competence in screening and assessment: Implications for services to young children with special needs ages birth through five.* Chapel Hill, NC: National Early Childhood Technical Assistance System (NECTAS) & Parent Advocacy Coalition for Educational Rights (PACER). (Available from PACER Center, 4826 Chicago Ave. South, Minneapolis, MN 55417, (612)827-2966.)

Bailey, D. B. (1989). Assessment and its importance in early intervention. In D. B. Bailey & M. Wolery (Eds.), *Assessing infants and preschoolers with handicaps* (pp. 1–21). Columbus, OH: Merrill.

Barrera, I. (1992). Personal communication.

Barrera Metz, I. (1991). Learning from personal experience. In M. Anderson & P. F. Goldberg, *Cultural competence in screening and assessment: Implications for services to young children with special needs ages birth through five* (pp. 8–10). Chapel Hill, NC: NECTAS & PACER.

Bazron, B. J., Dennis, K. W., & Isaacs, M. R. (1989). *Toward a culturally competent system of care: A monograpgh on effective services for minority children who are severely emotionally disturbed.* Washington, DC: The National Institute of Health, Child, and Adolescent Servie System Program (CASSP). (Available from CASSP Technical Assistance Center, Georgetown University Child Development Center, 3800 Reservoir Road, NW, Washington, DC 20007 - 202/687-8635.)

Beery, K. E. (1982). *Developmental Test of Visual Motor Integration—Revised.* Chicago: Follett Educational Corporation.

Bender, L. (1946). *The Bender Gestalt Test.* San Antonio: The Psychological Corporation.

Boehm, A. E. (1986). *Boehm Test of Basic Concepts—Preschool.* San Antonio: The Psychological Corporation.

Bracken, B. A. (1984). *The Bracken Basic Concepts Scale.* Columbus, OH: Merrill.

Brinkerhoff, J. (1976). *Portage Classroom Curriculum Checklist.* Portage, WI: Portage Project.

Burgemeister, B. B., Blum, L. H., & Lorge, I. (1972). *Columbia Mental Maturity Scale.* (3rd ed.) New York: The Psychological Corporation.

Campione, J., Brown, A., & Ferrara, R. (1982). Mental retardation and intelligence. In R. Sternberg (Ed.), *Handbook of human intelligence* (pp. 392–490). New York: Cambridge University Press.

Chan, S. (1983). *Assessment of Chinese-Americans: Cultural considerations.* Unpublished paper.

Duran, R. P. (1989). Assessment and instruction of at-risk Hispanic students. *Exceptional Children, 56*(2), 154–158.

Figueroa, R. (1989). Psychological testing of linguistic-minority students: Knowledge gaps and regulations. *Exceptional Children, 56,* 145–153.

Fradd, S. H., & Weismantel, M. J. (1989). *Meeting the needs of culturally and linguistically different students: A handbook for educators.* Boston: Little, Brown.

Garcia, S., & Ortiz, A. (1988). Preventing referrals of language minority students to special education. *New Focus, 5,* 1–11.

Goldman, S. R., & Trueba, H. T. (Eds.) (1987). *Becoming literate in English as a second language.* Norwood, NJ: Ablex.

Goldschmid, M. L., & Beatler, P. M. (1968). *Manual: Concept assessment kit—conservation.* San Diego: Educational and Industrial Testing Service.

Goodwin, W. L., & Driscoll, L. A. (1980). *Handbook for measurement and evaluation in early childhood education.* San Francisco: Jossey-Bass Publishers.

Hagen, E. (1989). *Communicating effectively with Southeast Asian patients.* Los Angeles: Immaculate Heart College Center.

Hanson, M. J., Lynch, E. W., & Wayman, K. I. (1990). Honoring the cultural diversity of families when gathering data. *Topics in Early Childhood Special Education, 10*(1), 112–131.

Kaufman, J. (1977). *Proceedings of a multicultural colloquium on non-biased pupil assessment.* Albany,

NY: New York State Department of Education, Bureau of School Psychological and Social Services.

Keogh, B., & Kopp, C. (1978). From assessment to intervention An elusive bridge. In F. Minifrie & L. Lloyd (Eds.), *Communication and cognitive abilities—Early behavioral assessment*. Baltimore: University Park Press.

Laosa, L. (1977). Nonbiased assessment of children's abilities: Historical antecedents and current issues. In T. Oakland (Ed.). *Psychological and educational assessment of minority children* (pp. 1-20). New York: Brunner/Mazer.

Leiter, R. G. (1966). *Arthur Adaptation of the Leiter International Performance Scale*. Chicago: Stoelting.

Leung, B. (1986). Psychoeducational assessment of Asian students. In M. K. Kitano & P. C. Chinn (Eds.), *Exceptional Asian children and youth* (pp. 24-35). Reston, VA: ERIC Clearinghouse on Handicapped and Gifted Children (ED 276178), Council for Exceptional Children.

Lynch, E. W. (1992). Developing cross-cultural competence. In E. W. Lynch & M. J. Hanson (Eds.), *Developing cross-cultural competence: A guide for working with young children and their families* (pp. 35-62). Baltimore: Paul H. Brookes.

Lynch, E. W., & Hanson, M. J. (1992). *Developing cross-cultural competence*. Baltimore: Paul H. Brookes.

McAdoo, H. (1978). Minority families. In J. H. Stevens & M. Matthews (Eds.), *Mother/child, father/child relationships* (pp. 177-195). Washington, DC: National Association for the Education of Young Children.

Mercer, J. R. (1979). *System of multicultural pluralistic assessment*. New York: The Psychological Corporation.

Mercer, J. R., & Ysseldyke, J. (1977). Designing diagnostic intervention programs. In T. Oakland (Ed.), *Psychological and educational assessment of minority children* (pp. 70-90). New York: Brunner/Mazel.

Nuttall, E. V., Landurand, P. M., & Goldman, P. (1984). A critical look at testing and evaluation from a cross-cultural perspective. In P. C. Chinn (Ed.), *Education of culturally and linguistically different exceptional children* (pp. 42-62). Reston, VA: Council for Exceptional Children.

Oakland, T., & Matuszek, P. (1977). Using tests in nondiscrimiatory assessment. In T. Oakland (Ed.), *Psychological and educational assessment of minority children*. New York: Brunner/Mazel.

Ortiz, A. A. (1987). The influence of locus of control and culture on learning styles of language minority students. In J. J. Johnson & B. A. Ramierez (Eds.), *American Indian exceptional children and youth* (pp. 9-16). Reston, VA: ERIC Clearinghouse on Handicapped and Gifted Children, Council for Exceptional Children.

Randall-David, E. (1989). *Strategies for working with culturally diverse communities and clients*. Washington, DC: Association for the Care of Children's Health.

Roberts, R. N. (1990). *Workbook for developing culturally competent programs for families of children with special needs* (2d ed.). Washington, DC: Georgetown University Child Development Center. (Available from Georgetown University Child Development Center, 3800 Reservoir Road, NW, Washington, DC 20007 - 202/687-8635.)

Sattler, J. M. (1988). *Assessment of children*. San Diego: Author.

Schilling, B., & Brannon, E. (1986). *Cross-cultural counseling: A guide for nutrition and health counselors*. Washington, DC: United States Department of Agriculture/Department of Health and Human Services.

Tharp, R. G., & Gallimore, R. (1988). *Rousing minds to life. Teaching, learning, and schooling in social context*. New York: Cambridge University Press.

Thurman, S. K., & Widerstrom, A. H. (1985). *Young children with special needs: A developmental and ecological ap̣   ı.* Boston: Allyn and Bacon.

Uzgiris, I. C., & Hunt, J. McV. (1975). *Assessment in infancy: Ordinal scales of psychological development*. Urbana, IL: University of Illinois Press.

Vincent, L. J., Salisbury, C. L., Strain, P., McCormick, C., & Tessier, A. (1990). A behavorial-ecological approach to early intervention: Focus on cultural diversity. In S. J. Meisels & J. P. Shonkoff (Eds.), *Handbook of early childhood intervention* (pp. 173–195). New York: Cambridge University Press.

Vygotsky, L. S. (1978). In M. Cole, V. John-Steiner, S. Scribner, & E. Soubermen (Eds.), *Mind in society: The development of higher psychological processes.* Cambridge, MA: Harvard University Press.

Walton, J. R., & Nuttall, E. V. (1991). Preschool evaluation of culturally different children. In E. V. Nuttall, I. Romero, & J. Kalesnik (Eds.), *Assessing and screening preschoolers: Psychological and educational dimensions* (pp. 281–299). Boston: Allyn and Bacon.

Wayman, K., Lynch, E., & Hanson, M. (1990). Home-based early childhood services: Cultural sensitivity in a family systems approach. *Topics in Early Childhood Special Education, 10*(4), 56–75.

$$Chapter \quad 7$$

Children with Severe Disabilities

LENORE B. LUCIANO

The challenge of assessing the skills of a young child intensifies when severe disabilities present (Bagnato & Neisworth, 1991). The use of standard assessment procedures becomes less reliable when motor, sensory, health, or affective deficits inhibit a child's participation in the assessment process. Under these circumstances, when a child does not successfully perform a task, it becomes difficult to determine whether the child lacks the problem-solving ability with which to complete the task or whether the mode of expected response places unrealistic demands on the child. When is it the task that is inhibiting performance? When is it the method? Is the child able to perform the task in another way?

A good first step in assessing children with severe disabilities is to be aware of and sensitive to the impact of a known disability on overall functioning. Adapting the environment, the materials, and/or the approach in order to assess developmental skills can facilitate a more meaningful evaluation. Note that such adaptations may alter the validity of some measures and preclude the use of standard scores. What is lost in item validity, however, is often gained in valuable, descriptive information about a child's functioning. It is essential that all modifications be described and justified and that responses to such changes be interpreted as estimates of functioning (Gerken, 1991).

The challenge involves finding the most reliable means of assessing a child's skills with the least penalty to the child for his or her specific disability. It is important to know what a given test expects of a child in the way of responsiveness in order to select the most appropriate and efficient measure for the job (DuBose, 1981). The goal is to maximize the child's opportunity to perform using his or her most intact modalities, while sufficiently maintaining the content and focus of the test to allow the most accurate measurement possible.

Extensive work has been done in the area of adaptive assessment of the young child with disabilities (Bailey & Wolery, 1989; Neisworth & Bagnato, 1987; Simeonsson, 1986; Wachs & Sheehan, 1988; Ulrey & Rogers, 1982). Highlights of important guidelines and tools for use with children with severe disabilities are presented here by type of deficit for ease of discussion. Keep in mind, however, that a deficit in one area may impact on multiple areas of developmental functioning. For example, motor and sensory impairments limit a child's exploration of the environment and may inhibit cognitive development. Communication impairments often hinder the development of social interaction skills.

Some tests have been devised for use with children with disabilities, but more often the examiner/practitioner must use more generalized material sensitively and meaningfully. Careful review of a test and its development will assist in the selection of an appropriate assessment instrument. Once selected, the test items and procedures may require adaptation, modification, and flexibility in order to be fair and useful with infants and preschoolers who are disabled.

Motor (or Neuromotor) Impairments

To achieve effective and meaningful developmental assessment of a child with motor impairment, one must minimize the hardship placed on the child by the disability itself. Bagnato and Neisworth (1991) emphasize the importance of "circumvent[ing] the neuromotor deficits as much as possible, in order to isolate evidence of intact conceptual, problem solving, and social communication skills" (p. 50). They caution us about the importance of time and proper positioning to maximize the child's opportunity for success. The authors describe the following four key points relevant to assessment of motor-impaired children:

1. Team with an occupational or physical therapist.
2. Remember to properly position the child.
3. Use adaptive equipment to minimize response limitations.
4. Determine (and use) the child's most reliable mode of response (p. 50).

The importance of proper positioning cannot be stressed enough, especially for the child with cerebral palsy:

> *Proper positioning alters muscle tone, reduces the negative effects of persistent primitive reflexes, and aligns the head and body for optimal facial orientation, reaching and grasping, and manipulating* (Bagnato & Neisworth, 1991, p. 50).

Two particularly useful books on handling and assessing the young child with cerebral palsy are *The Developmental Potential of Preschool Children* (Haeussermann, 1958) and *Handling the Young Cerebral Palsied Child at Home* (Finnie, 1975).

Rogers (l982) points out that even excellent positioning will not allow the severely disabled child to efficiently reach, grasp, and manipulate assessment materials. She suggests adapting or modifying test items and procedures in consideration of the following:

1. A child may respond by pointing or, if necessary, by eye gaze.
2. Markers may be easier to write/draw with than pencils or crayons.
3. Extended time to respond (in words or actions) is needed when muscle control is compromised.
4. Labored movement makes for greater fatigue, making multiple, briefer assessment sessions appropriate.

Positioning and Equipment

The frequently described adaptive equipment and modified materials are designed to afford the physically impaired child greater access to and more independent interaction with the environment. An individual who is constantly trying to maintain a comfortable and/or stable posture cannot attend well to learning tasks or even to social interaction. The fatigue that naturally accompanies such effort is significant as well.

Positioning equipment might include supportive seating devices with inserts, wedges, and strapping that assist in maintaining an upright posture. Corner chairs and side-lying devices are also useful in helping the child bring hands together at the midline. Lap boards may be attached to chairs or wheelchairs to provide a more accessible tabletop than traditional furniture might allow (Bagnato & Neisworth, 1991). In some cases, standing or prone boards with attached table surfaces offer the most stable and comfortable position in which a child may be "freed up" to engage in learning and assessment activities (Wilhelm, Johnson, & Eisert, 1986; Bagnato & Neisworth, 1991).

Adapted materials that utilize switches, peglike handles on puzzle pieces, hand splints and straps, and modified utensils may be used to allow children with poor grasps to participate in activities that would otherwise be impossible for them. Adapting the tabletop with a nonslip substance (i.e., a product called Dycem is useful) will keep materials and toys from sliding around (Bagnato & Neisworth, 1991).

The goal is to understand a child's physical capabilities as well as limitations in order to stage the most appropriate and meaningful assessment experience. Knowledge of a child's motor needs also will play a significant role in designing effective intervention programs.

Alternative Responsiveness

Robinson and Fieber (1988) present adapted assessment strategies that involve positioning of the child, positioning of the materials, and modification or substitution of materials themselves. Such levels of adaptation do not necessarily alter the task or the conceptual level of difficulty of a response. The goal is to maximize the child's opportunity to manipulate the materials in order to demonstrate understanding, intent, or mastery with respect to a given task.

These authors further address alternative ways in which the child may respond to tasks that provide an indication of skill level. A child's eye gaze or eye pointing can be a useful mode of responsiveness as long as no oculomotor problems are present. A child's attempted responses may not yield success but may be rather clear in intent. It is important to acknowledge and verify these efforts through repeated demonstration. Affective responses of the child also may provide an indication of cognitive awareness and recognition of desired responses.

Assisted Movement

Robinson and Fieber (1988) also describe techniques of assisted movement, whereby the examiner helps minimize the effects of the motor disability by providing hand/arm stability, strength, or improved grasp. The intent is to allow the child to demonstrate cognitive awareness and problem-solving skills that usually are inhibited by impaired motor dexterity. Apply these techniques with caution, and interpret tentatively. Even the most skilled and experienced practitioner/examiner can unintentionally guide a response not clearly intended by the child. Anticipated responses, assumption of estimated skill, or even reaction to involuntary muscle movement can lead or influence the child's response or our interpretation of it.

Process Approach

Adaptive assessment allows the practitioner/examiner to explore the child's responsiveness to the learning process. How the child learns and under what conditions he or she can perform tasks, or portions of tasks, is the goal of such assessment. This process-oriented or child-referenced approach offers an alternative to traditional assessment, which is typically focused on actual level of development rather than the process by which the child learns.

Some believe that a process-oriented approach to the assessment of strengths and weaknesses is the only meaningful way to assess the skills of young children with severe or multiple disabilities (Rosenberg and Robinson, 1990). We are cautioned not to take a child's access to learning activities for granted when motor or sensory impairments present. Through task analysis one can examine the child's ability to perform different levels of a task and obtain information useful to the development of an intervention program. (See the section on task analysis later in this chapter.)

Interactive Competencies

Early interentionists offer an alternative approach to the assessment of infants and preschoolers with disabilities (McLean, Bruder, Baird & Dunst, 1991; Dunst

& McWilliam, 1988). A recommended model, OBSERVE, examines a child's ability to learn new behaviors by matching learning conditions with the child's response capabilities. With this model, the child is observed within a variety of contexts that may have social and nonsocial expectations attached to them. The child's developmental interactions are observed and identified as he or she moves through daily routines. Following Piaget's sequence of cognitive development, the OBSERVE model utilizes five levels of interaction. Table 7–1 is an example of how this system could be used with an infant who is severely disabled.

Examiner Skill

Wilhelm, Johnson, and Eisert (1986) point out the importance of examiner skill and experience in the assessment of children with motor impairments. They note that collaboration and consultation with physical, occupational, and speech therapists are vital to a meaningful assessment of any aspect of the child's development. Examiners/practitioners need to be aware of their biases and prejudices when confronted with a child's motor or speech disabilities. It is easy to form false impressions about a child's disabilities and potential to perform when observing his or her very visible motor difficulties. These authors also describe the risk of the *halo effect* in the administration and interpretation of tests. Prejudged impressions of how a child might respond to tasks, or how one might wish them to respond, can inadvertently cue or influence a response (Wilhelm, Johnson, & Eisert, 1986). One must strive for objectivity during the assessment process.

Minimizing Barriers

For both assessment and intervention, the practitioner must identify and help the child overcome barriers to active participation. Rosenberg and Robinson (1990) summarize the strategies needed to increase a child's participation in program activities (including assessment) as: (1) increasing a specific skill through instruction, (2) modifying the environment, (3) identifying alternative behaviors through which the child may perform, and (4) adapting activities in order to circumvent the barriers that prevent the child's participation in them.

Visual Impairments

Blindness impacts on all aspects of a child's development. It affects awareness of spatial relationships and object permanence, self-help and social skills, coordination and motor dexterity, and as a result, impacts on complex cognitive and language development as well (DuBose, 1981). The blind infant does not have the benefit of the facial cues given by caregivers to enhance socialization, increase anticipation, and communicate satisfaction in the early months. Without sight these infants come to recognize and anticipate events through touch and ultimately

TABLE 7-1 Selected Findings from Using the OBSERVE to Map a Child's Topography of Behavior

Context of Assessment

Levels of Development	Circle Time	Free Play	Group Time	Meals	Outside Play	Bathroom
Attentional interactions: The capacity to attend to and discriminate between stimuli	1. Looks at caregiver when she's talking or singing. 2. Orients toward different caregivers and children when they talk.	1. Attends to caregiver's actions. 2. Laughs at funny events. 3. Tracks objects moving in and out of visual field.	1. Smiles when talked to. 2. Attends to other children. 3. Looks with interest at toys placed on his travel chair tray.	1. Watches other children at the table. 2. Searches for sources of sounds.	1. Orients toward voice when her name is called. 2. Pays attention to sights and sounds on the playground.	1. Tracks children and caregivers as they come and go.
Contingency interactions: The use of simple, undifferentiated forms of behavior to initiate and sustain control over reinforcing consequences	1. Reaches for child to initiate interaction. 2. Vocalizes to get adult's attention.	1. Makes kite (suspended from ceiling) move using a string attached to his arm. 2. Swipes at wind chimes to make them move. 3. Rolls over to reinitiate social interaction.	1. Smiles or laughs to get adult to continue activity. 2. Picks up toys and "examines" them.	1. Finger-feeds self with some difficulty.	1. Vocalizes to have an adult continue activity (e.g., swinging).	

104

TABLE 7-1 *(Continued)*

			Context of Assessment			
Levels of Development	Circle Time	Free Play	Group Time	Meals	Outside Play	Bathroom
Differentiated interactions: The coordination and regulation of behavior that reflects elaboration and progress toward conventionalization	1. Responds to "What do you want to sing now?" using arm movements to indicate which song he wants to hear (nonconventional gestures). 2. Imitates actions of other children and caregivers. 3. Engages in reciprocal turn-taking during interactive episodes.	1. Moves toward play activity in walker. 2. Points to items on shelf. 3. Uses objects and toys to initiate play with caregiver. 4. Demonstrates complex motor action with objects (rolls car). 5. "Talks" and holds pretend phone conversations.	1. Chooses "favorite" activity among several options. 2. Points to items she wants if out of reach. 3. Associates sound with action (attempts car sounds). 4. Hands toys and objects to adults to have them activated. 5. Shows ability to feed doll using spoon and bottle.	1. Uses head shake or facial expression to indicate yes or no. 2. Reaches for or grasps spoon to help with feeding. 3. Uses spoon to eat with (although with considerable difficulty).	1. Moves toward children (in walker) to engage in play episodes. 2. Will imitate motor actions made by other children. 3. Plays cooperatively with other children (takes turns trying to throw ball).	1. Indicates yes or no when asked if he has to go to the bathroom.
Encoded interactions: The use of conventionalized forms of behavior that		1. Engages in pretend play (makes hotdogs, puts them	1. Displays problem-solving abilities in getting objects and	1. Uses symbol board to select food item she wants.	1. Chooses from approximately 10 outside activities	

(Continued)

TABLE 7-1 (*Continued*)

			Context of Assessment			
Levels of Development	Circle Time	Free Play	Group Time	Meals	Outside Play	Bathroom
are context bound and that depend on referents as a basis for evoking the behaviors		in the oven to cook). 2. Pretends to "drive" car, vocalizations in attempt to make a motor sound. 3. Uses communication board to indicate desired activity. 4. Engages in pretend eating and drinking in doll corner.	activities he wants. 2. Puts dolls in appropriate situations when playing house (e.g., baby in bedroom, car in garage, stove in kitchen).		on communication board. 2. Follows series of two related commands.	
Symbolic interactions: The use of conventionalized forms of behavior to communicate a message in the absence of reference giving cues				1. Uses symbol board to signal desire to go to kitchen and eat.		

Source: From Wachs, T. D., & Sheehan, R. (Eds.). *Assessment of Young Developmentally Disabled Children* (pp. 230–231). Copyright © 1988. New York: Plenum Publishing. Reprinted with permission.

through auditory cues—sounds, voice, language—that may be learned more slowly and over an extended period of time (Fraiberg, 1974).

Exploration

When assessing the young child with visual impairment, it is essential to keep these developmental consequences in mind. One must investigate, although not prejudice, anticipated developmental delays due to the absence of sight. Alternative strategies of exploration and learning may already be developing for the child and must be evaluated as well. Without the benefit of sight, the child will need to *explore* the environment using other senses (i.e., hearing, touch, smell), which is likely to take more time. Also, in the learning or assessment environment, it is difficult for the child to know which stimuli should be *weeded out* as extraneous to the activities at hand; therefore, keep distractors to a minimum.

Assessment Considerations

Hansen, Young, and Ulrey (1982) offer the following principles of assessment when working with children with visual impairments:

1. Assess over time rather than in one session.
2. Give child ample time to explore and become familiar with surroundings.
3. Give ample time for child to become familiar with each test item (and its materials).
4. Be familiar with normal and abnormal behaviors in visually impaired children (such as repetitive behaviors).
5. Maintain flexibility in testing and observation (adapted from p. 111).

Note that these are valuable considerations that, in large part, apply to the assessment of any child with disabilities.

Bagnato and Neisworth (1991) further suggest that the examiner:

1. Consult with visual specialists;
2. Provide a distraction-free, well-defined work area;
3. Provide multisensory toys and tasks;
4. Emphasize touching, sounds, and verbal descriptions.

Adapted Techniques

Modification or adaptation of aspects of the assessment may be warranted in order to best examine the child's competencies and functioning. Moore and McLaughlin (1992) point out that individualized modifications in test administration may require changes in the test items, the task instructions, and/or the mode of response required by the child. They warn us not to assume that we can substitute a tactile version of a visual stimulus as the representations are not synonymous. Forms of simple structure and minimal detail may be adapted in some cases.

Impact of Visual Impairment

Davidson and Legouri (1986) emphasize the difficulty of assessing overall cognitive development of young children with visual impairments in light of the far reaching impact the disability has on the child's experiences, opportunity to learn, and processing of information. They recommend serial evaluations at short intervals (i.e., every three months) from early infancy in order to monitor and estimate the child's cognitive development during the first few years of life. This type of evaluation employs formal and informal techniques, using nonvisual items and measures, so the child is not penalized for the disability itself.

Materials

Other items to consider when selecting materials and conditions to use in the assessment of children with visual impairments include: brightness (although protection from glare is essential); contrast in color combinations of materials (i.e., black on white/buff, yellow on black, blue, purple); time required for the child who is visually impaired to identify and attend to events; distance from which the materials are to be viewed (the examiner may need to experiment with distance until the optimal distance for presentation of stimuli is found); size of image (i.e., of graphics, shapes, letters, etc.); setting conditions (must be free of auditory distractors; notice how child positions himself in the environment); materials that offer more than just visual appeal (i.e., spinning toys, pinwheels, brightly colored yarn, pop beads, slinky toys, lollipops); special aids (i.e., magnifying lenses, audio cassette recordings) (Fewell, 1991; Harley & Lawrence, 1977).

Limited Research

Little formal research has been conducted with respect to the development of young children who are visually impaired and how it resembles or departs from that of sighted children (Moore & McLaughlin, 1992; Warren, 1984; Fewell, 1991). While the impact of visual deficit on learning is noted, the specific ways in which sight or blindness affect the many ways a child learns have not been clearly established. This suggests that assessment efforts should proceed with caution and that global generalizations regarding the abilities and potential of a child based a on short-term evaluation should be avoided.

Selected Measures

Some measures that have been adapted or standardized for appropriate use with children with partial sight or blindness include: the Child Behavior Checklist (Achenbach & Edelbrock, 1981) for children 4 to 16 years of age; the *Reynell-Zinkin*

Developmental Scales—Visually Impaired (Reynell & Zinkin, 1979) ages 0 to 5 years; a Braille version (Catin, 1975) of the *Test of Basic Concepts* (Boehm, 1971) for use in kindergarten through the second grade; and the *Perkins-Binet Tests of Intelligence for the Blind* (Davis, 1980) for children 3 to 18 years of age (Davidson and Legouri, 1986). Moore and McLaughlin (1992) offer an annotated list of tests (see Table 7–2) that may be used with varying levels of confidence and success with the young child with a visual impairment.

Hearing Impairments

Communication

Communication is the most significant behavior of concern with respect to the child with hearing impairment (Mullen, 1992). The extent to which a child may develop receptive and expressive language skills has a great deal to do with the amount of hearing the child has as well as: (1) how early in life the hearing loss occurred, (2) at what point it was identified, and (3) how and when intervention was provided. How effectively the child interacts with others, communicating wants, needs, or ideas, may be impacted on by these factors as well. The mode of communication used by the child also is affected (Mullen, 1992).

Assessment Considerations

When assessing the child with hearing loss or deafness, do not rely on tasks that are dependent on verbal instructions, questions, auditory cues and models, or language concepts. Tests that require oral/verbal responses also penalize the child who is deaf (DuBose, 1981). Nonverbal performance items are essential. Bagnato and Neisworth (1991) suggest that the examiner/practitioner consider the following:

1. Consult with sensory specialists.
2. Provide a distraction-free, well-defined work area.
3. Select brightly colored, moveable, multisensory, multifunctional materials.
4. Be demonstrative in gesture and in facial expressions.
5. Stress a total communication approach.
6. Provide demonstrations and manually guide the child through practice items to teach a desired response mode.
7. Physically prompt the child to look at and orient toward the task.
8. Include smiles, touch, and clapping in your rewards for the child's efforts.

They further caution that shyness, hesitance, and social withdrawal are not uncommon behaviors for children who are deaf and that rapport-building is important.

TABLE 7–2   **Selected Assessment Instruments for Use with Young Children with Visual Impairments**

Adaptive Behavior Measure

Vineland Adaptive Behavior Scales—Expanded Form

Authors   Sara S. Sparrow, David A. Balla, and Domenic V. Cicchetti

Available from   American Guidance Service

Date of Publication   1984

Age Range   0–18 years

Comments   A norm-referenced, standardized test with supplementary norms for a relatively large visually handicapped sample aged 6 years to 12 years 11 months. The domains are Communication, Daily Living Skills, Socialization, Motor Skills, and Maladaptive Behavior. Various items in all domains are inappropriate for visually handicapped (VH) preschoolers or require careful adaptation. Judicious use of the Maladaptive domain only with children 5 years or older is advised.

Cognitive/Conceptual Understanding Measures

Kaufman Assessment Battery for Children

Authors   Alan S. Kaufman and Nadeen L. Kaufman

Available from   American Guidance Service

Date of Publication   1983a, 1983b

Age Range   2.5 to 12.5 years

Comments   A norm-referenced, standardized test that assesses intelligence and achievement, defining intelligence as mental processing or problem-solving ability. Minimum developmental level of 3.5 to 4 years is advised for VH children in order to establish a basal level and range of deficits above and below it. Only subtests appropriate for blind children are Number Recall and Riddles. Subtests that may be appropriate for low-vision children include Hand Movements, Number Recall, Triangles, Word Order, Expressive Vocabulary, Faces & Places, Arithmetic, and Riddles. Careful modifications or adaptations may be required for low-vision children, depending on functional vision.

Stanford-Binet Intelligence Scale, Fourth Edition

Authors   Robert L. Thorndike, Elizabeth P. Hagen, and Jerome M. Sattler

Available from   Riverside Publishing Company

Date of Publication   1986

Age Range   2 years–adult

Comments   Norm-referenced, standardized test that assesses intelligence. Adaptations for children with visual impairment are general and were not field-tested. Handbook recommends attempting to administer all tests in standard format to low-vision children, modifying Vocabulary, Quantitative, Comprehension, Number Series, Verbal Relations, and Equation Building as necessary. For blind children, omit Bead Memory, Pattern Analysis, Absurdities, Copying, Memory for Objects, Matrices, and Paper Folding & Cutting, and present only Memory for Sentences and Memory for Digits without modifications. Use of Braille is recommended, but caution is necessary because most preschoolers have not learned Braille and the type of discriminations required with Braille are different and sometimes more difficult.

TABLE 7-2 *(Continued)*

Cognitive/Conceptual Understanding Measures *(Continued)*

Tactile Test of Basic Concepts

Author Hilda Caton

Available from American Printing House for the Blind

Date of Publication 1986

Age Range 5–9 years

Comments Tactile analogue to the Boehm Test of Basic Concepts, Form A (1971), adapted by permission of The Psychological Corporation, designed to assess mastery of "concepts commonly found in preschool and primary grade instructional materials and essential to understanding oral communications" (p. 2). Fifty raised-line drawings of simple geometric forms with detailed instruction for administration are provided. Items may be used as criterion-referenced measure of spatial knowledge for blind preschoolers.

Developmental Measures

Battelle Developmental Inventory

Authors Jean Newborg, John R. Stock, Linda Wnek, John Guidubaldi, and John Svinicki

Available from Teaching Resources Corporation/DLM

Date of Publication 1984

Age Range 0–8 years

Comments Norm-referenced, standardized developmental battery designed to aid in making decisions regarding special education eligibility and placement, and to plan specific classroom programs. Modifications and adaptations for children with visual impairments are included, but were not field-tested and no score adjustments are given. Domains are Personal-Social, Adaptive, Motor, Communication, and Cognitive. For severely low-vision and blind, each domain contains items that must be scored 0; most are in Cognitive, thus invalidating this domain and the total scores. Valid scores may be obtained only for low-vision children with good usable vision.

Brigance® Diagnostic Inventory of Early Development

Author Albert Brigance

Available from Curriculum Associates

Date of Publication 1979

Age Range 0–6 years

Comments A criterion-referenced instrument designed to provide specific information for planning educational programs. No adaptations are suggested for children with visual impairment, but few are needed below the age of 3 years; for the remaining items, careful adaptations are necessary, especially for testing early academic skills. Eleven sections include Preambulatory Motor, Gross Motor, Fine Motor, Self-Help, Pre-Speech, Speech & Language, General Knowledge & Comprehension, Readiness, Basic Reading, Manuscript Writing, and Math.

The Callier-Azusa Scale

Editor Robert Stillman

Available from Callier Center for Communication Disorders

Date of Publication 1978

Age Range 0–9 years

(Continued)

TABLE 7-2 *(Continued)*

The Callier-Azusa Scale (Continued)

Comments Criterion-referenced test for deaf-blind and severely impaired children designed to provide information for planning instructional programs. Eighteen subscales assess behaviors in six domains: Motor Development, Perceptual Abilities, Daily Living Skills, Cognition, Communication and Language, and Social Development.

Growing Up: A Developmental Curriculum

Authors Noel B. Croft and Lee W. Robinson

Available from Parent Consultants

Date of Publication 1984

Age Range 0–5 years

Comments An informal criterion-referenced assessment procedure accompanying a curriculum guide based on Piaget's work originally developed for use with infants and preschoolers with visual impairments, designed to provide information for planning instructional programs. It also is useful with nonhandicapped children or children with mental and/or physical impairments, including children with profound levels of impairment. Items are coded with approximate age equivalents for sighted children (for use as a reference when sequencing skills), but were not field-tested. Recommendations for teaching 901 specific skills are provided. Six areas of development are assessed and curriculum suggestions given, with subdivisions called "strands" within each: Physical Development, Fine Motor Development, Self-Help Skills, Social Personal Development, Language Development, and Intellectual Development.

Informal Assessment of Developmental Skills for Visually Handicapped Students

Authors Rose-Marie Swallow, Sally Mangold, and Phillip Mangold

Available from American Foundation for the Blind

Date of Publication 1978

Age Range 0–16 years

Comments A compilation of informal criterion-referenced checklists or inventories developed by teachers of the visually handicapped. Part Two: Informal Assessment of Developmental Skills for Younger Visually Handicapped and Multihandicapped Children was developed to aid in assessment and formulation of teaching objectives for infants and preschoolers with visual impairment. Part Two provides five checklists: Self-Help, Psychomotor, Social-Emotional, Language, and Cognition.

Oregon Project for Visually Impaired and Blind Preschoolers

Authors Donneise Brown, Vickie Simmons, and Judy Methvin

Available from Jackson County Education Service District

Date of Publication 1979

Age Range 0–5 years

Comments A criterion-referenced instrument designed for assessment and educational program planning for young children with visual impairments. Items are assigned one-year age levels appropriate for sighted children, and separate codes are provided for skills that take longer for children with visual impairment to acquire, for specialized skills required because of visual impairment, and for items inappropriate for blind children. Recommendations for teaching each skill are extensive. Six areas of development are assessed: Cognitive, Language, Self-Help, Socialization, Fine Motor, and Gross Motor.

TABLE 7-2 *(Continued)*

Southern California Ordinal Scales of Development

Authors   Donald I. Ashhurst, Elaine Bamberg, Julika Barrett, Ann Bisno, Artice Burke, David C. Chambers, Jean Fentiman, Ronald Kadish, Mary Lou Mitchell, Lambert Neeley, Todd Thorne, Doris Wents

Available from   Western Psychological Services

Date of Publication   1985

Age Range   0–13 years

Comments   A criterion-referenced ordinal scale, designed for handicapped, developmentally delayed, or learning-disabled children, to assess functioning on the basis of a Piagetian framework. Manuals provide behaviors to be sampled, recommended administration materials, general procedures to be followed, and the criteria for scoring. Scoring system measures the quality of responses. Although field testing included a small sample of blind children, specific adaptations for visually handicapped children are not given, and knowledge of visual impairment as well as careful adaptations are necessary. The six scales are Cognition, Communication, Fine Motor Abilities, Gross Motor Abilities, Practical Abilities, and Social-Affective Behavior.

Ecological Measures

Early Childhood Environment Rating Scale

Authors   Thelma Harms and Richard M. Clifford

Available from   Teachers College Press

Date of Publication   1980

Age Range   Infant–Kindergarten

Comments   A field-tested, criterion-referenced, observational inventory to assess the quality of caregiver environments and interpersonal interactions outside the home. Minimal, if any, adaptations are necessary. Thirty-seven items are rated on a seven-point scale, from 1—minimal to 7—excellent, with all criteria specifically defined, to develop a profile for each room observed. The seven subscales are Personal Care Routines of Children, Furnishings and Display for Children, Language-Reasoning Experiences, Fine and Gross Motor Activities, Creative Activities, Social Development, and Adult Needs.

Home Observation for Measurement of the Environment, Revised Edition

Authors   Bettye M. Caldwell and Robert H. Bradley

Available from   Center for Research on Teaching and Learning, University of Arkansas at Little Rock

Date of Publication   1984 revision

Age Range   Infant–Preschool

Comments   A field-tested, criterion-referenced, observational inventory to assess the stimulation potential and quality of early developmental environment within the home. Four separate versions are available: Infant and Toddlers, Preschool, Infants with Severe Handicaps, and Preschool with Severe Handicaps. The Preschool with Severe Handicaps version includes items to assess presence of adaptive aids for children with visual, hearing, orthopedic, and mental impairments, such that more than one handicapping condition can be included as necessary. The seven subscales are Physical Environment, Emotional and Verbal Responsivity, Acceptance of Child's Behavior, Organization of Environment, Provision of Play Materials, Parental Involvement with Child, and Opportunities for Variety.

(Continued)

TABLE 7-2   *(Continued)*

Orientation and Mobility

Preschool Orientation and Mobility Screening

Authors   Bonnie Dodson-Burk and Everett Hill

Available from   Association for Education and Rehabilitation of the Blind and
Visually Impaired

Date of Publication   1989

Age Range   0–5 years

Comments   A criterion-referenced screening inventory for orientation and mobility
(O & M) skills which was developed in part by an HCEEP federal model demonstration grant for services to young children with visual impairment. O&M Screening A
was designed for younger (0–2), delayed, or nonambulatory children. O&M Screening B was designed for older (2–5) ambulatory children and assesses Background
Information, Home and Community Experiences, Body Parts and Planes, Positional
Concepts, Visual Functioning, Gross Motor Skills, Auditory Skills, Tactile Skills,
Mobility Skills, and Orientation Skills.

Language

Receptive Expressive Language Assessment for the Visually Impaired

Authors   Gloria Anderson and Annette Smith

Available from   Ingham Intermediate School District

Date of Publication   1979

Age Range   0–5 years

Comments   A three-dimensional adaptation of the Preschool Language Scale (Zimmerman, Steiner, & Pond, 1979) and language items from the Maxfield-Buchholz
Scale of Social Maturity for Preschool Blind Children (Maxfield-Buchholz, 1957).
Designed to measure receptive and expressive language of young children with
visual impairments through predominantly auditory and tactile responses. Real objects are utilized and an audio cassette tape of environmental sounds is provided.
Limited field testing with sighted children and a small number of children with visual
impairments dictates judicious interpretation.

Source: From Nuttall, E. V., Romero, I., & Kalesnik, J., *Assessing and Screening Preschoolers:
Psychological and Educational Dimensions,* pp. 358–364. Copyright © 1992. Reprinted with
permission of Allyn and Bacon.

Auditory Assistive Devices

The examiner/practitioner also needs to be aware of whether the child utilizes
a hearing aid or other amplification system (Mullen, 1992). If so, the device needs
to be in good working order and in use during the assessment. If the examiner
is not experienced with the mechanics of such devices, an audiologist or
speech/language pathologist should be on hand (or consulted) to rule out
mechanical malfunctions or distorted sound output. Caregivers also may be
familiar with the workings of the child's hearing device and should be consulted
as to its function as well as its perceived effectiveness.

Primary "Language"

Evaluators of the child with hearing impairments also should have competence in the child's primary mode of communication (Mullen, 1992). Assessment in a child's primary *language* is an essential right of the child and family and must be a component of any meaningful evaluation process.

Multidisciplinary Importance

A comprehensive, multidisciplinary assessment is crucial in determining the overall functioning of the child with a hearing impairment, as is the case for all children with low-incidence disabilities. In addition to the language/communication, cognitive, adaptive behavior, and social-emotional evaluations that are the basis of any in-depth assessment, an audiological test is crucial in assessing the child presenting with, or suspected of having, hearing impairment (Mullen, 1992).

Multiple Measures

Rogers and Soper (1982) point out the importance of using more than one test when assessing the developmental skills of the young child with a hearing impairment. This is a helpful suggestion for several reasons:

1. Multiple measures provide greater opportunity to become familiar with the child and his or her skills as well as familiarize the child with assessment procedures and expectations.
2. A broader sample of skills and behaviors can be observed and measured through the use of a battery of tests rather than a single test (note the different *types* of tasks included in different tests).
3. Discrepancies in scores can suggest greater skill and potential than might be identified through the use of only one measure.

It is recommended that observations of the child's play and social interactions with parents and peers be included among the measures to employ. Such observations can reveal important information about how the child communicates his or her wants and needs as well as provide some indication of the child's self-concept and self-esteem.

Selected Measures

Simeonsson (1986) suggests the availability of selected measures of cognition and communication for young children with a hearing impairment. These include the *Smith-Johnson Nonverbal Performance Scale* (Smith & Johnson, 1977) for children 2 to 4 years old; and the *Adaptation of the WPPSI for Deaf Children* (Ray & Ulissi, 1982) for use with children 4 to 6½ years old. Selected behavioral and personal/social measures include the "Socio-Emotional Assessment Inventory" (Meadow, 1983) — a preschool inventory for children 3 to 6 years old; the "Empathy Task" (Borke, 1971) for use with children 3 to 8 years old; and the "Modification of AAMD Adaptive Behavior Scale" (Suess, Cotten, & Sison, 1983) for ages 3 to 30.

Mullen (1992) has compiled a useful list of assessment instruments to be considered when evaluating the preschooler with a hearing impairment. She offers comments and suggestions for appropriate use with respect to measures across several domains: language and basic concepts (see Table 7–3), cognition (see Table 7–4), social-emotional and adaptive behavior (see Table 7–5). A list of scales of a developmental/criterion nature (see Table 7–6) is also provided.

Affective/Behavioral Impairments

Assessing a child with markedly distorted emotional and behavioral responses calls for considerable flexibility on the part of the examiner due to the unpredictability of the child. Readiness to modify testing procedures and methods of assessment as one proceeds will facilitate the broadest determination of the child's range and pattern of responsiveness. DuBose (1981) notes that poor communication skills (both verbal and social) are likely to be evident in children with severe behavioral and emotional problems. In the case of children who are autistic, auditory and/or visual problems may be present as well.

General Considerations

Waterman (1992) suggests procedures for the developmental assessment of the child with emotional disabilities (see Table 7–7). These procedures represent good practice for assessing this population. However, the author suggests that the examiner attempt to include *all* levels of the procedure described rather than selecting alternative methods based on lack of success with one. Gathering data through a combination of formal measures, observations, play, parent report, and a home visit is recommended when assessing a child whose responses and behaviors may be variable at different times and under different circumstances.

Multiple Measures

Bagnato and Neisworth (1991) further alert us to the need for reducing ambiguity and hasty or inaccurate interpretation of measurements by conducting "a multisource, multidimensional survey that synthesizes information from parent interview, observation of parent-child interaction, ratings of atypical and func-

TABLE 7-3 Selected Language and Basic Concept Assessment Instruments

> **Key**
> A. Name of instrument
> B. Age range, availability of norms for hearing-impaired
> C. Psychometric data
> D. Description
> E. Evaluation
> F. Year, author, publisher

A. *Assessment of Children's Language Comprehension*
B. 3-0 to 6-5, no norms for hearing-impaired.
C. Standardized on 311 nursery and elementary children. Limited statistical data provided.
D. Designed to assess comprehension of utterances one to four "critical elements" in length. Examiner reads word or phrase and child points to one of four pictures on test plate.
E. Provides practical information about length of utterance child can comprehend and if he or she tends to miss particular parts. Test can be signed and used as a criterion-based versus norm-referenced test. May be evaluating lipreading (speechreading) skill in children who do not use sign.
F. 1973, Foster, Gidden, and Stark, Consulting Psychologists Press

A. *Bare Essentials in Assessing Really Little Kids (BEAR)*
B. Developmental assessment process, not normed.
C. Criterion-referenced. No reliability or validity data.
D. Based on developmental models of language acquisition, BEAR designed to assess language mastery. Includes concept analysis, syntactic/morphological analysis, phonological analysis, and semantic/pragmatic analysis.
E. Yields developmental information useful in program planning, but no standard scores.
F. 1982, Hasenstab and Laighton (in Hasenstab & Horner), Rockville, MD: Aspen Systems.

A. *Bracken Basic Concepts Scale*
B. 2-6 to 7-11, no norms for hearing-impaired.
C. Standardized on nationally representative sample (N = 1,109). Reliability and validity data presented.
D. Measures receptive vocabulary thought to be essential to success in kindergarten, with a conceptual sentence format ("Show me . . . ," "Which is . . . ," "Who is . . .") Includes color, letter identification, numbers, counting, comparisons, shapes, direction/position, size, social/emotional, time/sequence, and texture/material concepts.
E. Language demands of test may be too difficult for many deaf children. Difficult to determine if child does not understand language or not know actual concept being tested. However, limited response requirements (i.e., pointing or short verbal response) are an advantage assuming child understands verbal questions. Provides potential information for programming. May be signed if used as criterion-referenced test, but iconicity of signs in some categories (e.g., shapes) may prove problematic.
F. 1984, Bracken, Psychological Corporation

(Continued)

TABLE 7–3 *(Continued)*

A. *Carolina Picture Vocabulary Test for Deaf and Hearing Impaired*
B. 2-6 to 16-0, norms for hearing-impaired provided.
C. Standard scores, age equivalents, percentiles. Standardized on 767 children with hearing impairments. Reported standard error of measure considerably larger for children below age 6.
D. Designed to measure receptive sign vocabulary. Examiner signs a word and child points to one of four pictures on test plate.
E. Good tool for assessment of preschool children who have been exposed to sign language. Limited usefulness below age 4. Although test authors suggest that stop-action pictures depicting sign production allow for administration by examiners inexperienced in signing, this practice is *not* recommended.
F. 1985, Layton and Holmes, Modern Education Corporation

A. *Environmental Language Inventory (ELI)*
B. Developmental assessment instrument, not normed.
C. Manual reports results of three research studies using ELI. Standard score comparisons not provided, but frequency, proportion and rank-ordering of the semantic/grammatical forms are available.
D. Designed to assess early semantic/grammatical expressive rules through imitation, conversation, and free play. Included are agent–action, action–object, modifier-possession, negation, location–agent, location–object, and introducer.
E. Assuming some level of receptive understanding, ELI can yield diagnostic information about expressive skills for use in program development. Designed for use with a variety of children, including autistic, mentally retarded, and hearing-impaired.
F. 1978, MacDonald and Horstmeier, Charles E. Merrill Publisher

A. *Environmental Pre-Language Battery (EPB)*
B. Behavioral assessment process, not normed.
C. Criterion-referenced, no reliability or validity data.
D. Designed to yield behavioral descriptions of very early language skills (one word stage or below) primarily through structured play situation. Skills included are nonverbal skills of object permanence, attention, gesture communication, picture and object identification, and following directions; verbal skills of naming objects, naming actions, repeating, two-word imitations, and two-word answers to questions. Can be adapted for use with children with a variety of handicapping conditions.
E. Yields criterion-referenced information for use in program development. Teaching strategies built into assessment process can be helpful in developing intervention strategies.
F. 1978b, MacDonald and Horstmeier, Charles E. Merrill Publisher

A. *Grammatical Analysis of Elicited Language, Pre-Sentence Level (GAEL-P), Simple Sentence Level (GAEL-S), and Complex Sentence Level (GAEL-C)*
B. 2-6 to 11-11, norms for hearing-impaired provided.
C. GAEL-P standardized on 150 children with hearing impairments aged 3-0 to 5-11 and 75 hearing aged 2-6 to 3-11. GAEL-S standardized on 200 orally educated children, severe to profoundly hearing-impaired aged 5-0 to 7-6 and 200 hearing children aged 2-6 to 5-0. Norms for children using total communication on GAEL-S are reported in Geers, Moog, and Schick (1984). GAEL-C standardized on 270 orally educated, severe to profoundly hearing-impaired aged 8-0 to 11-11 and 240 hearing aged 3-0 to 5-11.

TABLE 7-3   *(Continued)*

D. Designed to elicit and evaluate spoken or signed English through both prompted and imitated utterances. (GAEL-P assesses communication concepts versus English skill.)
E. Good tools for communication assessment and among few normed for hearing-impaired. GAEL-P provides good communication baseline for young children without testing English skill. Levels S and C test English syntax and allow comparisons to both hearing-impaired and hearing children. However, neither pragmatics nor semantics are directly measured at the S and C levels. Length of administration can be a drawback.
F. 1983, Moog, Kozak, and Geers (GAEL-P), 1979, Moog and Geers (GAEL-S) and 1980, Moog and Geers (GAEL-C), Central Institute for the Deaf

A. Scales of Early Communication Skills for Hearing Impaired Children
B. 2-0 to 8-11, norms for hearing-impaired provided.
C. Standardized on 372 orally educated hearing-impaired from 14 different programs across six states. Means and standard deviations provided in seven age groups. Data provided on reliability but not validity.
D. Teacher-administered instrument designed to measure speech and language development in hearing-impaired. Included four scales: receptive language, expressive language, nonverbal receptive, and nonverbal expressive.
E. Useful and easily administered screening instrument.
F. 1975, Moog and Geers, Central Institute for the Deaf

Sources: Some of the information presented here was adapted from the following materials:
Mullen, Y., & Spragins, A. B. (1987). *Deaf students and psychological services: What psychologists need to know.* Workshop presented at the National Association of School Psychologists Convention, New Orleans, Louisiana
Spragins, A. B., & Blennerhassett, L. (1989). *Intellectual, adaptive behavior, social-emotional, developmental/criterion-based, language and basic concept assessment instruments used with preschool deaf children.* Workshop materials presented at the National Association of School Psychologists Convention, Boston, Massachusetts.
Spragins, A. B., Blennerhassett, L., & Mullen, Y. (1987). *Intellectual adaptive behavior, social-emotional, developmental/criterion-based, language and basic concept assessment instruments used with preschool deaf children.* Workshop materials presented at the National Association of School Psychologists Convention, New Orleans, Louisiana.

Source: Reprinted with the permission of Allyn and Bacon. From Nuttall, E. V., Romero, I., & Kalesnik, J., *Assessing and Screening Preschoolers: Psychological and Educational Dimensions,* Copyright 1992.

tional characteristics, and appraisal of verbal and . . . nonverbal concept development and problem solving" (p. 51). Their inclusion of observations of parent-child interactions provides the opportunity for a better understanding of long-term patterns and established modes of responsiveness than tests and checklists usually permit. Indications of the child's self-concept, self-esteem, and dependence-independence tendencies also may be demonstrated through parent-child observations.

TABLE 7–4   Selected Cognitive Assessment Instruments

Key

A. Name of instrument
B. Age range, availability of norms for hearing-impaired
C. Psychometric data
D. Description
E. Evaluation
F. Year, author, publisher

A. CID Preschool Performance Scale (CID)
B. 2-0 to 5-5, norms for hearing-impaired provided.
C. Standard scores. Reliability and validity data available. Standardized on 978 children, hearing, and hearing-impaired.
D. Totally nonverbal measure of general cognitive functioning. Subtests included Manual Planning, Manual Dexterity, Form Perception, Perceptual Motor, Preschool Skills, and Part/Whole Relations.
F. 1984, Moog and Lane, Stoelting

A. Columbia Mental Maturity Scale, Third Edition (CMMS)
B. 3-6 to 9-11, no norms for hearing-impaired.)
C. Standard scores. Reliability and validity data available for hearing population. Standardized on nationally representative stratified sample.
D. Totally nonverbal test of reasoning abilities. Consists of a series of pictorial or figural classification items with demonstration and/or pantomime of directions.
E. Nonverbal format, sample/teaching items, and brief administration time makes CMMS good supplemental tool. Should not be used in isolation given the limited range of cognitive processes sampled. Particularly useful in evaluating children with motor problems, as test is untimed and child need only point or nod for response. However, heavy loading of test with visual-perceptual items makes CMMS a poor choice for children with perceptual problems.
F. 1972, Burgemeister, Blum, and Lorge, The Psychological Corporation

A. Hiskey-Nebraska Test of Learning Aptitude (H-NTLA)
B. 3-0 to 18-6, norms for both hearing and deaf provided.
C. Standard scores. Reliability and validity data available for both hearing and hearing-impaired populations.
D. Performance-based test of learning aptitude consisting of 12 subtest sampling a variety of areas, including visual attention, matching memory, classification, spatial reasoning, eye-hand coordination, and so on.
E. Developed, standardized and normed specifically for use with hearing-impaired, H-NTLA used frequently to assess this population, despite dated norms and materials. Test samples fairly broad behavioral base. Most subtests are untimed or very generous in limits. Tasks frequently hold interest of young children. However, test's length is sometimes problematic. Beware, small differences in raw scores may translate into significant differences in "Learning Age." Also may score low in preschool children compared to other cognitive measures. Best used in conjunction with other assessment techniques.
F. 1966, Hiskey, Mr. M. S. Hiskey

TABLE 7-4 *(Continued)*

A. Kaufman Assessment Battery for Children (K-ABC)—Nonverbal Scale
B. 4-0 to 12-6, no norms for hearing-impaired.
C. Standard scores. Reliability and validity data provided. Small number of children with hearing impairments included in standardization sample for proportional representation.
D. Nonverbal scale can be used to derive separate Mental Processing Composite scale score based on selected subtests from Simultaneous and Sequential Processing Scales of the K-ABC used to tap two different thinking styles.
E. Nonverbal scale of K-ABC appears generally appropriate for use in assessing hearing-impaired children aged 4 years or above. Not recommended at younger age levels as number of nonverbal subtests is too small to constitute scale. Most subtests are untimed and role of language is kept to minimum. Pantomimed instructions provided. Teaching items included and standardized. Research still lacking on use with preschool-aged hearing-impaired.
F. 1983a, 1983b, Kaufman and Kaufman, American Guidance Service

A. Leiter International Performance Scale—Arthur Adaptation (AALIPS)
B. 3-0 to 8-0, no norms for hearing-impaired.
C. Mental age and ratio IQ score. Limited norms, reliability, and validity data provided.
D. Age scale with four items at each level. Test items and instructions totally nonverbal with some demonstration. Subtests untimed with constant response format as task complexity increases. Yields measure of nonverbal intelligence based on traditional ratio IQ formula.
E. Despite significant psychometric weaknesses (see Ratcliff & Ratcliff, 1979), AALIPS is still used with some frequency in assessing young children with hearing impairments. Greter variability in scores of hearing-impaired relative to standardization sample. Scores for preschool-aged hearing-impaired frequently appear inflated. AALIPS should never be used in isolation, and obtained scores need to be interpreted with great caution.
F. 1952, Arthur, Stoelting

A. Merrill-Palmer Scale of Mental Tests (MPSMT)
B. 1-6 to 6-0, no norms for hearing-impaired.
C. IQ score. Dated norms. Reliability and validity data lacking.
D. Test of general intelligence, including both visual-motor and language items.
E. Helpful supplemental tool. Possible to eliminate verbal items and still obtain total score for child with hearing impairment. Flexibility in format allows for demonstration and some reordering of item administration, and does not penalize child for items refused or omitted. Useful with some hard-to-test children. However, large number of motor and/or timed tasks makes MPSMT inappropriate for evaluating children with motor difficulties.
F. 1931, Stutsman, Stoelting

A. Smith-Johnson Nonverbal Performance Scale (SJNPS)
B. 2-0 to 4-0, norms provided for hearing and hearing-impaired.
C. Test performance in each of 14 categories is compared to normative sample and scored as above, below, or within the average range for children of similar age, sex, and hearing status. Yields no global score. Reliability data provided. Validity data lacking. However, test items are drawn from other well-established and standardized tests.

(Continued)

TABLE 7-4 *(Continued)*

D. Nonverbal developmental assessment instrument consisting of 14 different categories of items tapping broad range of skills and cognitive processes. Tasks require minimal instruction and appear to hold the interest of children.

E. Though limited in age range, SJNPS is a very useful tool for assessing young children with hearing impairments. Provides data about individual strengths and weaknesses, as well as giving a general sense of child's overall performance level, despite lack of global score.

F. 1977, Smith and Johnson, Western Psychological Service

A. *Wechsler Preschool and Primary Scale of Intelligence (WPPSI): Performance Scale—Ray & Ulissi Adaptation*

B. 4-0 to 6-6, no separate norms for hearing-impaired provided.

C. Standard scores. Sample of 120 children with hearing impairments matched proportionally for demographic characteristics to original standardization sample of WPPSI (Wechsler, 1967). No significant differences found between hearing and hearing-impaired when adapted instructions are used. Reliability and validity data available for hearing populations.

D. Ray and Ulissi provide modified instructions simplifying complexity of the language and including practice items for the original WPPSI Performance scale.

E. Despite its nonverbal format, the original WPPSI-PS is usually not the instrument of choice among experienced evaluators of young hearing-impaired because of complexity of language of instructions and difficulty in conveying tasks. Ray and Ulissi attempt to circumvent these difficulties in administration and present data suggesting use of standard norms may be appropriate with hearing-impaired.

F. 1982, Ray and Ulissi, Steven Ray Publishing; 1967, Wechsler, The Psychological Corporation

---

Sources: Some of the information presented here was adapted from the following materials:

Mullen, Y. & Spragins, A. B. (1987). *Deaf students and psychological services: What psychologists need to know.* Workshop presented at the National Association of School Psychologists Convention, New Orleans, Louisiana.

Spragins, A. B., & Blennerhassett, L. (1989). *Intellectual, adaptive behavior, social-emotional, developmental/criterion-based, language and basic concept assessment instruments used with preschool deaf children.* Workshop materials presented at the National Association of School Psychologists Convention, Boston, Massachusetts.

Spragins, A. B., Blennerhassett, L., & Mullen, Y. (1987). *Intellectual, adaptive behavior, social-emotional, developmental/criterion-based, language and basic concept assessment instruments used with preschool deaf children.* Workshop materials presented at the National Association of School Psychologists Convention, New Orleans, Louisiana.

TABLE 7-5   Selected Social-Emotional and Adaptive Behavior Scales

> **Key**
> A. Name of instrument
> B. Age range, availability of norms for hearing-impaired
> C. Psychometric data
> D. Description
> E. Evaluation
> F. Year, author, publisher

A. *Joseph Pre-School and Primary Self Concept Screening Test*
B. 3-6 to 9-11, no norms for hearing-impaired.
C. Normed on 1,200 children from Illinois. No hearing-impaired reported in sample, but some children receiving special education services were included.
D. Scale provides general measure of self-concept. Consists of 15 items. Child chooses between two pictures: "Which is most like you?" Instructions can be pantomimed (although process is not standardized), and scoring allows for both a "don't know" and/or a "confusion" response.
E. Despite limited data on use with hearing-impaired, appears to provide good format for structured interview in screening for potential adjustment difficulties. However, should be used only by examiners skilled in communication with young children with hearing impairments.
F. 1979, Joseph, Stoelting

A. *Meadow/Kendall Social-Emotional Assessment Inventories for Deaf and Hearing-Impaired Students—Preschool Form*
B. 3-0 to 6-11, norms for hearing-impaired provided.
C. Percentiles. Normed on population of 857 preschool children with hearing impairments in a variety of residential and day school programs. Reliability and validity data provided for school-aged but not for preschool form.
D. Rating scale of observable behaviors, including some specific to hearing loss. Yields scores on four scales: communicative behaviors, dominating behaviors, developmental lags, and compulsive behaviors.
E. Despite lack of reliability and validity data for preschool form. Meadow/Kendall appears to be a very useful assessment tool and is one of the few with deaf norms. Can be used to gather information fairly easily from multiple informants working with the child in different settings, providing a more complete, though often varied, picture of child's functioning. Geared to identify developmental problems, may bias focus toward pathology versus normal development.
F. 1983, Meadow, Gallaudet University

A. *Scales of Independent Behavior*
B. Developmental Scale, no norms for hearing-impaired.
C. Standard scores, percentiles, age scores, adaptive level. Normed on representative national sample of 1,764 regular education children, infants, preschoolers, and adults. Reliability and validity data available for hearing population. No hearing-impaired reported in sample.
D. Measures motor, social/communication, personal independence and community independence skills through interview with a caregiver.
E. Although data are still limited on use with hearing-impaired, seems potentially useful as assessment tool. Relatively few questions involve auditory or communication behavior.
F. 1984, Bruininks, Woodcock, Weatherman, and Hill, DLM Teaching Resources

(Continued)

TABLE 7-5 *(Continued)*

A. *Vineland Adaptive Behavior Scales Revised—Survey Form*
B. 0 to 18-11, no norms for hearing-impaired below age 6 years.
C. Standard scores, percentiles, age scores, adaptive level. Standardized on nationally representative sample of 3,000. (Supplemental norms provided based on sample of 300 hearing-impaired children aged 6 to 12 in residential facilities.) Reliability and validity data available.
D. Assesses communication, daily living skills, socialization, and motor skills based on semistructured interview of caregiver.
E. Survey form recommended over other formats for assessing preschool hearing-impaired, as it included fewer items related to communication. Manual provides procedure for excluding individual domain score (i.e., Communication) in Adaptive Behavior Composite. However, individual domain scores are generally more useful than composite score with this population, allowing communication to be viewed independently from other skill areas. Length is a drawback.
F. 1984, Sparrow, Balla, and Cicchetti, American Guidance Service

Sources: Some of the information presented here was adapted from the following materials:
Mullen, Y. & Spragins, A. B. (1987). *Deaf students and psychological services: What psychologists need to know.* Workshop presented at the National Association of School Psychologists Convention, New Orleans, Louisiana.
Spragins, A. B., & Blennerhassett, L. (1989). *Intellectual, adaptive behavior, social-emotional, developmental/criterion-based, language and basic concept assessment instruments used with preschool deaf children.* Workshop materials presented at the National Association of School Psychologists Convention, Boston, Massachusetts.
Spragins, A. B., Blennerhassett, L., & Mullen, Y. (1987). *Intellectual, adaptive behavior, social-emotional, developmental/criterion-based, language and basic concept assessment instruments used with preschool deaf children.* Workshop materials presented at the National Association of School Psychologists Convention, New Orleans, Louisiana.

Source: From Nuttall, E. V., Romero, I., & Kalesnik, J., *Assessing and Screening Preschoolers: Psychological and Educational Dimensions.* Copyright ©1992 by Allyn and Bacon. Reprinted with permission.

Behavioral Observation

Observation is an essential component of any meaningful assessment, but nowhere is it as critical as in the case of a child who is emotionally or behaviorally different. Observing the child over time, in a variety of settings, under different conditions, and with different persons is recommended.

Some suggestions for guided observation include those outlined by Sattler (1988) and shown in Table 7-8. By providing more than a dozen characteristics of play to consider when observing (i.e., initiation, tempo, manipulations, tone), Sattler guides the observer through well-organized questions about the nature and appropriateness of the child's play behavior.

Linder's (1990) *Transdisciplinary Play-Based Assessment* (TPBA) offers another excellent model through which to learn about the child's affective as well as overall development. Linder guides the observer through carefully grouped questions about the child's actions and interactions. TPBA goes a step further in assisting

TABLE 7-6   Selected Developmental/Criterion-based Scales

Key

A. Name of instrument
B. Age range
C. Description and psychometric information
D. Evaluation
E. Year, author, publisher

A. Battelle Developmental Inventory
B. 0 to 8 years
C. Provides assessment of personal-social, adaptive, motor, communication, and cognitive domains. Yields standard scores, percentile ranks, and age equivalents.
D. Modified instructions provided for use with hearing-impaired. Appears to have good potential for use with this population.
E. 1984, Newborg Stock, Wnek, Guidubaldi, and Svinicki, DLM

A. Callier-Azusa Scale
B. 0 to 8 years
C. Developmental scale designed specifically for assessment of deaf-blind and children with severe handicaps. Areas assessed include motor, perceptual, cognitive, social, communication and language development, and daily living skills. Scale not normed. Developmental ages for items drawn from other sources. Limited reliability and validity information.
D. Useful in assessment of severely multihandicapped children.
E. 1978, Stillman, Callier Center

A. Developmental Activities Screening Inventory (DASI-II)
B. 1 month to 5 years
C. Provides assessment of fine-motor coordination, cause. effect and means. end relationships, association, number concepts, size discrimination, memory, spatial relationships, object function, and seriation. Scores provide developmental age and a developmental quotient. No norms given.
D. Useful in assessing specific skills development of children with hearing impairments, particularly those suspected of having additional handicaps.
E. 1984, Fewell and Langley, Pro-Ed

A. Developmental Profile II
B. 0 to 9 years
C. Developmentally sequenced items provide assessment of physical skills, self-help ability, social competence, academic skills, and communication ability primarily through parent interview and direct observation. Children with handicaps were purposely excluded from standardization sample in order to represent normal developmental expectations.
D. Can provide useful information in assessing specific skills development, despite some items that may be inappropriate for children with hearing impairments (i.e., telephone use).
E. 1980, Alpern, Bold, and Shearer, Psychological Development Publications

(Continued)

TABLE 7-6 *(Continued)*

A. *Inventory of Early Development (Brigance®)*
B. 0 to 6 years
C. Combines norm- and criterion-based elements in a developmental task analytic model. Links assessment to curriculum goals. Developmental age norms for items are drawn from other sources. Allows for pragmatic modification of tasks and response styles.
D. Useful in assessing skill development for educational planning.
E. 1978, Brigance, Curriculum Associates

A. *Southern California Ordinal Scales of Development*
B. N/A (Piagetian type developmental scales).
C. Provides assessment of cognitive, communicative, fine-motor, gross-motor, social-affective, and life skills behaviors. Scales nor normed, but general developmental ages/stages drawn from other sources. Children with hearing impairments were included in the standardization process.
D. Useful tool in assessment of children with various handicaps because of the flexibility in procedures. Use of sign language encouraged if appropriate.
E. 1985, Ashurst et al., Foreworks

A. *Uniform Performance Assessment System*
B. 0 to 6 years
C. Criterion-referenced. Provides assessment of preacademic/fine motor, communication, social/self-help, and gross-motor skills for use in educational program development. Adaptations, such as providing support or signing, are coded on answer sheet.
D. Potentially useful in assessing children with hearing impairments and more limited functioning levels.
E. 1981, White, Haring, Edgar, Alfred, and Hayden, Psychological Corporation

Sources: Some of the information presented here was adapted from the following materials:
Mullen, Y. & Spragins, A. B. (1987). *Deaf students and psychological services: What psychologists need to know.* Workshop presented at the National Association of School Psychologists Convention, New Orleans, Louisiana.
Spragins, A. B., & Blennerhassett, L. (1989). *Intellectual, adaptive behavior, social-emotional, developmental/criterion-based, language and basic concept assessment instruments used with preschool deaf children.* Workshop materials presented at the National Association of School Psychologists Convention, Boston, Massachusetts.
Spragins, A. B., Blennerhassett, L., & Mullen, Y. (1987). *Intellectual, adaptive behavior, social-emotional, developmental/criterion-based, language and basic concept assessment instruments used with preschool deaf children.* Workshop materials presented at the National Association of School Psychologists Convention, New Orleans, Louisiana.
Source: From Nuttall, E. V., Romero, I., & Kalesnik, J., *Assessing and Screening Preschoolers: Psychological and Educational Dimensions.* Copyright © 1992 by Allyn and Bacon. Reprinted with permission.

the observer in that it guides some of the observer's responses to questions as well as by using multiple-choice options. Linder offers detailed descriptions of developmental expectations across a variety of domains, based on a compilation of such findings from a broad cross-section of the literature. TPBA provides an excellent format that links observation, analysis of findings, and program development in a most functional way.

TABLE 7-7   Procedures for Developmental Assessment

1. Make a careful approach to child and build rapport
2. Attempt formal assessment
   a. Select appropriate instrument
      (1) Nonverbal conceptual tests
      (2) Infant tests
   b. Ensure maximal attentiveness
      (1) Provide distraction-free environment
      (2) Encourage eye contact through verbal and physical means
      (3) Allow for short sessions and frequent breaks
   c. Use tangible reinforcers

If unsuccessful:

3. Attempt play observations
   a. Allow spontaneous exploration of test materials
   b. Play together with child with developmentally oriented materials
   c. Observe child's spontaneous play

If unsuccessful:

4. Gather information from parents, **or**
5. Observe the child in home environment

Source: Adapted from Waterman, J. (1982). Assessment considerations with the emotionally disturbed child. In G. Ulrey, and S. J. Rogers (Eds.), *Psychological Assessment of Handicapped Infants and Young Children* (pp. 142-148). New York: Thieme Medical Publishers, Inc. Used with permission.

Autism

When assessing those children who present with extremely poor social relatedness, a need for sameness in the environment, significant communication impairments, and/or ritualistic behavior, one must be prepared to consider whether the child is autistic. Bagnato and Neisworth (1991) recommend the use of instruments specifically designed to help diagnose autism, such as the *Childhood Autism Rating Scale* (CARS) (Shopler, Reichler, & Renner, 1988), that elicit participation from all members of the multidisciplinary team. During the more structured aspects of assessment, they suggest alternating verbal, nonverbal, and reciprocal tasks. This strategy helps to minimize repetitive and self-stimulatory behaviors (by changing gears frequently).

Marcus and Baker (1986) have compiled characteristics of some commonly administered behavior rating scales that are used to help diagnose autism. These are shown in Table 7-9. They also offer some helpful strategies for the management of autistic tendencies during testing (see Table 7-10).

Developmental/Mental Retardation

Assessment of children with significant cognitive deficits entails using a combination of the techniques and guidelines described for other disabilities (Bagnato &

TABLE 7-8   Possible Observation Areas to Assess Children's Play

Entrance into the play room
- Does the child go into the playroom easily?
- Does the child ask to hold the mother's or interviewer's hand on the way?
- Does the child approach the toys, or does he or she cling to the mother?

Initiation of play activities
- Is the child a quick or slow starter?
- Does the child require help in getting started?
- Does the child need encouragement and approval?
- Is the child able to direct his or her own play?
- Does the child require active and steady guidance?
- Does the child show initiative, resourcefulness, or curiosity?
- Is the child impulsive?
- Does the child initiate many activities but seldom complete them, or does he or she maintain interest in a single activity?

Energy expended in plan
- Does the child work at a fairly even pace, or does he or she use much energy in manipulating the play materials, making body movements, and making verbalizations?
- Does the child seem to pursue an activity to the point of tiring himself or herself?
- Does the child start to work slowly and then gain momentum until the actions are energetic, or does he or she gradually lose momentum?
- Does the child seem listless, lethargic, lacking in vitality?

Manipulative actions in play
- Is the child free or tense in handling the play materials?
- Are movements large and sweeping or small and precise?
- Are movements smooth?
- Are play materials used in conventional or unconventional ways?

Tempo of play
- Does the child play rapidly or with deliberation?
- Is the pace of play hurried or leisurely?
- Does the pace of play vary with different activities or is it always about the same?

Body movements in play
- Does the child's body seem tense or relaxed?
- Are the child's movements constricted or free?
- Are the child's movements uncertain, jerky, or poorly coordinated?
- Are movements of hands and arms free, incorporating the whole body rhythmically, or are movements rigid, with only parts of the body being used?
- Does the child use the right hand, the left hand, or both hands?

Verbalizations
- Does the child sing, hum, use nonsense phrases, or use adult phrases as he or she plays?
- Does the child giggle appropriately?
- What is the general tone of the child's voice tones (for example, loud, shrill, excitable, soft, aggressive, tense, enthusiatic, or matter-of-fact)?
- What does the child say?
- What is the purpose of the child's verbalizations, judging from the intonation?

TABLE 7-8   *(Continued)*

Tone of Play
- What is the general tone of the child's play (for example, angry, satisfied, hostile, impatient)?
- Does the child throw, tear, or destroy play materials?
- Is the child protective of play materials?
- If aggression is present, does it have a goal or is it random?
- Does aggression increase, causing the play to get out of hand and posing a threat of damage to the playroom or interviewer?

Integration of play
- Is the play goal-directed or fragmentary?
- Does the play become more integrated over time?
- Does the play have form, or is it haphazard?
- Is the child's attention sustained or fleeting?
- Is the child easily distracted?
- Are there any peculiar elements to the play?

Creativity of play
- Is the play imaginative or stereotyped?
- Does the child use simple objects for play, or are special toys needed?
- Does the play show elements of improvisation or constriction?

Products of play
- What play materials are preferred?
- What objects are constructed or designs completed during play?
- Do the products have a recognizable form?
- How does the child achieve form?
- Does the child show interest in the product?
- Does the child tell a story about the product?
- Does the child show the interviewer and/or parent the product?
- Does the child want to save the product?
- Does the child want to give the product to someone?
- Does the child use the product for protective or aggressive purposes?
- Is the child overly concerned with neatness, alignment, or balance of the play materials?

Age appropriateness of play
- Is the play age-appropriate?
- Are there changes in the quality of the play?

Attitude toward adults reflected in play
- Does the child comply with adult request or do what he or she thinks adults expect of him or her?
- Does the child imitate adult manners accurately?
- Does the child protect himself or herself from adults?
- Does the child attempt to obtain tender responses from adults?
- Does the child follow his or her own ideas independently of adults?

Source: From *Assessment of Children*, 3rd edition, by J. M. Sattler, pp. 418–419. Copyright © 1988 by Jerome M. Sattler, Publisher. Used with permission from the publisher and author.

TABLE 7-9 Characteristics of Diagnostic/Behavior Rating Scales for Autistic Children

Scale	Domains	Age Range	Mode of Administration	Scoring
Autism Screening Instrument for Educational Planning	Sensory; relating; body and object use; language; social; and self-help	18 months	Checklist	57 items, sums of weighted items
Behavior Observation Scale	General language; language; response to stimuli; attending response; response to being helped; response to ball play; inappropriate response to pain; motility disturbances to stimuli	30–60 months	Observation in nine 3-minute intervals; combination of structured and unstructured; checklist	67 items, frequency count
Behavior Rating Instrument for Autistic and Atypical Children	Relationship to adult; communication; drive for mastery; vocalization and expressive speech; sound and speech reception; social responsiveness; body movement; psychobiological development	Up to 54 months	Descriptive ratings based on observations	10-scale score from severe autism to normal 3½–4 year level; cumulative score and profile
Childhood Autism Rating Scale	Relationship with people; imitation; affect; body awareness; relation to nonhuman objects; adaptation to environmental change; visual responsiveness; near receptor responsiveness; anxiety reaction; verbal communication; nonverbal communication; activity level; intellectual functioning; general impressions	All ages; has been used mostly with preadolescents	7-point rating scale based on observation of testing	(a) Scale scores (1–7) (b) Total score (15–60) (c) 3 categories; no autism; mild-moderate-severe autism
E-2 Checklist	Social interaction and affect; speech-motor manipulative ability; intelligence and reaction to sensory stimuli; family characteristics; illness development; physiological biological data	Up to 7 years	Checklist based on parental report, including retrospective recall	Multiple choice; items scored + or –; autism score the difference between pluses and minuses; +20 considered cutoff for Kanner syndrome

Source: From Marcus, L. M., & Baker, A. (1986). Assessment of autistic children. In R. J. Simeonsson (Ed.), *Psychological and Developmental Assessment of Special Children* (pp. 279–304). Boston: Allyn and Bacon. Reprinted with permission from Allyn and Bacon.

130

TABLE 7–10 Strategies for Management of Autistic Handicaps During Testing

Handicaps	Test Selection	Testing Structure	Test Administration	Use of Alternative Communication Systems
A. Severe communication deficits	Use of tests with limited language demands and many nonverbal items		1. Modification of verbal instructions; 2. Alternation of verbal and nonverbal instructions	1 Gestures; 2. Pictures; 3. Visual cues such as tokens or finished box
B. Deficits in social judgment & relating to people	Use of tests requiring minimal social interaction	Clear routines and expectations not dependent on social cues	1. Simple social interactions by examiner; 2. Low demands for response from child. 3. Awareness of child's skills in relating	
C. Attention, organization, and perceptual problems	Use of materials interesting but not overly distracting to child	1. Uncluttered room and work table; 2. Visually distinct work and play areas	1. Clear, simple presentation of materials; 2. Short work periods followed by breaks; 3. Careful pace and timing of testing to fit child's attentional patterns	
D. Uneven pattern of development	Use of more than one instrument if needed to cover range of child's skills		Awareness of child's strengths and weaknesses; modification of instructions and reinforcers on difficult items	
E. Motivational deficits			1. Flexible use of wide variety of reinforcers; 2. Sensitivity to child's sources of motivation; 3. Modification of or testing limits of items to provide success experiences	
F. Other atypical behaviors (e.g., motor stereotypes)	Avoidance of over-stimulating materials		Flexibility in deciding when to: interrupt behaviors; distract child; or allow behavior as a tension-relieving break	

Source: From Marcus, L. M., & Baker, A. (1986). Assessment of autistic children. In R. J. Simeonsson (Ed.), *Psychological and Developmental Assessment of Special Children* (pp. 279–304). Boston: Allyn and Bacon. Reprinted with permission from Allyn and Bacon.

Neisworth, 1991). Children who demonstrate severe retardation also are likely to exhibit characteristics that include: variable attention and moods; atypical muscle tone; limited language development; fleeting verbal and social communication; little or no initiation of activity or interaction; evidence of self-stimulatory behavior; and primitive, nonpurposeful play with or manipulation of objects.

Bagnato and Neisworth (1991) suggest that appropriate body position and careful selection of stimulating toys are essential in the assessment of the child's responsiveness to the environment. They also emphasize the importance of social interaction with the child—in close proximity (i.e., face to face) and in playful ways—to enhance the child's attention and arousal in response to the practitioner.

Huang and colleagues (1992) note that the training and experience of the multidisciplinary team, as well as the skill with which instruments and evaluation procedures are selected, are vital to meaningful assessment of the infant or child who is mentally retarded or multihandicapped. Adaptations and modifications of materials and testing procedures must be carefully determined, executed, and explained with attention to the individual needs and characteristics of the child with severe disabilities.

Assessment of the child with mental delays must include measures of adaptive behavior. Huang et al. (1992) define adaptive behavior as "an individual's ability to cope with social demands in a given social environment" (p. 320). How the child physically negotiates the environment, communicates and socializes with others, and acquires self-help skills, plays a significant role in the determination of mental retardation.

Selected Measures

Table 7–11 provides a list of measures, adapted from a list compiled by Huang et al. (1992), that are commonly used to assess the cognitive, educational, and adaptive behavioral functioning of infants and preschoolers suspected of developmental delay.

Health Impairments

Health and medical factors impact on the test performance of young children. Pain, fatigue, or hunger greatly alter a young child's already tentative motivation to perform on demand. Illness, or even the medication needed to treat it, may affect a child's alertness, consciousness, or overall behavior (Martin, 1982). Ear infections, particularly *otitis media*, have been associated with hearing difficulties, balance problems, and hindered communication skills. Irritability can be heightened by discomfort, illness, fatigue, or allergies as well as many medications used to treat and manage ailments.

TABLE 7-11   Tests Appropriate for Early Childhood Assessment

	Age in Months	Appropriate Categories[a]	Most Recent Publication Date/Company[b]	NR CR[c]
Cognitive tests				
Columbia Mental Maturity Scale	42–119	1, 2, 3	1972/PC	NR
Kaufman Assessment Battery for Children	24–72	1, 2, 3	1983/AGS	NR
McCarthy Scales of Children's Abilities	30–102	1, 3	1972/PC	NR
Pictorial Test of Intelligence	30–96	1, 2, 3	1964/HM	CR
Stanford-Binet Intelligence Scale IV	24–adult	1, 3	1986/RPC	NR
Wechsler Preschool and Primary Scale of Intelligence—Revised	36–84	1, 1	1989/PC	NR
Educational assessment tests				
Brigance® Diagnostic Inventory of Early Development	Birth–84	1, 2, 3	1979/CA	NR, CR
Developmental Assessment for the Severely Handicapped	Birth–72	2	1981/ER	NR
Developmental Programming for Infants and Young Children	Birth–48	1, 2, 3	1981/UM	NR, CR
HIGHCOMP	Birth–72	1, 2, 3	1982/MPC	NR, CR
Learning Accomplishment Profile	Birth–60	1, 2, 3	1974/KSS	NR, CR
Learning Accomplishment Profile—Infant	Birth–72	2	1977/UCP	NR
Uniform Performance Assessment System	Birth–72	1, 2, 3	1981/MPC	CR
Sensorimotor assessment tests				
Miller Assessment for Preschoolers	33–68	1, 3	1982/FKD	NR
Peabody Developmental Motor Scales	Birth–83	1, 2, 3	1983/DLM	NR
Southern California Postrotary Nystagmus Test	60–108	1, 2, 3	1975/WPS	NR
Southern California Sensory Integration Tests	48–120	1, 2, 3	1962/WPS	NR
Adaptive behavior assessment tests				
Adaptive Behavior Scale for Infants	Birth–72	1, 2, 3	1980/NC	NR, CR
Battelle Developmental Inventory	Birth–96	1, 2, 3	1984/DLM	NR
Callier-Azusa Scale	Birth–24	1, 2, 3	1978/UTD	CR
Behavioral Characteristics Progression Checklist	Birth–adult	1, 2, 3	1973/OSCSS	CR
Early Intervention Development Profile	Birth–72	1, 2, 3	1981/PC	NR, CR
Early Learning Accomplishment Profile	Birth–36	1, 2, 3	1978/KBS	NR

(Continued)

TABLE 7-1 *(Continued)*

	Age in Months	Appropriate Categories[a]	Most Recent Publication Date/Company[b]	NR CR[c]
Home Observation for the	Birth–36			
Measurement of the Environment	36–72	1, 2, 3	1984/DP	NR
Vineland Social Maturity Scale	Birth–360	1, 2, 3	1984/AGS	NR, CR
Speech and language tests				
Peabody Picture Vocabulary Test—				
Revised	30–adult	1, 2, 3	1981/AGS	NR
Bzoch-League Receptive Expressive				
Emergent Language Scale	Birth–36	1, 2, 3	1976/AP	NR
Carrow Elicited Language Inventory	36–72	1, 2, 3	1974/DLM	NR
Goldman-Fristoe Test of				
Articulation	48–adult	1, 2, 3	1986/AGS	NR
Houston Test for Language				
Development	Birth–72	1, 2, 3	1963/HTC	NR
Preschool Language Scale	24–72	1, 2, 3	1979/CEM	NR
Sequenced Inventory of				
Communication Development—				
Revised	4–48	1, 3	1984/UWP	NR
Test for Auditory Comprehension				
of Language	36–72	1, 2, 3	1981/LC	NR
Test of Early Language				
Development	36–95	1, 3	1981/PRO-ED	NR
Utah Test of Language				
Development	30–168	1, 2, 3	1967/CRA	NR
Verbal Language Development				
Scale	Birth–180	1, 2, 3	1959/AGS	NR

Source: From Nuttall, E. V., Romero, I., & Kalesnik, J., *Assessing and Screening Preschoolers: Psychological and Educational Dimensions,* Copyright © 1992. Reprinted with the permission of Allyn and Bacon.
[a]Categories: 1 = mental retardation; 2 = multihandicapped/orthopedically impaired; 3 = epilepsy.
[b]See Appendix B, "Test Publishers."
[c]NR = norm-referenced; CR = criterion-referenced.

General Considerations

Even short-term ailments can have an impact on a child's functioning or on performance during an assessment. Some guidelines to keep in mind include:

1. Ask the child's caregiver about current and recent health status and illnesses (also prior or chronic illnesses).
2. Ask if the child is on medications currently, and, if so, for what.
3. Ask the caregiver if the child's assessment behavior is unusually different or exaggerated in any way.
4. Ask if the child has any known allergies.

5. Ask if the child has had seizures or staring spells.
6. Avoid scheduling assessment sessions at a child's typical nap or meal time.

Severe Illness

Children who are chronically ill or medically compromised provide a particular assessment challenge to practitioners/examiners. Their developmental functioning and educational responsiveness depend on the impact of their condition or status on alertness, endurance, and ability to attend to others and to the task. Pain, discomfort, disorientation (due to illness or medication), or fear can have short- and long-term effects on the child's "availability" to learn. Fatigue, nausea, dizziness, pain, shortness of breath, and other symptoms of illness can hamper a child's ability to respond even to familiar tasks. Multiple, brief evaluation efforts will likely offer a more representative sample of the child's demonstrable strengths and weaknesses during the assessment period. Results of the ill child's performance should be interpreted with caution; ongoing monitoring of skills and progress is recommended.

Hospitalization

An environment in which infants and preschoolers with disabilities typically spend time is the hospital, and most often in the neonatal intensive care unit (NICU) or a pediatric unit (Bailey & Wolery, 1989). Although the health of the child is of primary concern during hospital stays, it is important to attend to the emotional and developmental needs of the child in such environments as well as to the needs of the caregivers. The developmental specialist can offer suggestions to improve the hospital environment for the child and caregivers as well as address the types of experiences needed for overall stimulation, personal-social responsiveness, and adaptive behavior. These might include considerations with respect to lighting, noise level, handling, and early learning opportunities (Wolke, 1987a, 1987b; VandenBerg, 1982).

The goals of assessing hospitalized infants and children may include evaluation of the child's affect and adaptiveness to the hospital setting and procedures. Close and frequent observation of the child's state and responsiveness to stimuli (visual, auditory, tactile, social) is necessary in order to understand the child's behaviors and potential developmental needs.

It also is essential to work with families and caregivers to determine their need for information, support, stress reduction, and strategies for helping and stimulating their child within the hospital environment. A vital service that can be provided to families of the hospitalized infant or toddler is to link them with the appropriate community resources and early intervention systems while still at the hospital, facilitating a smooth transition to continued special education and related services and resources as needed.

Task Analysis

When assessing (or teaching) the infant/child with severe or multiple disabilities, a useful procedure is task analysis. In the task analysis approach, a skill is broken down into smaller subskills that are requisite to the performance of the one being evaluated. In this way, the practitioner is able to determine the extent to which a child achieves portions of a skill as well as the most appropriate points at which to assist or begin intervention. Through task analysis one is better able to identify aspects of the child's difficulty in performing a task as well as the impact of specific disabilities on that performance. Skill sequencing and chaining of responses are two approaches to task analysis.

Skill Sequencing

In this approach to task analysis, a sequence of skills leading to mastery of a more advanced skill is identified (Benner, 1992; Browder, 1987). Benner (1992) offers an example with respect to independent toileting skills. Subskills of muscle control, anticipation of need, dressing/undressing, standing and/or sitting balance, general hygiene concepts, and an ability to follow a multistep process are necessary in order to achieve independent toileting competence. Which of these subskills (or even smaller steps within a given subskill) are areas of accomplishment or difficulty for a child that should be assessed. The specificity of strengths and weaknesses is enhanced as is the appropriateness of targets for intervention.

Chaining of Responses

This approach to task analysis involves the identification of specific behaviors as they occur during the completion of a task (Benner, 1992). In Benner's toileting example, the practitioner lists the subskills needed to succeed (in as detailed a fashion as is necessary to observe the finer nuances of the child's capabilities and inabilities) and records the exact point (or *link*) where the chain breaks. With this information, the practitioner begins the process of intervention, utilizing the least intrusive assistance needed (i.e., a least-prompts method) to increase the child's independence.

Summary

The assessment of a child with severe disabilities challenges the practitioner/examiner to understand the impact a disability has on specific areas of functioning, on overall development, and on a child's ability to communicate what he or she does know. Rather than being inhibited by the dearth of materials designed for use with children who exhibit a variety of disabilities, the practitioner needs to take the initiative to discover meaningful and creative ways to tap a child's skills. This calls for additional assessment competencies, knowledge, and experience in the realm of adaptive materials and procedures, and the insight to recognize the impact of alternative methods on a child's opportunity to perform or participate. The effort and training required to better understand the capabilities as well as the disabilities of infants and young children are well worth the commitment. The subsequent knowledge gained also has considerable relevance and application in the work of effective intervention planning for the child with a disability.

Suggested Group Activities

1. Discuss various adaptation techniques that would help in the assessment process without interfering with the testing results. Address a variety of disabilities and physical involvements. Allow for individual differences, styles, and needs.

2. List circumstances that could elicit behavioral observations in both the home and school environment. How would one document the information? What considerations would have to be made regarding the behaviors?

3. Devise a list of questions that could be asked of a caregiver or adult familiar with a child's abilities, needs, and routines prior to the testing situation. Include information about health, behavioral concerns, adaptation devices or strategies, and known or suspected developmental delays.

4. Have the instructor distribute cards with common tasks or activities that would be appropriate for a young child to master (e.g., tying shoes, dressing, feeding, sorting colors). Each participant develops a task analysis on the activity and tries to teach the skill to another adult. Were any steps omitted? Decide how to use each sequence to interpret the performance diagnosis and future instructional programming.

5. Using a developmental checklist from a commercial assessment instrument, observe the motor skills of several children of various ages and abilities. Determine their current functioning level as a result of this information. Were any difficulties encountered with either the disabled or nondisabled population? What adaptations, if any, were necessary?

References

Achenbach, T. M., & Edelbrock, C. S. (1981). Behavioral problems and competencies reported by parents of normal and disturbed children aged 4 through 16. *Monographs of the Society for Research in Child Development, 46*(Serial Nos. 1 & 188).

Bagnato, S. J., & Neisworth, J. T. (1991). *Assessment for early intervention: Best practices for professionals.* New York: Guilford Press.

Bailey, D. B., & Wolery, M. (1989). *Assessing infants and preschoolers with handicaps.* Columbus, OH: Merrill.

Benner, S. M. (1992). *Assessing young children with special needs: An ecological perspective.* New York: Longman.

Boehm, A. E. (1971). *Boehm test of basic concepts.* New York: Psychological Corporation.

Borke, H. (1971). Interpersonal perception of young children: Egocentrism or empathy. *Developmental Psychology, 5,* 263–269.

Browder, D. M. (1987). *Assessment of individuals with severe handicaps: An applied behavior approach to life skills assessment.* Baltimore: Paul H. Brookes.

Catin, H. R. (1975). The development and evaluation of a tactile analog to the *Boehm Test of Basic Concepts.* Doctoral dissertation, University of Kentucky, Lexington, KY.

Davidson, P., & Legouri, S. A. (1986). Assessment of visually impaired children. In R. J. Simeonsson (Ed.), *Psychological and developmental assessment of special children.* (pp. 217–239). Boston: Allyn and Bacon.

Davis, C. . (1980). *Perkins-Binet Tests of Intelligence for the Blind.* Watertown, MA: Perkins School for the Blind.

DuBose, R. F. (1981). Assessment of severely impaired young children: Problems and recommendations, *Topics in Early Childhood Special Education, 1*(2), 9–21.

Dunst, C. J., & McWilliam, R. A. (1988). Cognitive assessment of multiply handicapped young children. In T. Wachs & R. Sheehan (Eds.), *Assessment of young developmentally disabled children* (pp. 213–238). New York: Plenum.

Fewell, R. R. (1991). Assessment of visual functioning. In B. Bracken (Ed.), *The psychoeducational assessment of preschool children* (pp. 317–340). Boston: Allyn and Bacon.

Finnie, N. R. (1975). *Handling the young cerebral palsied child at home.* New York: E. P. Dutton.

Fraiberg, S. (1974). Blind infants and their mothers: An examination of the sign system. In M. Lewis & L. Rosenblum (Eds.), *The effects of the infant on its caregivers.* New York: Wiley.

Gerken, K. C. (1991). Assessment of preschool children with severe handicaps. In B. A. Bracken (Ed.), *Psychoeducational assessment of preschool children* (pp. 392–429). Boston: Allyn and Bacon.

Haeussermann, E. (1958). *The developmental potential of preschool children,* New York: Grune & Stratton.

Hansen, R., Young, J., & Ulrey, G. (1982). Assessment considerations with the visually handicapped child. In G. Ulrey & S. Rogers (Eds.), *Psychological assessment of handicapped*

infants and young children (pp. 108–114). New York: Thieme-Stratton.

Harley, R. & Lawrence, A. (1977). *Visual impairments in the schools.* Springfield, IL: Thomas.

Huang, A. M., Hunter, L. R., Reinert, H. R., & Wishon, P. M. (1992). Assessment of children with mental retardation and other handicapping conditions. In E. V. Nuttall, I. Romero, & J. Kalesnik (Eds.), *Assessing and screening preschoolers: Psychological and educational dimensions* (pp.311–326). Boston: Allyn and Bacon.

Linder, T. W. (1990). *Transdisciplinary play-based assessment: A functional approach to working with young children.* Baltimore: Paul H. Brookes.

Marcus, L. M., & Baker, A. (1986). Assessment of autistic children. In R. J. Simeonsson (Ed.), *Psychological and developmental assessment of special children* (pp. 279–304). Boston: Allyn and Bacon.

Martin, H. P. (1982). Neurological and medical factors affecting assessment. In G. Ulrey & S. J. Rogers (Eds.), *Psychological assessment of handicapped infants and young children* (pp. 86–94). New York: Thieme-Stratton.

Martin, R. P. (1991). Assessment of social and emotional behavior. In B. Bracken (Ed.), *The psychoeducational assessment of preschool children* (pp. 450–464). Boston: Allyn and Bacon.

Meadow, K. P. (1983). An instrument for assessment of social-emotional adjustment in hearing-impaired preschoolers. *American Annals of the Deaf, 128,* 826–884.

McLean, M. E., Bruder, M., Baird, S., & Dunst, C. J. (1991). Techniques for infants and toddlers with multiple or severe disabilities. In S. A. Raver (Ed.), *Strategies for teaching at-risk and handicapped infants and toddlers: A transdisciplinary approach* (pp. 234–259). New York: Macmillan.

Moore, M. S. & McLaughlin, L. (1992). Assessment of the preschool child with visual impairment. In E. V. Nuttall, I. Romero, & J. Kalesnik (Eds.), *Assessing and screening preschoolers: Psychological and educational dimensions* (pp. 345–368). Boston: Allyn and Bacon.

Mullen, Y. (1992). Assessment of the preschool child with hearing impairment. In E. V. Nuttall, I. Romero, & J. Kalesnik (Eds.), *Assess-*

ing and screening preschoolers: *Psychological and educational dimensions* (pp. 327–343). Boston: Allyn and Bacon.

Neisworth, J. T., & Bagnato, S. J. (1987). *The young exceptional child: Early development and education.* New York: Macmillan.

Nuttall, E. V., Romero, I., and Kalesnik, J. (Eds.) (1992). *Assessing and screening preschoolers: Psychological and educational dimensions.* Boston: Allyn and Bacon.

Ray, S., & Ulissi, S. M. (1982). *Adaptation of the Weschler Preschool and Primary Scales of Intelligence for deaf children.* Natchitoches, LA: Steven Ray.

Reynell, J., & Zinkin, K. (1979). *Reynell-Zinkin Developmental Scales – Visually impaired.* Chicago, IL: Stoelting Co.

Robinson, C., & Fieber, N. (1988). Cognitive assessment with motorically impaired infants and preschoolers. In T. Wachs & R. Sheehan (Eds.), *Assessment of developmentally disabled children.* New York: Plenum.

Rogers, S. J. (1982). Assessment considerations with the motor-handicapped child. In G. Ulrey & S. Rogers (Eds.), *Psychological assessment of handicapped infants and young children* (pp. 95–107). New York: Thieme-Stratton.

Rogers, S. J. & Soper, E. (1982). Assessment considerations with hearing impaired preschoolers. In G. Ulrey & S. Rogers (Eds.), *Psychological assessment of handicapped infants and young children* (pp. 115–122). New York: Thieme-Stratton.

Rosenberg, S. A., & Robinson, C. (1990). Assessment of the infant with multiple handicaps. In E. Gibbs & D. Teti (Eds.), *Interdisciplinary assessment of infants: A guide for early intervention professionals* (pp. 177–188). Baltimore, MD: Paul H. Brookes.

Sattler, J. M. (1988). *Assessment of children.* San Diego: Author.

Schopler, E., Reichler, R. J., & Renner, B. R. (1988). *Childhood Autism Rating Scale* (CARS). Los Angeles, CA: Western Psychological Services.

Simeonsson, R. J. (1986). *Psychological and developmental assessment of special children.* Boston: Allyn and Bacon.

Smith, A. J., & Johnson, R. E. (1977). *Smith-Johnson Nonverbal Performance Scale.* Los Angeles: Western Psychological Services.

Suess, J. F., Cotten, P. D., & Sison, G. F. P., Jr. (1983). The American Association on Mental Deficiency – Adaptive Behavior Scale: Allowing credit for alternative means of communication. *American Annals of the Deaf, 126,* 814–818.

Ulrey, G., & Rogers, S. J. (1982). *Psychological assessment of handicapped infants and young children.* New York: Thieme-Stratton, Inc.

VandenBerg, K. A. (1982). Humanizing the intensive care nursery. In A. Waldstein, G. Gilderman, D. Taylor-Hershel, S. Prestridge, & J. Anderson (Eds.), *Issues in neonatal care* (pp. 83–105). Chapel Hill, NC: TADS, University of North Carolina.

Wachs, T. D., & Sheehan, R. (1988). *Assessment of young developmentally disabled children.* New York: Plenum.

Warren, D. (1984). *Blindness and early child development* (2nd ed, rev.). New York: American Foundation for the Blind.

Waterman, J. (1982). Assessment considerations with the emotionally disturbed child. In G. Ulrey & S. J. Rogers (Eds.), *Psychological assessment of handicapped infants and young children* (pp. 142–148). New York: Thieme-Stratton.

Wilhelm, C., Johnson, M., & Eisert, D. (1986). Assessment of motor-impaired children. In R. J. Simeonsson (Ed.), *Psychological and developmental assessment of special children* (pp. 241–278). Boston: Allyn and Bacon.

Wolke, D. (1987a). Environmental and developmental neonatology. *Journal of Reproductive and Infant Psychology, O,* 17–42.

Wolke, D. (1987b). Environmental neonatology. *Archives of Diseases in Childhood, 62,* 987–988.

P a r t **III**

Developmental and Educational Assessment: Stages in the Assessment Process

This part provides an overview of each step in the assessment process from screening to program evaluation. The process begins with a broad view of developmental functioning and then focuses on the specific child and his or her abilities and disabilities. The initial stage of screening provides a general look at a child's overall functioning. The purpose is to identify children who may need special assistance. After identifying children through the screening process, the next steps in the assessment process can be taken.

It is now necessary to verify that there really is a disability; to do this, an interdisciplinary team conducts a developmental assessment to determine a child's needs and eligibility for special education services. The purpose of this stage is to determine the nature and extent of any problems. The information collected provides the basis for treatment that could include placement in an early intervention program. Recommendations also may be made regarding treatment by the therapists such as speech and language pathologists or occupational and physical therapists.

The educational assessment provides guidance as to the instructional programs that need to be offered to the child on a daily basis. Information is obtained about the child's specific strengths and weaknesses, and the skill areas for specific instruction and therapy from related service professionals are delineated.

The assessment process also involves examining ecological and environmental variables. An ecological assessment is done by observing the child in his or her natural settings in a variety of contexts with a variety of individuals. Examining environmental variables includes analyzing antecedents and consequences of behavior that provide the examiner with more information. Careful diagnosis and evaluation of the child in isolation produces very accurate and informative details about the child's current functioning under specific conditions and in a particular setting. It may not reveal, however, whether such skills are generalized to other situations and settings (i.e., at home, in school, in peer group). Examining the ecological and environmental factors increases the accuracy and relevance of an assessment.

The final step to include in the assessment process is program evaluation. Early interventionists need to assess the progress of children and the efficacy of the total intervention program. This step provides guidance and gives service providers an idea of whether the kinds of services they are giving are meeting the needs of the children they are serving.

Chapter *8*

Screening and Identification

Child Find

The first step in the assessment process is to conduct public awareness activities. These activities are called "child find" and are intended to inform the general public about typical and atypical child development. Unlike older children, who are conveniently grouped and observed in schools, infants, toddlers, and preschoolers typically are not clustered in one place. Parents and the professionals who come in contact with these young children must be aware of any indications of a child's need for early intervention services.

Activities in the child find process alert parents and professionals to warning signs—developmental conditions that are considered to be disabling or that may lead to abnormal growth and development. The purpose of this stage is to point out the signs that indicate a need for early intervention, why early intervention is important, and where parents can find professionals to help them determine if a child needs to be screened for possible developmental delays.

Child find is a systematic process of identifying infants and children who are eligible or potentially eligible for enrollment in early intervention programs. Child find activities are required by P.L. 94-142 and P.L. 99-457. Peterson (1987) summarizes a number of strategies to use to gain referrals and recruit children for screening (see Table 8–1).

Screening

A screening is a brief examination aimed at identifying those infants/children who may be demonstrating developmental delays or differences as compared with standard expectations and is an important part of child find programs. Through

TABLE 8-1   Strategies for Casefinding

Task	Description	Strategies
Building community awareness	Purpose is to (a) educate the public about importance of early identification and intervention with handicapped and high-risk children, (b) alert the public of the availability of screening services and special early intervention programs, and (c) enlist assistance of public agencies, organizations, and local citizens in making referrals and in supporting services for young children with special needs.	1. Announcements alerting public about screening clinics and the importance of identifying children who need special help, through newspaper features, radio/TV spots, posters, or distribution of brochures/letters/information sheets to community leaders, service agencies, and professional practitioners 2. Presentations to PTAs and other parent groups, church and civic groups, local professional organizations, special interest groups, and staffs of local service agencies. 3. Creation of an advocacy group among influential citizens and personnel in key positions within organizations who can bring visibility and local support to recruitment efforts.
Setting up system for referral and eliciting referrals	Purpose is to establish network of informed agencies and individuals who come into contact with a large number of children and who will take initiative to refer appropriate children for screening. Task is to (a) provide these persons or agencies with information on screening clinics and service programs for handicapped/high-risk children, (b) provide information and written literature on contact person and procedures for making referrals, and (c) establish working relationships between referral agents and intake/screening contact person.	1. Direct contacts with officials of key community agencies to establish formal linkages for sending and receiving referrals (e.g., public schools, local preschool and day-care programs, churches, mental health clinics, social service and welfare offices, health clinics, and agencies serving the handicapped—such as Easter Seal, United Cerebral Palsy, Association for Retarded Citizens). 2. Direct contacts with private practitioners who serve young children and their parents and who are in a prime position to make referrals (e.g., pediatricians and other medical professionals, dentists, psychologists and family counselors, psychiatrists, social workers, and therapists in private clinics, such as speech-language-hearing clinics or mental health clinics).

TABLE 8-1   *(Continued)*

Task	Description	Strategies
Canvassing community for children who need screening	Purpose is to conduct a systematic survey of children in the designated age range and geographical area to identify those for whom screening is needed and who may not be referred through other sources (often the mildly handicapped or developmentally delayed). The task is not only one of systematically canvassing the community to gain direct or indirect contact with the target population of children, but also to offer guides for helping parents and others identify child characteristics that suggest referral for a screening evaluation	1. Direct observation of children or consultation with staff and parents associated with local preschool or day-care centers, local churches, parents' and women's groups, or any other major organization through which a large group of community members are brought together. 2. Direct door-to-door canvassing of community to share information on how to make referrals and to offer checklist guides for helping parents discern situations when a child should be referred for screening. 3. Distribution of information on screening services and referral procedures by sending materials home with school-age students or under-school-age youngsters enrolled in local preschool, day-care, and Head Start programs.
Maintaining local publicity and contacts with referral sources	Purpose is to maintain a continual flow of referrals from various sources by (a) keeping the network of individuals and agencies continually informed about the screening system and the current contact person(s), (b) sharing information on the ongoing activities of the screening placement system, and (c) providing yearly reports on the number of children identified for early intervention, and on the success of the screening system in linking children with community services.	1. Yearly renewal of official contacts with key citizens, agencies, and organizations in referral network, to provide updated information on referral procedures for new persons who may become involved as a result of normal turnover in agency personnel and organization membership. 2. Replenishment of written materials disseminated to the network of referral agencies and citizens so that casefinding activities are continued and do not fizzle out over time. 3. Dissemination of year-end written reports summarizing data on the number of children referred, number screened, and percentage of children subsequently placed in special service programs, to allow referral sources to see the outcomes of their efforts.

Source: From *Early Intervention for Handicapped and At-risk Children: An Introduction to Early Childhood–Special Education* (pp. 288–289) by Nancy L. Peterson, 1987. Denver: Love Publishing. Reprinted by permission.

screening, professionals, service providers, and parents become aware of any need for further or fuller assessment of the child.

The screening process enables specialists to survey multiple developmental domains (e.g., cognitive, language, motor, adaptive, social) in order to detect/identify abnormal development. It is a detection process that is meant to highlight possible problems in development that warrant further assessment. Screening locates areas of suspected difficulty but does not provide specifics.

Planning Screening Programs

When screening at-risk infants and young children, professionals need to use an approach that allows for an overall scan of the child's functioning across a variety of domains as well as provides a view of family and environmental factors. Such an approach involves a pediatric examination, a family-responses developmental inventory, an evaluation of the development of motor, language, cognitive, social, and self-help skills, and a review of environmental status. This screening process also includes teacher judgments of the developmental readiness of children in their preschool classes.

There are a number of factors to consider when planning the screening of a particular population. Professionals need to determine the age of the group to be screened, how to access that age group, the geographical location to be served, and the likely range and prevalence of the developmental condition(s) for which screening is to be done.

The child's caregivers need to receive adequate information about the purpose of the screening procedures to ensure their full participation in the process. The scope and limitations of screening should be described to them in order to establish appropriate expectations regarding the possible outcome of a screening.

Professionals should be well qualified and experienced in performing screening tasks. All methods, instruments, and procedures to be used must be culturally sensitive. Cohn (1991) provides a summary of screening instruments that denote the areas evaluated and the standardization groups (see Table 8–2). Select scales that are similar in content to the skills expected to be learned and taught in early childhood programs. Use screening batteries that contain multiple skills for each age level. The National Center for Clinical Infant Programs has published an excellent reference on screening programs (Meisels & Provence, 1989). A list of selected screening instruments available is shown in Appendix A.

When planning screening programs professionals need to be careful that the procedures they use are adequate to separate infants/preschoolers with handicapping or potentially handicapping conditions from those with no potential problems. The failure to qualify for services based on one source of information should not prevent further evaluation if other risk factors are evident. All screening programs need to incorporate a follow-up component to track children who present significant risks for developmental delay. Ensuring and facilitating follow-up services helps minimize false positives and negatives.

TABLE 8-2 Summary of Screening Instruments

Instrument	Space	Time and Ease[a]	Age/Grade Range	Areas Evaluated	Standardization
Brigance® K & 1 screen (1982)	Stations, large room	10–20 1	K, 1	Motor, auditory, visual, and 14 others	Field test: 14 states
DDST-R (1975)	Small room	20 1	Birth to age 6	Personal-social, fine motor adaptive, gross motor	Denver area only; white, black, Hispanic surname; children with handicaps excluded
DIAL-R (1983, 1990)	Stations	20–30 3	2–5	Motor, concepts, language	National standardization, 1980 census; white, non-white, Hispanic; children with handicaps included.
ESI (1988)	Small room	15 1	4-0 through 5-1	Visual-motor, adaptive, language, cognition	465 from one urban community, all white; national standardization in progress
ESP (1990)	Medium room	20–25 2	2½–6½	Cognitive, motor, adaptive behavior	National standardization, 1990 census estimate; standardized 1987–1988; children with handicaps included.
MST (1978)	Medium room	20 3	4–6½	Right-left orientation, verbal memory, Draw-a-Design, number memory, concept grouping, leg coordination	MSCA national norms applied to MST; white, black, American Indians, Asians, Hispanics by race; children with handicaps excluded

(Continued)

TABLE 8–2   *(Continued)*

Instrument	Space	Time and Ease[a]	Age/Grade Range	Areas Evaluated	Standardization
MAP (1982)	Medium room	20–30 3	2-0 through 5-8	Sensory/motor, cognitive ability, and combined abilities in five areas	National; 1,204 normal: 86% white, 12% black, 2% other; additional 90 with handicaps excluded
PDI (1984, 1988)	Completed at home by mother	Untimed 1	3–6	General development, symptoms, behaviors	220 children in South St. Paul, Minnesota, who were in regular public school screening program

Source: From E. V. Nuttall, Ivonne Romero, & J. Kalesnik, *Assessing and Screening Preschoolers: Psychological and Educational Dimensions.* Copyright © 1992 by Allyn and Bacon. Reprinted with permission.

[a]Ease of administration: 1 = easier to administer than many; 2 = administration ease is average; 3 = more difficult to administer and score than many.

Screening is an initial step and cannot result in diagnosing or classifying the child until further assessment is complete. Screening programs are only one part of the services and interventions available to a population. If follow-up services are not available to at-risk infants, screening programs will have little or no impact. Including the considerations and recommendations above in planning a screening program will increase the precision and effectiveness of the individual child's assessment.

Problems with Screening Programs

Problems or dilemmas that arise with regard to screening programs for infants/young children include:

1. Failure to obtain informed consent from the caregiver.
2. Administration of screening instruments by personnel who are untrained or poorly trained.
3. Using screening tests that lack a high degree of validity or accuracy.
4. Failure to identify in quantifiable terms what the screening effort is to recognize.
5. Failure to differentiate between a positive screening result and a positive diagnosis (i.e., overreliance on an instrument not equipped to provide such complete information).

6. Administration of the screening tests by the same person(s) who provide(s) treatment, not being careful to avoid any conflict of interest.
7. Failure to "track" for rescreening those at-risk children who do not present with measurable delays currently but who are likely to in the future based on warning signs noted during the screening.
8. Screening for conditions for which treatment, diagnosis, or intervention services are not available.
9. Failure to properly monitor the screening program.
10. Failure to consider the cost/benefit of providing the screening program.
11. Failure to evaluate the long-term effectiveness of the screening program.

Summary

Keep in Mind . . .

Evaluators must remember that not every child has the same pattern of strengths and weaknesses. There are variations in the development of social behavior, language, gross- and fine-motor skills, and so on. Young children exhibit rapid changes in learning. Single screening or assessment sessions do not reliably capture these qualitative and quantitative changes; behavior is often situation- or person-specific.

Screening is only the first step in the evaluation process. If a problem is detected in the initial screening, the next step in the process needs to be initiated. Evaluators should not conduct a one-time assessment or use a single instrument—use a collection or battery of developmental measures. One professional with one point of view is not enough. An interdisciplinary team must conduct assessments.

Suggested Group Activities

1. Prepare a sample flyer that could assist in the *child find* process. Include the following information: (1) how to make families aware that there is a need for early intervention, (2) provide a brief explanation about why intervention is important, and (3) where parents can find professional guidance.

2. Role-play a discussion with a parent presenting a list of current educational options for their newly identified high-risk youngster.

3. Prepare two informational presentations, one to a parent group and another to a local service agency. How would the informational format differ?

4. Who might be members of an advocacy group? Discuss how they could be organized to bring information to the community.

5. Create a brief checklist that parents could complete to help evaluate whether their child could benefit from an early intervention program.

6. How can the screening process be adapted to address the needs of culturally and linguistically diverse populations? Discuss various methods and strategies that could be used to help foster cultural sensitivity on the part of the examiner.

References

Cohn, M. E. (1991). Screening measures. In E. V. Nuttall, I. Romero, and J. Kalesnik (Eds.), *Assessing and screening preschoolers: Psychological and educational dimensions* (pp. 83–98). Boston: Allyn and Bacon.

Meisels, S. J., & Provence, S. (1989). *Screening and assessment: Guidelines for identifying young disabled and developmentally vulnerable children and their families.* Washington: National Center for Clinical Infant Programs.

Peterson, N. (1987). *Early intervention for handicapped and at-risk children: An introduction to early childhood–special education.* Denver: Love.

Chapter 9

Norm-based Assessment: Determination of Eligibility

JUDITH BONDURANT-UTZ
LENORE B. LUCIANO

When a developmental screening indicates an area or areas of suspected delay for a child, a fuller evaluation is warranted. In order to determine the nature and extent of a child's potential need for special assistance, the family is now directed to pursue a multidisciplinary evaluation of the child's functioning, including strengths and weaknesses. The information gathered during such an evaluation becomes the basis for determining eligibility for special educational services.

Entitlement to Full Evaluation

As provided by P.L. 99-457, the child should be assessed in all areas related to the suspected disability, including, where appropriate, health, vision, hearing, social and emotional status, general intelligence, academic performance, communicative status (i.e., speech and language development), and motor abilities. The law states that the evaluation and assessment of the child must (a) be conducted by trained personnel who utilize appropriate methods and procedures; (b) be based on informed clinical opinion; (c) include a review of pertinent records related to the child's current health status and medical history; (d) evaluate the child's level of functioning in cognitive development, physical development (including vision and hearing), language and speech development, psychological development, and self-help skills; and (e) include an assessment of the family's strengths and needs related to enhancing the child's development. P.L. 99-457 further states that no single procedure is to be used to determine a child's eligibility for special educational services.

Diagnostic Process

This second stage in the assessment process involves a more in-depth or *diagnostic* look at the child than does a screening. The diagnostic process is designed to verify that a developmental delay or disability severe enough to require remediation exists. According to P.L. 99-457, each state must set forth guidelines and eligibility criteria to determine the severity of a delay that qualifies a child to receive early intervention services in that state. The diagnostic stage also serves to clarify the nature of the suspected problem (for example, determining whether the delay is global—affecting all aspects of the child's development—or specific—affecting one particular aspect of development such as speech or motor skills). The data gathered also provides information to use in the development of an intervention program, although an additional examination of a child's mastery of specific developmental and educational skills is needed.

Using Norm-based Assessment in Early Childhood

Norm-based assessment is often a required component in determining the degree or severity of a child's disability and in subsequently determining eligibility for special educational services. It is important for professionals evaluating infants and preschoolers to understand the problems inherent in the use of norm-based data alone in the planning of intervention programs. Norm-based assessment is only one of the procedures to use in evaluating and planning services that young children need. The purpose of this chapter is to explain norm-based assessment and provide guidelines for its use in early childhood special education.

Description and Purpose

Norm-based or norm-referenced tests compare a child's performance with that of a normative group consisting of children with similar characteristics (i.e., age, sex). Norm-based assessments have undergone standardization on a carefully chosen reference group. The reference group from which the norms are derived should be large and demographically representative of the population being tested. Norm-referenced tests use standardized or uniform procedures and materials to present selected tasks that will demonstrate specific skills. The child's performance is evaluated according to set criteria and then translated into a score that provides an indication of standing in the normative group.

Performance of the test items yields one or more raw scores. The raw scores are then transformed into standard or derived scores based on the distribution tables of the normative sample. Derived scores may be available in the form of developmental age equivalents (year and month), percentiles (i.e., a score at the 50th percentile indicates that 50 percent of the norm group attained scores below that of the child in question), developmental quotients (DQ), intelligence quotients (IQ), or other standard scores (i.e., T-scores, z-scores). Because scores are *standard* comparisons between them can be made—one may compare one child's scores with those of another child or to those of the normative group at large. The score reflects whether the child demonstrates average, below average, or above average assessed skills relative to the group. Also one may compare a child's score in one assessed area to that in another domain, yielding a pattern of strengths and weaknesses. Standard scores are comparable from test to test. (The confidence with which one makes those comparisons, of course, depends on the reliability and validity established for the given tests.)

The primary purpose in giving norm-referenced tests is to indicate a child's developmental level in relation to that of other children. Bagnato and Neisworth (1991) list three distinct purposes of norm-based assessment: (1) to describe the child's functional skills in comparative terms, (2) to classify the degree of the child's deficits using a preexisting diagnostic category, and (3) to predict the child's development in the absence of intervention or other major life changes. However, they also point out that the latter purpose is an abstract one at best. The very aim of early intervention is to create changes that stimulate and enhance development. Norm-referenced tests are generally appropriate in situations requiring selectivity such as determining whether a child demonstrates a significant enough developmental delay to be eligible for special education or early intervention services.

Commonly Used Norm-referenced Tests

The psychologist on the team typically administers the norm-referenced tests addressing intellectual or overall development during the initial phases of an evaluation. Often, diagnostic concerns and issues of program eligibility are in question at this point. Norm-referenced tests commonly used by psychologists in the assessment of infants and preschoolers include the *Bayley Scales of Infant Development* (Bayley, 1969), the *McCarthy Scales of Children's Abilities* (McCarthy, 1972), the *Kaufman Assessment Battery for Children* (Kaufman & Kaufman, 1983), the *Stanford-Binet Intelligence Scale, Fourth Edition* (Thorndike, Hagen, & Sattler, 1986), the *Wechsler Preschool and Primary Scale of Intelligence—Revised* (Wechsler, 1989), and the *Battelle Developmental Inventory* (Newborg et al., 1984). Some features of these and other measures are shown in Table 9–1.

Other professionals on the team (i.e., speech/language pathologists, occupational and physical therapists) also employ norm-referenced tools relevant to their areas of expertise when assessing a child's abilities and skills and determining the need for related special education services. (These will be referred to in the appropriate chapters in Part 4 of this book.)

TABLE 9-1 Norm-referenced Assessments

Test Name	Target Population and Age Range/Purpose	Domains Covered	Psychometric Data Available	Outcomes	Publisher/Vendor	Administration of/Time (minutes)
Bayley Scales of Infant Development (BSID) (Bayley, 1969)	Infant, 2–30 months; Comprehensive analysis of infant development skills	Mental Psychomotor Developmental	Yes	Develop mental quotient, developmental age	Psychological Corporation	Mental: 25–30
Stanford-Binet Intelligence Scale (Thorndike, Hagen & Sattler, 1986)	Children, 2 years–adult; Measure general intellectual ability	General Intelligence, (verbal, nonverbal)	Yes	Mental age: IQ	Riverside Publishing	60–90
McCarthy Scales of Children's Abilities (McCarthy, 1972)	Children, 2.5–8.6 years; Measure intelligence and identify children with possible learning disabilities	Verbal Perceptual Quantitative Cognitive Memory Motor	Yes	Scale index; general cognitive index	Psychological Corporation	40–45 for children below 5 60 for older children
Wechsler Primary Scale of Intelligence, Revised (Wechsler, 1989)	3–7.5 years	General Intelligence (verbal, nonverbal)	Yes	Scaled scores for 6 verbal and 5 performance subtests; verbal performance and full-scale IQs	Psychological Corporation	60–90
Battelle Developmental Inventory (Newborg, Stock, Wnek, Guidubaldi, Svinicki, & Allen, 1984)	0–8 years; Norm based/curriculum referenced; diagnosis, linkage and progress evaluation	Personal-social Adaptive; Motor Communication Cognitive	Yes	Developmental age equivalents; percentiles and standard scores (developmental quotients, z/t scores and normal curve equivalents)	DLM/Teaching Resources	*Screening:* 10–30 *Entire BDI:* 60–120 depending on child's age

TABLE 9-1 (*Continued*)

Test Name	Target Population and Age Range/Purpose	Domains Covered	Psychometric Data Available	Outcomes	Publisher/Vendor	Administration of/Time (minutes)
Kaufman Assessment Battery for Children (Kaufman & Kaufman, 1983)	2.5–12.5 years	Verbal and nonverbal intelligence Mental processing Sequential simultaneous processing Achievement	Yes	Achievement: Mental Processing Composite (MPC) Standard scores and scaled scores Percentile ranks Stanines	American Guidance Service (AGS)	45–50 for children below 5 years
Leiter International Performance Scale (Leiter, 1948)	2–18 years	Nonverbal Intelligence	Poorly described; very limited	Mental age: IQ	Chicago: Stoelting Co.	30–45
Extended Merrill-Palmer Scale (Ball, Merrifield, & Stott, 1978)	3.0–5.11 years	Content and process of thinking (cognition)	Yes, but no validity data	Weighted scores Percentile ranges and bands	Chicago: Stoelting Co.	60

Norm-referenced measures are designed to verify, through extensive direct assessment, the nature and extent of a child's developmental delay. Bagnato and Neisworth (1991) recommend an approach that requires the agreement of at least two independent sources of diagnostic information before affirming developmental delay. One source always involves the caregivers and the other the early intervention team or diagnostic specialist. Professionals are cautioned to remember that tests only provide an indication of a child's abilities and skills at a given time.

Advantages

Advantages of administering norm-referenced tests include the following:

1. Test results are expressed in terms of a child's standing among a group of peers of the same age and other characteristics (i.e., gender).
2. The child's performance can be compared with the performance of a normed, representative population, allowing for greater generalizability of findings.
3. Norms provide an indication of average or expected performance for age.
4. The derived scores of norm-referenced tests allow us to compare the child's performance on one test with his or her performance on other tests (i.e., helps identify strengths and weaknesses), as well as compare the performance on different scales or domains.
5. Test results can be expressed in the form of a developmental score, an age equivalent, a percentile, a standard score, and/or other derived scores, allowing for flexible and relevant use of the results as needed.

Cautions

As with any measure, one should take care to avoid misuse of or overreliance on this one type of assessment. Norm-based tests serve a purpose in early childhood assessment; it often is important to compare a child's abilities with those of age peers. This helps determine the child's relative standing with respect to expected performance for age. Norm-based tests, however, do not tell us all we need to know about a child's skills in order develop the best educational programs.

Norm-referenced measures were not developed to plan educational programs; the test items selected had to meet rigid statistical standards. The instructional relevance of these items was only a secondary consideration. Therefore, the items on scales, such as the *Bayley* or *McCarthy*, may not be good instructional targets. These scales are useful primarily for determining developmental status and indicating general areas in which instruction might be appropriate (Bailey & Wolery, 1984).

Norm-based tests are not designed to evaluate individual response to treatment or overall program effectiveness. These tests usually are not sensitive to small increments of change and often do not sample the types and scope of behaviors focused on in early intervention programs. Curriculum-based assessment is better suited to address such issues.

When selecting a norm-referenced measure for potential use, professionals need to carefully examine the test manual for a variety of features. It is important to note how the test was normed and determine whether the characteristics of the sample population are representative of the child or children with whom the measure is to be used. One should also examine the basis from which the norm-referenced scores were derived. Some instruments allow the generation of developmental age scores, but the instrument itself was never normed; rather, the developmental age equivalent is assigned to each item, or clusters of items, based upon norm-based sources such as the Bayley (1969) or the *Gesell Developmental Schedules* (Knoblock, Stevens, & Malone, 1980). Professionals should not rely on the accuracy of *age levels* drawn from non-normed measures.

Finally, note that children with disabilities are rarely included in a normative, sample group. The reason is that norms typically provide an indication of normal developmental sequences and milestones. The purpose of testing is to determine the nature and extent of deviation from the norm. Keep in mind, of course, that rigid adherence to standard procedures prevents an examiner from making adaptations to circumvent the child's impairments (Bagnato & Neisworth, 1991). If these impairments are not taken into account when testing, the child's score may not reflect an accurate representation of the child's abilities. When assessing young children with disabilities, the skilled and experienced examiner must administer tests and interpret results with utmost caution.

Limitations of Norm-based Assessment

Limitations or problems with norm-based tests may be summarized as follows:

1. With standardized tests, the examiner is confined to specific materials and procedures, thereby limiting his or her freedom to adapt to a child's particular interests and preferred materials.

2. The directions and questions through which the examiner must elicit responses are fixed, and they may include verbalizations that exceed the child's language development or differ from the usual context within which the child may have experienced similar activities. In such cases, *failure* of an item may reflect misunderstanding of directions rather than inability to perform a given task.

3. Rigidly adhering to standard procedures can be in direct conflict with the characteristics, style, and performance needs of the young child. The very nature of infants, toddlers, and preschoolers defies the notion of *performance on demand*. (See chapter 2 for considerations in accommodating the needs of young children.)

4. Specific disabilities in areas of vision, hearing, language, or motor development will hamper a child's performance on most standardized tests. Any adaptations in materials, manner of presentation, or criteria of evaluation challenge

standard procedures and the reliable interpretation of test results. Any modifications therefore, must be adequately described and justified by the trained examiner
and a determination made as to the potential impact of such changes on the test
results.

5. Norm-referenced tests are neither designed nor adequate for use in the
development and evaluation of educational programs. Their effectiveness in the
realm of early childhood education is ensured only when they are used as part
of a comprehensive assessment of a child's skills and needs.

Linking Norm-based and Curriculum-based Assessment

Both norm-based and curriculum-based measures are important to the evaluation of young children. They are complementary in that they differ in purpose
and qualities. Norm-based measures should be used if it has been established
that a child is at risk for developmental delay. A norm-based assessment can confirm a developmental problem, determine a child's level of functioning in one
or more domains, describe strengths and weaknesses in ability, and identify the
nature of a problem (i.e., global retardation, language delay, perceptual-motor
difficulties, attention deficits). Curriculum-based assessment is a more appropriate
measure for the planning and evaluation of a child's intervention program; it addresses the child's performance of learning tasks that arise in the educational
setting.

Linking norm-based and curriculum-based forms of assessment is most meaningful when both measures are adequately related to developmental milestones.
Some testing tools also strive for curricular relevance as well as the comparative
benefits of norm-referencing. Bagnato and Neisworth (1991) recommend the use
of an instrument such as the *Battelle Developmental Inventory* (BDI). It is an excellent example of a developmental scale that provides curricular objectives that
are norm-referenced. When a program's curriculum is based on an instrument
such as the BDI, a child's progress can be evaluated in terms of response to the
program's interventions as well as compared with peers in the national norm
group.

Summary

Norm-based measures constitute an important part of the evaluation process, particularly relative to the diagnostic criteria used to determine a child's special service needs. Norm-based assessment should be only one part of a comprehensive
assessment battery. Multidimensional assessment, or using multiple types of
assessment instruments, provides a broader, more valid and useful profile of a
child's abilities and needs. Professional judgment, as well as additional information from caregivers, health professionals, teachers, and so on, need to be used
when making eligibility or placement decisions and when developing intervention programs.

Suggested Group Activities

1. Choose several test items on the *Bayley Scales of Infant Development* and/or the *McCarthy Scales of Children's Abilities* that are inappropriate for instructional purposes. Rewrite them to target a more practical and educational goal.

2. Keeping the limitations of norm-based assessment in mind, discuss ways that can make testing circumstances and results more useful for the child who is developmentally delayed.

3. Compare a norm-based and curriculum-based assessment and find any items that are similar in nature. How might the structural demands of each item impact on the child's performance of the skill?

4. Using a real or imagined case study of an infant or young child, describe the child's functional abilities compared to a comparative population. Based on the information, could the child's future educational development without further intervention be predicted? Why or why not?

5. List several circumstances under which it would be important to administer and use the results of norm-referenced tests. Discuss situations where it would not be appropriate to use norm-referenced tests.

References

Bagnato, S. J., & Neisworth, J. T. (1991). *Assessment for early intervention: Best practices for professionals.* New York: Guilford Press.

Bailey, D. B., & Wolery, M. (1984). *Teaching infants and preschoolers with handicaps.* Columbus, OH: Merrill.

Bayley, N. (1969). *Bayley Scales of Infant Development.* San Antonio: Psychological Corporation.

Kaufman, A. S., & Kaufman, N. L. (1983). *Kaufman Assessment Battery for Children.* Circle Pines, MN: American Guidance Service.

Knoblock, H., Stevens, F., & Malone, A. F. (1980). *Manual of developmental diagnosis.* New York: Harper and Row.

McCarthy, D. (1972). *McCarthy Scales of Children's Abilities.* San Antonio: Psychological Corporation.

Newborg, J., Stock, J., Wnek, L., Guidubaldi, J., & Svinicki, J. S. (1984). *Battelle Developmental Inventory.* Allen, TX: DLM/Teaching Resources.

Thorndike, R. L., Hagen, E. P., & Sattler, J. M. (1986). *Guide for administering and scoring the Stanford-Binet Intelligence Scale.* Chicago: Riverside.

Wechsler, D. (1989). *Manual for the Wechsler Preschool and Primary Scale of Intelligence—Revised.* San Antonio: Psychological Corporation.

Chapter 10

Curriculum-based Assessment for Instructional Planning

Curriculum-based assessment (CBA) is a form of criterion-referenced measurement in which the curricular objectives act as the criteria for the identification of instructional targets and for the assessment of the child's status and progress (Bagnato & Neisworth, 1991). Criterion-referenced tests measure a child's mastery or performance of a skill or sequence of skills rather than comparing the child with other children.

CBAs are tests organized into a developmentally sequenced curriculum and include suggested teaching activities for each item on the scale. A CBA follows a child's achievement on the basis of certain objectives in the sequenced curriculum and performance is compared with past performance to monitor progress within the curriculum. CBAs typically address several areas of development such as gross- and fine-motor skills, cognition, language proficiency, self-help, and social/emotional functioning. Objectives in these areas vary from *landmark* goals to finely graded sequences of prerequisite behaviors that constitute a given skill objective (Neisworth & Bagnato, 1988).

Purpose of Curriculum-based Assessment

Developmental CBA can provide the major approach for: (1) identifying curricular entry points, (2) program planning, (3) progress monitoring, and (4) program evaluation (Neisworth & Bagnato, 1988). The information obtained from the CBA is directly relevant to the child's program.

P.L. 99-457 stipulates that the evaluation and assessment of the child must include the child's level of functioning in each of the following developmental areas: (a) cognitive development, (b) physical development, (c) language and speech development, (d) psychosocial development, and (e) self-help skills. Curriculum-based assessment facilitates this process by providing examination in most of these areas.

Using a CBA, the early interventionist is able to identify where the child falls within the range of objectives of the program's curriculum. The CBA scale also provides a profile of the child's specific strengths and weaknesses and direct information for use in writing instructional objectives. Bagnato and Neisworth (1991) compare CBA to a *map* that should be detailed enough to permit progress checks, accommodations for various handicaps, and comprehensive and balanced objectives. This map provides a better overall view to use when writing the Individualized Education Program and facilitates tracking of the child's progress throughout the year and at the end of the year. This method yields both formative and summative information about the efficacy of the program.

Types of Curriculum-based Assessments

Curriculum-imbedded Scales

One type of CBA is the curriculum-imbedded scale The assessment items and the curricular objectives of this scale are one and the same. The assessment items are taken directly from the program's curriculum. The teacher can track the child's progress through the curriculum by noting when mastery of specific objectives is achieved. The *Learning Accomplishment Profile* (LAP) (Sanford & Zelman, 1981), the *Early Learning Accomplishment Profile* (ELAP) (Glover, Preminger, & Sanford, 1978), the *Learning Accomplishment Profile: Diagnostic Edition* (LAP-D) (LeMay, Griffin, & Sanford, 1991), and *The HICOMP Preschool Curriculum* (Willoughby-Herb & Neisworth, 1983) are examples of widely used curriculum-imbedded measures (Bagnato & Neisworth, 1991).

Curriculum-referenced Scales

Another type of CBA is the curriculum-referenced scale. This scale samples objectives commonly emphasized in most developmental curricula but that are not integral to any particular curriculum. They are composites of curriculum sequences (Neisworth & Bagnato, 1988). Although the assessment and curricular items are not identical, they should be similar enough to place a child within a curriculum. The *BRIGANCE Diagnostic Inventory of Early Development—Revised* (Brigance, 1991) and *The Developmental Activities Screening Inventory II (DASI)* (Fewell & Langley, 1984) are well known examples of curriculum-referenced scales (Bagnato & Neisworth, 1991).

Considerations for Choosing a CBA

No one CBA is appropriate for all children and all programs. Teachers, program supervisors, and other professionals involved in choosing a CBA should be aware of the weaknesses inherent in these tests. In order to decide on an appropriate developmental curriculum-based assessment for a particular child or group of children, a number of items should be considered.

Compatibility with Program

The assessment instrument chosen should be compatible with the philosophy and theoretical orientation of the program and reflect the staff's philosophy of how children develop and how learning can be facilitated. For example, a program may choose a model based on developmental milestones, cognitive-developmental, or a functional model. Does the CBA chosen reflect the program's content and approach to child development?

Family-focused Assessment

The family, rather than the child in isolation, is the focus of the assessment and intervention. Curricula supporting family participation are more effective in helping the child generalize and maintain the skills taught in the intervention program. This minimizes the variability of at-school and at-home performance and behavior. Teachers can understand the conditions under which a skill is demonstrated better if the child is observed at home and as well as at school. Also, in keeping with family-focused intervention, present all findings and implications clearly so they can be easily interpreted by family members.

Multidimensional Assessment

Interventionists should not rely solely on one observation by one professional. Nor should professionals rely solely on one assessment instrument as the source for information. To obtain a truly accurate assessment, use several instruments over a period of time to determine what a child can and cannot do. Select instruments that examine different settings (e.g., preschool, home) and can be completed by different respondents (e.g., caregiver, teacher, speech/language pathologist). Multisession assessments conducted by more than one professional in a variety of settings provide a more representative picture of the child's abilities and skills.

Transdisciplinary Team Assessment

A transdisciplinary arena assessment eliminates unnecessary duplication. All members of the multidisciplinary professional team need information typically obtained from curriculum-based assessments. The team needs to plan how the assessment is to be conducted so duplication does not occur. An arena assessment allows the team to observe the administration of the CBA by one or two of its members. The observing team members offer input by commenting or making suggestions during the session or sessions. Then, the team discusses the results based on a common ground. As needed, additional assessment information can be obtained in further testing specific to a domain or discipline.

Developmental Age of Child

Choosing a CBA appropriate to the developmental level of a child is essential. Keep in mind that the child's developmental age may be different from his or her chronological age. A child's development also may vary across domains, being much lower in one area than another. If the curriculum chosen does not examine a wide enough age range, it may be necessary to use two curricula. If a child is functioning considerably below his or her chronological age, the examiner needs to adapt activities to maintain a more age-appropriate appeal of the curricular tasks.

Developmental Areas Assessed

The CBA selected should include developmental areas appropriate to the child. A relevant sampling of skills and behaviors that relates to the curricular needs of the child needs to be obtained. A crucial factor in using a CBA is choosing an appropriate curriculum. For example, assess children with emotional problems using a CBA that includes items relating to social interactions, self-esteem, and so on.

Small Steps

The steps between the assessment items of the CBA must be small enough to measure progress, especially for those children with more severe deficits. Skills should be related to one another and provide for the emergence of more complex skills. The items should be sequential and relevant to children with disabilities and organized in a logical order—easy tasks should precede more difficult ones.

Age-appropriate, Functional Norms

A CBA should be able to provide objectives that are as normal and age-appropriate as possible. Early interventionists should identify functional skills that are needed across environments and that will have an immediate and long-term, positive impact. The benefits of these functional skills are more likely to be seen when children are integrated, mainstreamed, or included with normal children.

Adaptive to Handicap

If the child has a severe handicap, a more specialized curriculum may be necessary. For example, for a child with a sensory or physical disability, the examiner may need to use specialized techniques and materials to accommodate the handicap. Some curricula were specifically developed for use with children with certain types or levels of disability and provide suggestions for making accommodations. Curricula that were developed for specific handicaps or that employ functional objectives are especially helpful for children with more serious sensory and/or response disabilities. The CBA chosen should be able to be easily adapted to various handicaps.

Form versus Function

Forms are the observable behaviors of the child. Functions are effects of these forms on the environment. CBAs tend to emphasize form over function. The examiner should realize the importance of both forms and functions and identify the functions needed for adaptive performance: Can the child impact on the environment effectively? Various forms of behaviors may exist that accomplish the same function. For example, verbally asking for help is a form; the function is to indicate in some way that help is needed. This could be communicated in a variety of ways, even by simply making eye contact, gesturing, or tapping on the shoulder. The teacher or examiner needs to determine what functions exist, which functions are most important, how the functions are related to one another, and which forms are most useful (Wolery, 1991). The focus should be on whether a child can get something done rather than how it is done.

Results Translatable to Program Planning

Can the results of the CBA be easily translated into information to use in program planning? Are the skills assessed important for learning? For example, learning that actions cause effects, sets the stage for meaningful exchanges with the physical and social environment. Identifying that a child is aware of cause-effect relationships (as a result of items in the CBA) allows for the development of goals and objectives in which the child learns how his or her actions impact on an activity, game, or social interaction.

Profile of Strengths and Needs

Do the CBA results express both strengths and needs that can become the focus of program planning? Many CBAs include a format for developing a profile of subscales of the test so scores may be compared across skill areas. The profile is a visual representation of the child's relative strengths and weaknesses and is helpful in communicating this information to parents and other professionals; it provides a way of setting priorities for teaching skills. Areas of weakness may be given a higher priority than areas of strength and identified strengths may be used strategically to remediate weaknesses.

Recordkeeping System

Most curricula offer mastery checklists or a way of keeping track of the objectives that have or have not been mastered. Progress is noted by writing plus (+), objective achieved; minus (−), objective not achieved; and plus/minus (±), emerging objective. Complete ongoing assessments at regular intervals after the initial assessment. This method provides formative evaluation information as the year progresses. Overall developmental age ranges also provide summative information for program evaluation.

Feasible and Cost-effective

The curriculum-based assessment chosen must be both feasible and cost-effective to implement. Early interventionists must have the time and skill to actually use the instrument. The cost of the instrument should not be excessive. Bagnato and Neisworth (1991) suggest that a commercially available instrument should not cost more than $100. Those that do usually include materials that can be easily found in a classroom. Useful questions to consider when determining the appropriateness of a CBA include: How long does it take to administer? Who is qualified to administer the assessment? How much staff training time is necessary? What equipment or materials are needed to administer it? Can these items be found in a classroom? Is the recording system practical?

Evaluation of Curriculum-based Assessments

The initial decision to purchase a curriculum-based assessment for a program should take all of the factors previously mentioned into consideration. A program director or early interventionist might use an evaluation form such as the one shown in Figure 10–1 from Bagnato, Neisworth, and Munson (1989).

Advantages

Using a multidomain CBA has become very popular in programs for young children with disabilities. Although we do not advocate the use of only one tool in the assessment process, the advantages of including a multidomain assessment are:

1. An agency can purchase one test and have subtests in all domains.
2. It is more cost-effective to purchase one test instead of five single-domain tests.

Scale _____ Publisher _____

Address _____ Phone _____

Ratings: 0 = Does not meet criterion 1 = Partially meets criterion 2 = Fulfills criterion

Developmental Base

_____ 1. Are the activities within the assessment measure hierarchically structured and sequenced according to a developmental task analysis or developmental process format?

_____ 2. Is the design of the scale based upon some reputable developmental orientation?

Multidomain Profile

_____ 3. Does the assessment measure organize items into several distinct yet interrelated subdomains?

_____ 4. Does the multidomain organization of competencies allow the detection of fully acquired (+), emerging (±), and absent (−) capabilities?

_____ 5. Does the scale offer separate scores/indexes for each subdomain?

Multisource Sample

_____ 6. Does the assessment measure integrate information obtained from several people (parent, professional) and methods (observation, ratings, performance, interview)?

_____ 7. Can several different team members independently contribute information to complete the scale?

Curricular Links

_____ 8. Is the assessment measure organized into developmental domains similar to those surveyed in the early intervention program's curriculum?

_____ 9. Does the scale contain tasks/items similar in content and behavioral demands to those included in the program's developmental curriculum?

Adaptive Options

_____ 10. Does the scale provide structured modifications of tasks to accommodate the sensory and response limitations of young children with sensory, motor, and adaptive deficits?

_____ 11. Can a professional "clinically" alter the tasks within the scale to accommodate children with various handicaps?

_____ 12. Does the scale provide or allow modifications for scoring the performances of young handicapped children?

Ecological Emphasis

_____ 13. Does the scale provide information on the child's interaction with the physical and social environment (e.g., attention to tasks, peer interaction, need for prompts and limits, ability to cope with new situations)?

_____ 14. Does the scale integrate information from both home and school?

Technical Support

_____ 15. Has research established the reliability, validity, and diagnostic utility of the assessment measure?

_____ 16. Has the scale been adequately standardized and/or field-tested in general?

_____ 17. Has the scale been field-tested and/or standardized on any handicap group?

_____ 18. Does the scale contain separate norms or any comparative data for young handicapped children?

_____ Total Evaluation Score

_____ /36 (total possible score) =_____ %

FIGURE 10–1 **Evaluation and Selection Criteria Rating Form for Prescriptive Developmental Assessment Measures**

Source: Reprinted from *Linking Developmental Assessment and Early Intervention: Curriculum-based Prescriptions,* 2nd ed., by S. J. Bagnato, J. T. Neisworth, & S. M. Munson, pp. 39–40, with permission of Aspen Publishers, Inc., © 1989.

3. Extensive training and experience are not needed for basic administrative purposes.

4. The test's items are sequenced or grouped by domain and age; suggestions for easily translating into instructional objectives and activities are included.

5. The assessment can be administered over and over again to the same child.

6. In many cases, it is possible to compare progress in one domain to that in another. (Consider the points in the Disadvantages section.)

7. Some tests have items clustered as a screening test.

8. Tests often span several ages and can provide continuity and evaluation over a period of years.

9. Developmental scores expressed in months make measurement of even small gains possible. (Adapted from Fewell, 1991, pp. 169–70.)

Disadvantages

Although CBA has many advantages, the examiner should be aware also of its limitations which include:

1. Age equivalents are from developmental schedules and not from normative samples rendering them less reliable than those obtained when using standardized or norm-referenced measures.

2. In some tests, age equivalents are not consistent within or across domains. The number of items needed to progress by six months in one section or part of a scale may not be comparable with that needed to indicate a similar gain in another section of the scale. Again, this may be a function of the lack of normative data in designing the scales.

3. Requirements in one domain on one age level may be far less demanding than those at the same age in another domain.

4. Because only a few of these tests are standardized, it is difficult to compare scores on one test to those of another test.

5. Some of these tests offer several scoring options that, if interpreted carelessly, may decrease the potential validity of the test results. An example of this is the developmental quotient on the *Battelle Developmental Inventory* (Newborg et al., 1984). When testing a child with severe handicaps, a negative developmental quotient can be derived. Beware of *derived* scores on a non-normed test.

6. Because the tests are curriculum-referenced, the early interventionist may tend to teach to the test and thus severely limits the facilitation of many other appropriate, developmentally relevant skills that may not be specifically represented in the instrument utilized. (Adapted from Fewell, 1991, p. 170.)

Examples of Curriculum-based Assessments

A number of assessment instruments have been developed specifically for use in instructional planning for young children with disabilities. Table 10–1 provides an overview of some of the most commonly used assessments. It is not comprehensive and is meant simply as a starting point for decision making. To determine the suitability of a particular CBA, individual early interventionists and program supervisors need to examine the instrument in relation to the children in their settings.

Helpful Tips for Conducting the Assessment

In most instances, curriculum-based assessments should be done when the child is at home or in the classroom. Assessments conducted in a familiar setting and over a period of time are much more valid than those that allow only a one-time session for the entire assessment battery. Using methods such as a transdisciplinary play-based assessment (Linder, 1990) also provide a much more accurate picture of the child.

Curriculum-based assessment provides a match between the assessment items and curriculum. The daily teaching activities should have assessment components in them and assessment should be viewed as an integral part of the intervention program. Ongoing, daily assessment provides program monitoring and is an essential part of the instructional program.

An example of how assessment and intervention are linked is found in the *Carolina Curriculum for Infants and Toddlers with Special Needs* (Johnson-Martin et al., 1991). The Curriculum Sequences section expands the curriculum item in the "Assessment Log." This section gives a description of the materials needed, procedures for encouraging the skill in the child's daily routines, adaptations for children with disabilities, and criterion for mastery. These items can be condensed into a few words and then conveniently located where the intervention normally takes place, e.g., a list of snack-time activities placed by the table where snack time occurs or self-care activities placed by the door. Simple forms for use at home and more complex ones for use at school can be made. The *Carolina Curriculum* (Johnson-Martin et al., 1991) also suggests writing each item on an individual activity sheet as an example of a helpful form to use in assessing and monitoring a child's progress (see Figure 10–2).

The Shopping List Approach

To ease the burden of completing the comprehensive lists of skills contained in most CBAs, Bagnato and Neisworth (1991) suggest preparing a *shopping list*. The examiner prepares a list of skills in a particular area that provides a systematic sampling of behavior. A sample communication skills shopping list is shown in Table 10–2.

The shopping list approach emphasizes the essential skills that need to be sampled rather than the order of or techniques for sampling. The examiner must be very knowledgeable in typical and atypical child development stages and patterns in order to choose the most appropriate skills to assess. Inventories or surveys of developmental skills can serve as appropriate models for the design

TABLE 10-1 Commonly Used Developmental Assessments

Test/Source	Age Range	Domains Assessed	Description
Brigance Diagnostic Inventory of Early Development, Revised (Brigance, 1991) Curriculum Associates	0–6 years	Preambulatory motor Gross motor Fine motor Self-help Speech and language General knowledge and comprehension Social and emotional development Readiness Basic reading skills Manuscript writing Basic math	Gives developmental age levels in each area; criterion-based test with norm-based qualities, and is useful for targeting instructional objectives.
Callier-Azuza (Stillman, 1982) Council for Exceptional Children	0–9 years	Motor Perceptual Daily living Socialization Language	Assesses deaf-blind and multihandicapped children; useful for targeting instructional objectives; criterion-referenced but not a curriculum; examples provide instructional suggestions.
Carolina Curriculum for Infants and Toddlers with Special Needs (Johnson-Martin, et al., 1991) Paul H. Brookes Carolina Curriculum for Preschoolers (Johnson-Martin, et al., 1990) Paul H. Brookes	0–2 years 3–5 years	Cognition Communication Social adaptation Fine motor Gross motor	Assesses children with severe disabilities (alternative behaviors provided); items ordered by logical teaching sequence; curriculum-referenced tool; individual assessment logs and developmental progress charts.
Early Learning Accomplishment Profile for Infants (ELAP) (Sanford, 1981) Kaplan School Supply	0–3 years	Gross and fine motor Cognitive Language Self-help Social Emotional	Helpful in programming for severe disabilities; adaptations needed for disabilities; curriculum-imbedded measure; profile for summative information; activity cards available in Spanish.
Hawaii Early Learning Profile and Help for Special Preschoolers (Furuno, et al., 1985) VORT Corporation	0–3 years 3–6 years	Cognitive Language Gross motor Fine motor Social-emotional Self-help	Precautions and suggestions for particular disabilities; based on developmental milestones; curriculum-referenced test; provides charts to identify current mastery of skills, needs, objectives, and recording progress; family guides available.

TABLE 10-1 *(Continued)*

Test/Source	Age Range	Domains Assessed	Description
Learning Accomplishment Profile, Diagnostic Edition, Revised (LeMay, Griffin, & Sanford, 1991) Kaplan School Supply	0–6 years	Fine and gross motor Language Cognitive Self-help	Provides profile of fully acquired, absent, and emergent skills; curriculum-imbedded with normal sequence of skills; useful for targeting instructional objectives.
Battelle Developmental Inventory (Newborg, et al., 1984) DLM Teaching Resources	0–8 years	Personal-social Adaptive Motor Communicative Cognitive	Includes screening measure and can be used in all assessment stages from screening to program monitoring; norm-referenced but integrates curriculum referenced features; general adaptations for various handicaps.
Hicomp Preschool Curriculum (Willoughby-Herb & Neisworth, 1983) Psychological Corp.	0–5 years	Communication Own care Motor Problem solving	Takes developmental task approach; suitable for use with developmentally delayed and multihandicapped children; each domain contains a comprehensive list of separate hierarchical objectives for a total of 800 objectives and lesson plans; HICOMP guide provides reference list of objectives identical in several domains; also provides individual graphs/charts for child data.
Developmental Programming for Infants and Young Children (DPIYC) (Brown & Donovan, 1985) University of Michigan Press	0–3 years	Perceptual/fine motor Cognition Language Social/emotional Self-care Gross motor	Developmental milestones; parents are focus; professionals offer training support and monitor progress; adaptations for handicaps noted; designed for use by interdisciplinary teams; no specific data sheet.
Arizona Basic Assessment and Curriculum Utilization System (ABACUS) (McCarthy, et al., 1986) Love Publishing	0–5.5 years	Body management Self-care Communication Preacademic Socialization	Developmental milestones; can be used to develop IEP and IFSP; home/parent teaching component; complete recordkeeping system.

(Continued)

TABLE 10-1   *(Continued)*

Test/Source	Age Range	Domains Assessed	Description
Portage Guide to Early Education (Shearer, et al., 1976) CESA 5	0–6 years	Infant stimulation Socialization Language Self-help Cognitive Motor	Adaptation needed for disabilities; assesses current level of performance with checklist; designed for home-based individual pro-grams, but can be used in center-based; includes manual and 580 activity cards for skill development; family involvement is integral part.
Uniform Performance Assessment System (UPAS) White, et al., 1981) Psychological Corporation	0–6 years	Preacademic Communications Social Self-help Gross motor	Criterion-referenced; func-tional, curriculum-based analysis of adaptive skills; assesses instructional needs and behaviors of children with moderate to severe disabilities; leads directly to IEP goals; assesses instruc-tional strategies; provides formative and summative data.
Assessment, Evaluation, and Programming System (AEPS Test) (Bricker, Gentry, & Bailey, 1992) Paul H. Brookes	0–3 years	Fine motor Gross motor Self-care Cognitive Social-communication Social	Designed to provide direct intervention activities and program evaluation; gen-erally appropriate for children up to 6 years; tracks child performance and used on individualized goals and objectives; includes a family report form and family interest survey for IFSP development; AEPS Child Progress Record for display-ing current abilities, interven-tion targets and child progress.

of the shopping lists. The *BRIGANCE Inventory of Early Development—Revised* (Brigance, 1991), the *Early Intervention Developmental Profile* (Rogers et. al., 1981) and the *Preschool Developmental Profile* (Brown et al., 1981) provide listings of developmental skills in cognitive, language, gross motor, perceptual/fine-motor, social/emotional, and self-care domains (Bagnato & Neisworth, 1991).

Name: _____ Week: _____
Location: _____

Situation for activities	Opportunity to observe					Mastered (date)
	M	T	W	Th	F	
Child on back (e.g., diapering, playing) Visually tracks in circle						
Turns head to search for sound						
Feet in air for play						
Child on back or sitting supported Glance from toy to toy when one in each hand						
Plays with toys placed in hand(s)						
Places both hands on toy at midline						
Looks or reaches for object that touches body out of sight						
Reacts to tactile stimulation with movement						
Repeats activities that get interesting results						
Social interactions, including meals Anticipates frequently occurring events in familiar games						
Responds differently to stranger and family members						
Laughs						
Repeats sounds when imitated						
Turns to name being called						
Repeats vocalizations that get reactions						
Smiles reciprocally						
Mealtime Munches food						
Vocalizes 5 or more consonant-vowel combinations						
Bathing and dressing Holds trunk steady when held at hips						

FIGURE 10–2 **Sample Weekly Record for Child Learning Objectives of the IFSP**

Source: From *The Carolina Curriculum for Infants and Toddlers with Special Needs,* copyright © 1991. p. 43. Used by permission of the authors (Johnson-Martin, N. M., Jens, K., Attermeier, S., & Hacker, B.) and Paul H. Brookes Publishing Co., Baltimore, MD.

Play-based Assessment

Observing and interacting with a child or children during playtime can provide much information in a variety of domains. Certain toys or materials may be provided for a group of children and then the examiner may observe and interact

TABLE 10-2   Shopping List for Communication
                        Skills

Developmental Area	Skills to Be Sampled
Pre-speech	
Orienting	Orients to sound
	Orients to voice
Responding	Responds selectively to voice
	Responds to name
Gesturing	Gives greetings
	Indicates needs
Vocalizing	Makes cooing, babbling
	Imitates sounds
Receptive language	
Identifying	Identifies body parts
	Identifies common objects
	Identifies colors
Following directions	Follows one-step direction
	Follows two-step direction
	Follows complex directions
Developmental areas	Skills samples
Expressive language	
Naming	Names people
	Names body parts
	Names common objects
Stating needs	States need to eat, drink
Describing action	Describes own actions
	Describes action of others
Speaking socially	Responds to questions
	Initiates discussion

Source: From Bagnato, S. J., & Neisworth, J. T. (1991). *Assessment for Early Intervention: Best Practices for Professionals*, p. 77. New York: Guilford Publications, Inc. Reprinted with permission.

with the children as they play, noting specific behaviors or skills that were outlined for observation prior to the session. The *Play Assessment Scale* (Fewell, 1986) is an example of how an examiner may assess multiple areas systematically through structured play routines.

Transdisciplinary Play Based Assessment (TPBA) (Linder, 1990) also provides both an assessment and intervention process. Information is gathered from the family concerning the developmental status of the child. This information is then used to design the play session. Toys and materials appropriate to the child's level of development are provided. The content and sequence of the play session are structured so that the examiner may observe the child across developmental domains. One of the members of the transdisciplinary team facilitates the play and the caregivers are included in certain phases of the session. The TPBA guidelines provide a structure for the observation of cognitive, social-emotional, communication and language, and sensorimotor development. It is a good idea to videotape the play session for analysis and documentation of the child's progress.

Group Assessment

Because CBAs do not have to follow rigid procedures, many of the skills may be assessed in group settings that are more natural than structured one-on-one test situations. Often, CBAs offer suggestions for group administration procedures. The *BRIGANCE* (Brigance, 1991) suggests ways to assess skills in group settings, e.g., observe children in outdoor activities to see if they are able to perform gross-motor skills such as running, hopping, and skipping.

Cue Card Approach

When conducting a CBA, early interventionists who are not familiar with a particular test often meticulously administer items in the sequence in which they are listed. To avoid this long and tedious experience, for both the examiner and the child, the examiner needs to become familiar with the instrument and its items prior to conducting an assessment. Then, developing a *cue card* will enable the examiner to keep track of the behaviors being assessed and the results. A sample cue card for using the LAP (Sanford & Zelman, 1981) is shown in Table 10-3. The listing of skills in each area enables the examiner to note the child's success or failure with the items and make brief behavioral observations at the same time. The examiner needs to be familiar enough with the test items to judge success or failure at a variety of developmental levels without referring to the manual. For example, how long must a child balance on one foot in order to receive credit for accomplishing the task.

Another example of the way to organize a cue card or planning sheet for a three-month-old infant is shown in Table 10-4 using the *Early Learning Accomplishment Profile (ELAP)* (Glover, Preminger, & Sanford, 1978). This example provides more detailed information than the previous one. The ELAP is organized around the position of the infant as opposed to the domain.

These are some examples of ways to organize an assessment session. The examiner also may develop a cue card based on the practical use of the materials (i.e., list together all block items, pencil tasks, shape concepts, table versus floor activities, or skill sequences). The idea is to conduct meaningful, smooth-flowing assessments. This enhances the child's performance and minimizes the distractions and transitions. Following the session with the child, the examiner records the information on the appropriate assessment forms. If additional items need assessment, this can take place later.

TABLE 10-3   Common Items by Domain on the Learning Accomplishment Profile

Gross motor
- Balance
- Walk
- Jump
- Ball (catch, throw)
- Step (alternate, which foot)

Fine motor
- Tower
- Lid
- Book pages
- Pegboard
- Beads
  - Pincer
  - String
- Scissors
- Fold paper
- Puzzle

Pre-writing
- − 1 + 0
- Draw body

Self-help
- Button
- Tie
- Zip
- Snap
- Buckle

Personal social (parent reports also)
- Imitates
- Turn taking
- Attentive to story
- Separates
- Make believe
- Age/name/address/family

Cognition
- Sort cubes
- Repeat digits
- Count
- Give objects
- Big/little
- Match (objects, pictures)
- Body parts
- Stack ring
- Missing object

Language
- Points-body parts
- 1-2-3 word phrases
- Plurals
- Pronouns
- Verbs
- Preps
- Telephone
- Names objects
- How/where/when/who
- If/then
- Retell story

Language samples
- Examiner should record examples of language obtained during assessment—both verbal and/or nonverbal

Assessment Results

Curriculum-based assessment activities assist with instructional program planning and need to identify:

- Skills the child demonstrates independently.
- Skills the child performs with support, adaptation, or assistance.
- Effective and efficient instructional strategies for teaching the infant or child.
- Variables that may influence the way intervention is implemented.

TABLE 10-4 Early Learning Accomplishments Profile Cue Card

Supine activities
* Dangling toy

Lean over and dangle toy over baby.

Responses: Excitable (legs and arms react)
Head position midline
Legs kick in sequence/cycles
Reaches for toy with both arms

Move toy 180° arc from one side to other 4–6″.

Response: Child follows visually
* Rolling

Prompt to roll to one side with toy.

* Sounds

Lean over baby 10″ from face. Talk in quiet voice.

Responses: Babbles/coos
Localizes eyes of speaker

Lean over baby. Play peek-a-boo.

Response: Child laughs
* Rattle

Touch handle of rattle to child's fisted fingers.

Response: Child holds it briefly.

Place rattle in hands. Observe exploration.

Response Brings to mouth, rubs, throws.
* Pull to sit

Hold child's hands and pull to sit.

Response: Head lags

Hold sitting supported.

Response: Head forward

Standing activities

Hold standing under arms across chest.

Responses: Extends legs, rises on toes
Head unsteady, bobbing
Sustains weight briefly, legs extend

Prone activities

Place child across your arms on stomach. Lower child to floor.

Response: Head level/raised

Observe in prone.

Responses: Head lifts
Hips lowered to floor at rest
Raises chest 2″ using arms
Legs extend, 1 arm flexed

Sitting activities
* Have parent set baby on lap facing parent

Approach baby from behind saying baby's name in low, quiet voice.

Response: Turns toward voice

Show rattle to baby briefly. When baby looking at parent, shake rattle 8–10″ opposite each ear out of range of vision.

Response: Head turns toward sound

This information helps identify environmental factors and developmental skills that are relevant targets for intervention. The teacher or examiner should consider variables that may enhance or interfere with a child's performance of a given task. (See also chapter 11, Ecological Assessment.)

When a child does not successfully complete a task, the examiner should ask: Why didn't the child succeed? Was it a function of the . . .

- Place where assessment occurred?
- Materials or tasks used?
- Level of task comprehension required?
- Mode of response expected?
- Rate of response needed?
- Mode of response needed?
- Quality of the response?
- Efficiency of the child's skill acquisition?

Then, the item or task is modified to help determine the conditions under which the child performs best. This information is used to improve the child's instructional program.

When compiling and reporting assessment information, it is important to include the following:

- Observations of the child's behavior when interacting with the examiner and others.
- Strategies that enhance the child's attention and on-task performance.
- Patterns of strengths and weaknesses.
- Developmental age (DA) equivalents for each domain measured (i.e., cognitive, language, personal-social, and so on).
- A narrative of the specific skills demonstrated in the developmental domains.
- Specific findings, which address a description of the areas of weaknesses noted, that become the instructional targets when planning the child's intervention program.

Summary

Curriculum-based assessment is an integral part of the assessment process. There are many CBA forms from which to choose. Each individual program, teacher, or examiner needs to decide which CBA is most appropriate based on that particular program's and individual's needs. Bagnato, Neisworth, and Munson (1989) suggest that useful assessment should consider certain attributes. Individuals choosing a CBA also might consider these attributes and ask whether the assessment is:

- Intervention- or program-based (i.e., linkable to program objectives)?
- Child-relevant (i.e., indicates a profile of strengths and needs accommodated by the program)?
- Sensitive to a child's progress (i.e., sensitive to small increases)?
- Adaptive?
- Able to provide informative reports?
- Complementary to other assessment devices?

Suggested Group Activities

1. Using a curriculum-based assessment, select several items and write a brief instructional program to teach those skills.

2. Discuss the similarities and differences between a curriculum-imbedded scale and a curriculum-referenced scale. Suggest examples of appropriate skills to use with each scale.

3. List examples of instruments to use in a multidimensional assessment. Include a variety of settings and respondents—caregiver, teacher, other service providers.

4. Compile a list of forms and functions. Discuss the function of each form and suggest possible adaptation options.

5. Divide into groups and assign each a particular *shopping list* for the examiner to prioritize the important subskills that need to be mastered.

6. In the same format as the previous activity, have the group members work together to construct a *cue card* to assist an examiner in the assessment process.

7. Divide into groups of two or three. Have students use the following case studies, choosing a particular CBA such as the *Carolina* or the *LAP* to use.

ETHEN

Ethen, age 3 years, 11 months, was brought to the center today by his mother. He has been referred to the center due to his mothers's concern about his development. He has been diagnosed as having a severe sensory-neural hearing loss. His mother would like to know the exact nature of his difficulties and what she can do to help him.

KIMBERLY

Kimberly, age 4 years, 0 months, was brought to the center by her mother and brother. She was referred by her pediatrician, Dr. Goodlad, with a speech delay problem as well as possible motor delay.

MIKE

Mike, age 2 years, 6 months, was brought to the center by his father. He was referred by Dr. McLaurin. The parents would like some general help and understanding of his overall problems. When Mike was born with a large occipital encephalocele, he was immediately transferred to intensive care for treatment for a short time. Medically, he is now fine, but his parents are concerned with the delays in his development.

ALAN

Alan, age 3 years, 1 month, was brought to the center by his mother and his 14-month-old sister. His mother expresses concern regarding Alan's behavior, which she describes as "aggressive." She also is concerned about Alan's resistance to toilet training.

Each group should work on the following items:

a. With what items and at which level should testing begin?

b. Examine the case study report and place the information in the appropriate strengths and weaknesses columns on the summary sheet.

c. Given the minimal information in the case study, what instructional objectives might be written for this child?

d. Discuss each group's case study with the rest of class by presenting a summary of strengths and weaknesses and written objectives.

References

Bagnato, S. J., & Neisworth, J. T. (1991). *Assessment for early intervention: Best practices for professionals.* New York: Guilford Press.

Bagnato, S. J., Neisworth, J. T., & Munson, S. M. (1989). *Linking developmental assessment and early intervention: Curriculum-based prescriptions* (2nd ed.). Rockville, MD: Aspen.

Brigance, A. H. (1991). *BRIGANCE Diagnostic Inventory of Early Development—Revised.* North Billerica, MA: Curriculum Associates.

Brown, S. L., D'Eugenio, D. B., Drews, J. E., Haskin, B. S., Lynch, E. W., Moersch, M. S., & Rogers, S. J. (1981). *Preschool Developmental Profile.* Ann Arbor: University of Michigan Press.

Fewell, R. R. (1991). Trends in the assessment of infants and toddlers with disabilities. *Exceptional Children, 58*(2), 166–173.

Fewell, R. R. (1986). *Play Assessment Scale (PAS)—Research Edition.* New Orleans: Tulane University.

Fewell, R. R., & Langley, B. (1984). *Developmental Activities Screening Inventory II.* Austin: Pro-Ed.

Glover, E. M., Preminger, J., & Sanford, A. (1978). *Early learning accomplishment profile (E-Lap).* Winston-Salem: Kaplan School Supply.

Johnson-Martin, N. M., Jens, K. G., Attermeier, S. M., & Hacker, B. J. (1991). *The Carolina Curriculum for Infants and Toddlers with Special Needs* (2nd ed.). Baltimore: Paul H. Brookes.

LeMay, D., Griffin, G., & Sanford, A. R. (1978). *Learning Accomplishment Profile—Diagnostic Edition (LAP-D).* Lewisville, NC: Kaplan School Supply.

Linder, T. W. (1990). *Transdisciplinary play-based assessment: A functional approach to working with young children.* Baltimore: Paul H. Brookes.

Neisworth, J. T., & Bagnato, S. J. (1988). Assessment in early childhood special education: A typology of dependent measures. In S. L. Odom & M. B. Karnes (Eds.), *Early intervention for infants and children with handicaps: An empirical approach* (pp. 23–49). Baltimore: Paul H. Brookes.

Newborg, J., Stock, J., Wnek, L., Guidubaldi, J., & Svinicki, J. S. (1984). *Battelle developmental inventory (BDI).* Allen, TX: DLM/Teaching Resources.

Rogers, S. J., Donovan, C. M., D'Eugenio, D. B., Brown, S. L., Lynch, E. W., Moersch, M. S., & Schafer, D. S. (1981). *Early Intervention Development Profile.* Ann Arbor: University of Michigan Press.

Sanford, A. R., & Zelman, J. G. (1981). *Learning Accomplishment Profile* (rev. ed.). Winston-Salem: Kaplan Press.

Willoughby-Herb, S., & Neisworth, J. T. (1983). *HICOMP Preschool Curriculum,* San Antonio: Psychological Corporation.

Wolery, M. (1991). Instruction in early childhood special education: "Seeing through a glass darkly . . . knowing in part." *Exceptional Children, 58*(2), 127–134.

Chapter *11*

Ecological and Behavioral Assessments

What Are Ecological and Behavioral Assessments?

Ecological and behavioral psychologies both recognize the important influence environment has on behavior. An ecological viewpoint sees the relationship between the child and her or his environment as interactive. A behavioral viewpoint focuses on how environment influences or controls the child's behavior.

Although there are major differences between ecological and behavioral approaches to assessment, they do have certain commonalities. Simeonsson (1986) identifies these common features relevant to assessment: (1) both strategies rely on systematic observation of the child, (2) both approaches can be used to assess children of any age, and (3) each approach tries to define the role of environment relative to a specific child. Based on these commonalities, this chapter focuses on both ecological and behavioral approaches to assessment and their relationship to the assessment process.

Importance of an Ecological and Behavioral Framework

Consideration of the influences of environmental and situational factors on an individual or a group (i.e., family, group of children) is an essential component of any effective assessment (Thurman & Widerstrom, 1985). The screening, diagnostic, and assessment stages presented in the previous chapters provide important information about the child's functioning under specific conditions in a specific setting with specific individuals. However, assessment results from one situation cannot be assumed to be generalizable across a variety of situations. An ecological approach to assessment helps the team to better understand the range of responses a child and family may exhibit under a variety of conditions.

How successfully assessment information can be used to prescribe intervention depends on the degree to which environmental factors are taken into account. An ecological and behavioral framework expands the concept of assessment to include environmental factors.

Simeonsson (1986) states that the ecological and behavioral approaches are valuable because they provide a way to assess the influences of environment on the performance of the child. The information obtained from ecological and behavioral assessment perspectives enhances what is obtained from other assessment strategies. Ecological assessment yields information about the context in which a child exhibits a certain behavior. Behavioral assessment results in a functional analysis that allows the examiner to make inferences about the causal relationships between stimuli in the environment and behavior.

The ecological and behavioral approaches should be integral to the daily, ongoing assessment process. All environmental factors that contribute to the child's status need to be considered. The goal of an early interventionist is to attempt to examine all antecedent, concurrent, and consequent events and variables that influence the child's development.

Ecological Assessment

The ecological approach sees the child as interacting with his or her environment. One perspective of human ecology sees the relationship between environment and child as static; environment is viewed as affecting the child's behavior. A more recent perspective views environment and child in a dynamic interplay— changes in one cause changes in the other (Carta, Sainato, & Greenwood, 1988). Major characteristics of ecological methods include: (1) focusing on naturalistic observation, (2) documenting behavior with minimal predetermination of criteria for recording observations, (3) making observations in as nonintrusive a manner as possible, and (4) making inferences about the interplay of behavior and environment after recording the information. The goal of the observer is to identify patterns and sequences of behaviors.

Behavioral Assessment

A behavioral approach views the child's behavior as a function of the antecedents and consequences. Behavioral assessment provides information about the setting or context in which a child's behavior occurs by using a functional analysis. This analysis permits making inferences about the relationships between stimuli and behavior.

Behavioral or functional analysis requires that the target(s) of observation be defined before the observation occurs. The method for collecting and recording data also is determined beforehand. Then, behavior is observed and recorded under controlled conditions. The frequency, intensity, and duration of a particular behavior are examples of dimensions or characteristics to measure.

Direct or systematic observation and recording of behavior are the fundamental procedures to use for behavioral assessment. It is possible to observe behavior under the following variety of circumstances or formats:

1. In vivo or naturalistic, e.g., in the home or classroom;
2. Simulated or staged where a situation and materials permit or occasion the target behavior, e.g., prearranging certain toys;
3. Role-play or prompt circumstances – the child is asked what she or he would do in a certain situation.

Characteristics and Features

Neisworth and Bagnato (1988) view ecological assessment as an interactive model that stresses behavior as a function of personal variables interacting with environmental variables. They categorize the variables or features in ecological assessment as follows:

Static or Physical Elements

- Organization and arrangement of classroom
- Number and arrangement of materials available
- Lighting
- Temperature control
- Number, properties, and arrangement of toys
- Number of children present
- Physical arrangement of children
- Teacher–student ratio and staffing pattern

Dynamic or Social Features

- Extent of peer interaction
- Caregiver sensitivity and responsiveness
- Provision for rewards and punishment

Both static and dynamic features or variables affect preschoolers' behavior. The interaction between these features is examined using learning or behavioral variables. These variables consist of:

- Setting events (what is occurring within the setting);
- Discriminative stimuli (stimuli that signal a particular response);
- Child's behavior;
- Consequences (what follows the behavior);
- Contingencies among all of the psychological/learning variables.

The static variables may set the stage for students to respond. For example, the arrangement of tables and chairs in the room influences the kind of interaction between children and teachers. Dynamic variables, such as teacher or parent behaviors, affect the ways students behave, but these variables may themselves be affected by student behavior (Carta, Sainato, & Greenwood, 1988). For example, the number of children and teachers in the room affects both the children's and the teachers' behavior. The greater the ratio of adults to children in the room, the greater the likelihood of interaction between adults and children.

Behavioral Methods of Data Collection

There are many different types and methods of data-recording systems to use to gather information about a child's performance or behavior. Observation is an essential technique that involves gathering qualitative and quantitative data about a child's behavior. Some observation systems are more formal and structured than others. To be as objective as possible in the interpretation of those behaviors, the examiner needs to focus on the actual events and behaviors.

Developmental Checklists

The teacher needs to use a formal or informal checklist to record a child's progress in mastering developmental milestones or skills and to track that child's progress in comparison to age level expectations. Such a list of skills usually is arranged in developmental sequence. The child is presented with specific tasks and demonstrates his or her proficiency level. There is no prescribed way in which tasks must be presented. Thurman and Widerstrom (1985) present an example of this process in Table 11–1. The teacher records the date on which the child demonstrates the skill as well as the level of proficiency displayed, and notes factors such as whether the child performs independently, with teacher assistance, or with physical or verbal prompts.

A good checklist clearly spells out the criteria for mastery. This increases the ease with which the tool can be used as well as the reliability of the data recorded. Some developmental curricula can be used as checklists. Often, teachers or early interventionists design their own checklists by compiling tasks or skills to examine from a variety of instruments.

In developing one's own checklist, use a task analysis to break down the skill into smaller components. This approach is useful for children with severe or multiple disabilities who may display gain in smaller increments or, in some cases, be able to perform only part of a skill. This method is discussed more fully in chapter 7.

Behavior Rating Scales

A rating scale or checklist may be used at regular intervals by the teacher or caregiver to make judgments about a child's behavior or environment. The

TABLE 11–1 Steps in Developing Skills Checklist

Guideline
1. Choose a developmental area in which the child needs special instruction. Pick a skill from this area to assess.

Self-help skills: feeding self
2. Observe several older children to find out what the specific components of the skill are. Use a commercial checklist to get you started. List the developmental steps in sequence.

Steps to self-feeding as presented in LAP	Observed
1.	a.
	b.
2.	a.
	b.
3.	a.
	b.
4.	a.
	b.

3. Transfer your skill sequence to a checklist format with room for recording date first assessed, date of mastery, and comments

Skill	Date Assessed	Date Mastered	Comments
1.			
a.			
b.			
2.			
a.			
b.			

Source: From Thurman, S. K., & Widerstrom, A. H. (1985). *Young Children with Special Needs: A Developmental Ecological Approach,* p. 159. Boston: Allyn and Bacon. Reprinted with permission.

checklist notes the absence or occurrence of specific behaviors or skills and may include appropriate or inappropriate behaviors to be evaluated. The rating usually consists of a simple yes-no response, a continuum ranging from always to never, or a qualitative judgment from excellent to poor. Although highly subjective, using a rating scale at regular intervals and having more than one individual rate behaviors increases the amount and reliability of the information obtained.

This type of judgment-based assessment provides an excellent means for input from the family and a variety of professionals who come in contact with the child. This input can challenge or support the information obtained from more formal assessment. This method also allows for more qualitative observation of a child's overall functioning than the specific items of direct testing methods typically allow. An example rating scale is shown in Table 11–2.

TABLE 11-2 Infant/Toddler Environment Rating Scale

	Inadequate 1	2	Minimal 3	4	Good 5	6	Excellent 7
10. Personal grooming	Little attention paid to child's personal grooming (Ex: no hand or face washing, wet clothes not changed quickly). Same towel or washcloth used for different children.		Children's hands washed as needed (Ex: after diapering/toileting, before and after meals, after messy play). Own towel/washcloth (paper or cloth) used for each child. Extra clothes available and children changed when needed.		Care given to children's appearance (Ex: faces washed, cleaned up after messy play, hair combed with own comb, bibs used if needed). Self-help encouraged in personal grooming as children are able (Ex: child cooperates in changing clothes, encouraged to wash own hands). Personal care activities made more acceptable to children (Ex: caregiver sings songs, gently washes baby's face and avoids making baby cry).		Personal grooming used as learning experience (Ex: learning names for body parts and clothing, letting child look in mirror). Individual toothbrushes properly stored and used for each toddler at least once during the day. Easy place for toddlers to wash hands (Ex: steps near sink).
Listening and talking 15. Informal use of language	Little or no talking to infants and toddlers. Little or no response to children's attempts to communicate through gestures, sounds, or words.		Talking used mainly to control child's behavior (Ex: "come here," "take this," "don't touch"). Some social talking to children (Ex: "What a pretty baby!"). Some response to children's attempts to communicate.		Caregiver frequently responds verbally to infants/toddlers' crying, gestures, sounds, words, and questions. Caregiver usually maintains eye contact while talking to child. Caregiver names and talks about many objects and actioons for infants/toddlers. Caregiver takes part in verbal play.		Caregiver talks to each infant and toddler during play and routines about child's activities. Caregiver repeats what toddlers say, adding words and ideas when appropriate. Caregiver adds to children's understanding of language all day (Ex: gives clear directions, repeats new words often). Caregiver maintains a good balance between listening and talking (Ex: does not overwhelm child with constant talk).

Source: Reprinted by permission of the publisher from Harms, Thelma, Cryer, Debby, & Clifford, Richard M., *Infant/Toddler Environment Rating Scale.* (New York: Teachers College Press, © 1990 by Thelma Harms, Deborah Reid Cryer, and Richard M. Clifford. All rights reserved.) Item 10, "Personal Grooming" from p. 19; Item 15, "Informal Use of Language" from p. 23.

Behavioral Observation Recording Methods

The first step in the process of behavioral observation is to select a system of data collection. The system selected needs to be appropriate to the behavior being observed.

It is possible to measure behavior across a number of dimensions, including: the rate (how often a behavior occurs within a specific time period), duration (how long a behavior lasts), latency (how long it takes before a child starts performing a behavior), topography (what the behavior looks like—verbal or nonverbal), force (the intensity of the behavior), or locus (where the behavior occurs).

The decision to use a specific recording method is made on the basis of the dimension of behavior that is to be observed. There are three general approaches to use when collecting data: (1) analyzing written records (anecdotal reports), (2) observing tangible products (permanent product recording), and (3) observing a sample of behavior (event, interval, time sampling, duration, and latency recording).

Anecdotal Reports

Written anecdotal reports provide as complete a description as possible of a child's behavior in a particular setting or at a particular time. The teacher, assistant, therapist, psychologist, or caregiver makes notes with respect to significant observations of a child's behavior or activities. This information may be factual or interpretive; the individual recording the information needs to indicate the nature of the data (i.e., fact, judgment, interpretation). The report might include specific circumstances or events that preceded and/or followed a behavior. The recorder often includes specific words the child used, and notes conditions under which the child exhibited certain behaviors. It is useful to record specific occurrences of a temper tantrum, seizure, or a notable social interaction.

The purpose of the anecdotal report is to describe individuals and interactions. This description assists the professional or caregiver in identifying the relationship between the child's behavior and what occurs just prior to or following a certain behavior. Anecdotal reports or records help teachers, parents, or early intervention professionals determine what factors are eliciting or maintaining behaviors. Wright (1960) suggests these guidelines for writing anecdotal reports:

1. Before beginning to write anecdotal data, describe the setting as you see it. In writing, describe the individuals in the setting, their relationships to one another, and the activity occurring as you are about to begin recording (e.g., snack time, free play).
2. Include everything the target student(s) says and does in the description, indicating to whom or to what.
3. Include everything said and done to the target student(s) and by whom in the description.

4. As you are writing, clearly differentiate fact from your impressions or interpretations of cause and reaction.
5. Provide some time indications in order to be able to judge how long particular
   responses or interactions are occurring.

After making observations, analyze anecdotal reports to determine the
behavior(s), if any, that may need to be the subject of a behavior change program. The anecdotal record usually concentrates on the content or style of behavior
rather than on precise measurement of its frequency or duration. Sometimes the
observations in the initial anecdotal format are difficult to separate into individual
behaviors and relationships. Bijou, Peterson, and Ault (1968) offer a system for
sequence analysis; they rewrite an anecdotal report in a form that reflects a
behavioral view of environmental interactions as shown in Table 11-3. This *ABC*
(i.e., antecedent–behavior–consequent event) analysis approach is very helpful
in discerning functional relationships that may exist (Sulzer-Azaroff & Mayer,
1977).

Permanent Product Samples

Another method of data collection involves gathering samples of the child's work
at regular intervals to be able to compare earlier works with later products. Permanent products to collect include arts and crafts work, pencil and crayon drawings, audiotapes of vocalizations, or videotapes of social behavior or task performance. This method of data collection is useful in demonstrating changes and
progress in a child's skills or behavior to caregivers and professionals. These
samples give concrete evidence of the child's progress over time and assist in program evaluation as well.

Observing Samples of Behavior

Several data collection procedures to use to gather ongoing performance information are described in the following six sections.

Event or Frequency Data
A behavior is monitored and recorded in terms of the number of its occurrences.
The teacher or caregiver counts the number of discrete instances of a particular
behavior as it occurs during an observation period. Examples of behaviors (see
Figure 11-1) that lend themselves to event recording are the number of tantrums
occurring daily, the number of times a child talks to another child, the number
of times a child requests assistance (Ruggles, 1982).

Duration Data
The observer records how long a behavior lasts. A stopwatch is used to measure
the total time a child engages in the targeted appropriate or inappropriate

TABLE 11-3 Structuring of an Anecdotal Record

Time	Antecedent	Response	Consequence
5:15 P.M.	1. Mother (M.) working at sink		
		2. Chris (C.) throws pans on floor.	
			3. M. picks up pans; tells C. to stop.
		4. C. spins lid.	
			5. M. restacks pans; closes cabinet.
	6. M. returns to sink.		
		7. C. throws lid across room; spills salt shaker.	
			8. M. stops cooking; cleans salt.
		9. C. spins pan lid.	
	10. M. opens refrigerator.		
		11. C. pulls refrigerator door.	
			12. M. holds door.
		13. C. screams.	
			14. M. slams door; talks to C.

Source: Reprinted with the permission of Merrill Publishing Company, an imprint of Macmillan Publishing Company, Inc., from *Applied Behavior Analysis for Teachers, Third Edition,* by Paul A. Alberto and Anne C. Troutman, Copyright © 1990 by Merrill Publishing Company.

behavior. A behavior appropriate for duration recording is how long a child plays with a toy or with another child.

Latency Data

The observer records the time that elapses before a child exhibits a particular behavior. A stopwatch is used to measure the elapsed time. The length of time it takes a child to begin to respond after instructions are given to a direction or command is appropriate for latency data collection.

Date _____	Time Observation Began _____		
Observer _____	Time Observation Ended _____		
	Total Minutes of Observation _____		
Child Name	Talley Behavior	Total	Summary Rate = $\dfrac{\text{number of instances}}{\text{minutes of observation}}$

FIGURE 11-1 Sample Data Sheet for Recording and Summarizing the Frequency of Children's Behaviors

Source: From K. Eileen Allen & Elizabeth M. Goetz, *Early Childhood Education: Special Problems, Special Solutions,* p. 87. Copyright © 1982. Rockville, MD: Aspen Publications. Reprinted with permission.

Interval Recording
The specific observation period is divided into a number of predetermined intervals (e.g., 15 or 30 seconds). Behavior is observed in terms of whether a defined behavior occurs within a specified time interval. Using a stopwatch or prerecorded tape with interval times, note the presence or absence of a behavior during each interval. Count the number of intervals in which the behavior occurs and divide by the total number of intervals observed to obtain a ratio of total intervals. Then, report this number as a percentage. Use the interval recording procedures when gathering data on behaviors that do not have a discrete beginning or end such as time on- or off-task. Figure 11–2 is a sample data sheet (Ruggles, 1982).

Time Sampling
Time sampling is similar to interval recording, but the intervals in time sampling are often minutes rather than seconds. Behavior is monitored by observing a child at designated time intervals to record the presence or absence of a specific behavior. The teacher predetermines the length of time between observations (e.g., 5 minutes, 30 minutes) and makes observations exactly at the defined time intervals. At the end of the observation period, the teacher counts the number of intervals in which the child exhibited the behavior and divides this number

Date _____   Total No. of Intervals Observed _____

Observer _____   Total Intervals Where Behavior Scored ____

Percentage of Intervals

Child Observed _____ $\left(\dfrac{\text{total intervals scored}}{\text{total int. observed}} \times 100\right)$ _____

E 1

E 2

E 3

E 4

E 5

FIGURE 11–2   Sample Data Sheet for Recording and Summarizing Interval Observations of a Single Child

Source: From K. Eileen Allen & Elizabeth M. Goetz, *Early Childhood Education: Special Problems, Special Solutions*, p. 90. Copyright © 1982. Rockville, MD: Aspen Publications. Reprinted with permission.

by the total number of intervals to obtain a percentage measure. One useful time sampling procedure is referred to as *mapping* (Ruggles, 1982). Mapping may be used to learn more about children's interactions with others or with particular areas of the classroom. The data sheet shown in Figure 11–3 might be used to record a child's behavior in a playground setting.

Rate Data

Behavior is recorded in terms of how fast a child performs a given skill. For example, the teacher may record how many buttons a child can button in one minute's time.

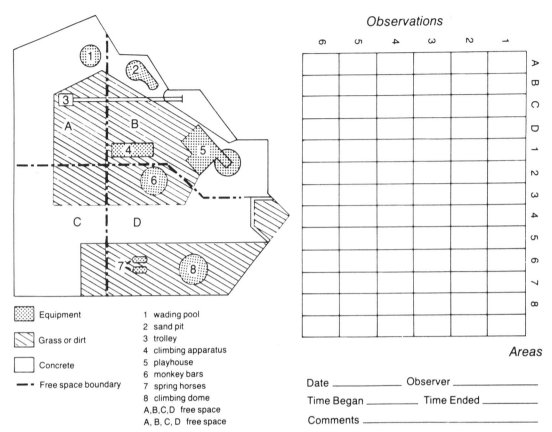

FIGURE 11–3 **Sample Data Sheet for Time Sampling Procedure of Mapping**

Source: From K. Eileen Allen & Elizabeth M. Goetz, *Early Childhood Education: Special Problems, Special Solutions,* p. 95. Copyright © 1982. Rockville, MD: Aspen Publications. Reprinted with permission.

Ecological Observation Recording Methods

Narrative Descriptions

Anecdotal Records

This record requires no particular length, time, or structure for recording information. It is simply a collection of descriptions about one child whenever there is something of interest to record. Although it often reflects the observer's own biases, it can help her or him gain information concerning a child's behavior and what conditions might be reinforcing them. For example, an aggressive child may react to certain children more than others or to certain kinds of statements from other children.

Brandt (1972) developed guidelines for researchers using anecdotal records. These guidelines also are useful for teachers:

1. Write down the anecdote as soon as possible after it occurs. Although this may be difficult for busy teachers, it is important to have as accurate information as possible.
2. Identify the basic action of the key person and what was said. Try to record word for word what was said by the child in question and the response. It may be necessary to paraphrase what other individuals have said, but the basic flavor of the conversation should be preserved.
3. At the beginning of the anecdote, include a statement that identifies the setting, time of day, and the basic activity. Record what is happening if it is different from what was expected.
4. Preserve the sequence of the episode. The anecdote should have a beginning, middle, and end.
5. Include three levels of action in the anecdote: (1) The molar level reports the main activity described in the anecdote. (2) The subordinate molar level records more specific information about the main activity. (3) The molecular level gives a qualitative description of the activity. (Adapted from Thurman & Widerstrom, 1985.)

Running Records

The running record provides more complete information than does the anecdotal record because it continues over a period of time. The writer of the running record must record behavior at scheduled, predetermined intervals. In a running record, an observer records everything that occurs within a given time period by taking notes or videotaping. It is a useful technique for the teacher to get a general idea of what is happening and the sequence of events. The running record is useful at any point in the assessment process, whether it is to make a placement decision, identify areas of child functioning that need further assessment, or for program evaluation.

Once the observation is complete, the observer has a large volume of information that is not organized in any meaningful way. The observer needs to convert the information into another form for analysis and interpretation. The way it is organized may significantly influence the meaning of the information. The observer studies the data in order to form categories or uses previously identified categories to study the data. The *Behavioral Coding System* (BCS) (Jones, Reid, & Patterson, 1975) is an example of a psychometrically validated and reliable coding system that reduces the likelihood of misinterpretation. The BCS contains 28 observable categories that can be noted during an observation.

Examples of Environmental Assessment Measures

Environmental assessment measures, which usually are used in the formative stages of development, vary in the amount of field-testing conducted and in their demonstrated technical adequacy. These scales use different types of assessment formats to obtain information. Examples of these formats include clinical rating scales, anecdotal records, criterion checklists, and normative assessments.

The *Home Observation for Measurement of the Environment* (HOME) (Caldwell & Bradley, 1972) measures the content, quality, and responsiveness of a young child's home environment. It is widely used and is appropriate for use with children ages birth to five years.

Another example of an ecological assessment is the *Early Childhood Environmental Rating Scale (ECERS)* (Harms & Clifford, 1980). It rates the quality of the classroom setting across a number of variables using a 7-point scale.

The authors of the ECERS also developed two additional measures that incorporate the same approach and framework for environmental assessment but focus on two types of environments. These instruments are *The Infant/Toddler Environment Rating Scale (ITERS)* (Harms, Cryer, & Clifford, 1990) and the *Family Day Care Rating Scale* (FDCRS) (Harms & Clifford, 1990). The ITERS is designed to assess the quality of care children under 30 months get. The FDCRS is designed to assess the quality of care in a day care setting. Although the ECERS, ITERS, and FDCRS focus on different settings, some subscales on each include: personal or basic care routines, furnishings and display for children, language-reasoning experiences, social development or interaction, creative or learning activities, and adult needs.

Quantifying Ecological Variables

Behavioral researchers have attempted to use the ecological perspective to quantify important classroom variables in early childhood settings. Observational instruments have been developed to incorporate all of the classroom activities and thus to quantify these variables. Researchers at the University of Pittsburgh (Carta, Sainato, & Greenwood, 1988) categorize six major areas of observational measures:

1. Topographic features
   - Type of activity
   - Presence of teacher(s)
   - Physical arrangement
   - Instructional grouping
2. Materials
   - Type
   - Location
   - Access
3. Teaching codes or categories of instruction
   - Child guided
   - Teacher guided
4. Response codes
   - Engagement
   - Quantity and/or quality of response
5. Classroom interactions (peers and teachers)
6. Transition codes (p. 225)

Observations have then been converted into percentages or frequency counts. For example, the time children spend in instructional groups and the type of instruction used has been compared between classrooms. The amount of child-guided and teacher-guided instruction in the regular preschool setting has been compared with special education preschool settings. This information then becomes the basis for describing the behaviors of a successful child in the least restrictive environment (Carta, Sainato, & Greenwood, 1988).

In 1985, Carta and Greenwood developed another system for observation. The authors attempted to assess how different dimensions interact in the classroom. These researchers wanted to learn more about how these variables influence children's development and achievement over time (Carta, Sainato, & Greenwood, 1988). *The Ecobehavioral System for Complex Assessment of Preschool Environments* (ESCAPE) (Carta, Greenwood, & Atwater, 1985) can be used to examine the interactions between ecological variables and student behaviors. Table 11–4 summarizes ESCAPE categories and codes.

Describing Relationships and Contingencies

Direct observation of children's behavior is useful for describing and analyzing behavioral-environmental relationships or contingencies. Appropriate uses for direct observation include:

1. Documenting whether a perception concerning a child is factual or representative of actual behavior;
2. Determining how a child behaves in a given setting under specified conditions;
3. Clarifying the child's presenting problem;
4. Selecting instructional materials and techniques;
5. Providing a clearer analysis or close-up of curricular skill attainment;
6. Evaluating progress (change) in specific aspects of development;
7. Providing concurrent validity measures of other forms of assessment;
8. Determining local or situational norms to provide the parameters of *normality* and *abnormality*;
9. Assessing low-functioning, nonverbal children who cannot or will not respond to traditional assessment situations. (Adapted from Neisworth & Bagnato, 1988, p. 44.)

Basic Guidelines

Neisworth and Bagnato (1988) summarize some basic guidelines to incorporate into an ecological assessment:

1. The family should be a significant partner in the process.
2. These assessments should focus heavily on naturalistic observations of the child's behavior in normal routines.

TABLE 11-4 Preschool Observation System for Measuring Ecobehavioral Interactions

	Description	Code examples
Ecological categories		
Designated activity	Subject of instruction	Free play, pre-academics, language, fine motor
Activity initiator	Classification of person choosing activity	Teacher, child, no one
Materials	Objects with which the student engages	Manipulatives, art materials, large motor equipment
Location	Physical placement of the observed student	On floor, at tables, on equipment, in chairs
Grouping	Size of group in same activity as observed student	Small group, large group, one-to-one
Composition	Mix of handicapped and nonhandicapped students in instructional group	All handicapped, mixed, all nonhandicapped
Teacher behavior categories		
Teacher definition	Primary adult interacting with observed student	Teacher, aide, student teacher, ancillary staff
Teacher behavior	Teacher behavior relative to observed student	Verbal instruction, physical assisting, approval, disapproval
Teacher focus	Direction of teacher's behavior	Target child only, target child and entire group, other than target child
Student behavior categories		
Appropriate behaviors	Specific on-task responses	Fine motor, gross motor, academic work
Inappropriate behaviors	Behaviors which compete with appropriate behaviors	Acting-out, off-task, self-stimulation
Talk	Verbalizations	Talk to teacher, talk to peer

Source: From Carta, J. J., Sainato, D. M., & Greenwood, C. R. (1988). Advances in the ecological assessment of classroom instruction for young children with handicaps. In S. L. Odom and M. B. Karnes (Eds.), *Early Intervention for Infants and Children with Handicaps: An Empirical Base,* pp. 217–239. Baltimore, MD: Paul H. Brookes Publishing. Reprinted with permission.

3. Assessment instruments should be nondiscriminatory, taking into account the child's cultural background, economic status, and family value systems.
4. The assessment should plan for the next most probable placement for the child.

Summary

Assessing environments helps determine whether they facilitate or hinder children's development. Teachers and examiners need to be aware of the complexities of environmental assessments, appreciate the dynamic and interactive nature of environments, and be familiar with a variety of assessment strategies. Information from ecological assessment has important implications with regard to a student's achievement. Information from an environmental assessment is useful when planning and implementing environmental changes (Bailey, 1989). Including ecological variables to evaluate preschool programs increases the ability to depict and explain the effectiveness of early intervention programs as well as to determine what factors contribute to their success.

Suggested Group Activities

1. Divide participants into groups and suggest various behaviors that could be observed through the following formats:

   - In vivo or naturalistic;
   - Simulated or staged;
   - Role-play or prompted circumstances.

   Have groups share their ideas with others.

2. The instructor distributes cards with tasks (e.g., tieing a shoe, washing hands, putting on a jacket). Have each person devise a developmental checklist by task to analyze a skill.

3. Design a brief rating scale to use with children that would address one of the following domains: cognitive, fine/gross-motor, self-help, or social skills.

4. Take turns role-playing socially interactive *scenes* (either group- or instructor-generated). The remaining participants should carefully write an anecdotal report and later compare their observational skills. Include the following information:
   - A description of the setting (as described in the vignette);
   - The relationship between the individuals;
   - The activity that is occurring;
   - Objective reporting of the actions;
   - Direct quotes, if possible;
   - Use of the *ABC* sequence analysis approach;
   - A description of the beginning, middle, and end of the interaction.

5. Suggest behaviors and/or skills that would be best assessed through the use of: (a) anecdotal reports, (b) event or frequency data, (c) duration data, (d) latency data, (e) interval recording, (f) time sampling, (g) rate data, and (h) running records.

6. Design an ecological study for either a home or school setting. Include items to address the needs of culturally and linguistically diverse children and their families. If possible, administer the instrument and write a brief interpretative analysis.

References

Alberto, P. A., & Troutman, A. C. (1986). *Applied behavior analysis for teachers.* Columbus, OH: Merrill.

Allen, K. E., & Goetz, E. M. (1982). *Early childhood education.* Rockville, MD: Aspen.

Bailey, D. B. (1989). Assessing environments. In D. B. Bailey & M. Wolery (Eds.), *Assessing infants and preschoolers with handicaps* (pp. 97–118). Columbus, OH: Merrill.

Bijou, S. W., Peterson, R. F., & Ault, M. H. (1968). A method to integrate descriptive and experimental field studies at the level of data and empirical concepts. *Journal of Applied Behavior Analysis, 1,* 175–191.

Brandt, R. M. (1972). *Studying behavior in natural settings.* New York: Holt, Rinehart, and Winston.

Caldwell, B., & Bradley, R. (1978). *Home observation for measurement of the environment (HOME).* Little Rock: University of Arkansas, Human Development.

Carta, J. J., & Greenwood, C. R. (1985). A methodology for the evaluation of early intervention programs. *Topics in Early Childhood Special Education, 5,* 88–104.

Carta, J. J., Greenwood, C. R., & Atwater, J. B. (1985). *ESCAPE: Ecobehavioral system for complex assessment of preschool environments.* Kansas City: University of Kansas, Juniper Gardens Children's Project, Bureau of Child Research.

Carta, J. J., Sainato, D. M., & Greenwood, C. R. (1988). Advances in the ecological assessment of classroom instruction for young children with handicaps. In S. L. Odom & M. B. Karnes (Eds.), *Early intervention for infants & children with handicaps: An empirical approach* (pp. 217–240). Baltimore: Paul H. Brookes.

Harms, T., & Clifford, R. M. (1990). *The family day care rating scale.* New York: Teachers College Press.

Harms, T., & Clifford, R. M. (1980). *Early childhood environment rating scale (ECERS).* New York: Teachers College Press.

Harms, T., Cryer, D., & Clifford, R. M. (1990). *Infant/toddler environment rating scale.* New York: Columbia University, Teachers College Press.

Jones, R.R., Reid, J. B., & Patterson, G. R. (1975). Naturalistic observation in clinical assessment. In P. McReynolds (Ed.), *Advances in psychological assessment* (Vol. 3). San Francisco: Jossey-Bass.

Neisworth, J. T., & Bagnato, S. J. (1988). Assessment in early childhood special education: A typology of dependent measures. In S. L. Odom & M. B. Karnes (Eds.). *Early intervention for infants and children with handicaps: An empirical approach* (pp. 23–50). Baltimore: Paul H. Brookes

Ruggles, T. R. (1982). Some considerations in the use of teacher implemented observation procedures. In K. E. Allen & E. M. Goetz (Eds.), *Early childhood education: Special problems, special solutions* (pp. 77–104). Rockville, MD: Aspen.

Simeonsson, R. J. (1986). *Psychological and developmental assessment of special children.* Boston: Allyn and Bacon.

Sulzer-Azaroff, B., & Mayer, G. R. (1977). *Applying behavior-analysis procedures with children and youth.* New York: Holt, Rinehart and Winston.

Thurman, S. K., & Widerstrom, A. H. (1985). *Young children with special needs: A developmental and ecological approach.* Boston: Allyn and Bacon.

Wright, H. (1960). Observational study. In P. J. Mussen (Ed.), *Handbook of research methods in child development* (pp. 71–139). New York: Wiley.

Chapter 12

Program Evaluation

Program evaluation is the process of determining the progress of children and the efficacy of the total intervention program in an objective and systematic way. Early interventionists must be accountable; they must evaluate the quality of the overall intervention program and document its impact on the children and families it serves.

The purpose of an evaluation is to determine the program's ability to achieve its stated goals. Program evaluation is the final link in the model presented by Bagnato, Neisworth, and Munson (1989). If the program is not accomplishing what it started out to do, changes can be made to improve its effectiveness.

It is important to make judgments about three aspects of a program: (1) overall child outcomes, (2) the efficiency and quality of program operations (e.g., staff performance), and (3) consumer satisfaction (Peterson, 1987).

Child Outcomes

The main reason to evaluate a program is to show that the child is progressing as a result of special services. The evaluation documents overall child outcomes by assessing the impact the program is having on children and families. Programs need to demonstrate that the intervention it is providing is effective. It is important to verify that the gains and progress are greater than would be attributable to maturation alone, that is, if the child and family were not participants in the program.

Efficiency and Quality of Program Operations

Are the children showing sufficient gains based on the cost of the special services? Is the program running smoothly and is the staff performing effectively? Programs need to provide evidence that money is being well spent. Positive program evaluation data justifies requests for funds. These data also provide the basis for improvements and changes in services for the children and families.

Consumer Satisfaction

What do parents of children enrolled think about the program? Do they feel the program is beneficial to their children? Ask caregivers to rate the program, the services they received, and the way in which the staff deals with them and their children (Peterson, 1987).

Obtaining feedback from individuals who are intrinsic and extrinsic to the program is important. When performing an evaluation, collect internal feedback from participants and staff working in a program and external feedback from individuals who are not directly associated with the program.

Considerations in Planning Program Evaluations

Consider these general guidelines when planning and implementing program evaluations:

1. The program philosophy, objectives, and evaluation should all relate to each other. The objectives of the program define the kind of content to be evaluated. The factors to be evaluated define the kind of documentation needed.

2. Perform a multidimensional evaluation of early intervention programs. Use a variety of assessment instruments and involve all of the professionals from all disciplines who participate in the program.

3. Plan the evaluation design carefully. Select instruments that assess the major thrust of the program and the population being served. Measure the specific goals of each child's intervention to determine program effectiveness. For example, if social interaction is a major component, choose assessment instrument(s) that will measure the gains made as a result of the intervention.

4. Assessment and evaluation strategies need to be feasible and practical: Will the staff have time to implement these strategies? Can the program afford the cost of internal and external reviews?

5. Be sure the program evaluation overlaps the entire assessment process used in the intervention program. The evaluation needs to be both formative (during the program) and summative (at the end of the services). Diagnosing individual children's capabilities and deficits at the beginning of the program also serves as baseline performance monitoring data or formative evaluation.

6. Programs also need to measure the outcomes of various family variables, such as the use of support networks or the family's ability to manage resources.

How to Begin Program Evaluation

Many programs operate without a consistent and well-planned system of evaluation. Program evaluation is most likely to be done if the methods used are the least intrusive and burdensome to program deliverers.

For programs new to the evaluation process it is a good idea to proceed in stages: Start with some simple indicators, provide feedback to staff, and then move to more in-depth evaluations. DeStefano, Howe, Horn, and Smith (1991) provided an example of a simple program assessment to use to begin program evaluation (see Figure 12–1).

One way to develop a system of program evaluation is to form a committee to decide how to conduct the evaluation. Include representatives from the groups—administration, teachers, and families—that are most affected by program policies. Effective program evaluation needs to have staff cooperation and people to implement any necessary changes.

The next step is for the committee to look at the program's philosophy, goals, and objectives to determine what the program is trying to accomplish. The committee also has to determine whether the program is adhering to its philosophy, goals, and objectives. Another factor to consider is what evaluation tools to use and how often an evaluation is to be done. Note that individuals collecting data need feedback about the data emerging from the process so they do not lose interest. After considering how to evaluate the program and implement the procedures selected, the committee is able to determine the weak and strong points of the program and its effectiveness.

Types of Evaluation Information

Federal legislation mandates yearly reviews for Individual Education Plan (IEP) and semiannual reviews for Individualized Family Service Plans (IFSP). Individual programs sometimes require more frequent updates. The two types of evaluation information to be collected are: (1) formative and (2) summative. Formative and summative evaluations provide the basis for selecting tools and deciding when to do an evaluation.

Formative Evaluation

Formative evaluation is periodic, i.e., done on a daily, weekly, or monthly basis. Examine individual assessment results to determine if each child is making progress in relationship to the goals of the program. A purpose of formative evaluation is to help program planners keep on target. The information obtained is used to make changes as the need arises and as the program is being developed. If program planners want to know how quickly the children are progressing on their IEP goals so timely revisions can be made, they need to evaluate often and then make immediate changes. This may be done on a monthly, weekly, or daily basis, depending on the child and the particular objective.

Best Practices
Evaluating Early Childhood Special Education Programs

Self-Assessment Form

Completed by _____ Date _____

Component 1: Curriculum Programming

This is an important part of my program. | I'd like my program to improve in this area. | I'm not sure why this is important | I'd like more information on this.

Child-Centered Assessments

☐ ☐ ☐ ☐ Do assessments consider the child's:
- needs in the current environment?
- current level of functioning?
- potential needs in future environments?

Curriculum Content

☐ ☐ ☐ ☐ Are skills chosen for training:
- useful for the child now?
- appropriate for the child's developmental age?
- teachable during various activities?
- intended to increase the child's ability to interact with people and things?
- taught during times in which using the skill is appropriate and makes sense?

☐ ☐ ☐ ☐ Are goals and objectives embedded into both naturally occurring daily activities and planned activities?

IEPs and IFSPs

☐ ☐ ☐ ☐ Do the IEPs and IFSPs you write—
1. Reflect family concerns, strengths, and needs?
2. Set objectives based on an analysis of the child assessments and the ecological inventory?
3. Identify training needs that are:
   - useful?
   - immediately applicable?
   - appropriate to the child?
   - appropriate to the family?
4. Allow the child to join in an activity even though unable to perform the skills without help?

Component 2: Organization of the Learning Environment

Settings

☐ ☐ ☐ ☐ Are settings based upon the individual needs of the child and family?

☐ ☐ ☐ ☐ Settings should be flexible, because those needs change over time. Are yours?

☐ ☐ ☐ ☐ Is your use of space efficient and safe? Do you have:
- clearly posted general safety guidelines?
- clearly delineated areas (listening/reading area, academic area, art area ...)?
- adequate space to move about?
- appropriate modifications in place (door closed to reduce noise, adequate lighting, carpeted area)?

Organization of Instruction

☐ ☐ ☐ ☐ Does the schedule:
- assign staff responsibilities?
- assign children to activities and classroom areas?
- allow adequate time for each activity?
- allow the use of appropriate equipment and materials?

☐ ☐ ☐ ☐ Are activities organized to:
- reflect the educational needs of each child?
- address appropriate educational objectives throughout the day?
- provide a balance of 1-to-1, small-group, and large-group instruction?
- promote integration with typical peers?

☐ ☐ ☐ ☐ Are activities:
- appropriate to the needs of the child and family?
- useful to the child?
- making use of naturally occurring cues?

FIGURE 12-1   Best Practices Form

This is an important part of my program.
I'd like my program to improve in this area.
I'm not sure why this is important.
I'd like more information on this.

☐ ☐ ☐ ☐ Are activities and materials within the settings:
- challenging but not too difficult?
- encouraging child responses?
- encouraging social interactions at home and school?
- using appropriate adaptive equipment?

☐ ☐ ☐ ☐ Are some materials accessible, so the child can explore independently? Are other materials hard to reach, so the child has to request them?

Monitoring Child Progress

☐ ☐ ☐ ☐ Are procedures for collecting data clearly understood?

☐ ☐ ☐ ☐ Are data analyzed on a regular basis?

☐ ☐ ☐ ☐ Is progress reported to the family on a regular basis?

☐ ☐ ☐ ☐ After the data are analyzed, are changes made by team consensus?

Component 3: Social Skills

Assessing Social Skills

☐ ☐ ☐ ☐ Do assessments take place in home and/or preschool settings, such as at play or at meals?

☐ ☐ ☐ ☐ Do you use scales that measure functional social interaction, such as:
- the *Maternal Behavior Rating Scale*?
- the *SCIP Checklist*?
- one designed by preschool staff?

☐ ☐ ☐ ☐ Do your assessments determine the:
- frequency (how often) of social interactions?
- quality (positive/negative) of social interactions?
- appropriateness (to the situation) of social interactions?

☐ ☐ ☐ ☐ Do your assessments analyze the level of continued interactions between children and/or between children and adults?

Training Social Skills

☐ ☐ ☐ ☐ Are the social skills you target for training:
- based upon results of child-centered assessments done within natural settings?
- skills the child needs in the current environment and/or in future environments?

☐ ☐ ☐ ☐ Are your training activities:
- done during naturally occurring times throughout the day? (Are they done during wake up, at meals, when getting ready to go outside, when saying hello or goodbye, and when the child needs assistance?)
- appropriate to the child's chronological age? (Do infants interact mostly with adults? Do toddlers interact more with other children?)
- encouraging generalization of skills by providing a variety of interactions with different people? (For infants, this may include parents, aunts, uncles, siblings, grandparents, baby sitters. Toddlers might also interact with other toddlers and nonrelatives.)
- designed to encourage continued interactions between the child and others? (Do they encourage the parents and the child to play together? Do they encourage modeling by parents and teachers, and tutoring by peers? Is the environment structured to encourage interactions?)

Arranging for Interaction

☐ ☐ ☐ ☐ Are materials, activities, and space arranged to encourage social interactions between the child and others, both children and adults?

☐ ☐ ☐ ☐ Is physical space arranged so that the child is near other?

☐ ☐ ☐ ☐ Do materials and activities encourage interactions between children? Are materials arranged so that several children can play together with them?

FIGURE 12-1   *(Continued)*

Component 4: Using Support Services

This is an important part of my program.
I'd like my program to improve in this area.
I'm not sure why this is important.
I'd like more information on this.

Using Support Services

☐ ☐ ☐ ☐ Does your use and coordination of support services take into account:
- the family's needs (as identified in the IFSP)?
- the child's needs (as identified in the IEP or IFSP)?
- the teacher's skill level?
- the specialists' knowledge?
- the team model (multidisciplinary, inter-disciplinary, or transdisciplinary)?

Using Support Services—Within the Preschool/Home-Based Program

☐ ☐ ☐ ☐ Do the instructional goals reflect the child's needs across all disciplines?

☐ ☐ ☐ ☐ Are specialists' recommendations incorporated within the child's daily routine, such as those of the:
- physical therapist (crawling to a snack)?
- vision therapist (object location—locating a chair)?
- nutritionist (orange juice for vitamin C)?

☐ ☐ ☐ ☐ Do parents, teachers, and specialists share information?

☐ ☐ ☐ ☐ Do the specialists and the preschool teacher share information in order to expand their own learning?

☐ ☐ ☐ ☐ Do activities promote generalization of skills?

Using Support Services— Among Agencies

☐ ☐ ☐ ☐ Do you use support services from many different agencies, such as the:
- child's preschool?
- Department of Health?
- Department of Human Services?
- hospital?
- elementary school?
- university speech and hearing services department?

This is an important part of my program.
I'd like my program to improve in this area.
I'm not sure why this is important.
I'd like more information on this.

☐ ☐ ☐ ☐ To coordinate services among agencies, do you:
- identify a case manager from the "lead" agency?
- encourage case managers to gather the information that helps them identify services appropriate for the child and family?
- share information with the family so the family can make decisions about the child's program?
- locate, obtain, and use community resources according to the needs of the individual child and family?

Component 5: Family Involvement

Family Assessment

☐ ☐ ☐ ☐ Are your family assessments individualized? Do they reflect family priorities?

☐ ☐ ☐ ☐ To achieve that, do you use:
- direct assessments (such as the *Family Needs Survey* [Bailey and Simeonsson] or the *Family Needs Scale* [Dunst, Trivette, and Deal])?
- reports from parents?
- professional observations?
- assessment?
- setting goals (via the IFSP)?
- intervention?
- program evaluation?

Family-Professional Partnership

☐ ☐ ☐ ☐ Do professionals work with the family, so that family members become partners in making decisions? Do families know about:
- their child's disabilities?
- how to solve problems?
- how to become effective advocates?
- relevant laws and their own rights?
- available community resources (such as day care, preschools, respite care . . .)?

FIGURE 12–1 *(Continued)*

The column headers (rotated) read, from left to right:
- This is an important part of my program.
- I'd like my program to improve in this area.
- I'm not sure why this is important.
- I'd like more information on this.

Communication Strategies

☐ ☐ ☐ ☐ Does the case manager make sure that the family and the service personnel (such as the social worker and the physician) communicate with each other?

☐ ☐ ☐ ☐ Does the case manager use progress notes and other written messages, personal contact, and telephone calls to keep communication channels open?

Component 6: Transition

Transition Planning

☐ ☐ ☐ ☐ When planning to move the child to a new setting, do you:
1. Select a transition coordinator from each setting?
2. Set a general timeline for transition?
3. Convene a family meeting to:
   • determine transition needs for child, family, and staff in the current setting?
   • develop and write transition goals for the current setting?
   • identify options for placement?
   • obtain the parents' consent to release the child's name to the future program?
4. Arrange for family and staff to visit and evaluate possible future programs?
5. Convene a family meeting to:
   • determine transition needs for child, family, and staff in the future setting?
   • develop and write transition goals for the future setting?
   • determine placement?
6. Update the child's file and send it to the next program staff?
7. Have parents and both staffs evaluate transition procedures?

Transition from Home or Other "Noneducational" Setting

☐ ☐ ☐ ☐ To build interagency cooperation and communication, do you:
• try to coordinate services with agencies that screen and serve children?
• identify a case manager(s) or transition coordinator?
• organize a referral system and share records and information between agencies?
• begin the transition process?

Transition Between Programs

☐ ☐ ☐ ☐ When you prepare to move the child to a new setting, do you organize a transdisciplinary team that includes various members, such as:
• family members?
• the baby sitter?
• the transition coordinator?
• the current teacher?
• the future teacher?

☐ ☐ ☐ ☐ Do assessments and curricula in current and future programs focus upon the current and future needs of the child and the family?

Is the child's individual transition plan:
• part of the IEP or IFSP?
• written and implemented by the transition team?

☐ ☐ ☐ ☐ Do you have a strategy for follow-up and evaluation to assess the success of the transition?

☐ ☐ ☐ ☐ Do you keep communication lines open through personal contact, telephone calls, and/or written messages, in case problems arise?

© 1991 by

Communication Skill Builders, Inc.
3830 E. Bellevue/P.O. Box 42050
Tucson, Arizona 85733
(602) 323-7500

Key

☐ This is an important part of my program.

☐ I'm not sure why this is important.

☐ I'd like my program to improve in this area.

☐ I'd like more information on this.

Item #8055

ISBN 0-88450-379-8
Catalog No. 7749
Printed in the U.S.A.

FIGURE 12–1 *(Continued)*

Source: From *Best Practices: Evaluating Early Childhood Special Education Programs* by Donna M. DeStefano, Ardin G. Howe, Eva M. Horn, and Bruce A. Smith, copyright © 1991 by Communication Skill Builders, Inc., P.O. Box 42050, Tucson, AZ 85733. Reprinted with permission.

Summative Evaluation

A summative evaluation is an assessment of overall gains at the end of a longer period of time. To evaluate how much progress the children make over the course of a year, one would want to evaluate at least twice—at the beginning of the year and at the end of the year. The product or outcome scores summarize the performance of participants in a program and allow judgments as to whether or not gain has been significant, thereby reflecting on the efficacy of the program.

Framework for Monitoring Child Progress

Bricker (1986) suggests a three-level framework, as shown in Figure 12–2, that provides a useful system for measuring child/family change and program impact.

Level 1: Measuring Progress Toward Weekly Training Targets

Specific data collection formats that relate to the child's objectives need to be devised to collect data on social interactions, language, and so on. Data collection procedures for monitoring child progress including ongoing performance data—frequency, percentage, rate, duration—might include trial-by-trial, probes, or observational samples. It is also possible to use permanent product samples, anecdotal recording, or diaries. This type of data collection is discussed in chapter 11.

While conducting the instructional program, data collection on progress can be accomplished. The interventionist records the behavior and teaches a new response at the same time. Bricker (1986) suggests the use of a grid format to record data. Table 12–1 is an example of how to use this type of format. This grid allows the teacher to target several different skills for each child across activity groups. The antecedent, response, and consequence written on the data grids are from the child's individual program plan.

Collect some form of weekly information and then systematically compare it with data from other weeks. Plot the data on individual graphs to show percentage, proportion, frequency, or rate of change over time. Program personnel need to choose a simple and useful way to examine and display their weekly data to monitor progress and make sound educational decisions.

Level 2: Measuring Progress Toward Long-range Goals and Training Objectives

Collect data on child and family progress toward long-range goals and objectives, and analyze the data in terms of total or subgroup scores if they are to be used in program evaluation. Bricker (1986) suggests that published instruments with

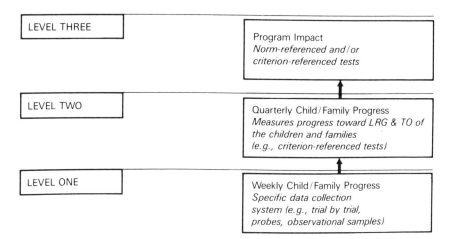

FIGURE 12–2   A Three-level Framework to Direct Selection of Instruments for Measuring Progress

Source: Reproduced from *Early Intervention for At-Risk and Handicapped Infants, Toddlers, and Preschool Children.* Copyright © 1989, Diane D. Bricker. Used by permission of VORT Corporation, Palo Alto, CA.

norms and/or reliability and validity information are the most useful. Use the same instruments that were used during the initial assessment when the child entered the program and that were used to develop the IEP and IFSP. In addition, use developmental checklists or behavior rating scales to provide information on child progress.

To analyze progress toward long-range goals, the predicted progress of each child and the group as a whole need to be compared to actual progress. Pretest data can be compared to posttest data. Another method is to establish timelines for goal attainment for the family and child and then compare the actual progress with these expectations. Use the outcome data to determine program effectiveness as well as to modify goals and expected rate of attainment as appropriate.

Level 3: Measuring Progress Toward Program Goals

It is possible to use assessment of progress toward program goals to evaluate child/family changes, but it is usually more useful for assessing the total impact of the program on the children. Norm-referenced and/or criterion-based tests generally are more desirable. However, the interventionist needs to consider the problems of using norm- and criterion-based tests to determine progress toward specific program objectives. (See chapters 9 and 10.) Choose a measure that is sensitive enough to detect change in children's performance and compatible with the program philosophy and goals.

TABLE 12-1 Sample Data Grid

> **Key**
> A = antecedent
> R = response
> C = consequence (error correction)
> 1–5 = number of trials

Domain	Teresa	Michael	Stephen

Communication	A: wants, needs, ideas
	R: sign and/or vocalize
	C: + receive object, praise
	  − repeat model (physical assistance to sign)
	
	1 2 3 4 5
		A: desired object
		R: vocalize
		C: + receive object
		  − model
		
		1 2 3 4 5
			A: teacher model of word
			R: word approximation
			C: + praise
			  − repeat model
			
			ball 1 2 3 4 5
			book 1 2 3 4 5
			dog 1 2 3 4 5

Social	A: peer offers toy (prompted by teacher) R: looks at peer and takes object C: + praise from peer − physical assistance 1 2 3 4 5		
Cognitive		A: verbal direction R: follow appropriately C: + praise − physical assistance "come here" 1 2 3 "sit down" 1 2 3	
Gross Motor			A: bell ringing; time to transition to next group R: pulls to standing & walks with one hand held to next group C: + plays with objects at next group − physical assistance 1 2 3 4 5

Source: From Diane D. Bricker, *Early Education of At-Risk and Handicapped Infants, Toddlers, and Preschool Children,* Second Edition, p. 328. Copyright © 1986. Glenview, IL: Scott, Foresman and Company. Reprinted with author's permission.

Linking Intervention and Program Evaluation

The AEPS System

Bricker and Cripe (1992) propose a system for linking intervention and evaluation activities in early intervention. The information obtained during the assessment phase in order to develop IEPs and IFSPs guides the selection of intervention content and strategies. The linked system is illustrated in Figure 12–3.

The first box is the assessment component that provides the information for developing the child's IEP/IFSP. The second box is the IEP/IFSP that outlines the intervention content by providing the goals and objectives for the child and family. The actual intervention is the third box. Bricker and Cripe (1992) suggest an activity-based approach to guide children's goals and objectives. The *Assessment, Evaluation and Program System* (AEPS) for infants and children (Bricker, Gentry, & Bailey, 1992) is the basis for this intervention in this model. Evaluation is the final step that provides systematic feedback on program effects.

Because the initial assessment is used to develop the IEP/IFSP and then forms the content of the intervention, it is extremely important that initial and follow-up assessments provide interventionists and caregivers with an accurate and comprehensive profile of the child. Notari, Slentz, and Bricker (1991) recommend using curriculum-based assessments to develop these intervention plans.

Content and Organization of the AEPS

The AEPS covers six curricular skill areas: fine-motor, gross-motor, self-care, cognitive, social-communicative, and social. The particular sets of skills or behaviors in each domain are sequenced developmentally and divided into strands that organize related groups of behaviors under a common category. Table 12–2 gives an overview of the six domains with their strands and shows how the behaviors under a common category are grouped (Bricker & Cripe, 1992).

Items on the AEPS are sequenced to facilitate the assessment of a child's ability to perform a particular skill within a developmental sequence. Each strand contains a series of test items called goals and objectives. Based on a child's abilities and needs, the AEPS goals can be used to develop annual goals on a child's IEP/IFSP. The goals are arranged in hierarchical skill sequence.

Three methods of data collection are allowed. The preferred method is observation. The examiner is able to view the topography or the form of the behavior, when and how frequently the behavior occurs, and the environmental events that may influence the infant's or child's performance. If the examiner does not have the opportunity to observe the behavior during classroom activities, a situation may be created to elicit the behavior. Sources of reported information from the examiner, family, therapists, or written documentation from medical reports also may be used for data collection. An example of a portion of a completed form for the gross-motor domain for a one-year-old child is shown in Figure 12–4.

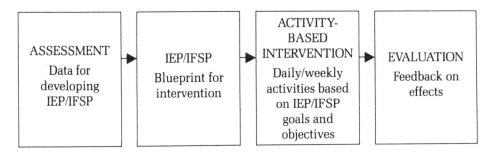

FIGURE 12-3   Linked Assessment, Intervention, and Evaluation System

Source: From Bricker, D. D., & Woods, J. J., *Activity-based Approach to Early Intervention*, p. 89, Figure 3. Copyright 1992. Baltimore, MD: Paul H. Brooks Publishing Co. Reprinted with permission.

The AEPS is an excellent example of how early interventionists efficiently and easily link assessment, intervention, and program evaluation. It is possible to use *any* curriculum-based assessment in this same way.

Other Systems for Linking Assessment to Program Evaluation

The AEPS system is one example of how to link assessment to program evaluation. Linder's (1990) *Transdisciplinary Play Based Assessment* (TPBA) also may be incorporated into both formative (ongoing) and summative (year-end) evaluations. The child is involved in play sessions throughout the year, and these sessions allow the team to record progress and modify the child's individual objectives. The team then repeats the TPBA process at the end of the year for pretest or post-test evaluation data. Other curriculum-based assessments to use are discussed in chapter 10.

This type of evaluation depends on the appropriateness of the objectives. There is no evaluation of the appropriateness of the objectives; it is simply a matter of whether or not the objectives are reached.

Advantages of this model are: (1) it is simple and easy to understand and interpret, (2) it focuses on measurable objectives and encourages accountability, (3) it provides the teacher with a way to demonstrate progress, and (4) the intervener is an integral part of the evaluation team.

The disadvantages include: (1) the evaluation process only includes objectives in the child's program; (2) it does not allow for evaluation of outcomes that are not easily written as objectives; and (3) the evaluation is only as good as the objectives, i.e., if the objectives are not appropriate, the evaluation is not valid.

TABLE 12–2 Overview of the AEPS Test Domains and Strands for Birth to 3 Years of Age

Domains	Strands
Fine motor	A. Reach, grasp, and release B. Functional use of fine motor skills
Gross motor	A. Movement and locomotion in supine and prone position B. Balance in sitting C. Balance in mobility in standing and walking D. Play skills
Self-care	A. Feeding B. Personal hygiene C. Undressing
Cognitive	A. Sensory stimuli B. Object permanence C. Causality D. Imitation E. Problem solving F. Preacademic skills G. Interaction with objects
Social. Communication	A. Prelinguistic communicative interactions B. Transition to words C. Comprehension of words and sentences D. Production of social-communicative signals, words, and sentences
Social	A. Interaction with adults B. Interaction with environment C. Interaction with peers

Source: From Bricker, D. D., & Woods Cripe, J. J., *Activity-based Approach to Early Intervention,* p. 96, Figure 5. Copyright 1992. Baltimore, MD: Paul H. Brookes Publishing Co. Reprinted with permission.

Additional Evaluation Models

Input-based Judgmental Evaluation

This model examines a program on the basis of the extent to which it is designed according to *best practices* as documented in the literature. The emphasis is on elements of planning and needs assessment and program structure (e.g., ratio of adults to children).

Output-based Judgmental Evaluation

An output-based judgmental or goal-free evaluation evaluates both the appropriateness of goals and objectives and the attainment of them. An outside

Gross Motor Domain

S = Scoring Key	Q = Qualifying Notes
2 = Pass consistently	A = Assistance Provided
1 = Inconsistent performance	B = Behavior Interfered
	R = Reported Assessment
0 = Fail consistently	M = Modification/Adaptation
	D = Direct Test

Name: Susy Smith

Test Period: I
Testing Date: 10/91
Examiner: DB

	IEP	S	Q	S	Q	S	Q	S	Q
A. Movement and locomotion in supine and prone position									
1. Moves body parts independently of each other		2	R						
1.1 Turns head past 45°		2	R						
1.2 Kicks legs		2	R						
1.3 Waves arms		2	R						
2. Rolls segmentally		2							
2.1 Rolls: back to stomach		2							
2.2 Rolls: stomach to back		2							
3. Creeps	✓	0							
3.1 Rocks in creeping position	✓	0							
3.2 Assumes creeping position		2							
3.3 Crawls		2							
3.4 Pivots on stomach		2							
3.5 Bears weight while reaching		2							
3.6 Lifts head/chest off surface		2							
B. Balance in sitting									
1. Assumes sitting	✓	0							
1.1 Assumes hands and knees position		0							
1.2 Regains sitting after reaching		0							
1.3 Regains sitting after leaning		0							
1.4 Sits on floor	✓	1							
1.5 Sits on floor with support		2							

FIGURE 12-4   **An Example of a Portion of the AEPS Gross Motor Domain Recording Form**

Source: From Bricker, D. D., and Woods Cripe, J. J., *Activity-Based Approach to Early Intervention*, p. 98, Figure 7. Copyright 1992. Baltimore, MD: Paul H. Brookes Publishing Co. Reprinted with permission.

evaluator, who has little knowledge of the program, determines the actual impact of the program, regardless of stated objectives. The premise is that preknowledge of program goals interferes with the evaluator's unbiased identification of program effects (Scriven, 1974). The evaluator does not need to know what the objectives are and only is concerned with identifying the actual impact of the program and whether this impact is intended or not.

The advantages are: (1) the evaluator is in a discovery role and is not limited to simply determining if goals were reached or not, (2) the person with a new perspective does not have tunnel vision and generally is open to seeing more results, and (3) the evaluation is more critical. The disadvantages include: (1) the lack of structure; (2) no standard to use consistently; and (3) this model doesn't include interveners and is conducted after the fact, thus, it is not an integral part of the program (Jordan et al., 1988).

Decision-Facilitation Evaluation

This model is designed to reduce or eliminate personal judgment. There are three steps in this process: (1) delineations of the information to be collected, (2) obtaining the information, and (3) providing information to decision makers (Stufflebeam, 1971, 1974). The evaluator gathers data that are presented to the program's decision makers for action. The program's decision makers are responsible for continuing, terminating, or modifying the program. This model is expensive and time-consuming and few programs are able to carry it out.

Naturalistic Evaluation

This model is based on an ethnographic approach to data gathering and includes case studies, observations, interviews, and participant surveys. A running record is kept of the individual child's behavior and a description of the context in which the behaviors are occurring. Through the analysis of patterns of individual behaviors, interactions can be discovered. These analyses can focus on specific goals of units and, thus, provide information on the child's attainment of goals (Benner, 1992).

Strategies for Program Evaluation

Peterson (1987) provides an excellent guide for questions and alternative strategies for evaluating the effectiveness of an early intervention program. Her chart, which concisely summarizes program evaluation information, is shown in Table 12–3. Program evaluation is not a simple procedure occurring at one time; ongoing assessment is a crucial part it and is at the heart of effective decision making (Peterson, 1987).

It is important to develop a data-collection method to obtain the needed information in as easy and as accurate a way as possible. Collect data from a variety

TABLE 12–3 Examples of Strategies for Evaluating Program Effectiveness

Evaluation Task	Possible Formative and Summative Questions to Be Asked	Potential Data Collection/ Evaluation Strategies

Evaluation of Efficiency and Quality of Program Operations	• Are program purposes, goals, and philosophy clearly defined and understood by all staff members?
	• Are operational procedures clearly defined and followed by staff?
	• Are staff activities organized and well coordinated?
	• Are individual staff members performing their jobs effectively and showing continuous growth in their own professional skills?
	• Are programs planned for individual children and based on objective evaluation information?
	• Does daily curriculum reflect children's IEP objectives, and are individualized programs carried out according to plan?
	• Does staff have objective means for assessing how well children are doing?
	• Are records up-to-date, readily available, well-organized, and used in effective ways?
	• Do staff members communicate on program matters in timely way and work together effectively as a team with children and in solving program issues?
	• Are things staff members say are important reflected in daily operations and services?
	• Is program in compliance with local and state regulations for education and for early childhood programs?
	• Do parents feel welcome, fairly treated by the program, and view their role as an important member of the intervention team? How do staff members view their relationships with parents?
	• Do parents understand the program and have sufficient information about its operations? Does staff think parents are given enough information and understand what the program is about?
		Internal Review Strategies
		• Regular staff business meetings to address issues and review progress
		• Regular consultations and interviews with individual staff by program director or coordinator
		• Formal review procedure for giving individual staff feedback on job performance at least once or twice a year
		• Formal staff evaluation of program operations using
		  –round table discussions
		  –checklist or questionnaire evaluation on program
		  –questionnaire or checklist for self-evaluation of job role and performance
		• Informal staff or client feedback using
		  –personal conferences
		  –suggestion box
		  –presentations by individual staff on activities or procedures, with discussion and reactions
		
		External review strategies
		• Observations and review by outside evaluation team
		• Comparison of program operations with those of other similar programs staff may visit
		• Review of program by state and local officials to determine compliance with regulations
		• Examination of program documents, records, and operational procedures by a consultant, advisory board members, representatives of funding agency, colleagues from otgher similar programs, or experts in the field
		• Formal and informal meetings between parents and staff, among staff members, or between staff and administrative personnel, for purposes of program review and problem solving

TABLE 12-3 *(Continued)*

Evaluation Task	Possible Formative and Summative Questions to Be Asked	Potential Data Collection/ Evaluation Strategies
	• Do parents have suggestions on how the program can be improved? What do parents view as strengths and weaknesses in the program? • Do staff members have suggestions on how the program can be improved? What do they view as program strengths and weaknesses? • How do other agencies who refer children to the program view its services and relationships with parents and with the community at large?	*Summative evaluation strategies* • Formal evaluation/feedback questionnaires or rating scales for parents and for staff • Formal interviews with parents or staff concerning perceptions of program and own role in program • Formal feedback using rating form from referring agencies • Review and data collection by outside party using observations, interviews, or questionnaires

of sources using a variety of methods. Typical data-collection methods include unobtrusive measures, observation, interviews, and questionnaires. Jordan et al. (1988) provide an excellent overview of these data-collection methods.

Unobtrusive Measures

These sources are nonreactive because children and families are not required to change their routine and may not even be aware that data is being gathered. Examples of unobtrusive measures include finding out how many books parents checked out of the resource library or the number of toys checked out of the toy-lending library (Casto, 1988).

Observations

Teachers or other professionals systematically record operationally defined behaviors in a normal setting. Definitions are based on observable, measurable characteristics of the behavior. (See chapter 11, Ecological Assessment.)

Interviews

Interviews are either unstructured, semistructured, or structured (Patton, 1980). In this method, the interviewer asks questions and records responses. The unstructured interview has a general objective, but respondents are allowed to respond in their own words and time. This type of interview is vulnerable to bias and often provides uninterpretable information.

The semistructured interview provides a list of questions to ask all respondents. If needed, however, the interviewer can pursue responses in greater depth. This also does allow for subjective biases, because the interviewer can lead the respondent to desired responses.

The structured interview is like an objective questionnaire. There is a specific set of questions to ask and sometimes respondents are even given a set of specific answers from which to choose. Responses are limited so that the interviewer cannot lead the respondent.

The following guidelines for engaging in the structured interview have been adapted by Johnson (1988) from Udinsky, Osterlind, and Lynch (1981):

1. *Word questions clearly and encourage effective communication between the interviewer and the respondent.*
2. *Make respondents aware of the purpose of each question they are asked.*
3. *Be sure that the population from which the respondents have been selected actually has the information being sought and that the interview questions permit the reasonable recovery of this information.*
4. *Avoid leading questions; that is, questions that suggest a desirable or preferred answer.*
5. *Ensure that a clear frame of reference is provided for each question, so that all respondents hear questions in the same way.* (p. 191)

Questionnaires

Data collection often involves using questionnaires. It is important to keep the purpose of the questionnaire in mind and limit its length. It also is imperative to state questions as simply and unambiguously as possible.

Questions need to be objective and provide a set of alternative responses. Using open-ended questions allows the respondent to explain answers and, thus, to provide more information. Specific statements may be rated by using a scale—strongly agree to strongly disagree. Udinsky, Osterlind, and Lynch (1981) recommend providing an even-numbered scale to force the individual to make an affirmative or negative decision about a statement.

Summary

A comprehensive evaluation plan enhances a program's ability to meet the needs of young children with special needs and their families, and it also will establish accountability for everyone involved.

Suggested Group Activities

1. Design a questionnaire for parents that would give them an opportunity to provide feedback to the program and its staff. When should it be distributed? Would all staff have access to the results of the questionnaire? How often should parents provide input?

2. Have participants assume roles of service providers during a mock program evaluation committee meeting. Discuss issues that might surface, offer suggestions for resolution, including reports on data collection.

3. Practice using Bricker's grid format (Table 12-1) to record data. Have the group suggest possible student activities that would include antecedents, responses, and consequences. Discuss its usefulness and practicality.

4. Brainstorm a list of unobtrusive measures that could provide information about children, families, and familiar environments.

5. Write several questions for an interview that would apply to these format styles: unstructured, semistructured, structured. What are the advantages and disadvantages of each? Would one style be more appropriate for a particular type of problem or issue?

6. Ask participants to list the kinds of evaluations used in their own programs. What type of evaluation is it—formative, summative, internal, external? What type might be used in the future?

References

Bagnato, S. J., Neisworth, J. T., & Munson, S. M. (1989). *Linking developmental assessment and early intervention: Curriculum-based prescriptions* (2nd ed.). Rockville, MD: Aspen.

Benner, S. M. (1992). *Assessing young children with special needs: An ecological perspective.* New York: Longman.

Bricker, D. D. (1986). *Early education of at-risk and handicapped infants, toddlers, and preschool children.* Glenview, IL: Scott, Foresman.

Bricker, D., & Cripe, J. J. W. (1992). *An activity-based approach to early intervention.* Baltimore: Paul H. Brookes.

Bricker, D., Gentry, D., & Bailey, E. J. (1992). AEPS test. In D. Bricker (Ed.), *Assessment, evaluation, and programming system (AEPS) for infants and children: Vol. 1. AEPS measurement for birth to three years.* Baltimore: Paul H. Brookes.

Casto, G. (1988). Research and program evaluation in early childhood special education. In

S. L. Odom and M. B. Karnes (Eds.) *Early intervention for infants and children with handicaps: An empirical base* (pp. 51–62). Baltimore: Paul H. Brookes.

DeStefano, D. M., Howe, A. G., Horn, E. M., & Smith, B. A. (1991). *Best practices: Evaluating early childhood special education programs.* Tuscon: Communication Skill Builders.

Johnson, L. J. (1988). Program evaluation: The key to quality programming. In J. B. Jordan, J. J. Gallagher, P. L. Hutinger, & M. B. Karnes (Eds.), *Early childhood special education: Birth to three.* Reston, VA: The Council for Exceptional Children. (ERIC Document Reproduction Service No. 302964)

Jordan, J. B., Gallagher, J. J., Hutinger, P. L., & Karnes, M. B. (Eds.) (1988). *Early childhood special education: Birth to three.* Reston, VA: Council for Exceptional Children. (ERIC Document Reproduction Service No. 302964)

Linder, T. (1990). *Transdisciplinary play-based assess-*

ment: *A functional approach to working with young children*. Baltimore: Paul H. Brookes.

Notari, A., Slentz, K., & Bricker, D. (1991). Assessment-curriculum systems for early childhood/special education. In D. Mitchell & R. Brown (Eds.), *Early intervention studies for young children with special needs* (pp. 160–205). London: Chapman and Hall.

Patton, M. Q. (1980). *Qualitative evaluation methods.* Beverly Hills: Sage.

Peterson, N. L. (1987). *Early intervention for handicapped and at-risk children: An introduction to early childhood—special education,* Denver: Love.

Scriven, M. (1974). Evaluation perspectives and procedures. In W. J. Popham (Ed.), *Evaluation in education: Current applications* (pp. 1–93). Berkeley: McCutchan.

Stufflebeam, D. L. (1974) Alternative approaches to educational evaluation: A self-study guide for educators. In W. J. Popham (Ed.), *Evaluation in education: Current application* (pp. 95–143). Berkeley: McCutchan.

Stufflebeam, D. L. (1971). The relevance of the CIPP evaluation model for educational accountability. *Journal of Research and Development in Education, 5*(1), 19–23.

Udinsky, F. F., Osterlind, S. J., & Lynch, S. W. (1981). *Evaluation resource handbook: Gathering, analyzing, reporting data.* San Diego: EdiTS.

Part IV

Assessment Within Domains

This part discusses assessment within each of the major domains in more depth. P.L. 99-457 specifies the evaluation and assessment of the child must include:

> (ii) *An evaluation of the child's level of functioning in each of the following developmental areas:*
> *(a) Cognitive development.*
> *(b) Physical development, including vision and hearing.*
> *(c) Language and speech development.*
> *(d) Psychosocial development.*
> *(e) Self-help skills.* (Federal Register, 1989, p. 26320)

Norm- and criterion-referenced assessments usually include some or all of these major areas. Some instruments include more skills within age ranges or assess a broader range of skills. Assessment in early childhood generally surveys the child's developmental status and skill level across the following domains:

- Cognitive development and preacademic skills
- Language skills (receptive and expressive)
- Social-emotional development
- Self-help skills
- Skills of daily living (play skills, adaptive skills, safety skills, functional living skills)
- Motor development (gross and fine)

In addition to assessment of developmental levels with norm- and/or criterion-referenced tests, specific skill areas that are of concern to the practitioner are assessed further by individual therapists in their treatment domain. Often, speech and language pathologists do further testing to more clearly assess the language development of a child, and an occupational therapist examines feeding and dressing skills. In both instances, the outcomes of these more detailed assessments are of concern to all the professionals involved with this child. The purpose is to provide a clearer picture of the child.

Interrelationships Across Domains

Organizing this final part into various domains helps organize and focus thinking in specific areas. However, examiners need to remember that most functional acts are based in multiple domains. Children's behavior cannot be segmented into separate domains. For example, a child requesting more juice requires motor movements of the mouth and possibly extending a cup to a teacher, the social awareness of another individual, the desire for more juice, and the communicative function of making a request. All domains interact with one another and these interactions are important to consider throughout the assessment process.

Infants view the world comprehensively—dividing the infant's capacities into separate domains is not possible in the early weeks of life and is somewhat artificial throughout the first three years. When a baby is asked to release a block into a cup, the examiner hopes to learn about the child's understanding of container and contained, about his or her motor control and about how she or he relates to instructions from an adult (McCune et al., 1990).

The primary goal of assessment is to determine the level of developmental accomplishment and the manner in which the child's organizing abilities appear to be operating at that time. Ideally, the assessment shows a pattern of performance in a range of developmental domains, provides information about strengths that are promoting development, and shows weaknesses that may be limiting the child's learning or performance (McCune et al., 1990).

The last part of this guide is intended to give a greater depth of understanding of the assessment process within the major domains. Each of the chapters provides the early interventionist with a general framework for assessment in these major domains, and presents a variety of commonly used instruments. Considerations for selecting assessment instruments are mentioned as well as factors to weigh in the decision-making process.

Within each domain, the examiner always needs to keep the reasons for a child's assessment in mind: Is the particular test appropriate for determining strengths and weaknesses or for developing instructional goals and strategies? Is the assessment instrument appropriate given the individual child's abilities and disabilities?

Chapter *13*

Cognition

What Is Cognition?

Cognition, as Neisser (1967) defines it, is the process by which sensory input is transformed, reduced, elaborated, stored, recovered, and used. In the infant, cognition is seen as sensorimotor intelligence – the integration and refinement of sensory and motor behaviors to produce adaptive responses to the environment in the child's first two years. Sensorimotor intelligence enables the child to solve problems through the integration of perception, postural adjustments, and movement. These skills begin with the simplest reflexive behaviors and provide the basis for acquiring increasingly more complex mental behaviors as children respond and adapt to sensory information through motor interactions with the environment (Langley, 1989).

Studies of infant perception that define it as the ability to learn or receive environmental information by using the senses of sight, hearing, smell, and/or touch, indicate that the senses are the starting point for the infant's expanding understanding of the world (Lockman, 1983). Normal infants experience a steady refinement of their perceptual and cognitive capabilities through early childhood (Yarrow, Rubenstein, & Pedersen, 1975). The heart of cognitive development is the infant's ability to organize and make sense of the environment that he or she is exposed to. The attainment of cognitive skills requires that the child take advantage of basic sensory input as she or he explores his or her environment. For the child to attain cognitive skills, three basic psychological processes need to be operating – attention, perception, and memory.

Cognitive development has been described as the progressive change in internal mental processes, such as thinking, reasoning, and remembering, or as the ability to function adaptively in the world by receiving information from the environment, understanding the meaning of this information, and using it to plan appropriate actions (Dunst, 1981; Piaget, 1952; Raver, 1991). The term *cognition* traditionally has been used to refer to symbolic and representational thought processes that do not necessarily depend on immediate perceptual input (Rossetti,

1990). Cognitive development, intelligence, and the ability to learn are all related concepts. Definitions of intelligence have three basic components in common: (1) the capacity to learn; (2) the sum total of knowledge an individual has acquired; and (3) the ability to adjust to various environments, particularly new situations (Robinson & Robinson, 1976).

The cognitive domain comprises a multitude of skills and abilities that are associated with intelligence. These skills are related to attention, discrimination, imitation, spatial relationships, temporal relationships, causality, reasoning, classification, sorting, sequencing, and problem solving (Benner, 1992). Early cognitive development is expressed by skills in communication, social, and motor development (Bayley, 1969; Dunst, 1981). Cognition is an area of development that is particularly difficult to isolate from other domains in assessment. Although it can be conceptualized as separate from other domains, such as motor or language functioning, the outward manifestation of cognition usually necessitates motor or language output. The separation of expressive actions and behaviors that provide evidence of cognitive understanding from cognitive understanding itself is crucial to the assessment process (Benner, 1992).

Tests for very young children, which purport to measure ability, intelligence, mental developmental age, and preacademic skills, all are considered measures of cognition. Often, they are based on the assumption that motor skills and/or language skills reflect cognitive ability. Cognition is much broader than the preacademic skills found on developmental instruments.

Cognition cannot be directly observed or measured but is inferred from the behavior of an individual within a specified context. Changes in behavior in similar contexts over time are assumed to reflect changes in cognitive functioning or structuring (Rossetti, 1990).

Theories of Cognitive Development

The basic perspectives regarding the cognitive development of young children are developmental theory, cognitive stages theory, behavioral theory, and information-processing models. These theories provide the framework for understanding the process of cognitive development and also provide the basis for assessment instruments.

Developmental Theory

The developmental or maturational theory is structured around the child's natural patterns of growth and development. A child develops cognitively as a result of his or her maturation. Maturation of the nervous system governs a child's physical, psychological, cognitive, and social development. Gesell (1925) and Knobloch and Pasamanick (1974) used developmental data on normal infants and children to identify motor milestones. They consider children who are unable to perform such tasks at certain ages to be developmentally delayed (Benner, 1992).

Cognitive Stages Theory

Cognitive stages theory focuses on a child's progression to higher cognitive functions in sequential stages. Jean Piaget put forth the most comprehensive theory of cognitive development. According to Piaget, movement from one stage to another results from environmental interactions characterized by assimilation and accommodation of the child's schemes, or understandings, of the world. A child assimilates information from the environment to fit his or her own schemes of the world. As she or he becomes aware that contradictions exist with his or her views of the world, disequilibrium occurs, and the child accommodates his or her thinking to alleviate the contradiction.

Behavioral Theory

An underlying foundation of the behaviorist theory is that all behavior is learned. The behaviorist model incorporates both classical conditioning, in which the child has no control over his or her response, and instrumental conditioning, where the child's response to stimuli determines consequences. Chapter 11, Ecological and Direct Observation, discusses this theory.

Information-processing Theory

Information-processing models of cognitive development are grounded in the functioning of the psychological processes of attention, perception, and memory. Information processing explains decision making, knowing, and remembering as processes. The mind is seen as a complex cognitive system such as a computer. Cognition becomes what the computer must know in order to produce a behavior. Most of the research on information-processing theory builds on Piaget's theory (Paget, 1989).

Techniques for Assessment

Age Differences

Benner (1992) points out that various techniques need to be used in the assessment of cognition depending on the age and characteristics of the child. Techniques that are appropriate for neonates are different from those used with one year olds. Langley (1989) provides a summary of assessment instruments appropriate for infants—examples are shown in Table 13-1. The same is also true for assessing the cognitive abilities of preschoolers as compared to toddlers. Preschool children are involved in traditional preacademic activities and have well-developed receptive and expressive language skills.

TABLE 13-1   Instrument Summaries

Instrument	Age Range	Areas Assessed	Unique Features
Adaptive Performance Instrument (Gentry, 1980)	Birth–24 months	Sensorimotor skills; physical intactness, reflexes and reactions, gross- and fine-motor, social, self-care, and communication skills	Particularly useful with severely and profoundly handicapped children; scoring criteria afford qualitative observations; suggestions for adaptations for physically, visually and hearing impaired and deaf/blind.
Comprehensive Developmental Evaluation Chart (Cliff, Carr, Gray, Nymann, & Redding, 1975)	Birth–3 years	Reflexes, gross-motor manipulation, vision, feeding, receptive and expressive language, cognitive-social, and hearing	May serve as a quick but thorough screening instrument and is particularly sensitive at the earlier ranges; very heopful in a team approach to screening children
Developmental Diagnosis (Knobloch, Stevens, & Malone, 1980)	Birth–3 years	Adaptive, gross motor, fine motor, language and personal-social behaviors	The manual provides excellent descriptions and illustrations of developmental skills; a must for anyone involved in the assessment of infants and young children
Generic Skills Assessment Profile (McLean, Snyder-McLean, Rowland, Jacobs, & Stremel-Campbell, no date)	2 weeks–30 months (approximate)	Object relationships, comprehensions, imitation, expressive communication, representation, and dyadic interaction	A graphic profile of early aspects of communication that may be used to chart the progression of language development; the profile may be scored from informal interactions and observations of children as they participate in developmental assessments; particularly useful in a team approach

Child Characteristics

Appropriate techniques also vary according to certain characteristics of each child. Techniques appropriate for children who have intact hearing and/or vision often are not suitable for children who are deaf or blind. Children with motor impairments and who may be nonverbal present tremendous challenges to anyone interested in assessing their cognitive functioning. Standard testing procedures do not work, are unfair, and need to be replaced with adaptive approaches (Benner, 1992).

Age Ranges

The age ranges for which instruments are intended vary widely. For example, the age range for the *Bayley Scales of Infant Development* are standardized on infants and toddlers from birth to 30 months. The *McCarthy Scales of Children's Abilities* (McCarthy, 1972) can be used with children age 2 years, 6 months to 8 years, 6 months. Instruments with wide age ranges have the advantage of being able to be used with many children. They also offer consistency for longitudinal studies. However, instruments that attempt to cover wide age ranges tend to be less accurate and test fewer skills. The number of items that can be included at each age level is often very limited on tests that cover a broad age span.

Multiple or Single Domain

Some instruments are designed exclusively for assessing cognitive functioning, while others include multiple domains. A list of common assessment instruments, ordering information, age range, and area(s) assessed (Raver, 1991) is shown in Table 13-2. Appendix A also presents typical cognitive assessment instruments available for use by the early interventionist. The *Bayley Scales of Infant Development* (Bayley, 1969), the *Battelle Developmental Inventory* (Newborg et al., 1984), the *Vulpe Assessment Battery* (Vulpe, 1977), and the *Infant Psychological Development Scales* (Uzgiris & Hunt, 1975) are commonly used to evaluate the cognitive functioning of infants and toddlers with disabilities.

Examples of Assessment Instruments

The majority of instruments used to assess cognitive functioning are based on the traditional psychometric methodology or the more recent developmental theory approach. Each approach can be helpful in assessing current functioning, detecting delayed or abnormal development, planning an intervention program, or evaluating the effectiveness of an intervention.

TABLE 13-2 Assessment Instruments for Cognition and Development

Instrument Name	Ordering Information	Age Range	Area(s) Assessed
Adaptive Performance Instrument (API)	Project CAPE Special Education Dept. University of Idaho Moscow, ID 83843	Birth– 2 years	All
Assessment in Infancy: Ordinal Scales of Psychological Development	Harper & Row 345 S. Lincoln Dr. Troy, MI 63379	Birth– 2 years	Cognition
Battelle Developmental Inventory	DLM Teaching Resources P.O. Box 4000 One DLM Park Allen, TX 75002	Birth– 8 years	All
Baley Scales of Infant Development	Psychological Corporation 757 Third Ave. New York, NY 10017	1 week– 30⅓ months	Mental Motor
Brazelton Neonatal Behavioral Assessment Scale	J. B. Lippincott Co. E. Washington Sq. Philadelphia, PA 19105	Approx. Birth– 28 days	Behavioral
Callier-Azusa Scale	Callier Center for Communication Disorders University of Texas–Dallas 1966 Inwood Rd. Dallas, TX 75235	Birth– 4 years	All
Carolina Curriculum for Handicapped Infants and Infants at Risk	Paul H. Brookes P.O. Box 10624 Baltimore, MD 21285-0624	Birth– 24 months	All
Diagnostic Inventory of Early Development	Pratt Education Media 200 Third Ave., SW Cedar Rapids, IA 32404	Birth– 7 years	All
Early Intervention Developmental Profile	University of Michigan Press 615 E. University Ann Arbor, MI 48109	Birth– 3 years	All
Early Learning Accomplishment Profile (E-LAP)	Kaplan School Supply 1310 Lewisville-Clemmons Rd. Lewisville, NC 27023	Birth– 36 months	All
EMI Assessment Scale	EMI Department of Pediatrics University of Virginia Medical Center Box 232 Charlottresville, VA 22908	Birth– 24 months	All

TABLE 13.2   *(Continued)*

Instrument Name	Ordering Information	Age Range	Area(s) Assessed
Gesell Developmental Scales (Revised)	Psychological Corporation 757 Third Ave. New York, NY 10017	4 weeks– 36 months	All
Hawaii Early Learning Profile (HELP)	VORT Corporation P.O. Box 11552-A Palo Alto, CA 94306	Birth– 3 years	All
Infant Scale of Communicative Intent (ISCI)	Speech & Language Svcs. St. Christopher's Hsptl. 5th & Lehigh Ave. Philadelphia, PA 19133	Birth– 18 months	Receptive/ expressive language
Minnesota Infant Development Inventory (MIDI)	Behavior Science Systems P.O. Box 1108 Minneapolis, MN 55440	1– 15 months	All
Peabody Developmental Motor Scales—Revised	Teaching Resources Corp. 50 Pond Park Road Hingham, MA 02043-4382	Birth– 7 years	Gross and fine motor
Play Assessment Scale	University of Washington Rebecca R. Fewell, Ph.D. EEU WJ-10 Seattle, WA 98195	Birth– 36 months	All
Receptive-Expressive Emergent Language Scale (REEL)	University Park Press 233 E. Redwood St. Baltimore, MD 21202	Birth– 36 months	Receptive/ expressive language
Rockford Infant Development Evaluation Scales (RIDES)	Scholastic Testing Svc. 480 Meyer Rd. Bensenville, IL 60106	Birth– 4 years	All
Sequenced Inventory of Communication Development (SICD)	Western Psych. Services 12031 Wilshire Blvd. Los Angeles, CA 90025	4– 48 months	Receptive/ expressive language
Sewall Early Education Developmental Profiles (SEED)	Sewall Rehab. Center 1360 Vine St. Denver, CO 80206	1– 42 months	All
Uzgiris-Hunt Ordinal Scales of Infant Psychological Development	PRO-ED 5341 Industrial Oaks Blvd. Austin, TX 78735	Birth– 2 years	Cognition
Vulpe Assessment Battery	National Institute of Mental Retardation 4700 Keele St. Downsview, Ontario M3J 1P3	Birth– 72 months	All

Source: Reprinted with the permission of Macmillan Publishing Company from *Strategies for Teaching At-Risk and Handicapped Infants and Toddlers: A Transdisciplinary Approach* by Sharon A. Raver. Copyright © 1991 by Macmillan Publishing Company.

Traditional Methodology

Traditional scales include norm- and criterion-referenced instruments that outline a sample of behaviors considered characteristic of a specific age range. Traditional tests produce scores such as a developmental quotient, developmental index, intelligence quotient, developmental age and mental age. Criterion-referenced tests that have similar content to the norm-referenced instruments also have been developed. The items on both types of tests represent developmental milestones in the child's maturation. These are used primarily for screening and diagnosis of cognitive ability.

One of the first instruments that provides a well-standardized methodology for assessing infant mental development is the *Bayley Scales of Infant Development* (Bayley, 1969). This scale of sensorimotor intelligence is most commonly used in programs with infants and children with handicaps (Simeonsson, 1986). The scale consists of three independent measures of mental, psychomotor, and social domains. The Bayley scales have well-respected standardization qualities, proven effectiveness in measuring skills of children with disabilities, and tests a large number and variety of behaviors at each age level. The Bayley scales need to be administered by psychologists trained to work with infants and young children and are most appropriate for children with cognitive delays and/or mild sensory and communication impairments (Langley, 1989).

The *Griffiths' Mental Development Scales* (Griffiths, 1954; 1979) are designed specifically for use with children with delays and deficits of various natures. The scales extend from birth to eight years with a separate instrument for measuring abilities during the first two years *(The Abilities of Babies)*. The *Griffiths* is British in origin, and thus experts question the applicability of the norms for today's U.S. children. Beail (1985) suggests that the Griffiths' scales be used interchangeably with the Bayley scales.

The *Battelle Developmental Inventory* (BDI) (Newborg et al., 1984) assesses all domains of development and allows the use of observations, interviews, and direct testing for evaluation. Langley (1989) suggests the most attractive features of the BDI are the suggested adaptations of items for specific handicapping conditions, the excellent and extremely comprehensive standardization data, and the provision for three methods of assessment—observation, interview, and direct testing. These researchers note the primary shortcomings to be the sparsity of items in each age range and the lack of items providing comprehensive assessment of the full range of sensorimotor cognitive abilities.

The *Vulpe Assessment Battery* (Vulpe, 1977), designed for children who are atypical, is not standardized and is to be used as a diagnostic-prescriptive assessment tool for instructional planning. The items on the Vulpe are all grouped in categories of behavior and a pattern of strengths and weaknesses may be derived. The Vulpe is comprehensive and is useful for informal assessment over a period of time.

It is important to remember that traditional assessment instruments cannot successfully assess all children. The child with profound sensory, motor, social, or intellectual deficits may exhibit insufficient behavior to be measured by such tools. This child warrants the use of nontraditional, process-oriented assessments to gain meaningful information for program planning (see chapter 7). Paget (1989) provides a comprehensive list of norm-referenced measures of cognitive development that should be helpful to early interventionists. This list reviews the utility of the tests in terms of preschoolers with disabilities (see Table 13-3).

Criterion-referenced and curriculum-referenced scales, such as the *Early Intervention Developmental Profile* (Rogers et al., 1981), and the *Hawaii Early Learning Profile* (Furuno et al., 1979), have Piagetian-based cognitive sections although they do not provide a thorough assessment of Piaget's sensorimotor concepts (Langley, 1989). In contrast, the *Carolina Curriculum for Infants and Toddlers with Special Needs* (Johnson-Martin, Jens, Attermeier, & Hacker, 1991) covers all developmental domains through 24 months and offers a comprehensive assessment of cognitive skills. This tool has a number of well-organized subsections for assessing Piaget's sensorimotor concepts. The purpose of curriculum-based assessment is to determine the child's level of functioning so that input to the child changes as the child's abilities change.

Developmental Theory Assessment Approach

Piaget (1952) describes the theoretical framework for sensorimotor and symbolic development during a child's first 24 months; it details the changing approaches infants use to solve problems as development progresses. A criterion-referenced instrument that is based on this Piagetian framework and used extensively in early intervention programs is the *Infant Psychological Development Scale* (Uzgiris & Hunt, 1975). These scales represent an approach toward cognitive assessment from the developmental theory perspective. They are ordinal—based on the assumption that early cognitive abilities involve movement from lower to higher levels of functioning—and most often do not include age ranges or equivalents.

Dunst (1980) expanded the application of these scales for use with infants with handicaps by the development of *A Clinical and Educational Manual for Use with Uzgiris and Hunt Scales of Infant Psychological Development*. Dunst's protocol assists interventionists in successfully developing programs from these scales. Test items were selected to represent an ordinal sequencing of cognitive development within each of six major concept areas: (1) object permanence, (2) means–end relationships, (3) imitation (vocal and gestural), (4) causality, (5) construction of object relations in space, and (6) development of schemes for relating to objects.

Although based on Piagetian theory, the scales are not designed to assign an infant to a specific sensorimotor stage. Infant performance on the scales provides a measure of current cognitive functioning. The scales make it possible to look for differences in rates of development in the six areas mentioned. Dunst (1980) has since provided a strategy to enable the assessor to obtain more standardized data following the administration of the scales. The procedures outlined by Dunst provide the assessor with additional insights concerning the child's sensorimotor capabilities and aid in the design of intervention strategies.

TABLE 13-3 Alternative Norm-Referenced Measures

Instrument	Age Range	Unique Aspects	Limitations
Arthur Adaptation of the Leiter International Performance Scale (Arthur, 1952)	3-0 to 7-11 months	Requires no verbal response or verbal understanding from child; a new handbook has been developed that facilitates administration and interpretation	Cumbersome test, difficult to administer; limited, outdated norm sample; no strong evidence that this test is more "culturally fair" than other norm-referenced tests
Columbia Mental Maturity Scale (Burgemeister, Blum, Lorge, 1972)	3-6 to 10-0 months	No verbal response required from child; good technical qualities; flexible directions; requires only 15.20 minutes	Only one item type; only one global score can be determined
Extended Merrill-Palmer Scale of Mental Tests (Ball, Merrifield, & Stott, 1978)	3-0 to 5-11 months	Only instrument based on Structure of Intellect Model (Guilford, 1956); evaluates process as well as content; founded on a theory of intelligence	Inadequate standardization; questionable reliability and validity; no evidence for fit of the model to young children's thinking
Griffiths Mental Development Scales (Griffiths, 1979)	Birth to 8 months	Comprehensive; enticing, childlike materials; measures a wide range of functioning; yields useful information from nonverbal children	Manual is difficult to read; limited guidelines for interpretation of scores
Nebraska Test of Learning Aptitude (Hiskey, 1966)	3-0 to 16-0 months	Can be administered entirely via pantomime; requires no verbal response; normed on deaf children	No adequate description of standardization; limited reliability; no mainstreamed deaf children in norm sample
Perkins-Binet Tests of Intelligence for the Blind (Davis, 1980)	4-0 to 18-0 months	Flexible administration; only such instrument available for the blind	Children under age 6 underrepresented in norm sample
Pictorial Test of Intelligence (French, 1964)	3-0 to 8-0 months	Nonverbal format allows pointing or eye movement response; well standardized; good reliabilities reported	Norms dated; no handicapped children in norm sample; format is unvaried and may be boring to some children
Woodcock Johnson Psycho-Educational Battery (Woodcock & Johnson, 1977)	3 years to adults	Attractive, well-organized test materials; designed for educational decision making	Not many preschool students in normative sample; limited information on reliability and validity for this age group

TABLE 13–3 *(Continued)*

Instrument	Age Range	Unique Aspects	Limitations
British Ability Scale (Elliott, Murray, & Pearson, 1983)	2½ to 17 years	Comprehensive: 23 scales cover 6 areas: speed of information processing, reasoning, spatial imagery, perceptual matching, short-term memory, retrieval and application of knowledge; oral, written, and performance tasks provided; evidence shows that sex and social class bias is negligible	Only British norms are available at present
Boehm Test of Basic Concepts-Preschool Version (Boehm, 1986)	3 to 5 years	Brief (10.15 minutes) and easy to administer; requires only a pointing response; measures child's understanding of each concept and situation; resource guide (up to grade 2) for teaching can be purchased	Limited in usefulness for visually impaired children
Bracken Concept Development Series (Bracken, 1986)	2½ to 8 years	Includes a basic concept scale *and* a concept development program: the Scale measures 285 basic concepts in 11 subtest categories; pointing response appropriate for motorically impaired children; concept development program provides colorful, creative materials with lesson plans for teaching; at-home worksheets suggest ways in which parents can reinforce child's conceptual understanding; normative sample carefully selected; Spanish translations available	Limited in usefulness for visually impaired children
Metropolitan Achievement Tests Sixth Edition (MAT 6), Pre-primer and Primer (Prescott, Farr, Hogan, & Balow, 1986)	Grades K-5 to 1-9	Preprimer level includes three tests: (1) the Reading Test measures visual discrimination, letter recognition, and auditory discrimination; (2) Mathematics Test	Norms not available for children with handicapping conditions; not easily adapted to children with handicapping conditions

(Continued)

TABLE 13-3   *(Continued)*

Instrument	Age Range	Unique Aspects	Limitations
		measures numeration, geometry, measurement, problem solving; (3) Language Test measures listening comprehension; parent folders provide parents with an understanding of the reasons for assessment and the results; scores are explained and recommended ways to improve child's scores are provided; sample items are included; materials are attractive, child-friendly	
Stanford Early School Achievement Test (SESAT): 2nd Edition (Madden, Gardner, & Collins, 1984).	Grades K-0 to 1-9	Measures listening comprehension, retention and organization, decoding and comprehension skills, knowledge of world, mathematics concepts and skills; listening test has advance organizers to allow children to organize their thoughts before and during listening process; a guide for classroom planning assists teachers with application of test results	Norms not available for children with handicapping conditions; not easily adapted to children with handicapping conditions

Source: Adapted and expanded from "Cognitive Assessment of Preschool Children" by J. Schakel, *School Psychology Review,* 1986, *15,* 200–215. Copyright 1986 by National Association of School Psychologists. Expanded and adapted by permission.

Source: From Bailey, Donald B., & Wolery, Mark, *Assessing Infants and Preschoolers with Handicaps,* pp. 286–289. Copyright © 1989 by the National Association of School Psychologists. Reprinted by permission of the publisher.

Other Piagetian-based assessment measures are the *Albert Einstein Scales of Sensorimotor Development* (Escalona & Corman, 1966), the *Casati-Lezine Scales* (Casati & Lezine, 1968), and the *Mehrabian and Williams Scales* (Mehrabian & Williams, 1971). McCune et al. (1990) caution examiners in the repeated use Piagetian-based measures to assess cognitive development. If ordinal scales are used with little variation in procedure, the infant may learn how to solve a particular problem (e.g., pulling a string brings an object) rather than learn a general principle. This is important especially if these tasks are also used for intervention.

Play as an Alternative Approach to Cognitive Assessment

Play and cognitive development interact. Play leads to more complex, cognitive behavior that then affects the content of play (Athey, 1984; Piaget, 1962). Play assessment is useful for observing a child's ability to organize his or her interactions with toys and play partners and thus for assessing cognitive functioning (McCune et al., 1990). A child who is nonverbal or has multiple disabilities may be observed during free or structured play to provide assessment information on cognitive functioning. The examiner also may observe the child as she or he organizes his or her interactions with toys and playmates. The manner in which children interact with objects is a reflection of their cognitive development. When using play assessments, the examiner primarily observes and scores the actions of the child but also may observe the complexity and variety of play behaviors.

Play is vital to and reflects a child's development. A child's play opportunities and experiences influence cognitive understanding, emotional development, social skills, language usage, and physical and motor development (Linder, 1990). A large body of research relates certain cognitive skills to various features of language development. Certain behaviors in a child's play express cognitive skills necessary for the development of language. Interventionists need to be familiar with play and play assessment as it relates to cognitive, social-emotional, and language development because observing the child's play skills can provide insight into the child's performance. Delays, defects, and deviations seen in a child's play may reflect problems in one of these domains. Although play assessment is introduced here, it is given further consideration when discussing language and social-emotional development in chapters 14 and 15.

Play Assessment Procedures

A variety of nonstandardized assessment procedures and guides for observing children's play with objects or toys are available. McCune (1986) describes a format for collecting a sample of play with the caregiver or examiner using a standard set of toys. The play behavior is observed and assigned to developmental levels based on Piaget's work (1962). Table 13–4 describes the play levels that have been identified.

The Manual for Analyzing Free Play (MAFP) developed by McCune-Nicolich (1980), uses a play sequence initially suggested by Piaget (1962). The MAFP includes strategies for viewing symbolic play, relational play, and manipulative play; it is possible to make a series of discrete judgments concerning the child's play behavior by categorizing the different types of play.

Linder's (1990) *Transdisciplinary Play-based Assessment* is a developmental profile that assesses all major domains using structured and free-play situations. The TPBA uses a transdisciplinary team to conduct a play-based assessment that can be adapted to various abilities. This assessment is process oriented and includes ecological and interactive variables and provides relevant information for intervention (Linder, 1990).

TABLE 13-4 Structure of Pretend Play, 10-24 Months (1977)

Levels and Criteria	Examples
Sensorimotor period	
Level 1. Presymbolic scheme: The child shows understanding of object use or meaning by brief recognitory gestures. 　No pretending 　Properties of present object are the stimulus. 　Child appears serious rather than playful.	The child picks up a comb, touches it to his or her hair, drops it. The child picks up the telephone receiver, puts it into ritual conversation position, sets it aside. The child gives the mop a swish on the floor.
Level 2. Auto-symbolic scheme: The child pretends at self-related activities. 　Pretending. 　Symbolism is directly involved with the child's body. 　Child appears playful, seems aware of pretending.	The child simulates drinking from a toy baby bottle. The child eats from an empty spoon. The child closes his or her eyes, pretending to sleep.
Symbolic stage 1	
Level 3. Single scheme symbolic games: *Child* extends symbolism beyond his or her own actions by: Level 3.1. Including other actors or receivers of action, such as a doll. Level 3.2. Pretending at activities of other people or objects such as dogs, trucks, and trains.	Child feeds mother or doll. Child grooms mother or doll. Child pretends to read a book. Child pretends to mop floor. Child moves a block or toy car with appropriate sounds of vehicle.
Level 4. Combinatorial symbolic games: Level 4.1. Single scheme combinations: One pretend scheme is related to several actors or receivers of action.	Child combs own, then mother's hair. Child drinks from the bottle, feeds doll from bottle. Child puts an empty cup to mother's mouth, then experimenter, and self.
Level 4.2. Multi-scheme combinations: Several schemes are related to one another in sequence.	Child holds phone to ear, dials. Child kisses doll, puts it to bed, puts spoon to its mouth. Child stirs in the pot, feeds doll, pours food into dish.
Level 5. Planned symbolic games: Child indicates verbally or nonverbally that pretend acts are planned ahead. Level 5.1. Planned single scheme symbolic acts—transitional type. Acivities from levels 2 and 3 that are planned. Type A: Symbolic identification of one object with another. Type B: Symbolic identification of the child's body with some other person or object. Level 5.2 Combinations with planned elements: These are constructed of activities from levels 2 to 5.1, but always include some planned element. They tend toward realistic scenes.	Child finds the iron, sets it down, searches for the cloth, tossing aside several objects. When cloth is found, he or she irons it. Child picks up play screwdriver, says ''toothbrush'' and makes the motions of toothbrushing. Child picks up the bottle, says ''baby,'' then feeds the doll and covers it with a cloth. Child puts play foods in a pot, stirs them. Then says ''soup'' or ''Mommy'' before feeding the mother. He or she waits, then says ''more?'' offering the spoon to the mother.

Source: From McCune, Lorraine, Kalmanson, Barbara, Fleck, Mary B., Glazewski, Barbara, & Sillari, Joan, An Interdisciplinary model of infant assessment. In Samuel J. Meisels and Jack P. Shonkoff (Eds.), *Handbook of Early Child Intervention*, pp. 234–235. Copyright © 1990. New York: Cambridge University Press. Reprinted with permission.

Benner (1992, p. 219) provides a list of free-play and structured or elicited assessments:

Free-play Assessments

Belsky, J., & Most, R. K. (1981). From exploration to play: A cross-sectional study of infant free play behavior. *Developmental Psychology, 17,* 630–639.

Bromwich, R. M. (1981). *Working with parents and infants: An interactional approach.* Baltimore: University Park Press.

Kearsley, R. B. (1984). *The systematic observation of children's play.* Unpublished scoring manual. (Available from the author, Child Health Services, Manchester, NH).

Lowe, M., & Costello, A. J. (1976). *Manual for the Symbolic Play Test.* Windsor, England: NFR Nelson.

McCune-Nicolich, L. (1983). A *manual for analyzing free play.* New Brunswick, NJ: Rutgers University, Department of Educational Psychology.

Rubenstein, J. & Howes, C. (1976). The effects of peers on toddler interaction with mothers and toys. *Child Development, 47,* 597–605.

Elicited and Structured-Play

Belsky, J., Garduque, L., & Hrncir, E. (1984). Assessing performance, competence, and capacity in infant play: Relations to home environment and security of attachment. *Developmental Psychology, 20,* 406–417.

Fewell, R. (1986). Play assessment scale (5th revision). Unpublished manuscript, University of Washington, Seattle (includes both free play and structured play).

Watson, M. W., & Fischer, K. W. (1977). A developmental sequence of agent use in late infancy. *Child Development, 48,* 828–836.

Fewell and Rich (1987) provide a list of the advantages of using play-assessment data over traditional testing, including:

1. The testing environment is nonthreatening and elicits better cooperation from the children.
2. The procedures are flexible enough to allow for the exchange of toys a child might find more appealing.
3. The procedures are easy to administer with few directions and no definite order of item presentation and freedom from time constraints.
4. The examiner may observe a child's preferred learning strategies and toy preferences.
5. Both accomplished and emerging skills can be noted.

Summary

The assessment of cognitive skills provides the early interventionist with a greater understanding of the child's behavior and development. Observation of cognitive skills serves as a basis for preparing an individualized plan for the child and family and furnishes the means for evaluating the child's progress. Most cognitive assessment instruments attempt to assess the efficiency with which the child uses motor and sensory skills to solve problems (Langley, 1989). It is possible to use both formal and curriculum-based measures to assess the effectiveness of intervention choices and thus evaluate the efficacy of the intervention program for the child.

Because cognition is a composite of skills across developmental domains, the assessor needs to be familiar with normal developmental skill mastery across all domains. Use of assessment instruments that include behaviors allows the child an opportunity to display behaviors across domains. Once a wide sampling of behaviors is obtained, the assessor can judge how well an individual child displays behaviors that reflect appropriate cognitive functioning.

The results obtained using assessment instruments generally are indicative of how the child did on that day and do not reflect potential; potential can only be estimated based on a series of tests over a period of time in a variety of settings and under varying circumstances.

When considering the cognitive domain, the assessor is examining processes that cannot be directly measured but only can be assumed on the basis of observed behaviors. Although several assessment instruments are available, ultimately, it is the assessor's observational skill and integrating ability that provides accurate and reliable judgments of cognitive functioning. Early interventionists always need to search for innovative ways to elicit behaviors to which significance may be attached concerning developmental skill mastery (Rossetti, 1990). Assessment instruments and strategies are only as good as the person using them.

Suggested Group Activities

1. Infants begin learning about the world around them through the use of their senses. Give a few examples for each sense that demonstrates that the infant can perceive or detect sensory input in his or her environment.

2. Using a varied selection of textbooks, developmental assessment checklists and similar sources, compose a list of activities to demonstrate the three basic psychological processes—attention, perception, and memory. Choose one of several ages to research and share information with the class.

3. Divide into groups with each assigned one of the following theories of cognitive development: developmental theory, cognitive stages theory, behavioral theory, and information processing theory. Discuss and select two to three assessment tasks to

use with young children that would be an example of the theory chosen. Share the tasks with the group. Could some of the tasks be used with more than one theory? Which theories include a wider variety of cognitive domains?

4. Select one of the infant assessment instruments described in this chapter and administer it to an infant or young child. Share the results with the class, including the following information:

   • Rationale for choice of instrument
   • Scope of instrument
   • Domains
   • Construction (reliability, validity, standardization)
   • Administration time
   • Adaptations, if any
   • Special features
   • Critique of the instrument and results

5. If possible, work with a baby (age 3 months to 1 year) and assess if he or she has entered any of the following cognitive developmental stages: object permanence, means–end relationships, imitation, causality, construction of object relations in space, the development of schemes for relating to objects. Report on the findings to the class and include the answers to the following questions:

   • Were any concepts more difficult to assess?
   • What problems were encountered?
   • Did the infant cooperate and if so, for how long?

Present some suggestions on improving assessment techniques based on this experience.

References

Athey, I. (1984). Contributions of play to development. In T. D. Yawkey and A. D. Pellegrine (Eds.), *Child's play: Developmental and applied* (pp. 9–28). Hillsdale, NJ: Lawrence Erlbaum Associates.

Bayley, N. (1969). *Bayley Scales of Infant Development*. New York: Psychological Corporation.

Beail, N. (1985). A comparative study of profoundly multiply handicapped children's scores on the Bayley and the Griffiths' developmental scales. *Child: Care, Health and Development, 11*(1), 31–36.

Belsky, J., Garduque, L., & Hrncir, E. (1984). Assessing performance, competence, and capacity in infant play: Relations to home environment and security of attachment. *Developmental Psychology, 20,* 406–417.

Belsky, J., & Most, R. K. (1981). From exploration to play: A cross-sectional study of infant free-play behavior. *Developmental Psychology, 17,* 630–639.

Benner, S. M. (1992). *Assessing young children with special needs: An ecological perspective.* New York: Longman.

Bromwich, R. M. (1981).*Working with parents and infants: An interactional approach.* Baltimore: University Park Press.

Casati, I., & Lezine, I. (1968). *Les étapes de l'intelligence sensorimotrice.* Paris: Editions de Centre de Psychologie Appliqué.

Dunst, C. J. (1981). *Infant learning: A cognitive-linguistic intervention strategy.* Hingham, MA: Teaching Resources Corporation.

Dunst, C. J. (1980). *A clinical and educational manual*

for use with the Uzgiris and Hunt Scales of Infant Psychological Development. Austin: Pro-Ed.

Escalona, S., & Corman, H. (1966). *Albert Einstein scales of sensorimotor development.* Unpublished paper. Albert Einstein College of Medicine, Department of Psychiatry, New York..

Fewell, R. R. (1986). *Play-assessment scale* (5th rev.). Unpublished manuscript. University of Washington, Seattle.

Fewell, R. R., & Rich, J. S. (1987). Play assessment as a procedure for examining cognitive, communication, and social skills in multihandicapped children. *Journal of Psychoeducational Assessment, 2,* 107–118.

Furuno, S., O'Reilly, K. A., Hosaka, C. M., Inatsuka, T. T., Allman, T.L., & Zeisloft, B. (1979). *The Hawaii Early Learning Profile and Activity Guide.* Palo Alto: VORT.

Gesell, A. (1925). *The mental growth of the preschool child.* New York: Macmillan.

Griffiths, R. (1979). *The nature of human intelligence.* London: Child Development Research Center.

Griffiths, R. (1954). *The abilities of babies.* London: University of London Press.

Johnson-Martin, N. M., Jens, K. G., Attermeier, S. M., & Hacker, B. J. (1991). *The Carolina Curriculum for Infants and Toddlers with Special Needs* (2nd ed.). Baltimore: Paul H. Brookes.

Kearsley, R. B. (1984). *The systematic observation of children's play.* Unpublished scoring manual. (Available from the author, Child Health Services, Manchester, NH).

Knobloch, H., & Pasamanick, B. (1974). *Gesell and Amatruda's developmental diagnosis: The evaluation and management of normal and abnormal neuropsychologic development in infancy and early childhood* (3rd ed.). New York: Harper and Row.

Langley, M.B. (1989). Assessing infant cognitive development. In D. Bailey & M. Wolery (Eds.), *Assessing infants and preschoolers with handicaps (pp. 249–274).* Columbus: Merrill.

Linder, T. W. (1990). *Transdisciplinary play-based assessment: A functional approach to working with young children.* Baltimore: Paul H. Brookes.

Lockman, J. J. (1983). Infant perception and cognition. In S. G. Garwood & R. R. Fewell (Eds.), *Educating handicapped infants: Issues in develop-*

ment and intervention (pp. 117–164). Rockville, MD: Aspen Publishers, Inc.

Lowe, M., & Costello, A. J. (1976). *Manual for the symbolic play test.* Windsor, England: NFR-Nelson.

McCarthy, D. (1972). *McCarthy Scales of Children's Abilities.* New York: Psychological Corporation.

McCune, L. (1986). Symbolic development in normal and atypical infants. In G. Fein & M. Rivkin (Eds.), *The young child at play: Reviews of research* (pp. 45–61). Washington: NAEYC.

McCune, L., Kalmanson, B., Fleck, M. B., Glazewski, B., & Sillari, J. (1990). An interdisciplinary model of infant assessment. In S. J. Meisels & J. P. Shonkoff (Eds.), *Handbook of early childhood intervention.* (pp. 219–245). New York: Cambridge University Press.

McCune-Nicolich, L. (1983). *A manual for analyzing free play.* New Brunswick, NJ: Rutgers University, Department of Educational Psychology.

McCune-Nicolich, L. (1980). *A manual for analyzing free play: Experimental edition.* New Brunswick, NJ: Rutgers University.

Mehrabian, A., & Williams, M. (1971). Piagetian measures of cognitive development for children up to age two. *Journal of Psycholinguistic Research, 1*(1), 113–126.

Neisser, U. (1967). *Cognitive psychology.* New York: Appleton-Century-Crofts.

Newborg, J., Stock, J., Wnek, L., Guidubaldi, J., & Svinicki, J. S. (1984). *The Battelle Developmental Inventory.* Allen, TX: Developmental Learning Materials.

Paget, K. D. (1989). Assessment of cognitive skills in the preschool-aged child. In D. Bailey & M. Wolery (Eds.), *Assessing infants and preschoolers with handicaps* (pp. 275–300). Columbus, OH: Merrill.

Piaget J. (1962). *Play dreams and imitation in childhood.* New York: Norton.

Piaget, J. (1952). *The origins of intelligence in children.* New York: International Universities Press.

Raver, S. A. (1991). *Strategies for teaching at-risk and handicapped infants and toddlers: A transdisciplinary approach.* Columbus, OH: Merrill Publishing.

Robinson, H. R., & Robinson, N. M. (1976). *The*

mentally retarded child (2nd ed.). New York: McGraw-Hill.

Rogers, S., Donovan, C. M., D'Eugenio, D. B., Brown, S., Lynch, E., Moersch, M. S., & Schafer, S. (1981). *Early Intervention Developmental Profile* (rev. ed.). Ann Arbor: The University of Michigan Press.

Rossetti, L. M. (1990). *Infant-toddler assessment: An interdisciplinary approach.* Boston: College-Hill Press.

Rubenstein, J., & Howes, C. (1976). The effects of peers on toddler interaction with mothers and toys. *Child Development, 47,* 597–605.

Simeonsson, R. J. (Ed.). (1986). *Psychological and developmental assessment of special children.* Boston: Allyn and Bacon.

Uzgiris, I., & Hunt, J. M. (1975). *Assessment in Infancy: Ordinal Scales of Psychological Development.* Urbana, IL: University of Illinois Press.

Vulpe, S. G. (1977). *Vulpe Assessment Battery.* Toronto: National Institute on Mental Retardation.

Watson, M. W., & Fischer, K. W. (1977). A developmental sequence of agent use in late infancy. *Child Development, 48,* 828–836.

Yarrow, L. J., Rubenstein, J. L., & Pedersen, F. A. (1975). *Infant and environment: Early cognitive and motivational development.* Washington: Hemisphere.

$C \quad h \quad a \quad p \quad t \quad e \quad r$ **14**

Communication and Language

BARBARA WEITZNER-LIN

Early interventionists have now become more aware of the importance of the early identification and remediation of communication disorders. To assess communication development in young children, the examiner needs a basic understanding of normal communication development.

Communication, Language, and Speech

Communication is a broad term that describes the process of exchanging information and ideas between interactants. Speech is only one aspect of communication; it occurs through other modes such as gestures, touch, facial expressions, or vocalizations (sounds). Infants communicate with their caregivers this way before language develops.

Language is a complex and dynamic system of conventional symbols that is used in various modes for thought and communication (ASHA, 1983). Language as a system of conventional symbols (words) has a set of rules that are used to combine those words into longer units (sentences). It is primarily a social system for conveying social meanings. Language can be used to control the environment, particularly the behavior of persons in the environment.

Speech is one mode to express language. Speech is a motor act and as such requires the precise coordination of the central nervous system and muscles to formulate the spoken output. Modes other than speech can be used to encode language as a means of communication.

Language can be used to communicate through other modes of expression. Sign language is a complete linguistic system with rules of its own and can successfully communicate the speaker's (signer's) intent. Augmentative and alternative communication systems utilize symbol systems other than the spoken or written word to represent language and to communicate.

Components of Language

When acquiring any language, children need to learn rules about its sounds, grammar, meanings, and uses. These rules are reflected in the four components of language: phonology, syntax, semantics, and pragmatics.

Phonology

Phonology refers to the aspect of language that is concerned with the rules for the formation of speech sounds or phonemes, and how phonemes are sequenced and distributed within words. A phoneme is the smallest linguistic unit of sound that signals a difference in meaning.

The acquisition of phonological competence has an anatomical aspect to it that must be considered. The sounds of the language are made by the muscles in the lips and tongue, the throat, palate, teeth, and vocal cords. Neuromuscular development, therefore, needs to be evaluated when assessing a child's phonological ability.

Speech sounds generally develop in a predictable sequence at certain ages (Sander, 1972). Research on phonological development has focused on the stages through which children go as they acquire the ability to produce more complex sounds and sound combinations. Researchers have identified a series of stages that describe the baby's development of sound-producing abilities (Oller, 1980; Proctor, 1989). Other authors (Ingram, 1976; Piaget & Inhelder, 1969) have studied phonological development as it relates to cognitive development and have described stages in the phonological process that correspond to and depend on the acquisition of certain cognitive skills (Thurman & Widerstrom, 1985).

Syntax

Syntax is the aspect of language concerned with the rules or grammar system used to combine words into phrases and sentences. Different languages have developed different syntactic or grammatical systems. The English language has certain grammatical forms to be used by a speaker to express an idea. These rules specify the parts of speech, word order, and the constituents of a sentence. Our syntactical rules specify which word combinations (sentences) are acceptable and which are not. Thus, a child who has developed syntactical competence knows if a sentence is acceptable or not. For example, the child knows that "The boy ate the cookie" is an acceptable sentence and "The ate cookie the boy" is not acceptable. Typically, the rules of syntax are acquired gradually by the child as he or she learns to put words together. Most children learn the grammatical rules that govern the language they are learning with little direct help from adults.

Semantics

Semantics is the aspect of language concerned with the rules for meanings of individual words and their relationship to one another. Words have many characteristics that establish their meaning, and a child has to learn which factors are critical in acquiring the use of a word. The total number and variety of words, the individual relationships among words, and the complexity of their meanings increase as the child develops. Children also need to learn that words can have different meanings depending on when or how they are used. Because words have alternative meanings, a child must use additional cues—in the sentences (linguistic cues), or in the physical, social context—to understand word meanings.

Pragmatics

Pragmatics is the aspect of language concerned with the use of language in social contexts and includes the rules that govern how language is used for the purpose of communication. Three different levels of pragmatics may be assessed. These levels are intentions, conversational discourse, and presupposition. The same sentence may have different meanings and reflect different intentions on the part of the speaker in different contexts (Thurman & Widerstrom, 1985). The first area of pragmatics deals with communicative intentions—the reasons a speaker talks. These reasons include requesting, commenting, protesting, and so on.

There are many taxonomies of communicative intent; see Roth and Spekman (1984) or Lund and Duchan (1993) for reviews of these. Researchers suggest a progression of the expression of communicative intent from the prelinguistic stage to the multi-word utterance level.

The second area of pragmatics deals with the rules of conversational discourse. These rules dictate how to participate in a conversation by taking a turn and by moving from one topic to another. In order to participate in a conversation the child learns to integrate the rules of conversational discourse and, therefore, to: (a) elicit a listener's attention, (b) speak clearly, (c) provide sufficient information to enable the listener to identify the topic, and (d) provide sufficient information for the listener to determine the intended semantic meaning (Roberts & Crais, 1989).

Presupposition is the third component of pragmatic skills. This is the ability to take the perspective of the listener. The child needs to monitor the conversation to determine what the listener is understanding and *repair* the conversation when there is breakdown.

Communication and Language Assessment

Speech and language assessments involve the study of a child's developmental milestones, communicative patterns of interaction (including functional communication), and/or structured language. Although there is considerable overlap of these three dimensions, each offers a somewhat different view of a child's communicative skills (Benner, 1992). Bailey (1989) indicates that there are seven characteristics to effective child assessment. Richard and Schiefelbusch (1990) have adapted these seven characteristics so that they are focused on speech and language assessment. They state that the characteristics indicate effective assessment:

1. Incorporates multiple sources and multiple measures;
2. Involves caregivers both as informants and significant partners;
3. Is comprehensive, covering all important developmental and behavioral dimensions of language and considering performance across natural settings;
4. Involves professionals from other disciplines;
5. Is ecologically valid;
6. Is nondiscriminatory;
7. Is capable of providing continuous progress information.

Although all seven of these characteristics are useful for effective assessment, it is important to fully understand the impact the first three have on speech and language assessment. If an assumption is made that an effective assessment requires information from multiple sources, utilizing multiple measures, then it is assumed that information will be obtained through interviewing the family, observing the child in natural contexts, and administering standardized and other direct testing procedures. Involving caregivers in the assessment process also is assumed. If caregivers are actively involved in the assessment process from the beginning, professionals can instill a sense of competence and trust in families. Caregivers can give important information about the child's use of language at home, in situations professionals cannot observe, and with different communicative partners; and they should be asked to identify priorities for intervention.

Finally, to be effective an assessment needs to be comprehensive—obtain information that concerns all aspects of speech and language performance across natural contexts. At the very least, language assessment must consider language comprehension, language production, and language use. When specific assessment procedures are discussed later in this chapter, these assumptions will be kept in mind and ways to obtain information by all of the means above will be reviewed.

Assessment Procedures

Interviews

Interviewing caregivers is one useful way to gather information. Typically interviews are used to gather background information and/or the family's perception of the child's abilities. However, to assess the competence of young children, it is important to obtain information from the child's natural social context—the home—and the information needs to be comprehensive. Even if the assessment team goes to the home, not all information can be obtained through observation. In a limited period of time it is not possible to observe the child using the full extent of his or her communicative abilities, for example, vocabulary. If the evaluator wants to determine the child's full range of words, one of the recently developed vocabulary scales (administered through parent interview or through having the parent complete the scale alone) needs to be included in the assessment. These vocabulary scales include the *Language Development Survey* (Rescorla, 1989) and the *MacArthur Communicative Development Inventories: Infant & Toddler* (Fenson et al., 1991).

Vocabulary size is not the only type of information that can be obtained through parent interview. Schuler and her associates (1989) suggest an interview procedure for obtaining information about the child's ability to express five basic communicative functions/intents. This procedure assesses the child's ability to express specific communicative intents by questioning the interviewee with regard to specific behavior observed in specific situational contexts. Schuler et al. (1989) indicate that they have found consistency between the reports of various informants. They also report that they have been able to confirm the interview findings through observation in natural contexts or through elicitation tasks. More traditionally, the *Receptive Expressive Emergent Language Scale-2* (REEL-2) (Bzoch & League, 1991) is a developmental checklist that obtains observational information about the child's expressive and receptive abilities through information supplied by parents or guardians.

The early interventionist also could use a form, such as the *Communication Report Form* designed by Roberts and Crais (1989), to obtain information from either the teacher or caregiver. A portion of this form is shown in Table 14–1. The teacher or caregiver is asked to describe the following: (1) what intentions the child uses, does not use, or is learning to express (e.g., requests for object or actions, or protests); (2) how those intentions are typically expressed nonverbally (e.g., gesture, body movement, and facial expression), verbally (speech or signing), or vocally (e.g., speech or nonspeech sounds); and (3) in what situation the child expresses these intentions.

Low-structured Observation or Observation in Natural Contexts and Elicitation

Observation is considered a critical aspect of an assessment because it provides information about the way children actually use or do not use certain skills.

TABLE 14-1 Communication Report Form

Instructions: Please check under level of use each communicative function and write in the communication mode.

Functions	Level of Use			Communication Mode Used[a]		Situations	
	Yes does this	Is learning this	Does not do this	Most often	Least often	In what situations?	Give example
1. *Requests objects*—Does your child communicate that he wants an object that is out of reach? (e.g., pushes adult's hands toward a cookie or says, "cookie")							
2. *Requests action*—Does your child communicate that she wants help doing something? (e.g., hands adult a jar to open or says, "open")							
3. *Attention seeking*—Does your child communicate that he wants you to attend to him or to something in the environment? (e.g., tugs on mother's pants or says, "Mama")							
4. *Comment on object*—Does your child communicate that she wants you to notice or comment on an object? (e.g., points to "dog" and smiles or says, "dog")							
. . .							
9. *Acknowledges*—Does your child do something to indicate that he has heard you speaking to him? (e.g., nods his head or says, "ok")							
10. *Social routines*—Does your child communicate routines such as "please," "thank you," "hi," and "bye"? (e.g., to indicate "bye bye" waves or says "bye")							

[a]GE = gesture, SP = speech, SO = sounds, SI = signing, BM = body movements, and FE = facial expressions.

Source: Reprinted with permission of Merrill, an imprint of Macmillan Publishing Company, from *Assessing Infants and Preschoolers with Handicaps* by Donald B. Bailey, Jr., and Mark Wolery. Copyright © 1989 by Merrill Publishing Company.

246

Informal observation in a comfortable setting may be more important for speech and language evaluation than the use of any specific standardized measure (McCune et al., 1990). Roth (1990) emphasizes that the use of meaningful contexts is especially important in the assessment of young and/or low-functioning children. Contrived assessment situations reduce the probability that the language behaviors are typical of a child's everyday performance (Roth, 1990).

Early language and communicative behavior is so dependent on the situation that children may be unwilling to display their skill to strangers in an unfamiliar environment. An advantage of language assessment through naturalistic observation is the ability to assess many components of the language system simultaneously. As the child's language develops, all forms of assessment come to depend more and more on the use of language both in understanding instructions and in producing responses.

To obtain a natural language sample in a setting outside the home or classroom, a play session between the baby and the caregiver may be set up with appropriate toys and picturebooks. This session could be recorded or videotaped and supplemented with observational notes. A home-based session allows more comfort and freedom on the part of the child and caregiver and, therefore, provides a richer language sample. The natural language sample becomes more important with age, and beyond 18 months becomes a critical feature of an assessment (McCune et al., 1990). Roberts and Crais (1989) offer the following list of suggestions on how to manage the context and setting to engage children in interactions:

1. *Choose developmentally appropriate toys and materials. Use play and motor scales to help in the selection.*
2. *Limit your own talking, especially questions. Pause often to encourage the child to initiate communication and take a turn.*
3. *Watch for and encourage any mode of communication demonstrated by child (eye gaze, point, shrug, word, etc.).*
4. *Parallel play with the child, mimicking her actions. Play animatedly with object or toy and occasionally comment on an object or action.*
5. *Place a few items within eye gaze but out of reach; partially hide a few objects as well. If necessary, point to or comment on objects to encourage a comment or request by the child.*
6. *Let the child choose objects and/or activities, particularly in the beginning (and throughout the interaction if possible). Be prepared to watch and interact/comment when the child shows interest.*
7. *Include parent or another child to help break the ice. Stay in the background and slowly get into the interaction.*
8. *Begin interaction with activities that require little or no talking, and gradually move to more verbal tasks.*
9. *Be genuine in your questions, and stay away from asking what is obvious to both you and the child.*

10. *Follow the child's lead in the interaction by maintaining the child's focus on particular topics and meanings.*
11. *Show warmth and positive regard for the child, and value his comments* (p. 351).

Observation of children interacting with caregivers in naturalistic contexts is one of the major means of sampling children's spontaneous communicative abilities. However, the result is often an incomplete picture of the young child's performance due to the variable of the context, as not all behaviors of interest will occur, or occur with adequate frequencies, to provide sufficient data on which to make recommendations. The absence of a particular behavior is not necessarily an indication that the skill is not part of a child's repertoire. The skill also must be demonstrated frequently enough to assess it adequately. Therefore, the most complete sampling of language behaviors is obtained through a combination of naturalistic observations and structured elicitations (Roth, 1990).

Coggins, Olswang, and Guthrie (1987) and Wetherby and Rodriguez (1992) compare the use of elicitation procedures to sampling in natural contexts to obtain information. Elicitation tasks do not guarantee a response; they increase the probability that the young child will produce the desired behavior in a given situation. Both sets of investigators studied young children's expression of requests and comments in spontaneous play and from elicitation tasks. Coggins et al. (1987) found that the children produced spontaneous comments in the play context but infrequently produced spontaneous requests. The results of both studies indicate that the elicitation tasks were more successful than the spontaneous-play context at sampling requests.

The inclusion of both low-structured observation and elicitation tasks supports the notion that multiple sources of information and multiple measures are the only adequate way to assess the communicative abilities of a young child. Therefore, the most complete sampling of language behaviors is obtained through a combination of naturalistic observations, elicitation tasks, and structured elicitations (Roth, 1990).

Structured Language Assessment

A complete assessment of language behaviors involves the analysis of structural and pragmatic components of the linguistic systems in both comprehension and production (Roth, 1990). A child's achievement of developmental milestones can serve as a basis for determining language delay in young children. Developmental milestones form the basic framework for many assessment instruments. Some of these developmental scales are highly structured, whereas others serve as informal checklists for the interventionist. Many of the norm-based and criterion- and curriculum-based assessments discussed in chapters 9 and 10 contain subtests or domains related to communication and language. The results of standard assessment procedures can allow the evaluator to make comparisons between the child being assessed and others at the same age or developmental level.

Wetherby and Prizant (1992) review the 10 instruments most frequently used in early identification of speech and language disorders. Their findings indicate that these test instruments do not comprehensively assess all developmental and behavioral dimensions of communicative abilities. Table 14–2 presents Wetherby and Prizant's review of assessment instruments and their ability to comprehensively assess communication skills. When using a standardized tool early interventionists need to ask whether the information being obtained provides a picture of the child's communication abilities or whether it provides only limited or incomplete information. Remember not to use standardized assessment tools alone; they do not provide the early interventionist with information about the child's performance across natural contexts because a testing environment is not natural.

Standardized Tests

The *Receptive Expressive Emergent Language Scale* (REEL/REEL-2) (Bzoch & League, 1971, 1991) is one of the most frequently used standardized instruments for infants (Roth, 1990). This test uses an interview format and looks at both receptive and expressive language behaviors; it covers the age range from birth to 36 months. The child's performance is scored as: typically exhibits, emerging, or not exhibited. The examiner scores high-frequency behaviors and arranges them in an ordinal sequence, producing scores for receptive language age, expressive language age, and combined language age. The primary strength of the instrument is its breadth because it includes phonological, semantical, syntactical, and pragmatic skills, and it is recommended for screening (Roth, 1990). However, this instrument has been criticized for its lack of a clearly delineated theoretical basis, the inadequacy of administration and scoring directions, and the lack of psychometric information (Roth, 1990).

Another frequently used instrument is the *Sequenced Inventory of Communication Development—Revised* (SICD-R) (Hedrick, Prather, & Tobin, 1984) that assesses communication skills of infants, toddlers, and preschoolers from four months to four years. The areas assessed are awareness of environmental sounds and speech sounds, discrimination of environmental sounds and speech sounds, understanding, initiating of communication, imitating communication, and responding to communication. Items are assigned age levels based on the performance of normally developing children included in the standardization sample. Scores in receptive and expressive communication ages are produced and can be compared to the chronological and/or mental age of the child. Note, however, that the standardization sample is restricted in race, social class, and geographic location. Alternative norms need to be developed for children who are culturally and/or linguistically diverse.

The *Preschool Language Scale—3* (PLS-3) (Zimmerman, Steiner, & Pond, 1992) is a highly structured scale based on normative findings of hundreds of Head Start children. The third revision is norm referenced. The norms are presented at three-month intervals from 0 to 11 months, at six-month intervals from 1 year to 4 years, and at 12-month intervals for ages 5 and 6. The scale assesses attention, vocal development, social communication, semantics (including vocabulary

TABLE 14–2   **Ten Routinely Used Assessment Instruments for Developmentally Young Children** (Rated for characteristics of assessment content and strategies)

	Assessment Instrument									
Feature	SICD	PLS	REEL	Denver	Birth to 3	Bayley Scales	ACLC	Ordinal Scales	Vine-land	ELI
Assesses functions of communication	L	–	L	L	L	L	–	L	L	–
Analyzes preverbal communication	L	–	L	L	+	L	–	–	L	–
Assesses social-affective signaling	–	–	–	L	L	L	–	–	L	–
Profiles social, communicative, and symbolic abilities	–	–	–	L	+	–	–	–	L	–
Uses caregivers as informants and assesses child directly	+	–	+	+	L	–	–	–	L	–
Uses spontaneous child-initiated communicative interactions	L	–	–	–	–	–	–	–	–	+
Uses caregivers as active participants	–	–	–	L	–	–	–	–	–	L

The assessment instruments are listed from left to right in descending order by number of university programs in speech-language pathology that use each instrument routinely (Crais & Leonard, 1990). (SICD = Sequence Inventory of Communication Development; PLS = Preschool Language Scale; REEL = Receptive-Expressive Language Scale; Denver = Denver Developmental Screening Test; Birth to Three = Birth to Three Checklist of Learning and Language Behavior; Bayley Scales = Bayley Scales of Infant Development; ACLC = Assessment of Children's Language Comprehension; Ordinal Scales = Ordinal Scales of Psychological Development; Vineland = Vineland Adaptive Behavior Scales; ELI = Environmental Language Inventory; + = characteristic addressed in depth; L = characteristic addressed to a limited extent; – = characteristic not addressed.)

Source: Reprinted with permission from Wetherby, Amy M., & Prizant, Barry M., Profiling young children's communicative competence, Figure 1, p. 220, "Assessment Instrument." In Warren, Steven F., and Reichle, Joe (Eds.), *Causes and Effects in Communication and Language Intervention* (Volume 1). Copyright © 1992. Baltimore, MD: Paul H. Brookes Publishing Co.

and concepts), structure (including syntax and morphology), and integrative thinking skills. The test also includes optional measures: an articulation screener, a language sample form and checklist, and a family information and suggestions form.

The *Communication and Symbolic Behavior Scales* (CSBS) (Wetherby & Prizant, 1990) examine communicative, social-affective, and symbolic abilities of 9- to 24-month-old children whose communicative abilities range from preverbal to verbal. The format of the CSBS is standard but flexible and includes both unstructured and elicitation tasks. The scales also include a form for parents to complete after the assessment to validate the results obtained by the professional. The scales include eight communicative temptations to determine communicative function and mode of expression, a series of play contexts to determine combinatorial and symbolic play abilities, and comprehension items.

Nonstandardized Tests/Protocols

Criterion-referenced assessments also may be used to assess structural and language abilities. These instruments assess achievement of language milestones exclusively.

The *Infant Toddler Scale* (Rosetti, 1990) is a criterion-referenced instrument designed to assess language skills of children from birth through 36 months. The following areas are assessed: interaction-attachment (the cues and responses that reflect a reciprocal relationship between the caregiver and the child), pragmatics (the way the child uses language to communicate with and affect others), gesture (the child's use of gestures to express thoughts and intent prior to the consistent use of spoken language), play (the changes in a child's play that reflect the development of representational thought), language comprehension (the child's understanding of verbal language with and without linguistic cues), and language expression (the child's use of preverbal and verbal behaviors to communicate with others). The scale includes a parent questionnaire that includes questions concerning interaction and communication development and a vocabulary checklist (for produced and understood words).

Assessing Linguistic Behaviors (Olswang, Stoel-Gammon, Coggins, & Carpenter, 1987) is an assessment protocol to use with children functioning below the age of two who are at risk for or suspected of impaired language development. There are five scales. The first scale is the "Cognitive Antecedents to Word Meaning Scale," designed to examine the cognitive skills for three early emerging semantic notions and their related pragmatic functions—nomination, agent, location. The second scale—the "Play Scale"—examines the child's practice play during the first year of the sensorimotor period, observing the child's actions on objects. The play scale also examines symbolic play that emerges during the second year of the sensorimotor period.

The "Communicative Intent Scale" is the third scale. It is a criterion-referenced measure of a child's intentional communication. The fourth scale is the "Language Comprehension Scale" that attempts to regulate some of the variables that affect early language comprehension such as: whether the referent was present or absent; how many words the child has actually attended to in order to comply; the particular semantic relations expressed; the probability of the action in the absence of a request; the availability of nonverbal cues and gestures indicating the speaker's intent, and the presence of supporting context (time, place, person) usually associated with the request. The final scale is the "Language Production Scale" that was designed to examine the vocalizations of 9- to 24-month-old children. The scale is divided into two major parts: one focusing on prelinguistic utterances (babbling) and the other on meaningful speech (linguistic productions).

The *Environmental Language Intervention Program* includes two highly structured developmental scales: the *Environmental Prelanguage Battery* (EPB) (Horstmeier and MacDonald, 1978) and the *Environmental Language Inventory* (ELI) (MacDonald, 1978). This program provides criterion-referenced measures describing prelanguage and early verbal behaviors (EPB) and semantic relations (ELI).

Dimensions of Speech and Language for a Comprehensive Assessment

A comprehensive evaluation of infants at risk for developmental problems needs to include a variety of speech and language techniques to assess a variety of components of speech, language and communication. In addition, a speech language pathologist should perform an oral-peripheral examination for both structure and function of the child's oral-motor skills. This examination helps to determine the infant's neurological potential for efficient respiration and feeding and for appropriate, volitional sound production (McCune et al., 1990). An audiological screening also needs to done to obtain an estimate of hearing ability and to identify children who should be referred for a complete audiological evaluation (McCune et al., 1990).

The components to be discussed here include assessing the child's: readiness to communicate pragmatic abilities, language production, language comprehension, and play abilities.

Assessing the Infant's Readiness to Communicate

Socio-communicative skills involve maternal-infant interaction and attachment, as well as the child's overall ability to comprehend and process language (Rossetti, 1991). The social interaction that takes place between the infant and the caregiver provides the foundation for the child's intentional use of language (Bates, 1979; Bruner, 1981). A comprehensive language assessment needs to examine both the caregiver-infant interaction and the infant's readiness to communicate.

Many instruments have been developed to facilitate the assessment of infant-caregiver interaction. Table 14–3 provides an overview of some measures of such interactions. Note, however, that interactional styles vary across families and cultures and that it may be difficult to qualify and quantify the exact nature of infant-caregiver interactions. When interpreting results obtained using any of the measures described in Table 14–3, it is important for the evaluator to focus on the positive behaviors of the caregiver and infant and the cultural variation in interaction patterns.

When assessing the infant's readiness to communicate, the following aspects need to be examined: the child's use of gaze, the attention to social stimuli and development of contingency, joint attention and joint action, and affective sharing.

Gaze is a powerful mode of communication. Infants respond to their caregiver's voice and face as early as age two weeks, fixing their gaze on the

TABLE 14-3 Measures of Parent-Child Interaction

Instrument	Description
The Dyadic Mini Code (Censullo, M., Bowler, R., Lester, B., & Brazelton, T. B., 1987).	This instrument is designed to measure adult-infant interaction synchrony from videotaped interaction.
The Greenspan-Lieberman Observation System (GLOS) (Greenspan, S., & Lieberman, A., 1980).	The GLOS provides a micro-analytic technique for assessing parent and child verbal and nonverbal behaviors.
Observation of Communicative Interaction (OCI) (Klein, M. & Briggs, M., 1986).	The OCI provides a framework for considering ten kinds of desirable maternal behaviors that may be used in mother-infant interaction in a check sheet format.
Ecoscales Manual (MacDonald, J., Gillette, Y., & Hutchinson, T., 1989).	The Ecoscales are designed to be used to analyze adult and child interactive and communicative skills and to establish treatment goals.
Diagnostic Interaction Survey (Owens, R., 1982).	The DIS is designed to identify parent-child interaction behaviors including reinforcement/punishment, nonverbal cues, conversation, verbal cues, and child register.
The Maternal (Parent) Behavior Rating Scale (Mahoney, G., Powell, A., & Finger, I., 1986).	This scale is designed to look at eight aspects of parent behavior in order to assess the quality of parent-child interaction.
Interaction Analysis Chart (McDade, H. & Simpson, M., 1984).	This chart provides ten categories for scoring parent communicative behaviors and four categories for scoring child behaviors.
Objective Observation Tool for Parent-Child Interaction (Russo, J. & Owens, R., 1982).	This tool is a ten-item taxonomy designed to assess parent and child interaction behaviors.
Parent Behavior Progression (Bromwich, R., Khokha, E., Fust, L., Baxter, E., Burge, D., & Kass, E., 1981).	Assesses infant-related maternal behaviors, such as apparent pleasure in proximity to infant, and ability to read infant cues.

Source: Reprinted from *Family-Centered Intervention for Communication Disorders: Prevention and Treatment* by G. Donahue-Kilburg, p. 131, with permission of Aspen Publishers, Inc., © 1992.

caregiver's mouth or eyes (Owens, 1992). Reciprocal interactions that involve gaze are thus found early on in the infant's repertoire.

The development of reciprocal social and communicative interaction depend on the ability to understand contingency, that is, the fact that actions of others affect oneself and that one's own actions affect others (Klinger & Dawson, 1992). Through contingent, predictable, and repetitive interactions with caregivers, infants develop a sense of control over their environments (Lamb, 1981) and begin to perceive themselves as effective social agents (Schaffer, 1977). Thus it is important to examine the contingency between the caregiver and the child. Likewise, the infant needs to be aware that social stimuli may signal the initiation of a communicative exchange.

Another aspect of early communication that needs to be documented is joint attention. Joint attention includes the triadic exchanges involving the caregiver, the infant, and objects. In these exchanges, caregivers and infants coordinate their attention around objects of mutual interest. Joint attention is observed through the use of referential looking between the object and caregiver (Klinger & Dawson, 1992). Joint action or routinized interaction games such as peek-a-boo are another important aspect to early communication. These interactional games provide the infant the opportunity to learn and practice important aspects of communication (Ratner & Bruner, 1978). In these interactions, the infant learns about turn-taking, event initiation, and structure, and because there is a close relationship between what is said and what is done, the infant can begin to make sense out of the language he or she hears.

Affective sharing involves the interpersonal coordination of affective expression between an infant and his or her caregiver. Typically, they experience mutual interest and pleasure in each other's smiling and vocalizations (Klinger & Dawson, 1992).

Assessing Pragmatic Ability

Pragmatics is the use of language for the purpose of communication. Roth (1990) summarizes the different levels at which communication skills can be analyzed. Any one message can be classified differently depending on the level of analysis selected. These levels are: (1) communicative intentions that a speaker wishes to convey, (2) presupposition that includes a speaker's message in relation to the specific information needs of a listener, and (3) organization of conversational discourse that involves maintaining a dialogue between partners over several conversational turns (Roth, 1990).

Communicative Intent

Communicative intentions concern the message a child is attempting to convey. At the preverbal level, intentions are attention seeking (i.e., to self or to events, objects, or other people), requesting (i.e., objects, action, or information), greetings, transferring, protesting or rejecting, responding or acknowledging, and informing. Intentions at the single-word level are similar but also include naming and commenting. Multiword-level intentions, which reflect a maturation and increased efficiency, are requesting information, requesting action, responding to requests, stating or commenting, regulating conversational behavior, and other performatives (e.g., teasing, warning, or conveying humor) (Roth, 1990).

At this assessment level, it is important to consider the intentions a child conveys and the effect these intentions have on a listener. The evaluation of communicative intentions involves an analysis of the range of intentions understood and expressed and the verbal and/or nonverbal forms in which they are coded (Roth & Spekman, 1984).

A comprehensive assessment of communication needs to include an assessment of the communicative intents expressed by the young child. Bruner (1981) indicates that children express three broad types of intentions by the end of the first year—regulatory behavior, social interaction, and joint attention.

Regulatory intentions are intents that are used to regulate another's behavior. Wetherby, Cain, Yonclas, and Walker (1988) indicate that the child can use acts that are requests for action, requests for object, or protests within this category of intents.

Social interactional intentions are those used to attract or maintain another's attention to oneself. Wetherby et al. (1988) indicate that within this category of intents the child may use acts that are requests for social routines, greetings, callings, requests for permission, acknowledgments.

Joint attention intentions are intents used to direct another's attention in order to share a focus on an event or an entity. Wetherby et al. (1988) include in this category comments, requests for information, and requests for clarification.

In order to attribute intentionality to young children, it is important to make some decisions on what behavior has communicative intent and what behavior does not. Note that Bates (1979) indicates that infants typically express intentionality between 8 and 12 months. The first social-communicative signals young children use are nonsymbolic vocalizations or gestures. When assessing the child's expression of intent, not only the reason the child communicates, but also the way in which the child expresses intentionality needs to be examined. It is important to examine the prelinguistic child's gestures (both conventional and unconventional) and the vocalizations the child uses both isolated from and in combination with gestures. As the child develops words, both the single words and later the multiword expressions of intent need to be examined.

Presupposition

Presupposition focuses on the ability of the child to take on the perspective of a communicative partner. Role-taking skills can be inferred from modifications a child makes when communicating with different partners for different purposes and in different situations. The examiner may ask, "Does the child talk differently to different people in different situations or have a different purpose to communicate?" (Roth 1990).

Conversational Discourse

Communication also involves the organization of conversational discourse (Roth, 1990). The child functions as both a listener and a speaker. Components of conversational discourse include socialized versus nonsocialized speech, turn taking and talking time, conversational initiation, and conversational maintenance (Roth, 1990). Assessment of the components of communication can be accomplished through structured observations in naturalistic settings. Specific components can be targeted for the observation (e.g., child initiations of conversation) depending on the individual needs of the child.

Language Production

There is a broad range of individual variations, yet it is important to consider vocal and verbal development. Variation is seen even in the youngest child's use of vocalizations. Just as we analyze the child's phonology once she or he begins to use words, we need to analyze the child's use of vocalizations prior to word use; by age three months different types of vocalizations may be produced in different contexts. There are many theoretical views of the development of vocalization. Proctor (1989) indicates that vocalization proceeds through five overlapping stages. She suggests observing the child in a variety of interactions, with known and unknown partners and with familiar and unfamiliar material, to determine the level of the child's vocalizations through our observations.

As the child begins to use single words, it may be important to determine the child's ability to utilize the phonological aspect of language. For a good review of what is typical versus atypical phonological development, see Stoel-Gammon (1991). When analyzing a young child's phonological system, it is useful to look at the number and type of initial consonants in the child's phonetic inventory, the number and type of different final consonants in the child's inventory, the variety of syllable/word structures used, and the number and type of vowels used.

Once the child begins to use conventional vocal forms, words, they use them to express the communicative intents that were previously expressed nonverbally. The assessment needs to document the number of words the child uses; one of the parent checklists discussed above is helpful. As the child begins to combine words into multiword utterances, an examination of the grammatical morphemes expressed by the child and an examination of the child's sentence structure (syntax) should be completed. Compute the mean length of utterance to determine the child's expressive language stage. For a complete review of how to analyze morphology and syntax, see Lund and Duchan (1993) and Miller (1981).

Language Comprehension

Comprehension is the ability to associate a symbol or sequence of symbols with meaning. Language comprehension, a child's ability to understand words and word combinations, must be included in any comprehensive assessment. James (1989) indicates that when assessing language comprehension there are two basic types of comprehension. The first type is linguistic comprehension—the ability to interpret a verbal stimulus using only linguistic cues and linguistic knowledge. The second type of comprehension is communicative—the ability to interpret verbal stimuli using all of the information available in the communicative situation.

When assessing a child's language comprehension, either linguistic or communicative, the early interventionist needs to keep in mind that young children often appear to understand words and sentences beyond their developmental level. Children rely on comprehension strategies (Chapman, 1978) to facilitate their understanding of the total event. Paul (1987) indicates that the strategies children use to facilitate comprehension change with development, incorporating new linguistic knowledge as it is acquired and integrated with the knowledge of the way things usually happen. The use of comprehension strategies makes the child *look good* receptively and simultaneously provides the child with a way to interact and provides the child with feedback on performance.

It is necessary to determine if the child understands a few single words in routinized contexts when assessing the young child between 8 and 12 months. Assessing the child's communicative comprehension also is important. To assess communicative comprehension, examine the child's understanding of single words paired with nonverbal cues such as gesturing. At this stage of development the child may use the following comprehension strategies: looks at objects that mother (adult) looks at, acts on objects the examiner has noticed, and imitates ongoing actions.

Between 12 and 18 months the child begins to comprehend single words. When assessing single word comprehension (linguistic comprehension), Paul (1987) indicates that the examiner needs to determine if the child is able to comprehend single words without the support of the nonlinguistic context—i.e., without gestures, without eye gaze toward the object, and not supported by the context (in the middle of eating, asking for the cup). The 12- to 18-month-old child also utilizes comprehension strategies to facilitate his or her understanding. The strategies the child uses include: attending to objects mentioned, giving evidence of notice (look/act on what mother looks at), and doing what another usually does (conventional manner).

The 18- to 24-month-old child understands two-word combinations and may understand the words for absent objects (linguistic comprehension). The child still uses comprehension strategies to facilitate his or her communicative comprehension. The strategies the child may utilize are: locate objects mentioned and give evidence of notice, put objects in containers or on surfaces, and act on the object in the way mentioned (the child is the agent). Paul (1987) indicates that, when assessing multiword comprehension, it is important to determine comprehension of early semantic relations such as agent-object, possessor-possession, action-affected object, agent-object, and entity-attribute.

The child between 24 and 36 months is now able to comprehend three term sentences, but context and past experience still play a part. The child does not understand that word order makes a difference in meaning. The comprehension strategies the child uses include: respond with probable locations, utilize probable events, and supply the missing information. Paul (1987) indicates that children, who succeed at the 24–36-month level in a nonstandardized assessment approach that incorporates the information described above, can be assessed using more formalized measures.

Play

There seems to be a relationship between young children's play and advances in language, particularly in symbolic play (McCune-Nicolich & Carroll, 1981). Symbolic play is make-believe play, or the knowledge that one object can be used to represent another. Pretending and language are both based on the capacity to represent, and advances in the complexity of play behaviors are usually accompanied by changes in language use and function in normally developing children (McCune-Nicolich & Carroll, 1981). Language assessment provides the early interventionist with some information about the child's ability to represent the world, and an assessment of play is another way to obtain information about representational capacity. For young children who are communicatively handicapped, a play assessment provides insight into the child's ability to represent, and in the absence of language, provides information about the child's potential to learn language.

A play assessment provides the early interventionist with information regarding the child's understanding of his or her world through analysis of the child's interactions with objects. Through an examination of the child's use of multiple action schemes, it also can provide information on what the child knows about objects, events, relationships between objects and events, qualities of objects, and their location in time and space. A play assessment also can provide information about the child's ability to engage in symbolic play.

Play can be assessed by providing the child with a variety of toys in a natural context and then coding the level of play (Westby, 1988). There are many assessment procedures that can be used to assess symbolic play; chapter 13 describes some of them. In addition, some of the assessment instruments described in this chapter have sections that assess a child's play. For example, the CSBS looks at the child's symbolic play and the child's combinatorial play by engaging the child in play with specified sets of toys. The ALB looks at two categories of play—practice play (actions on objects) and symbolic play (pretend play). This test also suggests using specified sets of toys to elicit play behavior. The *Infant Toddler Language Scale* also has a section to examine play.

Summary

When planning the assessment of infants, toddlers, and preschoolers, the early interventionist always needs to consider the mutual influences of social, motoric, and cognitive development on the child's efforts to communicate and learn language. The interactions of the infant with people and objects in the environment are the basis for the development of many nonverbal behaviors considered to be the beginning of language (Roberts & Crais, 1989). Behaviors such as eye gaze, touch, and attention getting are important antecedents of social and communicative development later in life.

The comprehensive assessment of communication needs to include multiple measures from multiple sources and active involvement of the caregivers in order to *be* comprehensive. If the early interventionist utilizes a variety of the assessment procedures and considers the various components of language described in this chapter, he or she is heading toward an effective assessment.

Suggested Group Activities

1. Observe a live or videotaped session with a baby or young child. Using both informal and formal means of assessment, collect information detailing the language and social interactions between child and adult (e.g., compare elicitation of requests/commands to a spontaneous sample and formal information on a test such as the REEL). Compare the results with others, and see how accurate the observational methods and data collecting procedures were.

2. Joint attention is an important component of the developing communication between infant and caregiver. Create a list of age appropriate toys and materials that could be used to elicit this form of behavior.

3. Observe an infant and a toddler and describe the different comprehension strategies they use to facilitate understanding of what is being said and done.

4. Create several situations that would allow the child to demonstrate the ability for symbolic and representational play (such as "feeding toys and dolls"). Describe what kinds of assessment opportunities would be made available through observing these behaviors.

5. Have several class members tape conversations with children of various ages. Play the tapes for the class and discuss some of the following:

   - Similarities and differences in interaction styles;
   - Mean length of utterances, grammatical structure, syntax, and so on;
   - Responses of child to adult questions and/or feedback.

References

ASHA Committee on Language. (1983). Definition of language. *ASHA, 22,* 44.

Bailey, D. B., & Wolery, M. (Eds.) (1989). *Assessing infants and preschoolers with handicaps* (pp. 1–21). Columbus, OH: Merrill.

Bates, E. (1979). *The emergence of symbols: Cognition and communication in infancy.* New York: Academic Press.

Benner, S. M. (1992). *Assessing young children with special needs: An ecological perspective.* New York: Longman.

Bruner, J. (1981). The social context of language acquisition. *Language and Communication, 1,* 155–178.

Bzoch, K., & League, R. (1991). *The receptive-expressive emergent language scale.* Austin: Pro-Ed.

Chapman, R. (1978). Comprehension strategies in children. In J. Kavanaugh & W. Strange (Eds.), *Speech and language in the laboratory, school, and clinic* (pp. 308–327). Cambridge, MA: MIT Press.

Coggins, T. E, Olswang, L. B., & Guthrie, J. (1987). Assessing communicative intents in young children: Low structured observation or elicitation tasks? *Journal of Speech and Hearing Disorders, 52*, 44–49.

Donahue-Kilburg, G. (1992). *Family-centered early intervention for communication disorders: Prevention and treatment.* Gaithersburg, MD: Aspen.

Fenson, L., Dale, P., Reznik, S., Bates, E., Thal, D., Hartung, J., & Reilly, J. (1991). *Technical manual for the MacArthur Communicative Development Inventory.* San Diego: San Diego State University, Developmental Psychology Laboratory.

Hedrick, D., Prather, E., & Tobin, A. (1984). *Sequenced Inventory of Communication Development—Revised.* Seattle: University of Washington Press.

Horstmeier, D., & MacDonald, J. (1978). *Environmental Prelanguage Battery.* New York: Psychological Corporation.

Ingram, D. (1976). Current issues in child phonology. In D. Morehead & A. Morehead (Eds.), *Normal and deficient child language* (pp. 3–27). Baltimore: University Park Press.

James, S. (1989). Assessing children with language disorders. In D. K. Bernstein & E. Tiegerman (Eds.), *Language and communication disorders in children* (2nd ed., pp. 157–207). Columbus, OH: Merrill.

Klinger, L. G., & Dawson, G. (1992). Facilitating early social and communicative development in children with autism. In S. F. Warren & J. Reichle (Eds.), *Causes and effects in communication and language intervention* (pp. 157–186). Baltimore: Paul H. Brooks.

Lamb, M. (1981). The development of social expression in the first year of life. In M. Lamb & L. Sherrod (Eds.), *Infant social cognition: Empirical and theoretical considerations* (pp. 155–176). Hillsdale, NJ: Lawrence Erlbaum Associates.

Lund, N., & Duchan, J. (1993). *Assessing children's language in naturalistic contexts.* Englewood Cliffs, NJ: Prentice-Hall.

MacDonald, J. D. (1978). *Environmental Language Inventory.* Columbus, OH: Merrill.

McCune, L., Kalmanson, B., Fleck, M. B., Glazewski, B., & Sillari, J. (1990). An interdisciplinary model of infant assessment. In S. J. Meisels & J. P. Shonkoff (Eds.), *Handbook of early childhood intervention* (pp. 219–245). New York: Cambridge University Press.

McCune-Nicolich, L., & Carroll, S. (1981). Development of symbolic play: Implications for the language specialist. *Topics in Language Disorders, 2*, 1–15.

Miller, J. (1981). *Assessing language production in children: Experimental procedures.* Austin: Pro-Ed.

Oller, D. K. (1980). The emergence of the sounds of speech in infancy. In G. H. Yeni-Komshian, J. F. Kavanaugh, & C. A. Ferguson (Eds.), *Child phonology: Vol.1. Production* (pp. 93–112). New York: Academic Press.

Olswang, L. B., Stoel-Gammon, C., Coggins, T. E., & Carpenter, R. L. (1987). *Assessing linguistic behaviors.* Seattle: University of Washington Press.

Owens, R. E. (1992). *Language development* (3rd ed.) Columbus,OH: Merrill.

Paul, R. (1987). A model for the assessment of communication disorders in infants and toddlers. *NSSLHA Journal, 14*, 88–105.

Piaget, J., & Inhelder, B. (1969). *The psychology of the child.* New York: Basic Books.

Proctor, A. (1989). Stages of normal noncry vocal development in infancy: A protocol for assessment. *Topics in Language Disorders, 10*, 26–42.

Ratner, N., & Bruner, J. (1978). Games, social exchange, and the acquisition of language. *Journal of Child Language, 5*, 391–402.

Rescorla, L. (1989). The language development survey: A screening tool for delayed language in toddlers. *Journal of Speech and Hearing Disorders, 54*, 587–599.

Richard, N. B., & Schiefelbusch, R. L. (1990) Assessment. In L. McCormick and R. L. Schiefelbusch (Eds.), *Early language intervention: An introduction* (2nd ed., pp. 117–156). Columbus, OH: Merrill.

Roberts, J. E., & Crais, E. R. (1989). Assessing communication skills. In D. B. Bailey and M. Wolery (Eds.), *Assessing infants and preschoolers with handicaps* (pp. 339–389). Columbus, OH: Merrill.

Rossetti, L. M. (1991). Infant toddler assessment: A clinical perspective. *Infant Toddler Intervention: The Transdisciplinary Journal, 1*, 11–28.

Rossetti, L. M. (1990). *Infant Toddler Language Scale.* East Moline, IL: LinguaSystems.

Roth, F. P. (1990). Early language assessment. In E. D. Gibbs & D. M. Teti (Eds.), *Interdisciplinary assessment of infants: A guide for early intervention.* Baltimore: Paul H. Brookes.

Roth, F. P., & Spekman, N. J. (1984). Assessing the pragmatic abilities of children: Part 1. Organizational framework and assessment parameters. *Journal of Speech and Hearing Disorders, 49,* 2–11.

Sander, E. (1972). When are speech sounds learned. *Journal of Speech and Hearing Disorders, 37,* 55–63.

Schaffer, R. (1977). *Mothering.* Cambridge: Harvard University Press.

Schuler, A. L., Peck, C. A., Willard, C., & Theimer, K. (1989). Assessment of communicative means and functions through interview: Assessing the communicative abilities of individuals with limited language. *Seminars in Speech and Language, 10,* 51–62.

Stoel-Gammon, C. (1991). Normal and disordered phonology in two year olds. *Topics in Language Disorders, 11,* 21–32.

Thurman, S. K., & Widerstrom, A. H. (1985). *Young children with special needs: A developmental and ecological approach.* Boston: Allyn and Bacon.

Westby, C. (1988). Children's play: Reflections of social competence. *Seminars in Speech and Language, 9,* 1–14.

Wetherby, A., Cain, D., Yonclas, D., & Walker, V. (1988). Analysis of intentional communication of normal children from the prelinguistic to the multiword stage. *Journal of Speech and Hearing Disorders, 31,* 240–252.

Wetherby, A., & Prizant, B. (1992). Profiling young children's communicative competence. In S. F. Warren, & J. Reichle (Eds.), *Causes and effects in communication and language intervention* (pp. 217–251). Baltimore: Paul H. Brooks.

Wetherby, A., & Prizant, B. (1990). *Communication and Symbolic Behavior Scales.* Chicago: Riverside.

Wetherby, A., & Rodriguez, G. (1992). Measurement of communicative intentions in normally developing children during structured and unstructured contexts. *Journal of Speech and Hearing Research, 35,* 130–138.

Zimmerman, I., Steiner, V., & Pond, R. E. (1992). *Preschool language scale–3.* San Antonio: Psychological Corporation, Harcourt Brace Jovanovich.

Chapter 15

Emotional, Social, and Personal Development

What Is Emotional, Social, and Personal Development?

Another major domain to include in the assessment process is the emotional, social and personal development of the child. This domain involves an extremely wide range of behaviors. Benner (1992) defines social and emotional development as the development of attachment, the growth of self, the emergence of emotions, and the development of adaptive behaviors that include self-care. The focus is on measures that reflect different aspects of a child's (1) characteristic traits, (2) emotional status, (3) sense of self, and (4) perceptions of others (Simeonsson, 1986). The assessment needs to consider the individual child's characteristics, the caregiver/parent–child interactions and relationships, social and environmental factors. The development of self involves the infant's knowledge of where she or he begins and ends (Benner, 1992). The development of emotions and emotional status are inferred from the child's behavioral responses to social and object interactions. The social and emotional status of a child often is determined by observing the child at play.

Assessment in this domain addresses areas ranging from self concept and locus of control to social competence and anxiety and temperament. Combining the areas of personal, social, and emotional into one domain allows consideration of measures that encompass a broader perspective of the child (Simeonsson, 1986). Therefore, this chapter begins by considering the child's emotional development, expands to consider the social aspects of development, and, finally, considers personal or adaptive behaviors.

General Considerations for Assessment

There are a variety of theoretical approaches to or philosophies of what to assess and measure with different tools or tests. For many special children simply using a psychometric base for psychological testing is inadequate. The particular problems of special children require that assessments be flexible and comprehensive; no one measure is exhaustive or all-inclusive. Early interventionists need to select materials based on the particular concern(s) or question(s) about a particular child.

It is necessary to look at personal-social behavior quantitatively and qualitatively. For example, quantitatively, the examiner is able to derive a developmental level for social skills. Qualitatively, one can consider aspects of social-emotional development e.g., behavioral style, temperament. (See also chapter 3, Qualitative Observations of Assessment Behavior.)

As in the other domains, consider the interaction between domains. The examiner also needs to keep in mind how cognitive and language competence influence an individual's perception of personal-social development. Questions to ask are:

Can the child comprehend thoughts/feelings?

Can the child generalize from one experience to another?

Can the child attend long enough to interact with the examiner?

What is the influence of affective relationships at home (bonding, separation, identity issues)?

Child Characteristics

Infants and young children display different temperament, readability, and behavior patterns (Huntington, 1988). These characteristics influence relationships and affect caregiver behavior.

Temperament

Thomas, Chess, and Birch (1968) identify 10 categories to use in assessing the temperament of infants and young children:

1. activity level (degree of activity displayed),
2. rhythmicity (regularity of behavioral patterns),
3. approach/withdrawal (tendency to approach or withdraw from new situation or person),
4. adaptability (ability to adjust to a new situation),
5. intensity of reaction (degree or level of reaction to different environmental situation),
6. threshold of responsiveness (degree of stimulation necessary to evoke a response),
7. quality of mood (general disposition),
8. distractibility (degree to which environmental stimuli can divert child's attention),
9. attention span (ability to keep attention focused), and
10. persistence (tendency to stick with task despite obstacles).

Readability

This characteristic involves the child's ability to provide caregivers with distinct signals and cues through overt behaviors (Benner, 1992). Infants with disabilities often provide unclear clues that may result in problems. Caregivers may not provide the appropriate response that also could lead to problems in the infant–caregiver relationship.

Mastery Motivation

The motivation a child shows as she or he attempts to learn new skills directly influences his or her opportunity for development. There is a growing body of research on the techniques for the assessment of children's mastery motivation (Benner, 1992). These techniques provide important information for the interventionist. Four forms of mastery motivation assessment currently are in use: (1) the structured mastery-task situation, (2) parental reports of observed mastery behavior, (3) global ratings of goal directedness, and (4) the free-play situation (Brockman, Morgan, & Harmon, 1988). The purpose of assessing mastery motivation is to provide insight into the developmental domains on which the child is focusing energy. The examiner should evaluate the degree of persistence, approach to problem solving, and effectiveness of efforts in each developmental area.

Assessing Child Characteristics

Formal checklists and rating scales are available that assess child characteristics; they also may be observed during multidomain assessments. The *Transdisciplinary Play-Based Assessment* (TPBA) (Linder, 1990) provides an excellent set of guidelines for observing social-emotional development. Table 15–1 gives examples from the TPBA for observation of child characteristics during the assessment. The TPBA also includes worksheets for team members to use to make notes.

Conducting a Comprehensive Assessment

Longitudinal

The most appropriate approach to comprehensive socioemotional assessment is a longitudinal procedure that includes several unstructured observations in the home for use in conjunction with more formal assessment procedures (Fraiberg, 1980). This procedure offers a much more valid and reliable picture of the baby's affective development. Generally, a longitudinal socioemotional assessment occurs during the beginning weeks of intervention. There are several advantages to unstructured home visits over formalized procedures as a means for assessing the mental health of an infant and caregiver. One of them is that the examiner is in a position to observe the infant's abilities and relationships with all members of the household present.

Observing over time increases the likelihood of a more accurate assessment

TABLE 15-1   Observation Guidelines for Social-Emotional Development

I. Temperament
   A. Activity level
      1. How motorically active is the child during the session?
      2. Are there specific times during the session when the child is particularly active?
         a. Beginning, middle, or end
         b. During specific activities
   B. Adaptability
      1. What is the child's *initial* response to new stimuli (persons, situations, and toys)?
         a. Shy, timid, fearful, cautious
         b. Sociable, eager, willing
         c. Aggressive, bold, fearless
      2. How does the child demonstrate his or her interest or withdrawal?
         a. Smiling, verbalizing, touching
         b. Crying, moving away, seeking security
      3. How long does it take the child to adjust to new situations, persons, objects, and so forth?
      4. How does the child adjust to new or altered situations after an initially shy or fearful response?
         a. Self-initiation (slowly warms up, talks to self)
         b. Uses adult or parent as a base of security (needs encouragement and reinforcement to get involved)
         c. Continues to resist and stay uninvolved
   C. Reactivity
      1. How intense does the stimuli presented to the child need to be in order to evoke a discernible response?
      2. What type of stimulation is needed to interest the child?
         a. Visual, vocal, tactile, combination
         b. Object, social
      3. What level of affect and energy are displayed in response to persons, situations, or objects?
      4. What response mode is commonly used?
      5. What is the child's response to frustration?

II. Mastery Motivation
   A. Purposeful activity
      1. What behavior demonstrates purposeful activity?
      2. How does the child explore complex objects?
   B. Goal-directed behaviors
      1. What goal-directed behaviors are observed?
      2. How does the child respond to challenging objects or situations?
         a. Looking
         b. Exploring
         c. Appropriate use
         d. Persistent, task-directed
      3. How often does the child repeat successfully completed, challenging tasks?

TABLE 15-1 *(Continued)*

4. How persistent is the child in goal-directed behavior?
   a. With cause-effect toys
   b. With combinatorial tasks
   c. With means-end behavior
5. Given a choice between an easy and more challenging task, which does the child select? (Examine if the child is over 3½ years old)
6. How does the child demonstrate self-initiation in problem solving?
   a. How frequently is assistance requested?
   b. How does the child organize problem solving?

III. Social Interactions with Parent
   A. Characteristics of child in interaction with the parent
      1. What level of affect is displayed by the child in interactions with the parent? Does the child appear to find the interactions pleasurable?
      2. How does the child react to the emotions expressed by the parent?
      3. How does the child respond to vocal, tactile, or kinesthetic stimulation by the parent?
      4. What type of cues does the child give the parent (vocal, tactile, kinesthetic)? How easily are these cues interpreted?
      5. What percentage of the time is the child active versus inactive in the play time with the parent? What amount of activity is directed toward interaction with the parent?
      6. How frequently does the child initiate an interchange with the parent?
      7. How many interactive behaviors is the child capable of maintaining?
      8. How does the child react to parental requests, limit-setting, or control?
   B. Characteristics of the parent-child interaction
      1. Describe the level of mutual involvement that is demonstrated.
         a. To what degree is there continuity of content in the play?
         b. To what degree is there synchonry of timing in the interactions?
         c. To what degree is there similarity in the level of intensity in the interactions?
         d. To what degree is there equality of turn-taking?
      2. To what degree do the interactions demonstrate a sequence of behaviors with a beginning, middle, and end?
         a. To what degree are themes repeated with variations or expansion?
         b. To what degree do parent and child anticipate the actions of each other?
         c. To what degree does the parent modify sequences to match the capabilities of the child?
      3. How do the parent and child indicate their enjoyment of the interactions?

Source: From Linder, Toni W., *Transdisciplinary Play-based Assessment: A Functional Approach to Working with Young Children*, pp. 139–140. Copyright © 1990. Baltimore, MD: Paul H. Brookes Publishing Co. Reprinted with permission.

and enables the examiner and caregivers to establish sufficient trust to permit relatively ordinary family interactions to occur during the visits.

Home Visits

The early interventionist who is collecting information on caregiver–infant interactions needs to observe the child and caregiver in a natural and comfortable setting for both, which is often the home. A play setting is an excellent time for observing, preferably a time when the child is active and alert. Chapter 2, The Assessment Experience, discusses additional considerations and how to conduct a diagnostic session. Most assessment instruments provide instructions for collecting the information needed.

Home visits also offer opportunities to observe the multiplicity of influences contributing to a developmental problem. Questions to consider are: Are there ample opportunities to explore the environment? Does the baby spend the day in the crib and lack adequate motor control and social experience? Are the effects of hospitalization or a disability affecting the frequency or depth of interactions offered the infant? Home visits allow the early interventionist to inquire about parental perception of the baby's spontaneous behavior as it occurs.

During the home visit record the data collected by using a structured instrument such as the *Home Observation for Measurement of the Environment Inventory* (Bradley & Caldwell, 1980; Caldwell & Bradley, 1972) or write clinical notes. The examiner needs to be sensitive so as not to detract from the spontaneity of the interaction. Generally, it is better to wait until after the visit to actually write and make notes.

The caregivers' previous experiences with other professionals prior to and during referral influence the emotional tone that they present at the assessment. Their feelings about treatment by other professionals often influences their expectations about the assessment process and the team members. The initial interview allows the caregivers the opportunity to ask questions in order to increase their security and sense of control. Assessment over a longer period of time allows the early interventionist to learn about the developmental history without immediately placing a questionnaire in front of the caregivers.

Attachment and Social-Emotional Development

The relationship between the infant and parent or primary caregiver and its influence on shaping subsequent social relationships is the focus of much research. There is general agreement that the infant's first relationship with the caregiver provides the basis for later social and emotional development (Teti & Nakagawa, 1990). Sroufe (1979) defines this first bond or attachment as "an enduring affective tie between infant and caregiver" (p. 495). Research shows that infants differentiate the primary caregiver very early (Lewis, 1987). Eventually attachment is established with secondary caregivers and family members. A stable affective bond is important for healthy emotional and cognitive development regardless of various childrearing practices across cultures (Lewis, 1987). A lack of attachment during the early months often results in later caregiving deficiencies such as child abuse, failure to thrive, and so on (Rossetti, 1990).

Assessment of Attachment and Emotional Development

The early interventionist is able to assess the quality of the attachment by observing the balance between the child's ability to explore and to seek and obtain comfort when distressed (Sroufe, 1979). The child's behavior when left by the caregiver with a stranger also can indicate secure or insecure attachment patterns.

Scales have been developed for structured observation of behaviors on which normal development can be rated. If the child displays normal attachment patterns, it is likely that normal interaction patterns will develop, and therefore, the child is developing emotionally and communicatively.

Avant (1982) describes an assessment strategy that is designed to examine maternal attachment behaviors. This scale is a one-page observation checklist of common attachment behaviors to observe (e.g., during feeding) early in the child's life. Four sets of scores may be obtained (i.e., overall attachment, affectionate behavior, proximity maintaining, and caretaking). The scale provides a simple, systematic, structured method for observing maternal behavior (Rossetti, 1990).

The *Ainsworth Strange Situation Procedure* (Ainsworth, Blehar, Waters, & Wall, 1978; Teti & Nakagawa, 1990) assesses the attachment relationships of children between the ages of 10 and 24 months. During 8, 3-minute episodes, the infant, primary caregiver, and an unfamiliar person follow through structured episodes in a laboratory setting. The infant's behavior is rated for the 2nd through 8th episodes using a 7-point scale on the following dimensions: (1) proximity- and contact-seeking behavior, (2) contact-maintaining behavior, (3) resistant behavior, (4) avoidant behavior, (5) distance interaction, and (6) search behavior during separations.

To use the *Ainsworth* procedure, the child must have established person-permanence and be able to engage in proximity seeking and contact maintenance. Teti and Nakagawa (1990) point out that some adaptations may be required for infants with sensory or other impairments. Many factors can affect the child's response pattern, such as hunger, illness, setting, and so on (Benner, 1992). This measure is meant to be used as the only measure to assess a child's emotional functioning.

The *Attachment Q-Set* (Waters & Deane, 1985), was developed to measure secure base behaviors in the home. This instrument contains 90 behavioral descriptors sorted into 9 groups of 10 each. The groups represent a range from "very much like the child" to "very much unlike the child." The results are compared to average sorting scores as determined by attachment experts as to how a *most secure child* behaves. Using a correlation coefficient measurement, the child's correlation score is compared with the hypothetical most secure child. A high correlation would indicate a similarity in secure base between the real and hypothetical children. Clinical impressions can be formed of a given child from the scores of specific *Q-set* items in relation to their scores on the criterion sort. It is possible to use the items as a basis for talking with caregivers about their relationship with their child and developing interventions (Teti & Nakagawa, 1990).

The *Greenspan-Lieberman Observation System for Assessment of Caregiver-Infant Interaction during Semi-Structured Play* (GLOS) (Greenspan, Lieberman, & Poisson, 1981; Greenspan & Lieberman, 1988) is another example of a test instrument to use in assessing a child's emotional functioning. This instrument provides a structured coding system of infant and caregiver behaviors using videotapes of the infant and caregiver behavior. The GLOS extends the Ainsworth system by providing specific behavioral criteria for assessing the quality of the infant-caregiver relationship from birth to four years of age (Teti & Nakagawa, 1990). It also provides the important ability to play back the video for clarification or further study or intervention with the caregiver(s).

Social Development

A social interaction occurs when the social behavior of one partner is intentionally directed to the second partner. Social development is the acquisition of skills necessary for interacting competently with adults and peers. Social competence is the competent use of those skills in appropriate contexts (Odom & McConnell, 1989). Social competence involves social maturity, self-confidence, self-help skills, independence, and interaction with others.

Two developmental skills or tasks need to occur in social development. It is important that humans establish a positive working relationship or attachment with at least one primary caregiver. This relationship begins as early as 3 to 4 months and continues on through adulthood. The second important task is to establish oneself as a member of a social network of peers. By age 3 children show a preference for playing with peers rather than objects and by age 5 have developed fairly sophisticated social interactions (Odom & McConnell, 1989).

Social development may break down for one of the following reasons: (1) the infant or child lacks the prerequisite skills for participating in successful social interactions (child does not have the motor skills or has not learned how to share toys); (2) the partner does not have sufficient skills for participating in the successful interactions (e.g., child is unable to engage his peers in mutually satisfying interactions because the peer group does not have the necessary skills); (3) both partners have some social skills, but there is a mismatch between the skills involved (e.g., the mother of a child who is blind may not understand that manual exploration is a social skill and may not respond to it). The assessment process needs to consider not only the level of development but also the reason the social development has broken down if the child is delayed in this area.

Adult–Infant Interactions

It is difficult to quantify the exact nature of quality adult–infant interactions. Although there are instruments to identify certain behaviors as representative of optimal interactional patterns, it is difficult to attach weighted values to these behaviors.

Interactional styles vary across families and cultures. Although caregiver–child interactional patterns show considerable variation, certain behaviors do seem to be important for the nurturing of the young child and may be worthwhile intervention goals. Generally, it is accepted that young children need experiences that support their emotional growth. According to Rossetti (1990), critical areas for socio-communicative intervention seem to be related to increasing and introducing experiences that foster the following in caregiver–child interactions:

- Attention and engagement
- Intentional, reciprocal gestures and cues
- Vocal/verba turn-taking
- Elaboration of emotional responsiveness
- Mutually pleasurable exchanges.

Eye contact, crying, quieting, attention to faces and voices, and body movements are interaction cues and responses of the normal newborn. In general, infant–caregiver interactions that are considered in synchrony with the infant's signals are thought to have beneficial long-term effects on cognitive, social, and linguistic skills (Sparks, Clar, Oas, & Erickson, 1988). (See also chapter 14, Communication and Language.)

Children with Disabilities

At times, it may be more difficult to establish a responsive relationship with young children with developmental disabilities. Many factors, such as adjustment to the diagnosis, additional caregiving demands, financial pressures, may affect initial parent–child interactions. In other cases, children are not allowed an optimal opportunity to establish a stable relationship with their primary caregiver. Infants who spend 4 to 10 weeks in an intensive care nursery use all of their physiological energy to survive. There is little energy left to develop a reciprocal relationship with any caregiver. Low birthweight infants spend considerable time during the first year in the hospital. Establishing optimal parent–infant interactional patterns in the early months of life with premature or sick infants definitely is difficult.

Some infants with disabilities experience disrupted social relationships with their parents/caregivers and are less socially accepted by peers than normally developing babies. Infants with disabilities, motoric in particular, cannot provide clear signals or enough information to the caregivers about when they are ready to interact. Some infants have delayed development of behavioral cues that are important for the caregiver (e.g., infants who are blind have muted smiles and an absence of eye contact). At times, stress factors within and from outside the family influence the responsiveness of the caregivers.

Research shows that children with mild, moderate, and severe disabilities interact less often with their peers than normally developing children (Guralnick, 1980; Guralnick & Groom, 1985; Guralnick & Groom, 1987). These data suggest that most preschoolers with disabilities have social interaction delays that exceed their developmental delay (Odom & McConnell, 1989). These peer relationships often cannot develop automatically even in integrated settings.

Social Interaction Assessment

Suggested Procedureal Considerations

Early interventionists need to be reminded of certain procedural considerations before assessment begins. They are:

1. Social interaction skills usually are observed in natural contexts and recorded by an observer or reported by a caregiver. Administering test items from standardized assessments usually is not appropriate for social interaction skills.
2. The setting affects the social behavior of infants and children. A natural setting is recommended, realizing that even the presence of the examiner may cause children to respond differently.
3. Social interaction is a reciprocal process. The interaction will be affected by the partners in the situation. The social context of the assessment needs to be reported when the information is interpreted.
4. Collect information from multiple sources. The more agreement there is across settings, the more confident the observer can be about the information.

Levels and Techniques for Assessment

It is possible to assess different levels of social interaction skill development. Information may be obtained on individual social behaviors, relationships, or comparisons with established norm. The particular level or approach chosen is based on the purpose of the assessment.

Several techniques exist for assessing the social interaction development of infants, toddlers, and preschoolers with disabilities. Each of the techniques provides slightly different information. Odom and McConnell (1989) suggest collecting assessment information through: (1) observation of infants and children in a social context, (2) rating scales, (3) sociometric nominations or ratings by peers, (4) criterion-referenced assessments, and (5) norm-referenced tests. Table 15-2 provides a summary of assessment of social behavior and interaction of infants and young children with disabilities. Chapter 11, Ecological and Behavioral Assessment, discusses methods such as anecdotal data collection, direct observation, rating scales.

TABLE 15-2 **Assessment of Social Behavior and Interaction of Infants and Young Children with Handicaps**

Type	Instruments	Age Range	Behaviors Assessed	Description
Anecdotal	Systematic Anecdotal Assessment of Social Interaction (Odom, McConnell, Kohler, & Strain, 1987)	Open	Behaviors generated by the teacher	A structured anecdotal recording system for collecting social interaction information
Direct observation	Social Interaction Scan (Odom et al., 1988)	Preschool	Isolate/unoccupied Proximity Interactive Negative Teacher Interaction	A system for scanning classrooms of children. Designed to measure both interaction play and social integration.
	Observational Assessment of Reciprocal Social Interaction (McConnell, Sisson, & Sandler, 1984)	Preschool	Initiations (five behaviors listed) Summative (four behaviors listed) Teacher behavior (two behaviors listed)	An interval-sampling system designed to measure components and durations of social interaction of peers
	Scale of Social Participation (Parten, 1932)	Preschool	Unoccupied Onlooker Solitary Parallel Associative Cooperative	An interval-sampling system designed to measure young children's participation in social interaction
	Parten/Smilansky Combined Scale (Rubin, 1983)	Preschool	In addition to Parten Scale (1932) above Functional Constructive Dramatic Games with rules	An interval-sampling system designed to measure cognitive play within a social context
	Bakeman & Adamson (1984)	Infancy	Unengaged Onlooking Persons Objects Passive Joint Coordinated Joint	Event-recording systems for measuring mother/infant interactions
	Guralnick & Groom (1987)	Preschool	Gains peer attention Uses peer as resource Leads peer in activity—positive Leads peer in activity—negative Imitates peer	Event-recording system for measuring peer interactions

(Continued)

TABLE 15-2 *(Continued)*

Type	Instruments	Age Range	Behaviors Assessed	Description
			Expresses affection to peer Expresses hostility to peer Competes for adult attention Competes for equipment Shows pride in product Follows peers activity without specific direction	
	Odom, Silver, Sandler & Strain (1983); Strain (1983); Tremblay, Strain, Hendrickson, & Shores (1980)	Preschool	Play organizer Share request Share Assistance Assistance request Affection Complimentary Negative Motor Gestural Negative Vocal Verbal	Event-recording system for measuring peer social interactions
Teacher Rating	Social Interaction Rating Scale (Hops et al., 1979)	Preschool-Elementary	Summary score	Eight items with 7-point Likert scale
	Teacher Rating of Social Interaction (Odom et al., 1988)	Preschool	Summary scores Positive and negative subscores	Eight items with a 5-point Likert scale
	Preschool Behavior Questionnaire (Behar & Stringfield, 1974)	Preschool	Summary score Hostile subscore Angry subscore Hyperactive subscore	30 items with a 3-point Likert scale
	Social Competence Scale (Kohn, 1977)	Preschool	Participation vs. disinterest subscore Cooperation vs. defiance subscore	
	Carolina Record of Individual Behavior (Simeonsson, Huntington, Short, & Ware, 1982)	Infant/ Preschool	State rating score Eight items related to orientation and communications Eight items related to task performance and responsiveness	Rating scale completed after 15–30 minute observation of infant/child

(Continued)

TABLE 15–2   *(Continued)*

Type	Instruments	Age Range	Behaviors Assessed	Description
	Carey Infant Temperament Scale (Carey & McDevitt, 1978)	Infant	Allows the classification of several patterns of infant temperament	95-item questionnaire completed by parents: items are scored on a 6-point scale
Rating scores on 14 behavioral outcomes of intervention	Teacher Rating of Intervention Behavior (Odom, McConnell, Kohler, & Strain, 1987)	Preschool	Rating scores on 14 behavioral outcomes of intervention	Rating scale for measuring social interaction target for intervention
Sociometric	McCandless & Marshall (1957)	Preschool	Summary score of peer nominations as friends	Peer nomination sociometric using photographs
	Asher, Singleton, Tinsley, & Hymel (1979)	Preschool	Summary score of peer rating by whole class	Peer rating scale using photographs
Criterion-referenced	Learning Accomplishment Profile (LAP) Early LAP (LeMay, Griffin, & Sanford, 1977)	Infancy-Preschool	Criterion items in the social strand	Criterion-referenced items provided in strands across developmental areas
	Battelle Developmental Inventory (Newborg, Stock, Wnek, Guidubaldi, & Svinicki, 1984)	Infancy-Preschool	Criterion items in the personal social strand, also provides norms	Assessment across developmental areas
	Portage Guide to Early Education (Bluma, Shearer, Frohman, & Hillard, 1976)	Infancy-Preschool	Criterion items in social abilities strand	Criterion-referenced items provided across developmental areas
Norm-referenced	Vineland Adaptive Behavior Scale (Sparrow, Balla, & Cicchetti, 1984)	Preschool and above	Age scores and percentile ranks for social age	General adaptive behavior scale with social competence subscale
	California Preschool Social Competency Scale (Levine, Elzey, & Lewis, 1969)		36-item rating yields raw score and percentile ranked norms	Scale designed to measure social competence of preschool children

Source: Reprinted with permission of Merrill, an imprint of Macmillan Publishing Company, from *Assessing Infants and Preschoolers with Handicaps* by Donald B. Bailey, Jr. and Mark Wolery. Copyright © 1989 by Merrill Publishing Company.

Individual Social Behaviors

There are several ways to assess individual social behaviors: (1) Count the frequency with which a social behavior occurs within a given time frame. (2) Make judgments of the affective quality of the social behavior (i.e., positive or negative). (3) The examiner or data collector indicates whether the child was initiating or responding to the social behavior of another child or adult.

Interactional Level

Social reciprocity is important at the interactional level. One form of social reciprocity is the immediate response of a social partner to a social behavior. In this type of social reciprocity the sequence or order of behaviors in an interaction is significant. Social behaviors that produce a response from a peer are reciprocal; behaviors that do not produce a response are not reciprocal. Examiners or data collectors need to identify the positive social behaviors that produce a response (Odom & McConnell, 1989).

Another type of reciprocity refers to the direction and frequency of social interactions with potential partners. To assess this type of reciprocity, the number of social behaviors a child directs to his peers and the number directed to him from his peers are counted. It also is possible to do this with caregivers and other children such as strangers, older children, or siblings.

The duration of interactions also may be assessed. Duration refers to the length of time an interaction continues as measured with a stopwatch—time the beginning to the end of the interaction. The examiner also can measure the number of behaviors in a social interaction chain by recording and counting the number of behaviors in each interaction.

Social Relationships

Infants are assessed based on achieving social developmental tasks, attachment, and social acceptance within a peer group. At the preschool level, social relationships with peers are most often measured by the use of a sociometric assessment. These assessments rate the popularity of the child as well as the level of acceptance the child has achieved in the peer group (Asher & Taylor, 1981). Peer preferences or relationships also can be examined.

With sociometric assessment procedures children are asked to provide general qualitative evaluations of the social acceptance, social preference, or likability of other children. Teachers usually gather sociometric information from intact groups of children. Teachers need to be cautious in interpreting information obtained from sociometric instruments. Sociometric measures cannot necessarily be expected to offer stable estimates of social preference (McConnell & Odom, 1986).

Two useful general types of sociometric assessment instruments are peer nominations and peer ratings. With peer nominations children are asked to identify those of their classmates who meet some general criterion (''best friend'' or the one "liked the least"). The criteria vary depending on the purpose of the assessment. Consider possible caregiver concerns when using negative nomination criteria. When peer ratings are used, children provide general qualitative ratings for each child in the class or play group. The criteria depend on the purpose of the assessment but are used to gather general statements of preference (e.g., How much do you like to talk to/ play with _____?) (Odom & McConnell, 1989).

Norm-based Assessment

When diagnosing or classifying a child, it is necessary to judge a child's social behavior against an established norm. In these cases, the examiner is concerned about the general performance of the child in relationship to the performances of other children. This requires the use of a norm-based instrument to document a child's current level of functioning and, thus, to diagnose a social problem and possibly qualify a child for special services.

The majority of norm-based assessments of social behavior and competence describe the child's performance on broad dimensions of social development. These norms are used to compare the development of an individual child to the overall status of other children at a similar age are usually are part of a broader assessment of development. Norm-based measures often rely on caregiver ratings, which are completed in interview formats, and teacher ratings completed in classroom situations.

An example of a newly developed, standardized, norm-referenced scale is the *Social Skills Rating System* (SSRS) by Gresham and Elliott (1990). This instrument assesses student social behaviors of preschoolers that may affect teacher-student relations, peer acceptance, and academic performance. The measure contains three behavior rating forms (teacher, parent, and student versions) and an integrative assessment and intervention planning record. The subdomains in both the parent and teacher ratings scales are cooperation, assertion, and self-control. The parent version also measures responsibility. Raters indicate how often a behavior occurs (never, sometimes, or very often).

During the administration of a standardized instrument, the examiner focuses on the baby's relationship with his or her caregiver to gain valuable information about socioemotional development. For example, McCune et al., (1990) suggest *The Bayley Infant Behavior Record* (IBR) for use as a psychosocial screening instrument to identify children at risk. Clinical observations made during a Bayley assessment often provide clues to socioemotional problems and to the impact of affective considerations on cognitive performance. The following lists from McCune et al. (1990) provide examples of behaviors that generally indicate problems in socioemotional development.

Doesn't take pleasure in interpersonal relationships:

- Mechanically builds tower
- Doesn't look to parent or examiner as social reference point
- Experiences private pleasure in tasks themselves, but doesn't share with others

- Doesn't warm up to examiner
- Unable to initiate a subsequent act without verbal encouragement

Difficulty in self-organization:

- Unwillingness to relinquish toys as testing proceeds
- Unwillingness to engage sufficiently with a particular set of materials to complete a required task
- may seem unwilling to reach for or touch objects
- May appear highly distractible or unable to focus on one task
- May be easily frustrated and unable to persevere with tasks that are not mastered easily
- May operate only on their own agenda and cannot become interested in any items that are presented

Difficulties in caregiver-infant relationship that may be observed may involve:

- Caregiver's responsiveness to infant's bids for caregiver attention or infolvement
- Caregiver's capacity to provide appropriate social cues, such as reassurance or encouragement
- An extremely anxious caregiver who is intrusive or tries to take over the assessment process
- Overanxious parent may be unwilling to allow examiner to attend to baby by demanding constant attention from examiner
- Caregiver who has withdrawn from relationship may turn baby over to examiner and act as if not present in room

Criterion-referenced or Curriculum-based Instruments

Curriculum-based instruments provide highly specific information regarding a child's current level of performance for multiple individual skills (Odom & McConnell, 1989). The following assessments provide information for planning individual interventions in the area of personal-social development:

Battelle Developmental Inventory (Newborg, Stock, Wnek, Guidubaldi, & Svinicki, 1984)

Carolina Curriculum for Handicapped Infants (Johnson-Martin, Jens, Attermeier, & Hacker, 1991)

Hawaii Early Learning Profile (Furuno, O'Reilly, Inatsuka, Hosaka, Allman, & Zeisloft-Falbey, 1985)

Early Learning Accomplishment Profile (Glover, Preminger, & Sanford, 1978)

Portage Guide to Early Development (Bluma, Shearer, Frohman, & Hillard, 1976)

The early interventionist needs to select the test based on the needs and strengths of the particular child.

Odom and McConnell (1989) provide the following guidelines for choosing criterion-referenced measures. The instrument should: (1) provide for direct and detailed assessment of a child's behavior across situations and settings, (2) focus on discrete social skills or components of social interaction (social initiation might include child's use of eye contact and/or proximity to peers during play, etc.), (3) arrange skills in a natural progression or hierarchy by task analysis or typical developmental progress, (4) be carefully linked to curricula or other intervention programs for children, and (5) be sensitive to small changes in behavior.

Chapter 10 discusses criterion-referenced or curriculum-based measures. A survey of the subdomains in the various multidomain, curriculum-based assessments shows the wide range of behaviors included in the personal-social and emotional domain. Table 15-3 summarizes subdomains found in some commonly used multidomain assessments.

Play

Chapters 13 and 14 discuss play in relation to a child's cognitive and language development. It is often possible to determine a child's social or emotional status by observing him or her at play. The interaction of the child's growing self-awareness, his or her cognitive understanding of objects in the environment, and attachment to and investment in caregivers allows the child to begin playing (Benner, 1992).

Researchers have identified several types of play. These types of play focus on interactions with people and with the exploration or use of objects. Parten's (1932) category system for social play is often used to classify social play. The six categories of play in which children typically engage unoccupied behavior, onlooker behavior, solitary independent play, parallel activity, associative play, and cooperative or organized supplementary play. Although this classification system appears to be sequential, other authors suggest that it is more useful when considered as a description of various types of social participation by young children, rather than as a developmental continuum (Benner, 1992; Rogers, 1982).

Several classification systems have been developed for identifying the types of play in which children engage. Wolery and Bailey (1989) summarize the various classification systems as shown in Table 15-4. Each of these may be defined operationally and used for assessing play (Wolery & Bailey, 1989). They are not meant to be seen as developmental sequences, but as different types of play for children during early childhood. Chapter 13, Cognition, summarizes various scales that have been developed to assess play.

The examiner who wants to assess play skills needs to directly observe play sessions to find out the types of social interaction and toy or object play the child demonstrates. The assessment of toy play should focus on at least three goals: (a) describing children's general contact with toys, (b) identifying children's

TABLE 15-3 Personal/Social Items on Assessment Instruments

Instrument	Domain/Subdomains	Number of Items
Arizona Basic Assessment and Curriculum Utilization (ABACUS) 2–5.5 years	**Socialization** awareness of self and others; awareness of feelings; social information; play behavior; interactive behavior	33 items
	Self-care	48 items
Battelle Developmental Inventory 0–8 years	**Personal/Social** adult interaction; express feelings/affect; self-concept; peer interaction; coping; social role; attention; eating	75 items
	Adaptive dressing; personal responsibility	59 items
Brigance Diagnostic Inventory of Early Development 0–6 years	**Self-help** feeding/eating; dressing/undressing; fastening/unfastening; toileting; bathing; grooming	137 items
	Personal/Social general social/emotional development; play skills and behavior; work-related skills and behavior	102 items
Carolina Curriculum for Infants and Toddlers with Special Needs 0–2 years	**Social skills** interaction and smiling; game playing; affection; sharing; comforting skills; imitation; using words or signs to express wants	47 items
	Self-help skills feeding; grooming; dressing	35 items
	Self-direction makes choices; plays alone; explores	9 items
Carolina Curriculum for Preschoolers 3–5 years	**Self-concept**	15 items
	Interpersonal	21 items
	Self-help	32 items
Learning Accomplishments Profile 0–6 years	**Personal/Social**	40 items
	Self-help	60 items
Hawaii Early Learning Profile 0–3 years	**Social/Emotional** physical contact; eye contact; (play) interactions; mirror interaction; stranger interaction; mother interaction; imitating behavior; expresses feelings/emotions	94 items
	Self-help	93 items
Inside Help Hawaii Early Learning Profile— 1992 Edition	**Social/Emotional** attachment/separation/autonomy; development of self-esteem; expression of emotions/feelings; learning rules and social expectations; social interaction and play	113 items
	Self-help dressing; independent feeding; oral motor; grooming and hygiene; toileting; household independence and responsibility	82 items
Early Lap Accomplishment Profile 0–3 years	**Self-help**	49 items
	Social/Emotional eye contact with familiar adult; interactions with strangers; interactions with mirror	38 items
	Play interactions role-playing; initiates play; parallel play	
Vineland Adaptive Behavior Scales (classroom edition) 0–8 years	**Socialization** interpersonal relationship; play and leisure time; coping skills	53 items

TABLE 15–4 Examples of Different Taxonomies of Play

Author and Play Types (categories)	Description
Smilansky (1968)	
Functional play	Repetitive movements that appear playful and frequently involve objects
Constructive play	Use of objects to make or create something
Dramatic play	Use of pretend play with or without objects, frequently involving the child assuming a given role
Games with rules	Engagement in activities that involve compliance with the conventions and requirements of games and may involve competition with others
Chance (1979)	
Physical play	Action that is frequently social, may be competitive, and includes rough-and-tumble activities
Manipulative play	Actions on objects, designed to gain control of those objects
Symbolic play	Pretend play that may include objects being used to represent other objects
Games	Engagement in activities that involves compliance with the conventions and requirements of games and may involve competition with others
Wehman (1977)[a]	
Exploration	
Level I—Orientational responses	Relatively abrupt behavioral changes that occur as a result of external stimulation and appear to redirect the child's attention
Level II—Locomotor exploration	Movement about an environment that produces sensory feedback
Level III—Perceptual investigation and manipulation	Movements on objects that appear to provide the child with information about the characteristics of the object
Level IV—Searching	Seeking a new stimulus for exploration
Toy play	
Level I—Repetitive manual manipulation/oral contracts	Repetitive actions on objects with attention to sensory consequences
Level II—Pounding, throwing, pushing/pulling	Repetitive actions on objects that frequently involve gross-motor movements and a beginning awareness of cause/effect relationships
Level III—Personalized toy use	Use of toys to perform actions on the child's body, frequently uses miniatures of real objects to imitate common routines
Level IV—Manipulation of movable parts of toys	Movements on movable parts of objects; objects are viewed as having parts rather than being a whole
Level V—Separation of parts of toys	Movements on objects that result in separation of parts or of taking things out of containers

(Continued)

TABLE 15-4   *(Continued)*

Author and Play Types (categories)	Description
Level VI—Combinational use of toys	Movements on toys where two or more different objects are used together or where parts of objects are put back together
Sutton-Smith (1970)[b]	
Imitation	Copying the motor and/or verbal behavior of others
Exploration	Investigating what can be done with objects, and how they work
Prediction	Testing the effects of various actions on objects and the effects of different behaviors
Construction	Movements on objects to make or create something

[a]This classification is based on an adaptation of Wehman's (1977) hierarchies by Bailey and Wolery (1984).

[b]This categorization of play describes common modes of play seen throughout early childhood.

Source: Reprinted with permission of Merrill, an imprint of Macmillan Publishing Company, from *Assessing Infants and Preschoolers with Handicaps* by Donald B. Bailey, Jr. and Mark Wolery. Copyright © 1989 by Merrill Publishing Company.

reactions to and preferences for specific toys, and (c) assessing children's levels and types of play (Wolery & Bailey, 1989). The examiner also should assess the types of play displayed, the complexity of that play and any themes that exist in the play (Wolery & Bailey, 1989).

Guidelines for Setting Up a Play Session

Wolery and Bailey (1989) provide a number of factors to consider when setting up a play assessment session. These factors are summarized below:

   1. Children should be free to select various toys, have adequate space to play, and have peers available if assessing social play.
   2. When assessing peer interactions, the familiarity of the peers chosen, the sex, the toys chosen, and the competence of the peers will influence the type and amount of play.
   3. The type of activities will influence the amount of positive social interactions or play. To assess social play, the space should be small, peers should be available, and structured free-play activities should occur.
   4. The type and number of toys and materials influence the type and nature of play. When assessing children's social play, a limited number of social materials should be available. The examiner should use toys that will produce certain types of play, such as constructive or pretend, when assessing the nature of play.

5. Observation over a few days will provide a more representative sample of children's play skills.

6. Children who seem to have few play skills may need to be prompted to play and the level of assistance needed should be noted by the examiner. Children with motor disabilities may need to be provided with batter-operated toys and computer-activated switches. The examiner should observe the positions that allow the child to make movements, switches that are easily and efficiently activated, and children's toy preferences.

Adaptive Behavior and Self-care Skills

Adaptive behavior has been defined by the American Association on Mental Deficiency (AAMD) as "the effectiveness or degree with which individuals meet the standards of personal independence and social responsibility expected for age and cultural group" (Grossman, 1983, p. 1). Adaptive behavior may be defined physically, socially, and emotionally. Physical adaptive behaviors involve basic functions such as eating, keeping warm, and avoiding danger. Social adaptive behaviors include communicating basic needs, cooperative play skills, and appropriate use of toys. Emotionally, adaptive behaviors include the formation of relationships that promote self-esteem and identity (Benner, 1992). Self-care skills are an important component of adaptive behavior. The major self-care skill areas are dressing/undressing, eating/feeding, toileting, and grooming.

Interdisciplinary Involvement

The child's functioning with adaptive and self-care skills greatly depends on the child's movement skills. Therefore, physical and occupational therapists need to participate in the assessment and intervention planning. Speech and language pathologists can assist in assessing oral motor behaviors needed in eating. Nutritionists can assess the child's diet. Of course, caregivers are essential in providing information related to choosing self-care objectives and teaching the appropriate self-care skills.

Formal and Informal Assessment

As with other developmental areas, it is necessary to assess adaptive behavior both formally and informally in a variety of settings. Using standardized procedures provides a direct assessment of a child's performance in a particular setting and at a particular time. It is possible to use informants or third-party assessment by caregivers or teachers, but these methods rely on the memory and knowledge of the informant. Informal observation provides the opportunity for assessing behaviors in a variety of situations and allows the examiner to observe the child's responses to the environment. Informal checklists may also be used as a guide for discussing issues related to adaptive behaviors on an informal basis.

Harrison (1991) provides a checklist in age periods that offers some guidelines of behaviors to observe at given ages.

Assessment Instruments

The *Early Coping Inventory* (ECI) (Zeitlin, Williamson, & Szczepanski, 1988) measures the coping and adaptive behavior of children whose developmental level is between 4 to 36 months. *The Coping Inventory* (Zeitlin, 1985) can be used with children ages 3 to 16 years. The organization and administration of both are similar. The ECI contains 48 items that are divided into the following three categories: sensorimotor organization (i.e., behaviors used to regulate psychophysiological functions and to integrate sensory and motor processes), reactive behavior (i.e., actions used to respond to the demands of physical and social environments), and self-initiated behavior (i.e., self-directed actions intended to meet personal needs and to interact with objects and people).

The child is rated on a five-point scale according to the level of effectiveness that ranges from "the behavior is not effective" to "the behavior is consistently effective across situations." The manual provides many examples to clarify the rating scale that is based on the rater's subjective judgment. The ECI provides three types of information: sensorimotor organization, reactive behavior, and self-initiated. An adaptive behavior index provides a global measure of the child's coping competence. The examiner may also determine the child's coping profile; it compares the child's level of effectiveness in the three behavioral categories (i.e., sensorimotor organization, reactive behavior, and self-initiated behavior). This profile helps to determine the primary focus for intervention. The scorer also may list the most and least adaptive behaviors to identify the child's specific strengths and weaknesses. Table 15–5 presents some examples of behaviors from the ECI and the *Coping Inventory*.

The *AAMD Adaptive Behavior Scale—School Edition* (Lambert, Windmiller, Tharinger, & Cole, 1981) was developed for individuals from age 3 to 16 to measure personal independence and social responsibility. This assessment instrument contains 21 domains. The first 9 domains use a rating scale of dependence and independence and include independent functioning (i.e., eating, toileting, cleanliness, appearance, care of clothing, dresssing and undressing, and travel), physical development (i.e., sensory and motor development), language development (i.e., expression, comprehension, and social language development), responsibility, and socialization. The other 12 domains in the second part of the scale are rated according to the frequency with which a behavior occurs. Behaviors in this part include aggressiveness, rebelliousness, trustworthiness, mannerisms, and interpersonal manners. A percentile rank can be derived for each domain, and 5 clusters (i.e., personal self-sufficiency, community self-sufficiency, personal-social responsibility, social adjustment, and personal adjustment) can provide an analysis of the child's functioning. Table 15–6 shows examples of additional assessment instruments for adaptive behavior skills.

TABLE 15-5 **Sample Items from the Early Coping Inventory (4 to 36 months)—Zeitlin, Williamson, & Szczepanski, 1988**

Sensorimotor organization
Child demonstrates ability to self-comfort.

Reactive behavior
Child demonstrates an awareness that own behavior has an effect on people and objects.

Self-initiated behavior
Child applies a previously learned behavior to a new situation.

Source: Copyright © 1988 by Shirley Zeitlin and G. Gordon Williamson. Reprinted by permission of Scholastic Testing Service, Inc., from *Early Coping Inventory: A Measure of Adaptive Behavior.*

Sample Items from the Coping Inventory (3 to 16 years)— Zeitlin, 1985

Coping with self: Productive
Child, when presented with a new or difficult situation, finds a way of handling it.

Coping with self: Active
Child tells or shows others when he or she is angry or in disagreement.

Coping with self: Flexible
Child can manage high-stress situations (finds ways to reduce feelings of stress or finds solution to the stress-causing situation).

Coping with environment: Productive
Child functions with minimal amount of external structure (is self-directed, can create own routine or structure).

Coping with environment: Active
Child is stimulating to others (gets others started, enthused, involved).

Coping with environment: Flexible
Child accepts warmth and support (for example, responds to affection and encouragement from others, likes to be held, kissed, praised).

Source: Copyright © 1985 by Shirley Zeitlin. Reprinted by permission of Scholastic Testing Service, Inc., from *Coping Inventory—Observation Form.*

Assessing Survival Skills

As more and more preschoolers are being served in regular preschools and as they move into kindergarten, more emphasis is being placed on the skills children need to succeed in the regular kindergarten setting. Vincent et al. (1980) define preschool survival skills as behaviors that will facilitate referral to and maintenance in less restrictive environments when the child is ready for kindergarten or first

TABLE 15-6 Assessment Instruments for Adaptive Behavior

Measure	Age Range	Areas Assessed	Source
Adaptive Behavior Inventory (ABIC) (Mercer & Lewis, 1978)	5–11 years	Family Community Peer relations Earner and Consumer Self-maintenance	Psychological Corp. 555 Academic Court P.O. Box 839954 San Antonio, TX 78283
Adaptive Behavior Scale for Infants and Early Childhood (Leland, Shoace, McElwain, & Christie, 1980)	Birth–6 years	Coping with environmental demands	Ohio State University Nisonger Center Columbus, OH

Adaptive Behavior Scale, School Edition (Lamber, 1981)	3–17 years	Personal self-sufficiency
		  independent functioning; physical development
		Community self-sufficiency
		  economic activity; language development; numbers and
		  time
		Personal-social responsibility
		  withdrawal; self-direction; responsibility
		Social adjustment
		  aggressiveness; antisocial vs. social behavior;
		  rebelliousness; trustworthiness; habits; activity level;
		  symptomatic behavior
		Personal adjustment
		  mannerisms; appropriateness of interpersonal habits;
		  vocal habits
			Publishers Test Service
			McGraw-Hill
			Princeton Road
			Hightstown, NJ 08520

Behavior Evaluation Scale, 2 (McCarney, Leigh & Cornbleet, 1990)	Grades K–12	Learning problems Interpersonal difficulties Inappropriate behavior Unhappiness and depression Physical symptoms and fears	Pro-Ed 8700 Shoal Creek Blvd. Austin, TX 78758-6897

Behavior Problem Checklist, Modified Version for Preschool (BPC) (Quay & Peterson, 1983)	Grades 1–12	Conduct
		  negativism; disruptiveness; destructiveness;
		  impertinence; fighting
		Personality
		  feelings of inferiority; shyness; lack of self confidence;
		  anxiety
		Social withdrawal
		  social withdrawal; sluggishness; preoccupation; doesn't
		  have fun; aloofness
			Journal of Abnormal Psychology, 5(3), 277–287

TABLE 15-6 (*Continued*)

Measure	Age Range	Areas Assessed	Source
Child Behavior Checklist (CBC) (Achenbach, 1981, 1986)	*Two versions:* 2–3 years; 4–16 years	Attention seeking attention seeking; jealousy; wanting help Hyperactivity restlessness; hyperactivity; easily startled; tension; rowdiness Distractibility distractibility; short attention span; clumsiness Depression Aggression Somatic complaints Hyperactivity	University of Vermont Burlington, VT
Children's Adaptive Behavior Scale (Richmond & Kicklighter, 1980)	5–10 years	Language development Independent functioning Family role performance Economic-vocational activity Socialization	Humanics Publishing 1482 Mecaslin St., NW P.O. Box 7400 Atlanta, GA 30357
Comprehensive Behavior Rating Scale for Children (Neeper & Lahey, 1988)	6–14 years	Inattention and disorganization Linguistic and information processing Conduct disorder Motor hyperactivity Anxiety and depression Sluggish tempo Social competence	Psychological Corp. 555 Academic Court P.O. Box 839954 San Antonio, TX 78283
Comprehensive Test of Adaptive Behavior (CTAB) and Normative Adaptive Behavior Checklist (Adams, 1986)	Birth. 21 years	Self-help skills toileting; grooming; dressing; eating Home living skills living room; kitchen (utensil, cooking); kitchen (cleaning); bedroom; bath and utility; yard care Independent living skills health; telephone; travel; time-telling; economic; vocational Social skills self awareness; interaction; leisure Sensory and motor skills sensory awareness, discrimination; motor skills Language concepts and academic skills language, math, reading, writing	Merrill Publishing Co. Test Division 1300 Alum Creek Drive P.O. Box 508 Columbus, OH 43216

TABLE 15-6 *(Continued)*

Measure	Age Range	Areas Assessed	Source
Developmental Profile II (Alpern, Ball, & Shearer, 1980)	Birth–9 years	Physical skill Self-help Social Academic Communication	Psychological Development Publishing P.O. Box 3198 Aspen, CO 81611
Kohn Social Comp. Scale, Research Edition (Kohn, 1986)	Preschool–K	Social and emotional functioning (cooperative-compliant vs. angry-defiant; interest vs. apathetic)	Psychological Corp. 555 Academic Court San Antonio, TX 78283
Scales of Independent Behavior (Bruininks, Woodcock, Hill, & Weatherman, 1984)	Infant–Adult	Motor skills Social interactions and communication skills Personal living skills; community living skills Broad independence Internalized maladaptive behavior Asocial maladaptive behavior Externalized maladaptive behavior General maladaptive behavior	DLM Teaching Resources One DLM Park Allen, TX 75002
Social Emotional Dimension Scale (Hutton & Roberts, 1986)	5.5–18.5 years	Physical and fear reaction Depressive reaction Avoidance of peer interaction Avoidance of teacher interaction Aggressive interaction Inappropriate behaviors	Pro-Ed 8700 Shoal Creek Blvd. Austin, TX 78758-6897
Vineland Adaptive Behavior Scales (Harrison, 1985)	Infant–18 years	Communication receptive; expressive; written Daily living skills personal; domestic; community Socialization interpersonal; play and leisure time; coping skills Motor skills gross; fine	American Guidance Serv. Publishers' Building P.O. Box 99 Circle Pines, MN 55014-1796

grade. Behaviors that have been identified as survival skills were originally identified and researched by Walter (1979). Best practices literature for early childhood special education services advocates teaching skills that have future utility for young children (McDonnell & Hardman, 1988). Early interventionists need to assess and then include survival skills in the preschoolers instructional program.

McCormick and Kawate (1982) found that few of the behaviors considered important for participation in regular kindergarten and first-grade classes are being assessed when using the most common preschool assessment instruments. They recommend that practitioners examine the instrument(s) currently in use in their settings to determine if these behaviors are being assessed. Table 15–7 presents the survival skills, rated as ''very important'' or ''absolutely essential,'' from Walter's list (McCormick & Kawate, 1982).

Summary

The emotional, social, and personal areas of development encompass a broad range of behaviors. This chapter attempts to touch on the variety of behaviors involved. Assessment of these behaviors must involve the family and all the professional members of the multidisciplinary team. As with the total assessment process, use of multimethod, multisource, and multidimensional evaluations is essential.

Suggested Group Activities

1. Devise a questionnaire to use with caregivers who are with the child at home. Be sure to include areas of emotional and social development as well as to provide family members with the opportunity to share any concerns or needs they have about the child.

2. List situations or circumstances that might demonstrate a child's ability to explore his or her environment. How could the examiner determine if the child is behaving in an age- appropriate manner?

3. Brainstorm a list of events that could cause a child to seek comfort due to distress. Include any circumstances that may occur in the home and school environment. How could the behaviors be recorded? If possible, include a checklist for the caregiver to refer to when considering these consequences.

4. Divide participants into groups and assign an age to each group (i.e., 0 to 4 months, 4 to 8 months, and so on). Have each group make a list of social skills to determine social competence that would be appropriate for that particular age. Groups can later share their lists and copy them, if desired.

5. Develop a social rating scale that could be used with young children. Include a variety of behaviors, interactions, and social/emotional experiences or situations.

TABLE 15-7 Kindergarten Survival Skills (Hawaii Version)

Independent task work
Begins work within an appropriate time without extra teacher direction
Stays on task without extra teacher direction
Completes tasks within allotted time
Completes task at criterion
Follows routine at end of work session (e.g., waits, puts materials away)

Group attending/participation
Sits appropriately
Does not disrupt peers
Focuses visual attention on speaker(s), shifting focus appropriately
Participates and/or follows task directions in a small group
Participates and/or follows task directions in a large group
Participates at appropriate time (e.g., waits for turn) in a group

Following class routine
Locates *own* possessions and returns them to appropriate locations
Locates materials and replaces or puts them in order when finished
Goes to various areas in the room when requested and/or directed
Makes transitions from one activity to the next with general group verbal cue
Makes transition from one activity to the next using contextual cues
Follows general rules and routines established in classroom

Appropriate classroom behavior
Works/plays without disrupting or bothering peers
Waits appropriately
Modifies behavior when provided with verbal direction
Reacts appropriately to changes in the routine
Uses time between activities appropriately

Self-care
Takes care of own toileting needs without supervision
Washes hands without supervision
Undresses without supervision (except for help with fasteners)
Dresses without supervision (except for help with fasteners)

Direction following
Complies with simple directions provided by adult to the child
Complies with simple directions by an adult to the group
Follows two-step direction

Social/Play skills
Spontaneously begins play activities during play time
Maintains play activity for an appropriate length of time
Interacts verbally with peers
Maintains play with peers for an appropriate length of time
Participates appropriately by performing game actions according to rules

Functional communication
Asks for information
States needs

Source: From McCormick, Linda, & Kawate, Janice, Kindergarten survival skills: New directions for preschool special education. In *Education and Training of the Mentally Retarded,* 17(3): 249, October 1982. Copyright © 1982. Reprinted with permission of Slack, Inc.

References

Ainsworth, M. D. S., Blehar, M. C., Walters, E., & Wall, S. (1978). *Patterns of attachment: A psychological study of the strange situation.* Hillsdale, NJ: Lawrence Erlbaum Associates.

Asher, S. R., & Taylor, A. R. (1981). Social outcomes of mainstreaming: Sociometric assessment and beyond. *Exceptional Education Quarterly, 1,* 13–30.

Avant, P. (1982). A maternal attachment assessment strategy. In S. Humenick-Smith (Ed.), *Analysis of current assessment strategies in the health care of young children and childbearing families.* Norwich, CT: Appleton-Century-Crofts.

Bayley, N. (1969). *Bayley Scales of Infant Development.* New York: Psychological Corporation.

Benner, S. M. (1992). *Assessing young children with special needs.* White Plains, NY: Longman.

Bluma, S. M., Shearer, M. S., Frohman, D., & Hillard, J. M. (1976). *Portage Guide to Early Education.* Portage, WI: The Portage Project.

Bradley, R., & Caldwell, B. (1980). The relation of home environment, cognitive competence and IQ among males and females. *Child Development, 51,* 1140–1148.

Brockman, L. M., Morgan, G. A., & Harmon, R. J. (1988). Mastery motivation and developmental delay. In T. D. Warhs & R. Sheehan (Eds.), *Assessment of young developmentally disabled children.* New York: Plenum.

Caldwell, B., & Bradley, R. (1972). *Home observation for measurement of the environment.* Little Rock: University of Arkansas.

Fraiberg, S. (Ed.). (1980). *Clinical studies in infant mental health: The first year of life.* New York: Basic Books.

Glover, E. M., Preminger, J., & Sanford, A. (1978). *Early learning accomplishment profile (E-Lap).* Winston-Salem: Kaplan School Supply.

Greenspan, S. I., & Lieberman, A. F. (1988). A clinical approach to attachment. In J. Belsky & T. Nezworski (Eds.), *Clinical implications of attachment* (pp. 387–424). Hillsdale, NJ: Lawrence Erlbaum Associates.

Greenspan, S. I., Lieberman, A. F., & Poisson, S. S. (1981). *Greenspan-Lieberman observation system for assessment of caregiver-infant interaction during semi-structured play (GLOS).* Bethesda: National Institute of Mental Health, Mental Health Study Center.

Greesham, F. M., & Elliott, S. N. (1990). *Social skills rating system.* Circle Pines, MN: American Guidance Service, Inc.

Grossman, H. J. (1983). *Classification in mental retardation.* Washington: American Association on Mental Deficiency.

Guralnick, M. J., & Groom, J. M. (1987). The peer relations of mildly delayed and nonhandicapped preschool children in mainstreamed playgroups. *Child Development, 58,* 1556–1579.

Guralnick, M. J., & Groom, J. M. (1985). Correlates of peer-related social competence of developmentally delayed preschool children. *American Journal of Mental Deficiency, 90,* 140–150.

Guralnick, M. J. (1980). Social interaction among preschool handicapped children. *Exceptional Children, 46,* 248–253.

Harrison, P. L. (1990). Assessment of adaptive behavior. In B. A. Bracken (Ed.), *The psychoeducational assessment of preschool children,* 2nd ed. (pp. 168–186). Boston: Allyn and Bacon.

Huntington, G. S. (1988). Assessing child characteristics that influence family functioning. In D. B. Bailey & R. J. Simeonsson (Eds.), *Family assessment in early intervention* (pp. 45–64). Columbus, OH: Merrill.

Johnson-Martin, N. M., Jens, K. G., Attermeier, S. M., & Hacker, B. J. (1991). *The Carolina Curriculum for Infants and Toddlers with Special Needs* (2nd ed.). Baltimore: Paul H. Brookes.

Lambert, N., Windmiller, M., Tharinger, D., & Cole, L. (1981). *AAMD Adaptive Behavior Scale-School Edition.* Monterey, CA: CTB/McGraw-Hill.

Lewis, M. (1987). Social development in infancy and early childhood. In J. D. Osofsky (Ed.), *Handbook of infant development.* New York: Wiley.

Linder, T. W. (1990). *Transdisciplinary play-based assessment: A functional approach to working with young children.* Baltimore: Paul H. Brookes.

McConnell, S. R., & Odom, S. L. (1986). Sociometrics: Peer-referenced measures and the assessment of social competence. In P. Strain, M. Guralnick, & H. Walker (Eds.), *Children's social behavior: Development, assessment, and modification* (pp. 215–286). New York: Academic Press.

McCormick, L., & Kawate, J. (1982). Kindergarten survival skills: New directions for preschool special education. *Education and Training of the Mentally Retarded, 17*(3), 247–252.

McCune, L., Kalmanson, B., Fleck, M. B., Glazewski, B., & Sillari, J. (1990). An interdisciplinary model of infant assessment. In S. J. Meisels & J. P. Shonkoff (Eds.), *Handbook of early childhood intervention* (pp. 219–245). New York: Cambridge University Press.

McDonnell, A., & Hardman, M. (1988). A synthesis of "best practice" guidelines for early childhood services. *Journal of the Division for Early Childhood. 12*(4), 328–341.

Newborg, J., Stock, J., Wnek, L., Guidubaldi, J., & Svinicki, J. S. (1984). *Battelle Developmental Inventory (BDI).* Allen, TX: DLM/Teaching Resources.

Odom, S. L., & McConnell, S. R. (1989). Assessing social interaction skills. In D. B. Bailey & M. Wolery (Eds.), *Assessing infants and preschoolers with handicaps* (pp. 390–427). Columbus, OH: Merrill.

Parten, M. (1932). Social participation among preschool children. *Journal of Abnormal and Social Psychology, 27,* 243–269.

Rogers, S. J. (1982). Techniques of infant assessment. In G. Ulrey & S. J. Rogers (Eds.), *Psychological assessment of handicapped infants and young children* (pp. 59–64). New York: Thieme-Stratton.

Rossetti, L. M. (1990). *Infant-toddler assessment: An interdisciplinary approach.* Boston: College-Hill Press.

Simeonsson, R. J. (Ed.) (1986). *Psychological and developmental assessment of special children.* Boston: Allyn and Bacon.

Sparks, S., Clark, M., Oas, D., & Erickson, R. (1988). *Clinical services to infants at risk for communication disorders.* Paper presented at the annual convention of the American Speech-Language Association, Boston, MA.

Sroufe, L. A. (1979). Socioemotional development. In J. D. Osofsky (Ed.), *Handbook of infant development* (pp. 462–516). New York: Wiley.

Teti, D. M., & Nakagawa, M. (1990). Assessing attachment in infancy: The strange situation and alternate systems. In E. D. Gibbs & D. M. Teti (Eds.), *Interdisciplinary assessment of infants: A guide for early intervention* (pp. 191–214). Baltimore: Paul H. Brookes.

Thomas, A., Chess, S., & Birch, H. G. (1968). *Temperament and behavior disorders in children.* New York: New York University Press.

Vincent, L. J., Salisbury, C., Walter, G., Brown, P., Gruenwald, L. J., & Powers, M. (1980). Program evaluation and curriculum development in early childhood/special education: Criteria of the next environment. In W. Sailor, B. Wilcox, & L. Brown (Eds.), *Methods of instruction for severely handicapped students* (pp. 303–328). Baltimore: Paul H. Brookes.

Walter, G. (1979). *The "survival skills" displayed by kindergarteners and the structure of the regular kindergarten environment.* Unpublished master's thesis. University of Wisconsin, Madison.

Waters, E., & Deane, K. E. (1985). Defining and assessing individual differences in attachment relationships: Q-methodology and the organization of behavior in infancy and early childhood. In I. Bretherton & E. Waters (Eds.), *Growing points of attachment theory and research. Monographs of the Society for Research in Child Development, 50*(1–2, Serial No. 209), 41–65.

Wolery, M., & Bailey, D. B. (1989). Assessing play skills. In D. B. Bailey & M. Wolery (Eds.), *Assessing infants and preschoolers with handicaps* (pp. 428–446). Columbus, OH: Merrill.

Zeitlin, S. (1985). *Coping inventory.* Bensenville, IL: Scholastic Testing Service.

Zeitlin, S., Williamson, G. G., & Szczepanski, M. (1988). *Early Coping Inventory.* Bensenville, IL: Scholastic Testing Service.

Chapter *16*

Sensorimotor Development

SHELLY J. LANE

Sensorimotor versus Perceptual Motor

In searching the literature for information pertinent to sensorimotor development and assessment, it quickly becomes apparent that there is some confusion within this domain. Is sensorimotor the equivalent of perceptual-motor? If these terms are defined differently, does assessment of sensorimotor skill differ from assessment of perceptual-motor skill? Can sensory development and motor development be meaningfully studied as separate entities? Can and should we, as clinicians, assess sensory processing and motor output individually? As one reads this literature, answers to both sides of each question stated can be found. How can the child best be served?

Strictly speaking the terms *sensory* and *perceptual* do differ. An assessment of sensory systems alone implies testing the integrity of the sensory receptors and pathways to answer the question of whether or not the information is taken in at the receptor level and transmitted appropriately to the central nervous system (CNS). Perception extends beyond this aspect of sensory input to include the processing of sensory input within the CNS and the subsequent attachment of meaning to the input, in preparation for the development of a motor response. However, when used together, as in *sensory-motor*, there is an implication that the sensory input is processed and used to prepare the motor output or response. Therefore, the phrase *sensorimotor assessment* is often used interchangeably with the phrase *perceptual-motor assessment* and functionally for a child these phrases often are equivalent.

Any assessment of motor skill requires some degree of sensory processing, or perception. Asking a child to perform a task requires that she/he process a verbal cue or direction; demonstrating a task with no verbal directions requires that the child process the task requirements visually and translate them into motor action; and even passively placing a child in a position or guiding his/her motor performance through a task requires that the child use his/her tactual/proprioceptive/kinesthetic senses to repeat the action. As a result, no assessment can be considered solely motor in nature, and performance needs to be assessed based on both aspects of the task: the perceptual and the motor.

The domain of sensorimotor development and assessment in this chapter will include the processes involved in sensory intake, interpretation and integration of sensory input, the use of sensory input in the preparation of a motor response, and, finally, the motor response itself. Clinicians rarely want, need, or are able to assess strictly sensory input. Instead, the most helpful assessment tools look at a combination of sensory input, processing, and motor output and, therefore, allow the early interventionist to provide the best guidance to the family and child.

Development of Sensorimotor Skills in Infancy

Numerous authors document motor development throughout infancy; and many excellent texts exist to provide the clinician with detailed information in this area (e.g., Short-DeGraff, 1988; Schuster & Ashburn, 1992). It is important that the clinician commit to memory some *key* aspects of development to help him or her identify infants and children in need of a detailed skills assessment. Some of these key points in development are described in the following pages, although many clinicians prefer to develop a list of developmental milestones that they consider to be critical. Sensory developmental milestones are more difficult to ferret out of the literature on infancy. Responses to sensory input seem subtle and may be difficult to identify by the untrained eye. These, too, are discussed in order to give the clinician some guidelines for knowing when to pursue evaluation.

Birth to Three Months

There are some key motor skills developing during this first quarter year that warrant mentioning. Many reflexes are present at birth that become integrated as the first year of life unfolds, including the rooting, grasping, and walking reflexes, along with asymmetrical and symmetrical tonic neck reflexes. Head control develops throughout the first year, but some degree of head control is expected even at term age. Beginning shortly after birth, infants should be able to lift their heads, slightly and briefly, when on their stomachs, and turn their heads from side to side. When supported in a sitting position they should be able to both lift the head off the chest briefly and bring the head forward if it is dropped all the way back. Hand-to-mouth skills also begin at this early age. In spite of the presence of the asymmetrical tonic neck reflex, infants can get at least one hand to the mouth, and begin sucking on the fist, early in development. By the close of the first quarter year, many infants can get both hands to their mouth and will likely enjoy the sucking activity that goes along with this.

During the first quarter year babies do not seem to "do" much. They sleep a great deal, and awaken primarily to eat. However, during this period of time, when motor skills are at a minimum, sensory processing is not only highly active, it is highly important. At this age babies enjoy being picked up, and enjoy the comfort of close contact with a parent. Even the newborn will respond to sounds and light in his or her environment. The response is often one of *stilling* of motor movement, along with some searching movements of the eyes. Infants can orient to changes in sound and light in their environment. This initial orientation may involve turning of the head or eyes in the direction of the new sound or change in light. Habituation to sounds and lights in the environment will occur with repeated or constant presence of the stimuli. This is an important skill in that it allows the infant to block out sensory stimulation, which for the time being is meaningless, permitting rest and sleep that are critical for optimal development.

Newborns also visually track an object up to 90 degrees if the object is appealing (Schuster & Ashburn, 1992). At this early age babies are most attracted to visual objects with high contrast, hence the recent appearance of black-and-white infant toys and mobiles. Infants are fascinated with faces. The ability to discriminate faces continues to develop throughout the first year of life. In addition to these visual skills, the infant is beginning to look at his or her hand and may begin to move an arm purposefully toward an object in the visual field. These skills are important in that they lay the foundation for visually directed grasp and reach (Short-DeGraff, 1988).

Four to Six Months

Between 4 and 6 months of age babies gain control of their heads and begin to get control of the trunk as well. Rolling both prone to supine and supine to prone develops within this time frame along with sitting, first with assistance and by 6 months, independently. At this age infants are still unable to get into and out of a sitting position independently. When on their stomachs, four-month-old babies can push up onto their hands, and will be able to play with a toy for a brief period of time by shifting their weight to one arm, freeing the other arm for toy manipulation. This is also the period of time when babies find their knees, feet, and toes and develop the stomach muscles needed to bring these body parts close to their hands and face. As stomach muscles develop during this time frame, babies demonstrate minimal head lag when pulled to a sitting position.

During this period, babies develop an interest in watching their hands and fingers move, and the fingers begin to move somewhat independently. The thumb is released during this stage to allow purposeful thumb-sucking. Babies at this stage may help hold the bottle with one or both hands, extending their ability to get hands to the midline of the body developed in the first quarter year. This skill translates into being able to bring any number of graspable objects to the mouth—the primary tool of exploration at this age.

Grasp at this stage is considered immature, but babies are able to correctly direct their hand toward a toy and pick up large objects such as blocks, initially with the thumb in line with the fingers and later with the thumb opposed. Grasping small objects still presents a significant challenge to most babies, although some babies show some degree of pincer grasp by age 6 months.

Volitional release of objects is a skill attained at about four months of age. Up to this point release was accidental. With the attainment of this skill, the baby begins to transfer objects from one hand to the other. There is continual refinement of this skill throughout the first year of life as the baby takes great pleasure in watching mommy or daddy play "fetch" with the toys and utensils the infant gleefully drops out of the playpen or crib or off the highchair tray.

Tickling may now be responded to with a smile or even a giggle, and some motor squirming. Bath time continues to be fun for most babies. As they gain security in the tub, babies of this age and older often splash and play with vigor. Being held continues to be an enjoyable activity. As the baby becomes more active she or he may prefer to play in the parents lap in addition to enjoying cuddling and close time. Most babies in this age range enjoy movement. They do not object to being picked up from sitting or lying down, and they often laugh when a play activity moves them quickly up and down. Visual and auditory skills are developed—they can see things across the room and respond to auditory input by turning their head and sometimes their body.

Seven to Twelve Months

During the last half of the first year, infants develop many new motor skills. Between 8 and 10 months they begin to creep, thereby increasing their ability to explore the environment. An interesting skill that goes along with this new ability to creep is the ability to get into and out of sitting and creeping postures. These transitional movements are critical both to overall motor development and to the baby's development of independence and, yet, rarely are such transitional movements listed on a developmental scale. If a baby can sit very steadily, but cannot get into and out of a sitting position, one may question whether or not sitting is truly a functional skill. Similarly, if a child can creep when placed on all fours, but cannot get into the all fours position independently, minimal environmental exploration will take place with the baby's initiation.

By the end of the first year, creeping is expected to give way to walking. Pulling up to stand, cruising while holding onto furniture, and walking with the hands held are skills that precede walking independently. The presence of these skills is a good sign that walking is on its way. It is critical to keep in mind that while the *average* baby will walk by 12 months of age, the *range* for walking is approximately 8 to 18 months of age. Variability in the time of skill attainment is present in most skills, but since walking is considered by many parents to be a pivotal skill, when a child does not walk by 12 months the parent may become unnecessarily worried. A clinical assessment at this point is critical in either identifying a delay, or putting the parent's mind at ease. A 12-month-old who is sitting independently, creeping and more importantly, getting into and out of these positions but not walking may be merely a *late bloomer*. Alternatively, if a 12-month-old seems stuck in sitting or prone, or seems to have stiff or floppy muscles and is not walking, referring the child to an occupational or physical therapist for a more comprehensive assessment may be appropriate.

Hand skills blossom during the second half of year one, as the baby develops and refines both pincer and whole-hand grasp. Along with skillful grasp comes the banging of objects on a table or tray and later the banging of 2 objects together at midline. In addition, peek-a-boo and pat-a-cake become fun activities now as the infant improves his or her midline hand skills.

Toward the end of the first year, the pincer grasp becomes well refined, allowing the baby to pick up small objects such as raisins and Cheerios with great precision. As the baby develops the ability to isolate finger movements, he or she also begins object exploration by poking with the finger. Finally, by 12 months of age, infants begin to meaningfully play with and use objects such as cups and spoons. The 12-month-old can hold a cup and drink from it, but assistance is recommended.

Within the sensory systems babies begin to demonstrate true intrasensory integration. The visual guidance of reach and grasp may already be present, and as the baby gains hand skills, the combination of visual and touch exploration of objects becomes more apparent. Although babies continue to obtain a great deal of touch information about objects with their mouths, the hands participate more and more with the visual system taking a backseat to touch exploration. Twelve-month-old infants generally derive great pleasure from movement, both self-initiated and adult-initiated; this is the time when "rough-and-tumble" play becomes popular.

Twelve to Twenty-four Months

The drive to explore the environment continues to thrive and skills develop to support this drive. Before they are 18 months old children learn to manage stairs, first by crawling and later by walking both up and down them. In addition, at this age babies learn to walk quickly, seeming to run from place to place. They develop sufficient balance and motor skills to allow them to stoop and recover without support and pivot while standing. Ball skills such as rolling, throwing, and kicking with purpose are also part of this stage. Toward the latter part of the second year, toddlers can walk a balance beam with one foot on the floor and begin jumping down, forward, and up.

Fine motor skills pertinent to this age range include turning thick pages in a book, stacking blocks into towers or two or more cubes, inserting shapes into simple puzzles, and scribbling with a crayon. Grasp develops from a pronated crayon grasp toward a mature pattern, and the pincer grasp is perfected such that visual guidance of pincer grasp and release permits the toddler to place small pellets into a jar with a small opening.

As motor skills become refined, the observer has a greater opportunity to see the extent of perceptual development that is taking place. The ability to direct the foot in kicking a ball and the hand in throwing a ball indicates that visual motor skills are progressing. Fine motor skills such as putting pellets into a jar further indicate the precision of visual perception. Spatial perceptual skills become apparent as the child is able to correctly position a shape and place it into a simple formboard, and develops the ability to imitate strokes with a crayon, first vertical and later horizontal.

Twenty-four to Thirty-six Months

Gross motor refinement occurs during this period of time with the continued development of balance and equilibrium skills and muscle strength. Stair climbing in this stage can be accomplished using alternating feet for going both up and down. As trunk rotational movements become more readily useable by the child throwing begins to look more mature. Very brief one-foot standing, hopping, and tiptoe walking also develop as the child attains the skill of weight shift while upright. Jumping continues to be a favorite activity and by three years of age, children can jump over low obstacles, jump forward a good distance, and jump down from heights of two feet or more. Some children may develop fears about some forms of movement during this time. They may dislike swinging high and feel insecure doing other activities that take their feet off the ground. Although this may be worrisome to a parent, and in an older child may indicate a problem, processing movement sensations in many two- to three-year-old children is a normal stage of gross motor development.

Fine motor skills are now closely linked with visual perception. Without a formal assessment, it may be difficult to determine whether a fine motor deficit is due to poor motor performance or inadequate visual perception. Writing implements now are held in the fingers rather than in the fist, and drawing takes on new precision. Horizontal lines are now copied as are circles and imitation is not always necessary.

The control needed to construct a tower of 8 to 10 cubes should be present, and cubes also may be used to make other structures. Children at this age may be able to unfasten buttons and pull socks on, although the socks are unlikely to be pulled on with the heel in the proper position. Performance of fine-motor tasks is beginning to speed up, and as such, accuracy may suffer to some degree. Visual-tactile integration is further refined at this point, and toward the close of the second year, a child will be able to feel a familiar object and identify its picture without seeing the actual object. The continued cultivation of tactile perception is thought to be necessary as a foundation for more precise fine-motor skills. Unless the child has a good "feel" for objects used by the hand (pencils, scissors, and so on) manipulating them for skilled use may be less than adequate (Ayres, 1973).

Thirty-six to Forty-eight Months

During the third year of life, children are working hard to refine their motor skills as they strive for independence. At times there will be frustration because the desire to be independent is not matched by the motor skills that permit it. In the gross-motor area, walking and running skills become more coordinated, incorporating reciprocal arm movements and longer strides so the pattern more closely resembles that of an adult. Stairs are now managed with alternating feet going both up and down.

Balance develops further and the three- to four-year-old child can jump over obstacles and manage several hops in place. The two- to three-year-old who seemed afraid of movement will likely begin to challenge himself or herself again with swinging and climbing activities. Balance also plays a role in the child's ability to kick a ball with some preparatory backswing. More trunk rotation is notable at this age in many activities including the kicking already mentioned. In addition, trunk rotation allows the child to raise from the floor to standing using a half-kneel position. This is a good age to introduce the tricycle if it has not been done before. The three-year-old can learn to pedal a tricycle and steer it to avoid running into things.

Within the fine-motor domain the three-year-old is beginning to master reciprocal movements of the fingers, and usually to develop preference for handedness. This allows the child to work with scissors so that by the end of the third year most children can cut straight lines with a surprising degree of skill. Bilateral hand use is apparent both in scissor use and in activities such as stringing of beads, which can be done with small beads, by the second half of this year. Most of the time, pencil/crayon grasp has developed to a tripod grip most of the time, although the pattern appears somewhat stiff. The maturation of fine-motor skills facilitates the development of daily living skills and the three-year-old can undress independently, including being able to unfasten even small buttons, and can put on most clothes with little or no assistance. At this age children also can wash and dry their hands with no help, permitting the three-year-old to be independent in toileting.

As daily living skills emerge, along with the strong drive to "do it myself," parents and/or teachers may find themselves frustrated with the speed and accuracy with which the child can accomplish such tasks. Socks often are donned with the heel up, shirts put on inside out and/or back to front, pants may be put on backwards, and shoes put on the wrong feet. However, bear in mind the effort taken in the task, and the pride taken in "I did it myself" before offering to fix the *error!*

The visual system is becoming increasingly important as a tool for obtaining information from the environment, and in the development of the fine motor skills mentioned above. At this age, visual perception has progressed to the point where children can copy lines and circles rather than needing to imitate their production. Tactile perception refines and the child is able to identify three-dimensional shapes with his or her hand and visually find a match. Cuddling and close contact are still sought as a form of tactile comfort even by the fiercely independent three-year-old.

Forty-eight to Sixty Months

Improvements in all motor skills take place during this last preschool year. It is amazing to watch the three-year-old struggle with climbing on a jungle gym, looking longingly at the older children able to maneuver themselves through and around the bars, transform into the four-year-old with daring and skill. Development in balance, trunk rotational skills, and bilateral and reciprocal arm and leg use give the child the ability to jump and hop well, climb with ease, walk on tiptoes and on a balance beam with good balance reactions, throw a ball with a reciprocal pattern, gallop well, and skip in an uncoordinated fashion.

Later in the third and into the fourth year children often are seen to be challenging their motor skills by attempting to discover new ways to accomplish the same old task. Thus, once a child has mastered a slide on his or her bottom, the child will try to figure out how to go down the slide on his/her tummy, back, soles of the feet, or upside down. Children in this age range are seemingly unable to merely walk down the street. Instead, they must walk sideways or backwards, balance on the curb, or avoid the sidewalk cracks. This drive to change the activity to challenge the developing motor skills is an excellent example of the development of motor planning skills in preschoolers. Motor planning begins early and is refined throughout life.

Fine motor skills also improve during this year. The tripod grasp begins to become more fluid and writing skill improves. Four-year-olds can accurately cut on a curved line with scissors. Daily living skills improve, and frustration decreases, as the fingers become more deft. The able fingers of a four-year-old are also now readily engaged in more complicated songs with finger plays, and counting on the fingers becomes easier as the fingers are less awkward in independent movement.

Visual-perceptual skills developed during this year allow the child to connect vertical and horizontal lines to form squares and rectangles. These shapes were recognized before this time, but in most children, the ability to reproduce them is just now developing. This advancement is needed to prepare the child for writing letters and numbers before starting school. The drawing of diagonal lines may be learned at the age of four but is more likely to be seen in a five-year-old child. Reproduction of block designs is at the stage of the *gate* in which the child is asked to correctly perceive and position both blocks and spaces. The transfer of tactile-visual information has progressed to the point where children in this age range are beginning to be able to feel an object and point to the object's *picture*, rather than needing to have the three-dimensional object present.

Assessment

The most frequently used frame of reference in assessing sensorimotor skills is developmental, especially with children from birth to age five. However, any developmentally based assessment of these skills needs to be carried out using an overall systems approach to be able to evaluate not just the child but also the environment. The systems approach looks at the child within his or her own environment, as an entity within a **family** system, which is an entity within a **neighborhood** or a **cultural** system, which eventually answers to the bigger systems of education.

Assessing skills in an appropriate environment may be difficult to arrange, but the astute clinician quickly realizes that it may not be relevant to the child or the family if the child cannot stack 8 inch cubes during the confines of an assessment. Failure to view the specific skills and deficits noted during a sensory-motor assessment from a systems perspective may make the results of such an assessment meaningless to the child and the family.

A detailed discussion of family-centered assessment and a systems approach to assessment is beyond the scope of this chapter. However, the clinician always needs to bear in mind that the presence or absence of a skill(s) may or may not have functional significance within the system of which the child is a part. By working to understand the system as well as the specifics of performance the child demonstrates, the clinician is able to be sure that assessment results and recommendations meet the needs of the child and his or her family.

Several assessment tools are briefly discussed in the next sections. All the tools available for use in the birth to five-year-old population cannot be addressed; the reader should view those presented here as a sampling. An excellent text that addresses many tools in greater detail is available—*A Therapist's Guide to Pediatric Assessment* by King-Thomas and Hacker (1987).

Newborn Assessment

In the period of time immediately following birth, several areas of development can be assessed. These include sensory processing, muscle stiffness or tone, the presence of early reflexes and state organization. *State organization* refers to the newborn's ability to control his or her behavioral state in response to environmental stimuli. Assessment tools exist that cover all of these areas in a comprehensive manner. One such tool is the *Neonatal Behavioral Assessment Scale* (NBAS) (Brazelton, 1984). This tool was developed to distinguish individual differences between normal infants, especially with regard and to social interactive behaviors. It has been adapted for use with high-risk and premature infants and has been successfully applied to these populations.

As can be seen in Figure 16–1, this tool contains 26 behavioral items that cover the areas of interaction, motor skill, state control, and response to stress and 20

	Ayres Clinical Observation of Sensory Integration	Miller Assessment for Preschoolers (MAP)	Developmental Profile II (Interview)	Denver Developmental Screening Test Revised (DDST-R)	Quick Neurological Screening Test	Therapist Generated Developmental Screening Checklists
AGE RANGE	5–8 years	2 years 4 months 5 years 8 months	0–9½ years	0–6 years	5–18 years	typically 0–9 years
TESTING TIME (minutes)	20 minutes	20–30 minutes	20–40 minutes	5–7 minutes	20 minutes	15–20 minutes
SCORING TIME (minutes)			10–20 minutes	5 minutes	5–10 minutes	
MAJOR AREAS TESTED: personal/social			X	X		X
communication			X	X		X
cognition		X	X			
self help			X	X		X
gross motor		X	X	X	X	X
praxis	X	X			X	X
reflexes	X					X
fine motor		X		X	X	X
visual-motor integration		X			X	X
visual perception		X			X	X
tactile	X	X			X	X
vestibular	X	X			X	X
TYPE OF TEST: norm referenced		X				
criteria referenced				X		
informal/ structured		X			X	X
observation	X		interview		X	X
SCORES OBTAINED: age level			X	X		X
percentile		X		X		
standard						
quantified observations	X					

FIGURE 16-1 Summary of Primary Characteristics of Screening Instruments Frequently Used by Occupational Therapists

Source: From *Pediatric Occupational Therapy: Facilitating Effective Service Provision.* Dunn, Winnie (Ed.), p. 13. Copyright © 1991. Thorofare, NJ: Slack, Inc. Reprinted with permission.

reflex items. In examining performance on the items one looks for *best* performance, not just the initial performance, and the response is graded as "exceptional," "average," or "worrisome." No total score is obtained. Instead examiners look at performance in the different areas and identify strengths and weaknesses.

A major focus of the NBAS is teaching a parent what to look for in the behaviors exhibited by the newborn. This tool was designed to be administered in the presence of the parent to be able to point out strengths, weaknesses, and general responses to the sensory input during the assessment process. In doing so, the NBAS becomes a teaching tool to assist parents in understanding and working with their infants. A major shortcoming of this assessment tool is that it requires extensive examiner training that is not available to all clinicians.

A second newborn assessment tool that covers similar areas is the *Neurological Assessment of Preterm and Full-term Newborn Infants* (NAPFI) (Dubowitz & Dubowitz, 1981). This is a criterion-referenced tool suitable for use by many different professionals working with infants. It is appropriately applied to full-term infants, or preterm infants as they approach term age. The NAPFI was designed to be easy to administer and does not require training like the NBAS. Scores are obtained for individual item responses in the areas of muscle tone and movement, reflex development, and neurobehavioral development; it also examines patterns of behavior. The examiner has the option of rating behavioral state on each item as it is administered to shed light on state modulation skills present in the infant. With practice, this tool can be administered in about 20 minutes and, thus, may be an ideal tool for use in a busy clinic.

Other tools for newborn assessment look primarily at reflex development. These tools do not allow the clinician to assess responsiveness to sensory input per se, but do offer insight into central nervous system production of normal reflexes. One such assessment tool is the *Milani-Comparetti Motor Development Screening Scale* (Milani-Comparetti & Gidoni, 1967; Kliewer, Bruce & Trembath, 1977). It is designed for use with children from birth to age two. It examines both spontaneous and elicited reflex behaviors and can be administered in 10 minutes by an experienced examiner. It can be useful for looking at this single domain of skill, and for providing a vehicle for discussion with parents since these reflexes are thought to be the foundation of what will develop in terms of motor skills later.

It is important to understand that none of these tools is *predictive* of later outcome. Instead they give a glimpse of performance today and may provide guidance to the parent on interacting with and handling an infant in the early months of life.

Infant and Toddler Assessment

General developmental and screening tools useful during this period include subscales that address sensorimotor development. Several scales, both standardized and criterion-referenced, are shown in Figure 16–1; some are described in chapter 13 along with the discussion of cognitive assessment. Scales, such as the *Bayley Scales of Infant Development* (Bayley, 1969) and the *Griffiths Mental Development Scales* (Griffiths, 1954), provide standardized assessment of motor development. The Bayley Scales examine motor development as a whole; they do not break fine- and gross-motor development apart when standard scoring is used. In contrast, an eye–hand and a gross-motor subscale in the Griffiths Scales permit more specific assessment of motor skills.

Criterion- and curriculum-referenced assessment of sensorimotor development can be found in general scales such as *The Developmental Programming for Infants and Young Children*—also known as the *Early Intervention Developmental Profile* (EIDP) (D'Eugenio & Moersch, 1979). This tool is available in two versions: 0 to

3 years and 3.5 to 6 years. It assesses perceptual/fine motor and gross motor skill along with cognitive, language, social and self-care skill development. Likewise, *The Carolina Curriculum for Handicapped Infants and Infants at Risk* (Johnson-Martin, Jens, Attermeier, 1986) (also discussed in chapters 10, 12, and 13) offers assessment of fine and gross motor skill development. Both tools are quick and easy to learn and administer.

One shortcoming of such tools is a small number of items for younger ages. This limits the clinician's ability to identify areas of strength and weakness. However, these assessment tools lend themselves well to repeated administration to update skills and goals that can be very beneficial in planning and implementing programs for children with delays. As with most general developmental assessments, the tools described here lend themselves well to multi- or interdisciplinary use, which is so important with children of this age.

A few more specific tools are available to examine motor skills and perceptual development. *The Peabody Developmental Motor Scales* (PDMS) (Folio & Fewell, 1983) is one such tool. Useful from birth through 72 months, the PDMS is norm-referenced and includes activity cards that may be incorporated into an intervention program. Administration and interpretation of the PDMS can be learned from the manual. It is divided into gross and fine motor sections with subsections for each area. A strength of this tool is that it has small age increments within the first two years of life and includes several skills at each age increment. This allows the clinician to have a good overall picture of gross and fine motor development in the early years. Age increment divisions enlarge after the first two years that may dilute the ability to make specific statements about the child's strengths and weaknesses.

Another assessment tool that focuses on motor skills is the *Movement Assessment of Infants* (Chandler et al., 1980). This assessment is most commonly used by occupational and/or physical therapists to assess muscle tone, reflex integration, and the development of automatic and volitional skills in the first year of life. It is a tool based on structured observation, with profiles of expected performance available for infants at both four and eight months of age. The use of this tool may assist in the identification of motor abnormalities, rather than motor delays, within the first year.

Assessments that focus on sensory or perceptual processing in the 0 to 3 population are less abundant. Visual perception is perhaps the best studied area of perception in the toddler age, yet few tools directly assess visual-perceptual skills in this age range. One tool that does attempt to measure these skills during toddlerhood is the *Test of Visual Motor Integration* (Beery & Buktenika, 1967). This assessment is appropriate for children beginning at age two; it is norm-referenced. Because it assesses visual-*motor* skills, the results of this assessment offer information about the processing of visual input to direct a motor response. Without further assessment, it is not possible to determine if identified problems are tied most closely to a visual-processing deficit or to the motor aspect of test performance.

At age four, some assessment tools are available that address visual processing in the absence of motor skill, but these are not appropriate for the child in the 0 to 3 age range. There is some evidence to suggest that low VMI scores predict kindergarten-grade reading difficulties (Klein, 1978). Therefore, it may be a useful tool for early identification of some academic deficits.

A newer tool, not listed in Figure 16–1, that attempts to assess sensory processing is the *Test of Sensory Function in Infants* (TSFI) (DeGangi & Greenspan, 1989). Currently, this assessment is used primarily by occupational therapists in an attempt to identify infants and young children experiencing over-sensitivity to touch or movement or difficulties with visual-tactile integration. According to the authors, it is norm-referenced on a small sample, and useful in the infant between 4 and 18 months of age. The variability in responses in the 4- to 6-month-old child make the application to this population tenuous. The TSFI can be learned by reading the manual, but it is recommended that further training and inter-rater reliability be established before it is used for clinical decision making (Adamitis & Lane, 1992). Administration time is approximately 15 to 20 minutes.

Given the paucity of assessment tools that skillfully examine sensory processing, many clinicians may still wish to use a Sensory History—a parent-oriented questionnaire that queries parents as to the reactions their children have to various sensory inputs and situations. It can be filled out by the parent alone, or information can be obtained from parent and early intervention personnel. This type of assessment tool requires a subjective interpretation of the results, and therefore, relies on clinical experience with a variety of children who show a variety of strengths and weaknesses.

When interpreting the information from the Sensory History, it is important to look for clusters of behaviors indicative of problems and not focus on isolated signs of over- or undersensitivity to sensory input. After identifying what she or he feels are the strengths and weaknesses in sensory processing experienced by the child, it is recommended that the clinician discuss these findings with the parent and be prepared to adjust the interpretation. In interpreting the information obtained, it also is important to describe the findings in functional terms. Just saying that a child is showing "signs of tactile defensiveness" is not very meaningful to most parents. However, saying that the child "appears to be very sensitive to touch and that may explain why the child resists activities such as hair combing, washing and cutting, prefers only certain types of soft clothing, and gets very angry when tickled," puts the problem into useful terms and assists the parent in understanding both the problem and some of the behaviors the child exhibits.

Preschool Assessment

Several of the standardized and criterion-referenced assessment tools listed previously are useful in the preschool years and will not be reiterated here. The Sensory History can be applied to a child of any age and is a useful tool to augment additional assessments for children during the preschool years. One additional tool useful in identifying strengths and weaknesses in the preschool population is the *Miller Assessment for Preschoolers* (MAP) (Miller, 1982). This standardized tool is applicable for children ages 2 years 9 months through 5 years 8 months and was developed to identify children at risk for the development of school-related problems.

Although strictly speaking this tool was designed as a screening tool, it provides a great deal more information about skills than do most screening tests. The MAP assesses skills in five domains of function: neuromotor foundations, motor coordination, verbal, nonverbal, and complex tasks. Functionally this screening test addresses areas of visual and tactual perception, balance and equilibrium, motor planning, expressive and receptive language. Scoring of the MAP is based on percentile cut-off scores that place a child in a normal, questionable, or at-risk category. The MAP has been shown to have predictive validity for the identification of preschool children at risk for academic difficulties. This makes it particularly useful. It is available to therapists, educators, and psychologists and can be learned by attending a training course.

As noted before, specific visual perception assessment tools for use with children beginning at age four are available that focus on visual processing and do not require motor skill. Two such standardized tools are the *Test of Visual Perceptual Skills* (TVPS) (Gardner, 1982) and the *Motor Free Visual-Perceptual Test* (MVPT) (Colarusso & Hammill, 1972). Both tools are relatively simple to administer and interpret and provide more specific information about the processing of visual input. The TVPS divides visual processing into seven subcategories—figure-ground perception, spatial relations, visual sequential memory, visual memory, visual discrimination, form constancy, visual closure. The MVPT measures performance in five areas—spatial relations, visual closure, visual memory, figure-ground, visual discrimination. These subdivisions may be helpful in identifying specific strengths and weaknesses in visual-perceptual performance areas, although it is not entirely clear whether or not such divisions of the domain of visual perception are justified.

Note that while the TVPS may assist in the identification of visual-perceptual difficulties, it has not been shown to have good diagnostic or predictive validity. On the other hand, the MVPT has been demonstrated to identify deficits in children with mental retardation and cerebral palsy. However, it may not correctly identify children with more subtle problems. Both tools are best used in conjunction with other assessment tools to substantiate and define strengths and weaknesses.

There is one final assessment tool to discuss that examines both motor performance and aspects of visual perception. *The Bruininks-Oseretsky Test of Motor Proficiency* (BOTMP) (Bruininks, 1978) is divided into gross and fine motor sections, each with its subsections of function. It was intended to be used with children with mental retardation, learning disabilities, or developmental delays as either a diagnostic or screening tool. The test is standardized for children ages 4.5 to 14.5.

This broad range of ages may be viewed as both a strength and a weakness of this assessment tool. The strength lies in the fact that it can be readily used to identify areas of growth and development, as well as areas of need for intervention, over a long period of time. In fact, it is a commonly used assessment tool for the school-age child for this reason. However, any assessment tool covering a 10-year-age span is likely to be limited in the depth with which it can assess function, and the BOTMP falls prey to this weakness to some degree. Bruininks has shown that the BOTMP total test score has adequate reliability and decision validity. Administration and scoring can be learned from the manual, although it is recommended that examiner reliability be checked.

Summary

During infancy and toddlerhood sensory processing and motor output are the best *windows* available to view the integrity of the developing nervous system. As a result, early assessment tools are primarily motor in focus, and motor skills are considered critical behaviors. Because sensory and motor development are inextricably linked, the assessment of sensory processing often accompanies that of motor skill. Clinically it often is difficult to determine if the expression of a motor deficit is due to inadequate sensory processing or poor motor-response accomplishment. The differentiation takes clinical skill and experience as well as a thorough understanding of normal development in these areas.

As the child develops more cognitive skills that can be directly measured, assessment of sensorimotor skills are but one aspect of an overall assessment. While sensorimotor skill may no longer correlate highly with cognitive performance, it is still an important aspect of development because environmental interaction is determined by these skills. Environmental interaction is very visible, and inadequate ability to interact with the environment may make a child look handicapped. For instance, a five-year-old child who cannot figure out how to get on a swing, or who still has an overhand, fisted, grasp of the crayon, is being impaired by sensorimotor difficulties. This child may not have cognitive deficits, yet assessment and intervention may be very appropriate. Therefore, assessment of strengths and weaknesses within the sensorimotor domain are essential components of any evaluation.

Suggested Group Activities

1. Discuss the terms *sensorimotor* and *perceptual motor*. How are the definitions alike and different? Cite several examples for each term.

2. Define the term *habituation* and its importance to the assessment of stimuli perception in the infant's environment. How can one determine if an infant exhibits this behavior? Brainstorm several nonintrusive strategies to elicit this response.

3. Divide the class into groups. Give each group a vignette about a child with suspected developmental delays. Each group should determine what reflexes, responses, and skills would be appropriate for the age of their child, and devise several strategies

to assess his or her current functioning status. Present the information to the class, demonstrating reflex responses on a doll, if desired. As interventionists, each group may discuss and suggest further evaluations and/or instructional programming recommendations.

4. Select one of the assessment instruments described in this chapter. After choosing a partner, take turns role-playing the part of an interventionist and a parent or caregiver. Explain the significance of each item as the administration of the instrument is simulated. Be sure to include a comfortable combination of professional and nonprofessional terms and descriptions. Remember to adhere to the systems approach to family centered assessment and its importance to the well-being and future development of the child.

5. As a group, design an informal developmental rating scale. Include a description of the behaviors that need to be looked for. The group may want to include a large range of ages and abilities, or gear it toward a particular age. With this list, would there be an opportunity to observe/describe the child's strengths and weaknesses? How could the information be turned into instructional guidelines and goals?

References

Adamitis, S., & Lane, S. J. (1992). Inter-rater reliability of the *Test of Sensory Function in Infants* as used with infants cocaine exposed in utero. Manuscript submitted for publication.

Ayres, A. J. (1972). *Sensory Integration and Learning Disorders*. Los Angeles: Western Psychological Corporation.

Bayley, N. (1969). *Bayley Scales of Infant Development*. San Antonio: Psychological Corporation.

Beery, K. E., & Buktenica, N. A. (1967). *Beery-Buktenica Developmental Test of Visual-Motor Integration*. Cleveland: Modern Curriculum Press.

Brazelton, T. B. (1984). *The Neonatal Behavioral Assessment Scale*. Philadelphia: J. B. Lippincott.

Bruininks, R.H. (1978). *The Bruininks-Oseretsky Test of Motor Proficiency*. Circle Pines, MN.: American Guidance Service.

Chandler, L. S., Andrews, M. S., Swanson, M. W., & Larson, A. H. (1980). *Movement Assessment of Infants*. Rolling Bay, WA: Movement Assessment of Infants.

Colarusso, R. P., & Hammill, D. D. (1972). *Motor-Free Visual Perception Test (MVPT)*. Novato CA.: Academic Therapy Publications.

DeGangi, G. A., & Greenspan, S.I. (1989). *Test of Sensory Functions in Infants*. LA: Western Psychological Corp.

D'Eugenio, D. B., & Moersch, M. S. (1979). *Developmental programming for infants and young children*. Ann Arbor, MI: University of Michigan.

Dubowitz, L., & Dubowitz, V. (1981). *The neurological assessment of preterm and full-term newborn infants*. Philadelphia: J. B. Lippincott Co.

Folio, M. R., & Fewell, R. R. (1983). *Peabody Developmental Motor Scales (rev. exp. ed.)*. Allen, TX: Developmental Learning Materials Teaching Resources.

Gardner, M. F. (1982). *Test of Visual-Perceptual Skills (Non-Motor)*. Seattle: Special Child Publications.

Griffiths, R. (1954). *The abilities of babies*. New York: McGraw-Hill.

Johnson-Martin, N., Jens, K. G., & Attermeier, S. M. (1986). *The Carolina Curriculum for Handicapped Infants and Infants at Risk*. Baltimore: Paul H. Brookes.

King-Thomas., L., & Hacker, B. J. (1987). *A therapist's guide to pediatric assessment*. Boston: Little, Brown.

Klein, A. (1978). The validity of the *Beery Test of Visual-Motor Integration* in predicting achievement in kindergarten, first, and second grades. *Educational and Psychological Measurement, 38,* 457.

Kliewer, D., Bruce, W., & Trembath, J. (1977). *The Milani-Comparetti Motor Development Screening Test: Administration Manual.* Omaha: Meyer Children's Rehabilitation Institute.

Milani-Comparetti, A., & Gidoni, E. (1967). A routine developmental examination in normal and retarded children. *Developmental Medicine and Child Neurology, 9,* 766.

Miller, L. J. (1982). *The Miller Assessment for Preschoolers.* Englewood, CO: KID Foundation.

Schuster, C. S., & Ashburn, S. S. (1992). *The process of human development. A holistic life-span approach.* Philadelphia: J. B. Lippincott.

Short-DeGraff, M. A. (1988). *Human development for occupational and physical therapists.* Baltimore: Williams and Wilkins.

Selected Infant
and Preschool Assessments

TABLE A-1   Selected Infant and Preschool Screening Tests

Assessment Devices	Age Range	Time in Minutes to Administer	Reliability	Mean & SD	Type							Validity	Purpose/Description/Comments
					Criterion	Normative	Group	Individual	Verbal	Nonverbal	Screening		
Denver Developmental Screening Test (DDST) 1975	0–6 yrs	20	TR .66 to .93			X		X			X	Concurrent validity with Stanford-Binet, Cattell, and Bayley = .74 to .97 *Sensitivity = .80 **Specificity = .90	The DDST is the best-known screening instrument. It screens across four developmental areas: personal-social, fine motor-adaptive, language, and gross motor. This test significantly under refers children.
Developmental Activities Screening Inventory (DASI-II) 1984 Pro-Ed	0–6 yrs	20–40	not reported		X			X		X	X	Concurrent validity .95 with DDST No sensitivity or specificity data	This test was designed for use with pre-school handicapped children. It is nonverbal in format. There are not enough data on it to validate its usefulness.
Developmental Indicators for the Assessment of Learning-Revised (DIAL-R) (1983) Childcraft Educational Corporation	2–6 yrs	25	TR = .87			X		X			X	Correlations with Stanford-Binet: Motor = .28; Concepts = .50; Language = .33; Overall = .40	This is a team-based screening test with weak predictive validity. The Communications/Language section would tend to under-refer children for further evaluation in this area.
Early screening Inventory (ESI) (1983) Teachers College Press	3–6 yrs	15–20	IR = .91 TR = .91			X		X			X	Concurrent validity with the McCarthy Scales of Children's Ability = .73 *Sensitivity x = .92 **Sensitivity x = .95	The ESI serves as a quick inventory to identify those children who may need further evaluation. This test has excellent psychometric properties and has a high "hit" rate, a quality lacking in many screening tests. A Spanish version is being standardized.

Instrument	Age	Time (min)	Reliability				Content validity	Description
Miller Assessment for Pre-schoolers (MAP) (1982) KID Technologies	2.9–5.8 yrs	20–30	TR = .81	X	X	X	Content validity	Provides a normative overview of a child's overall developmental status. All 40 items must be administered to score the test. Three categories are covered: sensory/motor cognition, and combined abilities.
Minneapolis Pre-School Screening Instrument (1980) Minneapolis Public Schools	3 yrs 7 mos to 5 yrs 4 mos	15	TR = .92	X	X	X	Concurrent validity with Stanford-Binet = .71 *Sensitivity = .63 **Specificity = .93	The MPSI is a 50-item test with an emphasis on classroom readiness tasks. The test underrefers children at risk.
Minnesota Child Developmental Inventory (MCDI) (1972) Behavior Science Systems	6 mos–6 yrs	20–30	X = .90	X	X	X	*Sensitivity X = .76 **Specificity X = .76	The MCDI is a 320 item Parent Report Inventory. It over-refers children not at risk. Some would question its use as a screening inventory.

Key: (TR) = Test-Retest; (SH) = Split-Half; (AF) = Alternate Form; (IR) = Inter-Rater; (SEM) = Standard Error of Measurement

* refers to proportion of children at risk correctly identified.

** refers to proportion of children not at risk who are correctly excluded from further testing.

313

TABLE A-2 Selected Developmental Inventories

Assessment Devices	Age Range	Time in Minutes to Administer	Reliability	Mean & SD	Type							Validity	Purpose/Description/Comments
					Criterion	Normative	Group	Individual	Verbal	Nonverbal	Screening		
Battelle Developmental Inventory (BDI) (1984) DLM Teaching Resources	0–8 yrs	45–90	TR = .71 to 1.0			X		X	X		X	Concurrent validity .66 with PPVT-R .66 with Pre-School Language Scale.	The BDI consists of 341 items grouped in 5 domains: (1) Adaptive, (2) Cognitive, (3) Communication, (4) Motor, and (5) Personal-Social. Is useful in depicting child progress in intervention programs. More validity data is becoming available.
Brigance Diagnostic Inventory of Early Development (1978) Curriculum Associates	0–7 yrs	45–60	N.A.	N.A.	X			X	X			Consensual validity by experts.	The Brigance assesses preambulatory motor skills and behaviors, gross-motor skills and behaviors, fine-motor skills and behaviors, self-help skills, prespeech and language skills, general knowledge and comprehension, and readiness. The items lend themselves readily to educational programming. Validity data not reported in manual.
Callier-Azusa Scales (1978) University of Texas	0–5 yrs	30–40	TR = .66 to .97	N.A.	X			X		X		Content validity only.	A scale designed for use with deaf-blind and severely handicapped. Eighteen subscales assess five areas: (1) Motor development, (2) Perceptual abilities, (3) Daily living skills, (4) Cognitive, communication, and language, (5) Social development. Ratings are obtained through direct observation.

Test	Age Range		Reliability						Validity	Description
Developmental Profile II. (1980) Psychological Developmental Publications	0.9 yrs	20.30	TR = 1.71 IR = .50 to .92	X			X	X	Content validity only.	A developmental scale that uses parent report to document growth in 5 areas: physical, self-help, social, academic, and communication. Because of weak standardization, it should not be used for classifying children for specific programs.
Gesell Developmental Schedules (1940) Nigel Cox (Cheshire, CT).	1 mo. 6 yrs	45.60	N.A.	N.A.			X	X	Consensual validity and content validity.	Provides a developmental diagnosis by assessing the quality and integration of children's development in 5 areas: adaptive, fine motor, gross motor, personal-social, and language.
Learning Accomplishment Profile (LAP-D) (1977) Kaplan School Supply	6 mos. 6 yrs	60.90	TR = .82 to .98	X			X	X	Content validity only.	The LAP consists of 323 items in five domains: (1) Cognitive, (2) Fine motor, (3) Gross motor, (4) Language/Cognitive, and (5) Self-help. The test is designed to evaluate a child's entry skills, and validate the effects of an intervention program. It is probably least useful in the last category because of inadequate norms.
Smith Johnson Non-Verbal Performance Scale (1982) Western Psychological Corp.	2.4 yrs	30.45	TR = .27 to .81		X	X	X	X	Content validity and correlations with Leiter.	Provides a useful format for observation of tasks frequently included in preschool curricula. Qualitative information is also obtainable. One of the few nonverbal tests available.
Uniform Performance Assessment System (UPAS) (1981) Charles E. Merrill	0.6 yrs	60.90	TR = .88 to .95	N.A.		X		X	Content validity only.	The UPAS assesses four curricular areas: (1) Communication, (2) Gross motor, (3) Preacademic, (4) Fine motor, and (5) Social/Self-help areas of development. The UPAS is best used to monitor a child's performance through a curriculum.

Key: (TR) = Test-Retest; (SH) = Split-Half; (AF) = Alternate Form; (IR) = Inter-Rater; (SEM) = Standard Error of Measurement

315

TABLE A-3 Selected Cognitive Assessment Devices

Assessment Devices	Age Range	Time in Minutes to Administer	Reliability	Mean & SD	Criterion	Normative	Group	Individual	Verbal	Nonverbal	Screening	Validity	Purpose/Description/Comments
								Type					
Bayley Scales of Infant Development (1969) Psychological Corporation	2 mos–30 mos	Mental 25–30	Mental Scale: .61 to .93	$\bar{x}$ = 100 SD = 16		X		X	X	X		Correlation of .57 was obtained with the Stanford-Binet for a sample of 120 (ages 24 to 30 mos) children in the standardization group.	One of the most widely used measures of intent development available. The Mental Scales evaluates a variety of activities and processes, including shape discrimination, sustained attention, purposeful manipulation of object, imitation/comprehension, etc. (also see motor).
Kaufman Assessment Battery for Children (KABC) (1983) American Guidance Service.	2.6–12.6 yrs	90	Ages 2½ to 4 Mental Processing Composite (MPC) = .90 Achievement = .93 Ages 12 and Over MPC = .91 Achievement = .97	$\bar{x}$ = 100 SD = 15 for four Global Scales		X		X	X	X		Concurrent validity ranging from .60 to .79 between the MPC and other intelligence tests (WISC-R, Stanford-Binet, and the McCarthy Scales) (GCI). From .75 to .86 between the achievement scales and other intelligence tests.	The K-ABC contains 16 subtests, 10 measuring the MPC and 6 achievement. The MPC is separated into a dichotomy of sequential processing (3 subtests) and simultaneous processing (7 subtests). The gamelike nature of the subtests help motivate preschoolers. Sociocultural norms are provided for minority subjects.

Instrument	Age Range	Administration Time (min.)	Reliability	Norms	(TR)	(SH)	(AF)	(IR)	(SEM)	Validity	Description
McCarthy Scales of Children's Abilities (1972) Psychological Corporation	2.6–8.6 yrs	45–50 for children below 5; 60 for older children	General Cognitive Index (GCI) = .93 Memory & Motor Scales = .79 to .88 (SH) GCI = .90 Memory & Motor Scales = .69 to .89	X	X	X			X	Concurrent validity is acceptable, with correlations ranging from .45 to .91 (median of .75) using the Stanford-Binet, WISC-R, and WPPSI as criteria.	The McCarthy Scales provides a general level of intellectual functioning (GCI) and a profile of verbal ability, nonverbal ability, number aptitude, short-term memory, and motor coordination. The scales contain 18 subtests grouped into one or more of six scales. Five verbal subtests and three quantitative tests are included in the GCI.
Stanford-Binet (Fourth-Ed.) (1985) Riverside Publishing	2 yrs–Adult	60–90	Ages 2 to 5 .74 to .88 Ages 6 to 13 .74 to .91 Ages 13 to 17 .85 to .93	$\bar{x} = 100$ $SD = 16$	X	X			X	Correlations obtained between the Stanford-Binet and the Bayley Scales .57 Between Stanford-Binet and KABC .82 to .89.	Stanford-Binet provides a continuous scale for assessing cognitive development from age 2 to adult. Assesses verbal reasoning, quantitative reasoning, abstract/visual reasoning, and short-term memory.
Uzgirus Hunt Ordinal Scales of Infant Psychological Development (1975) University of Illinois	0–18 mos	15–60	IR = .84 to .97	X	X	X				No validity data reported. Test is based on Piagetian constructs.	This test is constructed following Piagetian sequences: I. Visual Pursuit to object permanence, II. Instrumental Action, III. Vocal & Gestural Imitation, IV. Operational Causality, V. Object Relations in space, & VI. Developing Object Relations Schema.

Key: (TR) = Test-Retest; (SH) = Split-Half; (AF) = Alternate Form; (IR) = Inter-Rater; (SEM) = Standard Error of Measurement

TABLE A-4 Selected Communication Assessment Instruments

Assessment Devices	Age Range	Time in Minutes to Administer	Reliability	Mean & SD	Criterion	Normative	Group	Individual	Verbal	Nonverbal	Screening	Validity	Purpose/Description/Comments
Birth to Three Developmental Scale (1979) Teaching Resources	0–3 yrs	30	IR = .88 to .99		X			X	X	X	X	.70 to .80 with other language scales.	The Birth to Three Developmental Scale is designed for easy identification of developmental delays in four behavioral categories. It is most useful in identifying strengths and weaknesses and leads directly to educational programming. The test items are designed to be fair to individuals from culturally diverse backgrounds.
Early Language Milestone Screening Scale (ELM) (1983) Modern Education Corporation	0–3 yrs	1–3				X		X	X	X		Content validity only.	A communication screening test that covers auditory expressive, auditory receptive, and visual skills. Each behavior is developmentally sequenced and percentiles for each age are given.
Expressive One Word Picture Vocabulary Test (EOWPVT) (1979) Academic Therapy Publications	2–12 yrs	5–10	SH = .87 to .96			X		X	X	X	X	Content validity correlations with Peabody Picture Vocabulary Test –.29 to .59	Designed to assess verbal intelligence by means of acquired expressive picture vocabulary in a picture naming format. Useful in determining the quantity of expressive vocabulary.
Peabody Picture Vocabulary Test (PPVT-R) (1981) American Guidance Service	2½ yrs to Adult	10–20	.77 average for all studies	$\bar{x} = 100$ $SD = 15$		X		X	X	X	X	Concurrent validity .70 with Stanford-Binet and WISC.	The PPVT may be best described as a test of receptive vocabulary. It is most useful in longitudinal studies and in documenting changes in receptive vocabulary due to a language intervention program. Has excellent reliability and validity when used in this restricted way.

Test	Age Range	Time (min.)	Reliability	Norms				Validity	Comments
Receptive-Expressive Emergent Language Scale (REEL) (1976) University Park Press	0–36 mos	30			X	X	X	Content validity only.	Developed to fill the need for an instrument that could assess receptive and expressive language skills in very young children.
Receptive One Word Picture Vocabulary Test (ROWPVT) (1985) Academic Therapy Publications	2–12 yrs	10–15	SH = .87 to .96		X	X	X		Assesses children's single-word receptive vocabulary by requiring only a picture-pointing response. Has specific clinical ability for nonverbal children.
Sequenced Inventory of Communication Development (SICD) (1984) University of Washington	4–48 mos	Dependent on age 30–60	TR = .90 IR = .90	$\bar{x}$ = 100 SD = 15	X	X	X	Reviewers emphasize construct validity only.	A useful instrument in identification of broad areas in communication development that require intensive clinical prescriptive development. The SICD tests developmental milestones in areas of high validity, if one views communication development as best measured in terms of its interactive function among children and their environmental audiences and initiators. Particularly helpful in placing children along developmental grids.
Test of Early Language Development (TELD) (1981) Western Psychological Services	3–8 yrs	15–20	TR = .90	$\bar{x}$ = 100 SD = 15	X	X	X	.66 to .80 with Test of Language Development	The TELD assesses language content and syntax morphology and phonology. Syntax and morphology are assessed both receptively and expressively. Language quotients, percentiles, and language ages are reported.

Key: (TR) = Test-Retest; (SH) = Split-Half; (AF) = Alternate Form; (IR) = Inter-Rater; (SEM) = Standard Error of Measurement

TABLE A-5 Selected Motor Assessment Devices

Assessment Devices	Age Range	Time in Minutes to Administer	Reliability	Mean & SD	Criterion	Normative	Group	Individual	Verbal	Nonverbal	Screening	Validity	Purpose/Description/Comments
										Type			
Bayley Scales of Infant Development (1969) Psychological Corporation	2 mos– 30 mos	Motor: 20–25	Motor Scale: .68 to .92. However, reliabilities tend to be lower for the first 4 mos (ages 2 through 5 mos)	$\bar{x} = 100$ SD = 16		X		X		X		Correlation of .57 was obtained with the Stanford-Binet for a sample of 120 (ages 24 to 30 mos) children in the standardization group. No correlations for Motor Scale are reported individually.	One of the most widely used measures of infant development available. The Motor Scales covers gross- and fine-motor abilities, such as sitting, standing, walking, and grasping (also see Mental Scale).
Bruininks-Oseretsky Test of Motor Integration (1967) Follett Publishing Company	4½– 14½ yrs	45–60	Battery Composite: .86 to .89 Fine- and Gross-Motor Composite: .68 to .88 (TR)	Composite Scores: $\bar{x} = 10$ SD = 10 Individual Subtests: $\bar{x} = 15$ SD = 5		X		X		X		Construct validity was evaluated by the following methods: (1) relation of test scores to CA, (2) internal consistency of subtests, (3) factor structure of individual items. Correlations (product-moment) between subtest scores and CA for standardization sample range from .57 to .86.	The test contains 46 items with a framework of 8 subtests. Four subtests measure gross-motor skills, 3 measure fine-motor skills, and 1 measures both. Composite scores are obtained for the gross-motor subtests, fine-motor subtests, and total battery. A short form also is available that can be used as a brief survey of motor proficiency.
The VMI: Developmental Test of Visual Motor Integration (1989). (3rd Rev.) Modern Curriculum Press.	3–18 yrs	10–15	For 171 children: Boys = .83 Girls = .87 (TR) .90's (IR)	Given by age.			X	X		X		Concurrent validity of the test with CA is .89, with WISC-R is .49 (verbal) and .56 (performance), with PMA is .59, with Frostig is .72.	The VMI contains 24 geometric forms which the child is asked to copy and are arranged in order of increasing difficulty. The total raw score is converted into developmental equivalents and into scale scores, with separate tables for boys and girls.

Instrument	Age	Number of Items	Standardization	Reliability				Validity	Description
Milani-Comparetti Motor Development Screening Scale (Modified Edition) (1984) Meyer Children's Rehabilitation Institute	0–2 yrs	10			X	X		Content validity only.	Assesses control of head and body, protective responses, movement from one position to another, locomotion, reflexes, and the child's state. It can be repeated to monitor trends in motor development.
Peabody Developmental Motor Scales (PDMS) (1983) Teaching Resources Corporation	Birth–83 mos	45–60	Scaled Scores $\bar{x}=500$ $SD=100$ Develop. Motor Quotients (DMQ) $\bar{x}=500$ $SD=15$	Gross Motor = .95 Fine Motor = .80 TR Gross Motor = .97 Fine Motor = .94 (IR)	X	X	X	Concurrent validity between the PDMS Fine Motor total and the Bayley Mental and Psycho-Motor Scales are .78 and .36, respectively.	The PDMS is divided into two components: the Gross-Motor and Fine-Motor Scale. The Gross-Motor Scale contains 170 items divided into 17 age levels (10 items per level) and the Fine-Motor contains 112 items divided into 16 age levels (6 or 8 items per level). The Gross-Motor items are classified into five skill categories: reflexes, balance, non-locomotor, locomotor, and receipt and propulsion of objects. The Fine-Motor Scale items are classified into four skill categories: grasping, hand use, eye-hand coordination, and manual dexterity.

Key: (TR) = Test-Retest; (SH) = Split-Half; (AF) = Alternate Form; (IR) = Inter-Rater; (SEM) = Standard Error of Measurement

TABLE A-6 Selected Social/Emotional Assessment Devices

Assessment Devices	Age Range	Time in Minutes to Administer	Reliability	Mean & SD	Type Criterion	Type Normative	Type Group	Type Individual	Type Verbal	Type Nonverbal	Type Screening	Validity	Purpose/Description/Comments
Burk's Behavior Rating Scales: Preschool and Kindergarten (1977) Western Psychological Services	3–6 yrs	20–30	.74 to .96 on normal children	N.A.		X		X				A panel of 26 kindergarten teachers judged the appropriateness of each item.	The Burk's consists of 105 descriptive statements to be rated by parent or teacher. Eighteen scales are measured: Excessive . . . self-blame, anxiety, withdrawal, dependency, suffering, sense of persecution, aggressiveness, and resistance. Poor . . . ego strength, physical strength, coordination, intellectuality, attention, impulse control, reality contact, sense of identity, anger control, and social conformity.
Carolina Record of Infant Behavior (CRIB) University of North Carolina	0–3 yrs	10		N.A.	X	X		X				Research edition only available. One of the few infant behavior tests.	This test represents an attempt to modify the Bayley Behavior Test to make it useful in assessing infants.
Child Behavior Checklist Achenbach (1986) University of Vermont	2 yrs and up	30–40	TR = .87 to .89 Interparent Correlations = .67 to .74			X		X				Demonstrated that groups identified as disturbed had significantly higher behavior problem scores than did normal comparison groups. Overcontrolled (internalizing) and undercontrolled (externalizing) syndromes have been validated.	The Child Behavior Checklist is designed to record in a standardized format the behavioral problems and competencies of children. The checklist can be self-administered or administered by an interviewer. Separate editions of the profile are standardized for each sex at age 2 to 4, 6 to 11.

Test	Age Range		Reliability						Validity	Comments
Joseph Pre-School and Primary Self-Concept Screening Test (1979) Stoelting Co.	3½–9 yrs	7	TR = .87 SH = .59 to .81	N.A.	X	X	X	X	Concurrent validity = .66 with Slosson, .69 with YMI.	This test contains 15 items that assess self-concept. May be used as a screening or diagnostic instrument with handicapped pre-schoolers. Easy to administer and score.
Test of Early Social-Emotional Development (TOESD) (1984) Pro-Ed	3–8 yrs	30–50	TR = .70 to .85		X	X	X		Concurrent validity. Correlates well with other behavior measures.	The TOE SD is composed of 4 components: (1) a student rating scale, (2) a teacher rating scale, (3) a parent rating scale, and (4) a sociogram. Recently normed and provides percentiles and standard scores.

Key: (TR) = Test-Retest; (SH) = Split-Half; (AF) = Alternate Form; (IR) = Inter-Rater; (SEM) = Standard Error of Measurement

TABLE A-7 Selected Adaptive-Self-help Assessment Devices

Assessment Devices	Age Range	Time in Minutes to Administer	Reliability	Mean & SD	Type							Validity	Purpose/Description/Comments
					Criterion	Normative	Group	Individual	Verbal	Nonverbal	Screening		
Adaptive Performance Instrument (API) (1980) Office of Special Education and Rehabilitation Services	0–9 yrs	Open	No data	N.A.	X			X		X			The API measures functional skills in severely and multiply handicapped infants and young children. Assesses 8 domains: (1) Physical Intactness, (2) Reflexes and Reactions, (3) Gross Motor, (4) Fine Motor, (5) Self-care, (6) Sensorimotor, (7) Social, and (8) Communication. Computer assisted scoring.
Scales of Independent Behavior (SIB) (1984) DLM Teaching Resources	Birth and up	60–75	TR/IR = .74 to .94			X		X	X			Correlations between the SIB and Woodcock Johnson Cognitive area = .71 to .92.	This test consists of four adaptive behavior clusters: Motor skills, Social and communication skills, Personal living skills, and Community living skills. The Early Development Scale provides a developmental measure of adaptive behavior from infancy to three years.
Vineland Adaptive Behavior Scales (1984) American Guidance Service (AGS)	Birth–18 yrs 11 mos	20–30	Communication = .73 to .94 Daily Living = .83 to .92 Socialization = .78 to .94 Motor Skills = .70 to .95	$\bar{x} = 100$ SD = 15		X		X				Median correlations between the Vineland and the Adaptive Behavior Inventory = .58, between Vineland and the AAMD Adaptive Behavior Scale = .40 to .70	The scale assesses an individual's performance on the Daily Activities required for personality and social self-sufficiency. The scale assesses four domains: (1) Communication, (2) Daily living, (3) Socialization, and (4) Motor Development.

Key: (TR) = Test-Retest; (SH) = Split-Half; (AF) = Alternate Form; (IR) = Inter-Rater; (SEM) = Standard Error of Measurement

Source: All the tables in this appendix are from *Screening Assessment: Guidelines for Identifying Disabled and Developmentally Vulnerable Children and Their Families* by Samuel J. Meisels and Sally Provence with the Task on Screening and Assessment of the National Early Childhood Technical Assistance System (NEC/TAS). Reprinted with permission of the National Center for Clinical Infant Programs.

Test Publishers

PC/CEM	Psychological Corporation, 555 Academic Court, San Antonio, TX 78204
AGS	American Guidance Services, Inc., Publishers' Building, Circle Pines, MN 55014
HM	Houghton Mifflin Company, 1 Beacon Street, Boston, MA 02108
RPC	Riverside Publishing Company, 3 O'Hare Towers, 8420 Bryn Mawr Avenue, Chicago, IL 60631
CA	Curriculum Associates, Inc., 5 Esquire Road, North Billerica, MA 01862-2589
ER	Exceptional Resources, P.O. Box 9221, Austin, TX 78766
UM	University of Michigan Press, P.O. Box 1104, Ann Arbor, MI 48106
MPC	Charles E. Merrill Publishing Company, 1300 Alum Creek Drive, Columbus, OH 43216
KSS	Kaplan School Supply Corp., P.O. Box 609, Lewisville, NC 27023-0609
UCP	United Cerebral Palsy of the Bluegrass Child Development Center, P.O. Box 8003, 465 Springhill Drive, Lexington, KY 40503
FKD	Foundation for Knowledge and Development, 8101 East Prentice Avenue, Suite 518, Englewood, CA 80111
DLM	DLM Teaching Resources, One DLM Park, P.O. Box 4000, Allen, TX 75002
WPS	Western Psychological Services, 12031 Wilshire Boulevard, Los Angeles, CA 90025
NC	Nisonger Center, Ohio State University, Columbus, OH 43210
UTD	University of Texas at Dallas, Callier Center for Communication Disorders, 1966 Inwood Road, Dallas, TX 75235
OSCSS	Office of the Santa Cruz County Superintendent of Schools, 133 Mission Street, Santa Cruz, CA 95062
DP	Dorsey Press, 1818 Ridge Road, Homewood, IL 60430
AP	Anhinga Press, Route 2, Box 513, Tallahassee, FL 32301
HTC	Houston Test Company, P.O. Box 35152, Houston, TX 77035
UWP	University of Washington Press, P.O. Box 85569, Seattle, WA 98105
LC	Learning Concepts, 2501 North Lamar, Austin, TX 78705
PRO-ED	5341 Industrial Oaks Boulevard, Austin, TX 78735
CRA	Communication Research Association, Inc., Box 11012, Salt Lake City, UT 84111

Note: Test publishers for Table 7-11 in this book are listed in the order of appearance.

Author Index

327

Subject Index

Brazelton Neonatal Behavioral Assessment Scale, 226
BRIGANCE Diagnostic Inventory of Early Development, 111, 133
BRIGANCE Diagnostic Inventory of Early Development—Revised, 111, 162, 170, 172
Brigance K and 1 screen, 147
British Ability Scale, 231
Bruininks-Oseretsky Test of Motor Proficiency, 306
Bzoch-League Receptive Expressive Emergent Language Scale, 134

California Preschool Social Competency Scale, 275
Callier-Azusa Scale, 111–112, 133, 170, 226
Carey Infant Temperament Scale, 275
Carolina Curriculum for Handicapped Infants and Infants At-Risk, 226, 304
Carolina Curriculum for Infants and Toddlers with Special Needs, 170, 229
Carolina Curriculum for Preschoolers (Paul H. Brookes), 170
Carolina Picture Vocabulary Test for Deaf and Hearing Impaired, 118
Carolina Record of Individual Behavior, 274
Carrow Elicited Language Inventory, 134
Casati-Lezine Scales, 232
Characteristics of Diagnostic/Behavior Rating Scales for Autistic Children, 130
Child characteristics and development, 19–20, 36–38, 42–43, 164
  Emotional, social, and personal development, 263–290
Child Behavior Checklist, 287
Child find, 143
CID Preschool Performance Scale, 120
Cognition, 221–222
  Assessment of, 223–236
Cognitive development, 222–223
Columbia Mental Maturity Scale, Third Edition (CMMS), 120
Columbia Mental Maturity Scale, 133, 230
Communication and language, 241
  Assessment of, 244–252
  Components of, 242–244
  Dimensions of, 252–258
Communication and Symbolic Behavior Scales, 250
Communication Report Form, 245–246
Comprehensive assessment, 265–268
Comprehensive Behavior Rating Scale for Children, 287
Comprehensive Developmental Evaluation Chart,

Comprehensive Test of Adaptive Behavior and Normative Adaptive Behavior Checklist, 287
Conversational discourse, 255–256
Cultural diversity, of families, 74–76
Curriculum-based assessment, 7–9, 161–179

Data collection, 184–191
Data Collection Sheets, 189–190
Data Grid, 208
DDST-R, 147
Developmental Activities Screening Inventory II, 125, 162
Developmental Assessment for the Severely Handicapped, 133
Developmental/Criterion-based scales, 125–126
Developmental diagnosis, 224
Developmental Profile II, 125, 287
Developmental Programming for Infants and Young Children, 133, 171
Diagnostic Inventory of Early Development, 226
DIAL-R, 147
Direct selection of instruments for measuring progress, 207
Direct testing, 6

Early Childhood Environmental Rating Scale, 113, 193
Early Coping Inventory, 284, 285
Early Intervention Developmental Profile, 133, 172, 226, 229, 303
Early Intervention, models of, 61
Early Learning Accomplishment Profile, 133, 162, 177, 226
Early Learning Accomplishment Profile for Infants, 170
Ecobehavioral System for Complex Assessment of Preschool Environments, 194
Ecological and behavioral assessments, 181–196
  Characteristics of, 183–184
Ecological assessment, 12
EMI Assessment Scale, 226
Engagement in interactions, 247–248
Environmental Language Inventory (ELI), 118
Environmental Pre-Language Battery (EPB), 118
ESI, 147
ESP, 147
Evaluation and Selection Criteria Rating Form for Prescriptive Developmental Assessment Measures, 167
Examiner, 20–22
Extended Merrill-Palmer Scale of Mental Tests, 155, 230

Family Day Care Rating Scale, 193
Family interview, 6, 18, 49, 93